Contents

I am standing on the Pont des Arts in Paris. On one side of the Seine is the harmonious, reasonable façade of the Institute of France, built as a college in about 1670. On the other bank is the Louvre, built continuously from the Middle Ages to the nineteenth century: classical architecture at its most splendid and assured. Just visible upstream is the Cathedral of Notre-Dame — not perhaps the most lovable of cathedrals, but the most rigorously intellectual façade in the whole of Gothic art. The houses that line the banks of the river are also a humane and reasonable solution of what town architecture should be...

Kenneth Clark: Civilisation

John Murray (Publishers) Ltd/BBC Publications/Harper and Row Ltd.

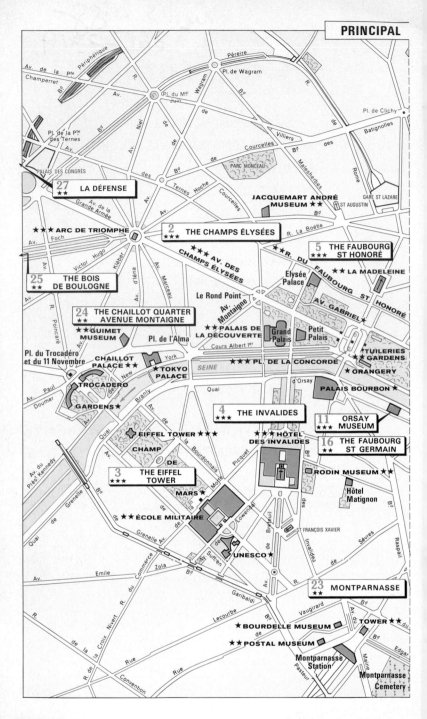

★★★ ARC DE TRIOMPHE

| 27 ★★ | LA DÉFENSE |

| 2 ★★★ | THE CHAMPS ÉLYSÉES |

JACQUEMART ANDRÉ MUSEUM ★★

| 5 ★★★ | THE FAUBOURG ST HONORÉ |

★★★ R. DU ★★ LA MADELEINE

★★★ AV. DES CHAMPS ÉLYSÉES

| 25 ★★ | THE BOIS DE BOULOGNE |

Elysée Palace

★★ GUIMET MUSEUM

| 24 ★★ | THE CHAILLOT QUARTER AVENUE MONTAIGNE |

AV. GABRIEL

★★ PALAIS DE LA DÉCOUVERTE

Grand Palais

Petit Palais

★★ TUILERIES GARDENS

CHAILLOT PALACE ★★

★ TOKYO PALACE

★★★ PL. DE LA CONCORDE

★ ORANGERY

TROCADERO

GARDENS ★

PALAIS BOURBON ★

| 4 ★★★ | THE INVALIDES |

EIFFEL TOWER ★★★

★★ HÔTEL DES INVALIDES

| 11 ★★★ | ORSAY MUSEUM |

CHAMP

| 16 ★★ | THE FAUBOURG ST GERMAIN |

| 3 ★★★ | THE EIFFEL TOWER |

DE

RODIN MUSEUM ★★

Hôtel Matignon

MARS ★

★★ ÉCOLE MILITAIRE

UNESCO ★

| 23 ★★ | MONTPARNASSE |

★ BOURDELLE MUSEUM

TOWER ★★

★★ POSTAL MUSEUM

Montparnasse Station

Montparnasse Cemetery

BUSES

Tickets. — Tickets are obtainable in booklets of ten for 34.50F and are valid on the *métro*. Booklets *(carnets)* can be purchased in *métro* booking halls, at tobacco counters, shops with the R.A.T.P. sign outside and on certain buses. Single tickets (5.50F) may be purchased on the buses.

Journeys are divided into stages — 1 ticket takes you two stages, 2 tickets almost any journey within the capital. Do not punch your tourist ticket *(p 8)* on the buses.

Hours. — All buses run from 7am to 8.30pm with some lines continuing later. Services may be reduced or suspended on Sundays and public holidays.

History. — In the mid 17C, on the initiative of the philosopher Pascal, there operated in Paris a network of carriages known as *fiacres* for which the fare charged was 5 *sols* or a few pence. The system worked well but eventually died, only returning in 1828 under the Restoration. In 1855 carriages known as Joséphines, Gazelles, Dames Réunies, Carolines, Hirondelles or Sylphides, and seen in all parts of Paris speeding along the streets, were united to form the General Omnibus Company. Horses were replaced in time by trams and buses. After 1918 all the road companies combined and in 1942 this joint company amalgamated with the underground. The present R.A.T.P. — Independent Paris Transport Authority — came into being in 1949.

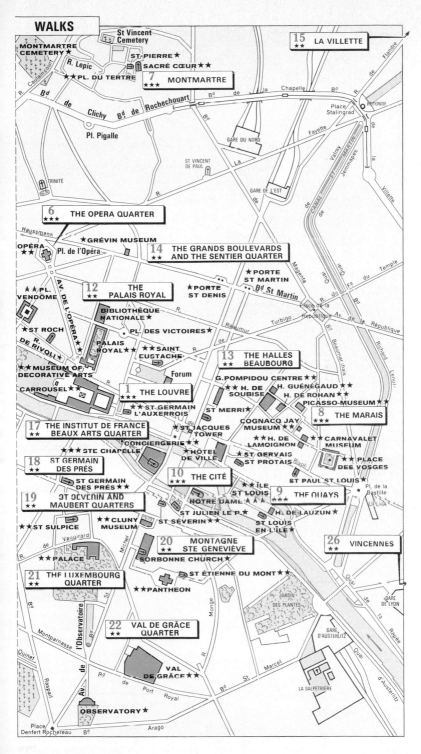

WALKS

	St Vincent Cemetery
	MONTMARTRE CEMETERY ★
	ST-PIERRE ★
	R. Lepic
	SACRÉ CŒUR ★★
	★★PL. DU TERTRE
7 ★★★	MONTMARTRE
15 ★★	LA VILLETTE

- Pl. Pigalle
- GARE DU NORD
- ST VINCENT DE PAUL
- TRINITÉ
- GARE DE L'EST
- Place Stalingrad
- ROTONDE

6 ★★★	THE OPERA QUARTER
OPÉRA ★★	
★ GRÉVIN MUSEUM	
Pl. de l'Opéra	
14 ★★	THE GRANDS BOULEVARDS AND THE SENTIER QUARTER
★ PORTE ST MARTIN	
★ PORTE ST DENIS	
★★ PL. VENDÔME	
12 ★★	THE PALAIS ROYAL
BIBLIOTHÈQUE NATIONALE ★	
★ ST ROCH	
★ R. DE RIVOLI	
PL. DES VICTOIRES ★	
PALAIS ROYAL ★★	
★★ SAINT EUSTACHE	
Place de la République	
★★ MUSEUM OF DECORATIVE ARTS	
CARROUSEL ★★	
Forum	
1 ★★★	THE LOUVRE
13 ★★	THE HALLES BEAUBOURG
G. POMPIDOU CENTRE ★★	
★★ H. DE SOUBISE	
H. GUÉNÉGAUD ★★	
H. DE ROHAN ★★	
PICASSO-MUSEUM ★★	
★★ ST GERMAIN L'AUXERROIS	
ST MERRI ★	
COGNACQ JAY MUSEUM ★★	
8 ★★★	THE MARAIS
17 ★★	THE INSTITUT DE FRANCE BEAUX ARTS QUARTER
★ JACQUES TOWER	
★★ H. DE LAMOIGNON	
CARNAVALET MUSEUM ★	
★★★ STE CHAPELLE	
CONCIERGERIE ★★	
★ HÔTEL DE VILLE	
★ ST GERVAIS ST PROTAIS ★★	
18 ★★	ST GERMAIN DES PRÉS
ST GERMAIN DES PRÉS ★★	
★★ PLACE DES VOSGES	
10 ★★★	THE CITÉ
ST PAUL ST LOUIS ★	
19 ★★	ST SÉVERIN AND MAUBERT QUARTERS
ST GERMAIN DES PRÉS ★★	
★★ ÎLE ST LOUIS	
9 ★★★	THE QUAYS
NOTRE DAME ★★★	
Pl. de la Bastille	
★★ ST SULPICE	
★★ CLUNY MUSEUM	
ST SÉVERIN ★★	
ST JULIEN LE P. ★	
H. DE LAUZUN ★	
ST LOUIS EN L'ÎLE ★	
20 ★★	MONTAGNE STE GENEVIÈVE
26 ★★	VINCENNES
SORBONNE CHURCH ★★	
21 ★★	THE LUXEMBOURG QUARTER
ST ÉTIENNE DU MONT ★★	
★★ PANTHEON	
JARDIN DES PLANTES	
GARE DE LYON	
22 ★★	VAL DE GRÂCE QUARTER
GARE D'AUSTERLITZ	
VAL DE GRÂCE ★★	
LA SALPÊTRIÈRE	
OBSERVATORY ★	
Place Denfert Rochereau	

PRIVATE CARS

There are about 1 000 000 private cars in Paris and it needs only 120 000 cars on the road at the same time to create bottlenecks, particularly as offices close in the evening. There are only 1 400km - 870 miles of highway and so any holdups have major repercussions. To try and alleviate the problem, road works have been and continue to be undertaken.

A west to east expressway (Georges Pompidou expressway, 13km - 8 miles) along the Right Bank has been created to speed up the flow of cars as well as a ring road (*boulevard périphérique,* 35km - 22 miles) running parallel to the outer boulevards which were built in 1919 along the line of the Thiers fortifications *(p 20)*. Parking sites have been built near the outlying stations to promote the use of public transport.

In the city, a blue zone *(zone bleue)* has been created with controlled parking only; also a grey zone *(zone grise)* with parking meters.

Obey the one-way and other signs, parking regulations etc with great care: the Paris police and meter maids are strict and show no particular leniency to tourists!

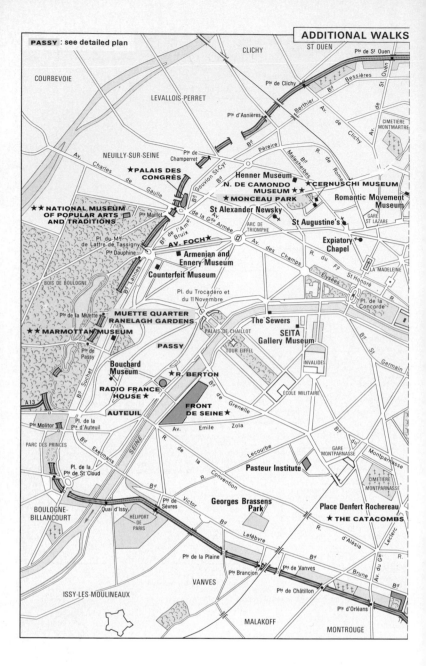

PASSY : see detailed plan

ST OUEN
CLICHY
COURBEVOIE
Pte de St Ouen
Pte de Clichy
Bessières
CIMETIÈRE
MONTMARTRE
LEVALLOIS-PERRET
Pte d'Asnières
Berthier
de
Clichy
NEUILLY-SUR-SEINE
Pte de Champerret
Péreire
R. de Rome
GARE ST LAZARE
★PALAIS DES CONGRÈS
Henner Museum
N. DE CAMONDO MUSEUM ★★
★CERNUSCHI MUSEUM
Romantic Movement Museum
★★NATIONAL MUSEUM OF POPULAR ARTS AND TRADITIONS
MONCEAU PARK
St Alexander Newsky
St Augustine's
ARC DE TRIOMPHE
Pl. du Mal de Lattre de Tassigny
Expiatory Chapel
Pte Maillot
AV. FOCH
Pte Dauphine
Armenian and Ennery Museum
Av. des Champs
R. du Fg St Honoré
LA MADELEINE
BOIS DE BOULOGNE
Counterfeit Museum
Élysées
Pl. de la Concorde
Pte de la Muette
Pl. du Trocadéro et du 11 Novembre
The Sewers
★★MARMOTTAN MUSEUM
MUETTE QUARTER RANELAGH GARDENS
PALAIS DE CHAILLOT
SEITA Gallery Museum
Germain
Pte de Passy
PASSY
TOUR EIFFEL
INVALIDES
Bouchard Museum
★R. BERTON
RADIO FRANCE HOUSE ★
AUTEUIL
ÉCOLE MILITAIRE
A13
FRONT DE SEINE ★
de Grenelle
Pte Molitor
Pl. de la Pte d'Auteuil
Av. Emile Zola
PARC DES PRINCES
SEINE
R. de la
Lecourbe
GARE MONTPARNASSE
Montparnasse
Pl. de la Pte de St Cloud
Convention
CIMETIÈRE MONTPARNASSE
BOULOGNE-BILLANCOURT
Pte de Sèvres
Pasteur Institute
Quai d'Issy
HÉLIPORT DE PARIS
Victor
Georges Brassens Park
Place Denfert Rochereau
★ THE CATACOMBS
Lefèbvre
d'Alésia
Leclerc
Pte de la Plaine
Brune
Pte Brancion
Pte de Vanves
ISSY-LES-MOULINEAUX
VANVES
Pte de Châtillon
Pte d'Orléans
MALAKOFF
MONTROUGE

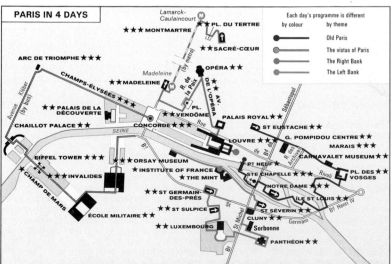

PARIS IN 4 DAYS

Lamarck-Caulaincourt
★ PL. DU TERTRE
★★★ MONTMARTRE
★ SACRÉ-CŒUR

Each day's programme is different
by colour   by theme
Old Paris
The vistas of Paris
The Right Bank
The Left Bank

ARC DE TRIOMPHE ★★★
Madeleine
OPÉRA ★★
CHAMPS-ÉLYSÉES ★★★★
★★ MADELEINE
★★ PALAIS DE LA DÉCOUVERTE
R. de la Paix
AV. DE L'OPÉRA
PL. VENDÔME ★★
PALAIS ROYAL ★★
CHAILLOT PALACE ★★
CONCORDE ★★★
Rue
★ ST EUSTACHE ★★
EIFFEL TOWER ★★★
LOUVRE ★★★
G. POMPIDOU CENTRE ★★
MARAIS ★★★
★★ INVALIDES
ORSAY MUSEUM ★
CARNAVALET MUSEUM ★★
CHAMP DE MARS
★ INSTITUTE OF FRANCE
PT NEUF ★
PL. DES VOSGES ★★
★ THE MINT
STE CHAPELLE ★★★
NOTRE DAME ★★★
★★ ST GERMAIN-DES-PRÉS
ILE ST LOUIS ★★
ÉCOLE MILITAIRE ★★★
★★ ST SULPICE
ST SÉVERIN ★★
★★ LUXEMBOURG
CLUNY ★★
Sorbonne
PANTHÉON ★★

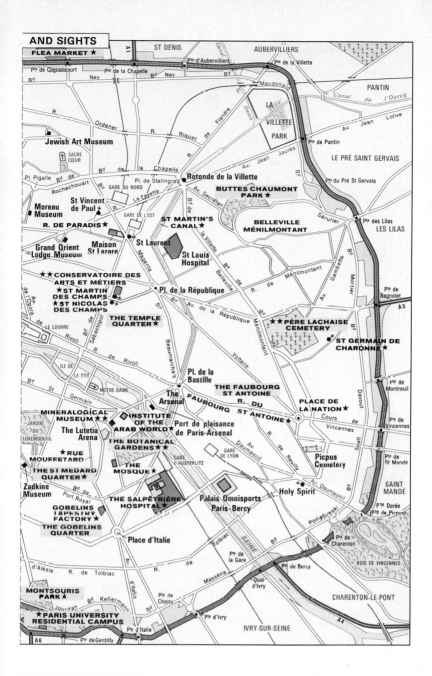

AND SIGHTS

FLEA MARKET ★

Jewish Art Museum

SACRÉ CŒUR

Moreau Museum

St Vincent de Paul ✝

R. DE PARADIS ★

Grand Orient Lodge Museum

Maison St Lazare

St Laurent

Rotonde de la Villette

ST MARTIN'S CANAL ★

BUTTES CHAUMONT PARK ★

BELLEVILLE MÉNILMONTANT

LES LILAS

★★ CONSERVATOIRE DES ARTS ET MÉTIERS

★ ST MARTIN DES CHAMPS

★ ST NICOLAS DES CHAMPS

St Louis Hospital

THE TEMPLE QUARTER ★

Pl. de la RÉPUBLIQUE

★★ PÈRE LACHAISE CEMETERY

ST GERMAIN DE CHARONNE ★

NOTRE DAME

ILE DE LA CITÉ

Pl. de la Bastille

The Arsenal

THE FAUBOURG ST ANTOINE

R. DU FAUBOURG ST ANTOINE ★

PLACE DE LA NATION ★

MINERALOGICAL MUSEUM ★★

INSTITUTE OF THE ARAB WORLD ★

Port de plaisance de Paris-Arsenal

The Lutetia Arena

THE BOTANICAL GARDENS ★★

★ RUE MOUFFETARD

THE MOSQUE ★

Picpus Cemetery

THE ST MEDARD QUARTER ★

Holy Spirit

Zadkine Museum

THE SALPÊTRIÈRE HOSPITAL ★

Palais Omnisports Paris-Bercy

SAINT MANDÉ

GOBELINS TAPESTRY FACTORY ★

THE GOBELINS QUARTER ★

Place d'Italie

BOIS DE VINCENNES

MONTSOURIS PARK ★

CHARENTON-LE-PONT

★ PARIS UNIVERSITY RESIDENTIAL CAMPUS

IVRY-SUR-SEINE

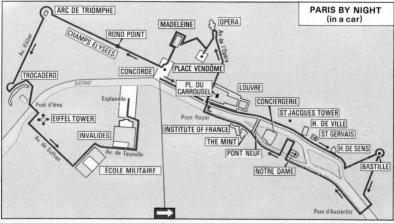

PARIS BY NIGHT (in a car)

ARC DE TRIOMPHE

MADELEINE

OPÉRA

CHAMPS ELYSÉES

ROND POINT

TROCADÉRO

CONCORDE

PLACE VENDÔME

PL. DU CARROUSEL

LOUVRE

CONCIERGERIE

ST JACQUES TOWER

H. DE VILLE

EIFFEL TOWER

INSTITUTE OF FRANCE

ST GERVAIS

INVALIDES

THE MINT

PONT NEUF

H. DE SENS

BASTILLE

ÉCOLE MILITAIRE

NOTRE DAME

All the year round: *Sundays to Fridays, sunset (5.15 to 10.20pm) to midnight (1am Saturdays and days before a holiday).*

In summer some boat companies give tours on the Seine *(details p 12)*.

7

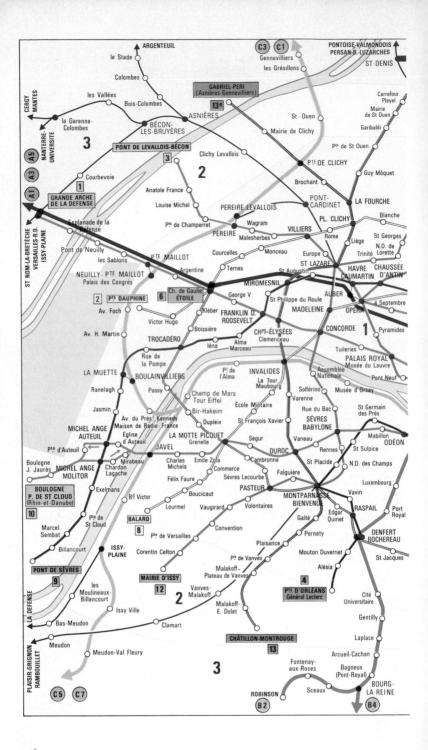

MÉTRO

Tickets. — Tickets are obtainable in booklets of ten for 34.50F — and are valid also on buses. Booklets *(carnets)* can be purchased in *métro* booking halls (also single tickets, price: 5.50F), on buses, at tobacco counters and at shops with the sign R.A.T.P. outside. Most journeys, apart from those on the R.E.R., require the flat rate of one ticket. Insert your ticket in the machine and keep it with you until you have left the *métro*.
Tourist tickets "Paris-Visite" can be bought on production of a passport, in larger *métro* stations, at Services Touristiques de la R.A.T.P., 53 ter, Quai des Grands Augustins, 6e and at the Paris Tourist Office, 127 Avenue des Champs-Élysées, 8e as well as in London, SNCF (Bureau officiel); price: 80F to 130F for unlimited journeys for 3 or 5 days respectively (tickets are also available at 150F and 185F and include access to Orly and Charles-de-Gaulle airports).

Construction. — Parisians first took the *métro* on 19 July 1900. The first Paris line was on the Right Bank, from Porte de Vincennes to Porte Maillot.
The engineer responsible was Fulgence Bienvenüe and the architect for what became the standard *métro* entrance *(illustration p 23)*, that master of the "noodle" style, Guimard.

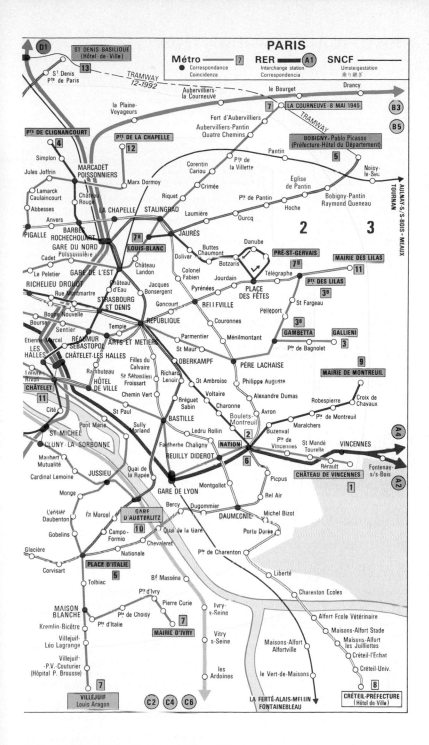

Facts and figures. — There are 199km - 124 miles of track for the 15 lines, apart from the R.E.R. and 368 stations of which 87 are interchanges. No point in the capital is more than 500m - 550yds from a métro station.
Some 6 million Parisians are transported daily — 1 360 000 million in 1989 — in 3 500 cars. In rush hours trains run every 95 seconds. 15 000 are employed in the *métro* service.

Modernization. — The system is being modernized technically and aesthetically to make it more efficient: moving walkways and escalators are being installed, tyres fitted to reduce noise and improve suspension.
Stations are being decorated with window displays and glass mosaics (Franklin-Roosevelt), good reproductions (Louvre, Varenne) and photographs (St-Germain-des-Prés, Hôtel de Ville).

The RER. — The Regional Express Network includes four lines: the A line from St-Germain-en-Laye to Boissy-St-Léger and Torcy; the B line from Robinson and St-Rémy-les-Chevreuse to Roissy and Mitry-Claye; the C line linking Versailles (south bank) and St-Quentin-en-Yvelines to Dourdan and Etampes and the D line from Le Châtelet to Villiers-le-Bel. A line to link up the RER and suburban lines of the north and southeast will eventually serve more than 200 stations. First class still exists in the RER.

PRACTICAL INFORMATION

BEFORE LEAVING

The French Government Tourist Office at 178 Piccadilly, London WIV OAL, ☎ 071 499 6911 (24-hour answering service with recorded message and information) or ☎ 071 491 7622 (urgent enquiries only) and 610 Fifth Avenue, Suite 222, New York 10020, ☎ 212 757 1125 will provide information and literature.

When to go. — In winter the streets are bright with Christmas illuminations, the shop windows brilliant; in summer you can sit beneath the trees or an awning with a long cold drink between seeing the sights or idle away an evening on a café terrace, or go on an open boat on the Seine; in the autumn Parisians are back from their own holidays and there is an air of energy and bustle; and Paris in the spring...

Where to stay. — There are hundreds of hotels and restaurants in Paris. Hotels range from the sumptuous to modest family *pensions*; restaurants equally can provide luxurious fare at frightening prices and very good food at reasonable cost — and the great advantage with French restaurants is that the menu, with prices, is displayed outside. For a comprehensive list including prices of hotels and restaurants look in the Michelin Booklet *Paris and Environs* (an extract from the Michelin Red Guide France). There are several youth and student organizations — apply to the French Government Tourist Office *(address above)*, the French Embassy Office, 23 Cromwell Road, London SW7, ☎ 071 581 5292 or the Central Bureau for Educational Visits and Exchanges, Seymour Mews House, Seymour Mews, London W18 H9PE, ☎ 071 486 5101.

How to get there. — You can go from London and other major cities in the United Kingdom directly by scheduled national airlines, by package tour flights, possibly with a rail or coach link-up or you can go by cross-channel ferry or by hovercraft and on by car or train. Enquire at any good travel agent — and remember, if you are going in the holiday season or at Christmas, Easter or Whitsun, to book well in advance.

CUSTOMS AND OTHER FORMALITIES

Passport. — Visitors entering France must be in possession of a valid national passport (or in the case of the British, a Visitor's Passport). In case of loss or theft report to the embassy or consulate and the local police.

Visa. — An entry visa is required for Canadian and US citizens (for a stay of more than three months) and for Australian citizens in accordance with French security measures. Apply to the French Consulate (visa issued same day; delay if submitted by mail). US citizens should obtain the booklet *Your Trip Abroad* ($ 1), which provides useful information on visa requirements, customs regulations, medical care etc for international travellers. Apply to the Superintendent of Documents, Government Printing Office, Washington, DC 20402-9325.

Customs. — Apply to the Customs Office (UK) for a leaflet on customs regulations and the full range of "duty free" allowances. The US Treasury Department (☎ 202 566 8195) offers a publication *Know before you go* for US citizens.

MOTORING IN FRANCE AND THE CAPITAL

Motoring. — The minimum age for driving in France is 18. Nationals of EC countries require a valid **national driving licence**; nationals of non-EC countries require an **international driving licence** (obtainable in the US from the American Automobile Club). For the vehicle it is necessary to have the **registration papers** (log-book) and a **nationality plate** of the approved size. There are no customs formalities for holidaymakers bringing their caravan into France for a stay of less than 6 months.

Insurance. — Insurance cover is compulsory and although an International Insurance Certificate (Green Card) is no longer a legal requirement in France it is the most effective proof of insurance cover and is internationally recognized by the police and other authorities.
The AA, RAC and Routiers (354 Fulham Road, London SW10 9UH) run accident insurance and breakdown service schemes for their members. Europ-Assistance (252 High St, Croydon CRO 1NF) also has special policies for motorists. Members of the American Automobile Club should obtain the brochure *Offices to serve you abroad*.

Car Rental. — There are car rental agencies at airports, air terminals, railway stations and on the main streets. European cars usually have manual transmission but automatic cars are available on demand. An international driving licence is required for non-EC nationals.

Parking regulations. — In the capital there are restricted and paying parking zones (blue and grey zones); tickets must be obtained from the ticket machine (*horodateurs* - small change necessary) and displayed (inside windscreen on driver's side); failure to display may result in a heavy fine. Beware where you leave your car — Paris meter maids are strict, even with tourists !

Taxis. — There are some 14 300 taxis in Paris, cruising the streets day and night and parked in ranks alongside the kerb close to road junctions and other frequented points beneath the signs labelled *Tête de Station*. Taxis may also be hailed in the street when showing the illuminated sign. The rate varies according to the zone and time of day. The white, orange or blue lights correspond to the three different rates A, B and C and these appear on the meter inside the cab. A supplementary charge is made for taxis from station forecourts, air terminals, and for heavy baggage or unwieldy parcels as well as for a fourth person and domestic animals.

GENERAL INFORMATION

Post. — Post offices are open Monday to Friday 8am to 7pm, Saturday 8am to 12noon. For post offices open at other times but only offering a limited service consult the Michelin publication no ▮▮. Postage via air mail to: UK letter 2.50F; postcard 2.10F; US aerogramme 4.20F; letter (20g) 3.80F; postcard 3.50F. Stamps are also available from newsagents and tobacconists.

Poste Restante mail should be addressed as follows: Name, Poste Restante, Paris and an arrondissement number. When no arrondissement number is given the mail may be collected from the post office at 52 Rue du Louvre, Paris 75001, ☎ 40 28 20 00. Take your passport as identification when collecting your mail.

Telephone. — Public phones using pre-paid phone cards *(télécarte)* are in operation throughout the capital. The cards (50 or 120 units), which are available from post offices, tobacconists, newsagents, railway and métro stations as well as all France Telecom agencies, can be used for inland and international calls. Calls can be received at phone boxes where the blue bell sign is shown.

Internal calls. — When calling within either of the two main zones (French provinces and Paris and its region) dial only the 8-digit customer's number. From Paris to the provinces dial 16 + 8-digit number. From the provinces to Paris dial 16 + 1 + 8-digit number.

International calls. — For Paris dial the country code 33 + 1 + 8-digit number. For the provinces the country code 33 + 8-digit number.

When calling abroad from Paris dial 19, wait until the continuous tone recurs, then dial the country code and dialling code and number of your correspondant. For international enquiries dial 19 33 12 + country code.

Telephone rates from a public telephone at any time are: Paris-London, about 5.60F for 1 minute; Paris-New York, 10.30F for 1 minute. Cheap rates with 50 % extra time are available on weekdays between 10.30pm and 8am, at weekends starting at 2pm on Saturdays.

Minitel. — The French Telecom videotex service offers a wide variety of information at your fingertips (fee charged). Minitel terminals are installed in hotel chains, post offices and certain petrol stations. Listed below are some of the telematic services offered:

3614 ED	electronic service in English
3615 TCAMP	camping information
3615 CORUS	mountain resorts: winter and summer
3615 METEO	weather report
3615 or 3616 HORAV	general airline information and flight schedules
3615 BBC	BBC news
3615 LIBE	USA TODAY
3615 MICHELIN	Michelin tourist and route information.

Medical treatment. — First aid, medical advice and chemists' night service rota are available from chemists (*pharmacie* — green cross sign).

It is advisable to take out comprehensive insurance cover as the recipient of medical treatment in French hospitals or clinics must pay the bill. Nationals of non-EC countries should check with their insurance company about policy limitations. Reimbursement can then be negotiated with the insurance company according to the policy held. American Express offers a service, "Global Assist", for any medical, legal or personal emergency — call collect from anywhere ☎ 202 554 2639. British citizens should apply to the Department of Health and Social Security for **Form E 111**, which entitles the holder to urgent treatment for accident or unexpected illness in EC countries. A refund of part of the costs of treatment can be obtained in person or by post on application to the local Social Security Offices (Caisse Primaire d'Assurance Maladie). For the addresses of the British and American (Blue Cross Member) hospitals see Useful Addresses.

Galerie Vivienne

Currency. — There are no restrictions on the amount of currency visitors can take into France. To facilitate the export of currency in foreign bank notes in excess of the given allocation visitors are advised to complete a currency declaration form on arrival.

Banks. — Banks are open from 9am to 12noon and 2 to 4pm and are usually closed on Saturday; some branches open for limited operations on Saturday. Travellers' Cheques are exchangeable at banks, or bureaux de change found at airports, terminals and the larger railway stations, and in some hotels and shops. A passport is necessary when cashing cheques in banks. Commission charges vary and hotels usually charge more than banks for cashing cheques for non-residents. Most banks have cash dispensers which accept international credit cards.

Credit Cards. — American Express, Carte Bleue (Visa/Barclaycard), Diners Club and Eurocard (Mastercard/Access) are widely accepted in shops, hotels, restaurants and petrol stations.

Shopping. — The big stores and larger shops are open Monday to Saturday from 9am to 6.30-7.30pm. Smaller, individual shops may close during the lunch hour. Food shops — grocers, wine merchants and bakeries — are open from 7am to 6.30pm; some open on Sunday mornings and are closed on Mondays.

Paris still has a vast number of individually-owned shops, which make every street a window-shoppers' paradise; for the fashion houses, the luxurious and the exotic, Avenue Montaigne, the Champs-Élysées, Place and Avenue de l'Opéra, Rue Tronchet, Rue Royale and Rue du Faubourg St-Honoré. The great names among jewellers are found in Rue de la Paix and Place Vendôme. For those looking for a particular item: shoes, hand bags, and leather goods (Rue St-Lazare and Boulevard St-Michel); off-the-peg French fashion (Rue de Passy and Rue de Sèvres); furniture (Rue du Faubourg St-Antoine); and crystal, glass and fine china (Rue Paradis). Antique and fine art shops are grouped in the Louvre des Antiquaires, Village Suisse, Carré Rive Gauche and the Flea Market. The Forum des Halles provides a varied selection of chain stores and fashion boutiques for the young and the avant-garde.

There are also lively street markets in every quarter.

SIGHTSEEING IN PARIS

To get the "feel", the atmosphere of Paris, besides seeing the sights described in the Guide you will want to sit at a café table on the pavement to sip a drink or go in one of the boats on the Seine, which enables you to see many of the major buildings from an unusual angle and rest at the same time, or go, one week-end, to the Flea Market.

Riverboats. — Many of the boats have glass roofs and you can sightsee spectacularly in the worst thunderstorm. The evening trips provide a more enchanted view of the capital's riverside buildings as floodlighting highlights the architectural details.

Bateaux-Mouches: embarkation — Alma Bridge, right bank (7e), ☎ 42 25 96 10.

Bateaux Parisiens Tour Eiffel: embarkation — Port de la Bourdonnais beside Iéna Bridge, left bank (16e), ☎ 47 05 50 00.

Vedettes du Pont-Neuf: embarkation — Square du Vert Galant, Pont-Neuf Bridge (4e), ☎ 46 33 98 38.

Vedettes de Paris-Ile de France: embarkation — Port de Suffren, between Iéna Bridge and Bir-Hakeim Bridge, left bank (15e), ☎ 45 50 23 79.

BatObus. — Riverboats operate a scheduled service on the Seine with five stops between Iéna Bridge and Ile de la Cité. *This daily service operates between 1 May and 30 September from 10am to 8pm. Day, 3-day and 7-day passes available.*

Sightseeing tours. — Apply to:

Cityrama Excursions: 4 Place des Pyramides, Paris 1er, ☎ 42 60 30 14.

Paris Vision: 214 Rue de Rivoli, Paris 1er, ☎ 42 60 31 25.

Panam 2002: ☎ 42 25 64 39. Cruises include either lunch or dinner on board.

Helicopter tours. — Apply to 4 Avenue de la Porte de Sèvres, 15e; Helicap ☎ 45 57 75 51; Hélifrance ☎ 45 57 53 67.

Paristoric. — Espace Hébertot, 78 bis Boulevard des Batignolles, Paris 17e, ☎ 42 93 93 46. *Daily on the hour from 9am to 6pm (9pm Fridays and Saturdays); time: 40mins; 45F, children 30F.*

This lively and interesting multi-media show presents the capital's important monuments from Lutetia's earliest ruins to the modern landmarks of today, such as the Great Arch at La Défense. It makes an ideal introduction to a visit to the city as it places the main sights in their historical context.

Museums, art galleries and exhibitions. — Some 100 museums, 200 art galleries and numerous temporary exhibitions keep up Paris' international reputation as a cultural and artistic centre. All national museums and art galleries are closed on Tuesdays and all those belonging to the City of Paris on Mondays. A special Museums and Monuments Pass *(Carte Musées et monuments)* gives access to 65 museums and monuments in the capital. It may be purchased in the museums themselves, in *métro* stations or from travel agents before leaving home. *Price: 55F, 110F or 160F for 1, 3 and 5 days respectively.*

Admission times and charges. — The visiting times indicate the hours of opening and closing and it is important to remember that many museums, churches etc refuse admittance from up to an hour before the actual closing time.

When guided tours are indicated, the departure time for the last tour of the morning or afternoon will once again be prior to the given closing time.

Most tours are conducted by French-speaking guides but in some cases the term guided tour may cover group visiting with recorded commentaries. Some of the larger and more frequented museums and monuments offer guided tours in other languages. Enquire at the ticket or book stalls.

The admission prices indicated are for adults; however reductions for children, students and parties are common. In some cases admission is free on certain days, eg Wednesdays, Sundays or public holidays.

Public holidays. — The following are days when museums and other monuments may be closed or may vary their hours of admission:

New Year's Day	France's National Day (14 July)
Easter Sunday and Monday	Assumption (15 August)
May Day (1 May)	All Saints' Day (1 November)
V E Day (8 May)	Armistice Day (11 November)
Ascension Day	Christmas Day
Whit Sunday and Monday	

In addition to the usual school holidays at Christmas, Easter and summer there are long mid-term breaks (10 days to a fortnight) in February and early November.

Entertainment. — Look in the *Officiel des Spectacles* (2F), *Une semaine de Paris-Pariscope (3F) and 7 à Paris (3F)* published weekly on Wednesdays and available at newspaper kiosks for a full programme of what's on in the theatre, cinema, nightclubs and for sporting and athletic fixtures, exhibitions, flower shows etc. Agencies and hotels will give details of the entertainments at the Folies-Bergère, the Lido, the Casino de Paris, the Crazy Horse Saloon, the Moulin Rouge, Olympia and Bobino's.

The following **Theatre Ticket Booths** offer, when available, half-price tickets for same-day performances:
Place de la Madeleine, to the west of the church; *open Tuesdays to Sundays including holidays 12.30pm to 8pm, closed Mondays;*
RER station Châtelet-les-Halles (opposite the FNAC); *open Tuesdays to Saturdays 12.30pm to 7.30pm, closed Sundays, Mondays and holidays;*
Montparnasse Station, on the parvis in front of the Montparnasse Tower; *operational in 1992.*

Tourism for the disabled. — Some of the sights described in this guide are accessible to disabled people. They are listed in the publication *Touristes quand même ! Access in Paris* is a guide for the disabled and those who have problems getting around. This carefully researched guide gives information about travel, accommodation and tourist attractions in Paris and is cross-referenced to Michelin maps and guides.

USEFUL ADDRESSES

Accueil de France, 127 Avenue des Champs-Élysées, 8ᵉ ☎ 47 23 61 72.
Accueil de la Ville de Paris, Hôtel de Ville, 29 Rue de Rivoli, 4ᵉ ☎ 42 76 40 40.
American Express, 11 Rue Scribe, 9ᵉ ☎ 47 77 77 07.
British Rail (Britrail Voyages), 55-57 Rue Saint-Roch, 1ᵉʳ ☎ 42 61 85 40.

Embassies

Australia, 4 Rue Jean-Rey, 15ᵉ ☎ 40 59 33 00.
Canada, 35 Avenue Montaigne, 8ᵉ ☎ 47 23 01 01.
Great Britain, 35 Rue du Faubourg St-Honoré, 8ᵉ ☎ 42 66 91 42.
    Visas: 16 Rue d'Anjou, 8ᵉ.
Ireland, 4 Rue Rude, 16ᵉ ☎ 45 00 20 87.
New Zealand: 7 ter rue Léonard de Vinci, 16ᵉ ☎ 45 00 24 11.
South Africa, 59 Quai d'Orsay, 7ᵉ ☎ 45 55 92 37.
United States, 2 Avenue Gabriel, 8ᵉ ☎ 42 96 12 02.
    Visas: 2 Rue St-Florentin, 1ᵉʳ, ☎ 42 96 15 88.

Hospitals

American Hospital, 63 Bd Victor Hugo, 93 Neuilly-sur-Seine (7.5 km - 5 miles from central Paris) ☎ 46 41 25 25.
British Hospital, 3 Rue Barbès, 92 Levallois-Perret (7.5km - 5 miles) ☎ 47 58 13 12.

Books in English

Attica, 84 Bd St-Michel, 6ᵉ ☎ 46 34 16 30.
Brentano's, 37 Avenue de l'Opéra, 2ᵉ ☎ 42 61 52 50.
Galignani, 224 Rue de Rivoli, 1ᵉʳ ☎ 42 60 76 07.
Nouveau Quartier Latin, 78 Bd St-Michel, 6ᵉ ☎ 43 26 42 70.
Shakespeare and Co, 37 Rue de la Bûcherie, 5ᵉ ☎ 43 26 96 50.
W. H. Smith, 248 Rue de Rivoli, 1ᵉʳ ☎ 42 60 37 97.

Air Terminals, Airports, Airline Offices

Aérogare de Paris: Les Invalides, coach connection with Orly. Aérogare de Paris: Porte Maillot, ground floor, coach connection with Charles-de-Gaulle. ☎ 43 35 61 61 or MINITEL 36 15 HORAV.
Charles-de-Gaulle Airport, Autoroute du Nord, ☎ 48 62 22 80 (27km - 17 miles from central Paris).
Orly Airport, Autoroute du Sud, ☎ 48 84 32 10 (16km - 10 miles).
Air France, 119 Avenue des Champs-Élysées, 8ᵉ ☎ 42 99 23 64.
Air Canada, 31 Rue Falguière, 15ᵉ ☎ 43 20 12 00.
Aer Lingus, 47 Avenue de l'Opéra, 2ᵉ ☎ 47 42 12 50.
British Airways, 12 Rue Castiglione 1ᵉʳ ☎ 47 78 14 14.
Quantas, 7 Rue Scribe, 9ᵉ ☎ 42 66 52 00.
T.W.A., 101 Avenue des Champs-Élysées, 8ᵉ ☎ 47 20 62 11.

*The **Domes of Paris***
*provide some of the most familiar silhouettes on the city's skyline. With their dignified and sweeping lines these masterpieces were the work of leading architects, François Mansart, Jacques Le Mercier and Louis Le Vau. The **Dome Church** (1677-1735 by J H Mansart) brought to perfection an idea developed in the **Church of the Val-de-Grâce** (1645-67 by F Mansart then Le Mercier) and the **Institut de France** (1663-70 by Le Vau). The **Pantheon's** dome by Soufflot dates from the 18C.*

Churches, Synagogues
American Church, 65 Quai d'Orsay, 7ᵉ — ☎ 47 05 07 99.
American Cathedral in Paris, 23 Avenue George-V, 8ᵉ — ☎ 42 27 28 56.
St Joseph's English Catholic Church, 50 Avenue Hoche, 8ᵉ — ☎ 42 27 28 56.
St Michael's English Church, 5 Rue d'Aguesseau, 8ᵉ — ☎ 47 42 70 88.
Church of Scotland, 17 Rue Bayard, 8ᵉ — ☎ 48 78 47 94.
St George's (Anglican), 7 Rue Auguste-Vacquerie, 16ᵉ — ☎ 47 20 22 51.
Liberal Synagogue, 24 Rue Copernic, 16ᵉ — ☎ 47 04 37 27.
Great Synagogue, 44 Rue de la Victoire or 17 Rue St-Georges 9ᵉ — ☎ 45 26 95 36.

Prices and tipping (mid-1992). — In shops and on menus, items are clearly marked; small extras cost approximately the following:

English newspapers (dailies) 10-15F
American newspapers (dailies, printed in France) 8.50F

Diesel (per litre) 4.00F
Petrol-Super (per litre) 5.60F
Petrol-unleaded 98 octane (per litre) 5.30F

English cigarettes .... 10 to 15F
American cigarettes .... 10 to 12F
French cigarettes .... 5.50 to 10F

Postage: to UK .... letter 2.50F; card 2.10F
         to USA — Airmail .... Aerogramme 4.20F; card 3.50F

Coffee — *un café* (black *espresso*) 4.50F
Coffee and milk — *un café au lait* .... 6.50 to 7.50F
Fresh lemon or orange juice — *citron pressé, orange pressée* ⁚ 16F
A beer (bottled) — *une bière bouteille* .... 9.50 to 15F
A beer (draught) — *une bière pression* .... 12 to 16F

Service is often included on the bill; if in doubt ask; if it is not, add on 15 %.

During the season, it is difficult to find hotel accommodation in Paris.
It is wise to book your hotel in advance by letter or by telephone.
*Or, apply to **Accueil de France**,*
127, Champs-Élysées, 8ᵉ, ☎ 47 23 61 72.

BOOKS TO READ

Artistic, architectural, historical and general background:
Paris — JOHN RUSSELL *(Thames & Hudson)*
The Sun King — NANCY MITFORD *(Hamish Hamilton)*
The French — THEODORE ZELDIN *(Collins)*
A Moveable Feast — ERNEST HEMINGWAY *(Granada Paperbacks)*
Paris Art Guide — FIONA DUNLOP *(A & C Black)*
Access in Paris (Disabled Tourists' Guide) — *Obtainable from Pauline Hephaistos Survey Projects, 39 Bradley Gardens, West Ealing, London W5*

Five English and American fiction classics:
CHARLES DICKENS — **The Tale of Two Cities**
BARONESS ORCZY — **The Scarlet Pimpernel**
ARNOLD BENNETT — **The Old Wives' Tale** (the 1870-71 siege)
HELEN WADDELL — **Peter Abelard**
ELIOT PAUL — **A Narrow Street**

There are English translations of the works of the major authors mentioned on p 23. There are also about 150 works of fiction with Paris as their setting which make amusing holiday or post-holiday reading. They range from the semi-biographical, semi-factual to light romances and fast-moving detective stories — you will find them listed in the Cumulative Fiction volumes.

TOURIST CALENDAR OF EVENTS

Last Sunday in January
Vincennes racecourse .... America Stakes

February
CNIT-La Défense — Porte de Versailles .... World Trade Fair on Tourism and Travel

Early March
Parc des Expositions — Porte de Versailles Agricultural Show

Late March
Floral Garden (Vincennes) .... International Bicycle Show

Easter Sunday
Auteuil racecourse .... President of the République Stakes

Palm Sunday to end of May
Vincennes (Reuilly Lawn) .... Throne Fair

April
Bagatelle (Bois de Boulogne) .... Azaleas
Floral Garden (Vincennes) .... Tulips
Grand Palais .... Book Fair

Late April — early May
Parc des Expositions — Porte de Versailles Paris Fair

Late April — early June
Floral Garden (Vincennes) .... Rhododendrons

Late May — early June
Roland Garros Courts .... French Open Tennis Championships

June
Parc des Princes Stadium .... Football Cup Final

Special venues .... Paris Festival (☎ 40 27 99 07)

Third Sunday in June
Auteuil racecourse .... Grand Steeplechase de Paris

Last Sunday in June
Longchamp racecourse .... Paris Grand Prix — Louis Vuitton

June — October
Bagatelle (Parc Floral) .... Roses

14 July
Champs-Élysées .... Military march-past, open air celebrations, fireworks

Mid-July
Champs-Élysées .... Finish of the Tour de France cycle race

Mid-July — early September
Special venues .... Paris Summer Festival (☎ 48 04 98 01)

September
Vincennes racecourse .... Summer Grand Prix

September — October
Floral Garden (Vincennes) .... Dahlias

Mid-September — Mid-December
Special venues .... Autumn Festival (☎ 42 96 12 27)

October
Parc des Expositions de Paris-Nord-Villepinte SICOB: Office Automation and Computing Fair

October *(even years)*
Parc des Expositions — Porte de Versailles Motor Show

First Saturday in October
Montmartre .... Wine Harvest Festival

First Sunday in October
Longchamp racecourse .... Prix de l'Arc de Triomphe

Seine — Eiffel Tower .... 6-hour Power Boat Race

Second Sunday in October
Rue Lepic .... Veteran cars hill race

Last fortnight in October
Municipal Flower Garden (Boulogne) .... Chrysanthemums

Late October
Grand Palais .... International Contemporary Art Fair
Parc des Expositions — Porte de Versailles D.I.Y. Show

1 November or nearest Sunday
Auteuil racecourse .... Montgomery Grand Prix

11 November (Remembrance Sunday)
Arc de Triomphe .... Military Parade

Late November — early December
Parc des Expositions .... Motorcycle Show

December
Parc des Expositions — Porte de Versailles Boat Show

ON A FINE DAY

Monuments

Arc de Triomphe — 19C
Place de la Concorde — 18C
The Invalides — 17C

The Louvre — 14-19C
Notre-Dame — 12-14C
The Eiffel Tower — 19C

Vistas, views

Arc de Triomphe (Platform)
Montparnasse (Tower)
Notre-Dame (Towers)
Sacré-Cœur (Dome)
The Eiffel Tower (stage 3)
Georges Pompidou Centre (5th floor)

Alexandre III Bridge
Place de la Concorde
Orléans Quay
Chaillot Palace (Terrace)
Tournelle Bridge
Viviani Square

Recreation areas

Bagatelle, Pré Catelan (Bois de
Boulogne)
Luxembourg Gardens

Botanical Gardens
Floral Garden (Bois de Vincennes)
La Villette Park

Open-air markets

Flowers (Place L.-Lépine)
Birds (Quai de la Mégisserie)

Stamps, post cards, phonecards, pin's (Avenue de Marigny)
Book stalls (The quays)

Attractions for children

Aquarium (tropical fish) (Museum of
African Art)
Amusement Park (Bois de Boulogne)

Zoo, vivarium (Botanical Gardens)
Zoo (Bois de Vincennes)

ON A RAINY DAY

Principal museums

Louvre (Paintings, sculpture)
Modern Art (Modern paintings)
Army (Arms, uniforms)
Decorative Arts (Furnishings, applied
arts)
Popular Art and Traditions (Crafts)
Carnavalet (History of Paris)
Cluny (Decorative arts of the Middle
Ages)
Conciergerie (Historic prison)
Palais de la Découverte (Scientific
discoveries)

Guimet (Oriental art)
Mankind (History of mankind)
Jacquemart-André (Furniture, paintings)
Maritime (Naval history, navigation)
French Monuments (Plaster casts, murals)
Rodin (Sculpture by Rodin)
Orsay (Arts from 1848 to 1914)
La Villette (Science and Technology)

Religious art

Ste-Chapelle (Stained-glass windows)
St-Germain-l'Auxerrois (Stained glass,
altarpiece, pew)

St-Étienne-du-Mont (Roodscreen)
St-Sulpice (Organ loft, murals)

Antique dealers

Cour des Antiquaires
Louvre des Antiquaires
Flea Market

Village Suisse
Nouveau Drouot

Shopping centres, galleries, arcades

Forum des Halles
Centre Beaugrenelle
Palais des Congrès
Centre Maine-Montparnasse

Quatre-Temps, La Défense
Champs-Élysées Arcades
Rivoli Arcades

*Versailles, St-Denis, Fontainebleau and Chantilly
are only some of the sights described
in the English edition of the
Michelin Green Guide Ile-de-France.*

MUSEUMS BY SUBJECT

Antiquities
Louvre★★★ p 29.

Army
Army Museum★★★ p 71; Museum of the Order of Liberation★★ p 75.

Art
Louvre★★★ p 29; *African:* African and Oceanian Art Museum★ p 224; Armenian Museum p 244; Decorative Arts: see below; *European:* Cognacq-Jay Museum★★ (18C) p 93; Jacquemart-André Museum★★ p 79; Nissim de Camondo Museum★★ (18C) p 250, Orsay Museum★★★ (19C) p 125; Petit Palais★, p 56; French Monuments★★ p 64; *Impressionism:* Orangery★ p 54, Orsay Museum★★★, p 125; Marmottan Museum★★ p 249; Jewish Art p 246; *Modern Art:* Palais de Tokyo p 210; National Museum of Modern Art★★★; Beaubourg p 148; *Nabis:* Orsay Museum★★★ p 125; *Naive* p 87; *Oriental:* see below; *Popular:* National Museum of Popular Arts and Traditions★★ p 253.

Artists; Sculptors
Bouchard p 240; Bourdelle★ p 206; Dali p 88; Delacroix p 178; Henner p 246; G. Moreau p 248; Picasso p 99; Scheffer (Romantic Movement Museum) p 254, Rodin p 169; Zadkine p 259.

Books, MSS, Prints, Maps, Posters
Bibliothèque Nationale★ p 137; Forney Library (Posters) p 101.

Coins, Medals, Orders
Army Museum★★★ p 71; Bibliothèque Nationale★ p 137; Legion of Honour Museum★ p 168; The Mint★ p 172.

Costume, Fashion
Costume and Fashion Museum p 140; Palais Galliera p 211.

Decorative Arts
Gobelins' Tapestry Factory★ p 245; Hotel de Cluny Museum★★ (Middle Ages) p 183; Museum of Decorative Arts★★ p 140.

Glass
Glass Museum★ p 250.

History
of Paris: Hotel Carnavalet Museum★★ p 96; Hotel de Cluny Museum★★ (Middle Ages) p 183; Hotel de Lamoignon (Historical Library) p 97; Museum of Old Montmartre p 89.
of France: Historical Museum of France★★ p 98.

Maritime
Maritime Museum★★ p 64.

Miscellaneous
Bricard Museum (Locks) p 99; Christofle Museum (Gold and silver ware) p 78; Counterfeit Museum p 244; Grand Orient Lodge Museum (Freemasonry) p 246; Museum of the Chase and of Nature p 98; Police Museum p 191; Postal Museum★★ p 206; SEITA Gallery Museum (Tobacco) p 257; Paris Hospitals' Museum p 105; Museum of Spectacles p 249; Sports Museum p 212; Wine Museum p 251.

Music
Musical Instruments Museum (Mechanical reproducers of music) p 150; Opera (Museum) p 83.

Oriental Art
Cernuschi Museum★ (Chinese) p 241; Ennery Museum (Chinese and Japanese) p 244; Guimet Museum★★ p 210; Institute of the Arab World★ p 239.

Personalities
Balzac p 252; Clemenceau p 251; Victor Hugo p 95; Mickiewicz p 124; Pasteur p 252.

Science
Anthropology: Museum of Mankind★★ p 65; *Astronomy:* the Observatory★ p 202; Palais de la Découverte★★ p 57; *Holography:* Holography Museum p 143; *Medicine:* Val de Grâce Museum p 201; *Mineralogy:* School of Advanced Mining Engineering★★ p 202; *Botanical* Gardens p 237; Mineralogical Museum★★ p 239; *Natural History:* Botanical Gardens p 237; *Radio and Television:* Radio France House p 233; *Science:* City of Science and Industry★★★ p 158; National Technical Museum★★ p 241; Palais de la Découverte★★ p 57; *Marine and Freshwater Centre* p 201; Oceanic Centre p 143.

Theatre, Cinema
Arsenal Library (Theatre Collection) p 233; Henri Langlois Cinema Museum★ p 65; Kwok-On Museum (Oriental Theatre) p 102.

Waxworks
Grevin Museum★ p 153; Grevin's Forum Annexe★ p 143.

HISTORICAL FACTS

Gallo-Roman period

3rdC BC	The Parisii settle on the Ile de la Cité.
52 BC	Labienus, Caesar's lieutenant defeats the Gauls under Camulogenes, who set alight and then abandon the Ile de la Cité.
1C AD	The Gallo-Romans build the city of Lutetia.
c 250	St Denis, first Bishop of the city, is martyred (p 86).
280	Lutetia destroyed by the Barbarians.
360	Julian the Apostate, prefect of the Gauls, is proclaimed by his soldiers Emperor of Rome when in the Cité. Lutetia becomes Paris.

Early Middle Ages

451	St Geneviève turns Attila away from Paris (p 112).
508	Clovis makes Paris his capital and settles in the Cité.
8C	Charlemagne makes Aix-la-Chapelle (Aachen) his foremost city. Paris, abandoned, declines.
885	Paris besieged by the Normans for the fifth time, is defended by Count Eudes who is elected King of France in 888 (p 112).

The Capetians

Early 12C	Abelard, first studies, then teaches, in Paris. Suger, Abbot of St-Denis and minister under Louis VI and Louis VII, rebuilds the abbey.
1163	Maurice of Sully undertakes the construction of Notre-Dame.
1180-1223	Philippe Auguste erects a wall around Paris and builds the Louvre.
1215	Foundation of the University of Paris (p 186).
1226-1270	Reign of St Louis: Pierre of Montreuil builds the Sainte-Chapelle, works on Notre-Dame and St-Denis. The king dispenses justice at Vincennes.
1253	Foundation of Sorbon College (p 188).
1260	The dean of the Merchants' Guild becomes Provost of Paris (p 106).
1307	Philip the Fair dissolves the Order of the Knights Templar (p 259).

The Valois

1358	Uprising under Étienne Marcel (pp 106, 118). The monarchy moves to the Marais and the Louvre.
1364-1380	Charles V builds the Bastille and a new wall around Paris (p 20).
1407	Duke Louis of Orleans is assassinated on the orders of John the Fearless (p 100).
1408-1420	Fighting between the Armagnacs and Burgundians. Paris handed over to the English.
1429	Charles VII besieges Paris in vain; Joan of Arc is wounded (p 140).
1430	Henry VI of England is crowned King of France in Notre-Dame.
1437	Charles VII recaptures Paris.
1469	The first French printing works opens in the Sorbonne.
1530	François I founds the Collège de France.
1534	Ignatius Loyola founds the Society of Jesus in Montmartre (p 87).
1559	Henri II is fatally wounded in a tourney (p 94).
1572	Massacre of St Bartholomew (p 107).
1578-1604	Construction of the Pont Neuf (p 122).
1588	The Catholic League turns against Henri III who is forced to flee Paris, after the Day of the Barricades (12 May).
1589	Paris is invested by Henri III and Henri of Navarre. The former is assassinated at St-Cloud.

The Bourbons

1594	Henri IV is converted to Catholicism; Paris opens her gates to him.
1605	Creation of the Place des Vosges.
14 May 1610	Henri IV is mortally wounded by Ravaillac (p 146).
1615-1625	Marie de' Medici has the Luxembourg Palace built.
1622	Paris becomes an episcopal see.
1627-1664	Development of the Ile St-Louis.
1635	Richelieu founds the French Academy.
1648-1653	Paris disturbed by the Fronde (p 235).
1661	Mazarin founds the College of Four Nations, the future Institut de France (p 173).
1667	Colbert establishes the Observatory (p 202) and reorganizes the Gobelins Tapestry Factory (p 245).
17C	Construction of Versailles; development of the Marais.
Late 17C	Erection of the Louvre Colonnade and the Invalides.
Early 18C	Construction of the Place Vendôme and development of the Faubourg St-Germain.
1717-1720	John Law's Bank (p 146).
1722	Creation of the first Fire Brigade.
1727-1732	End of the Jansenist crisis; the St Medard "Convulsionnaires" (p 255).
c 1760	Louis XV has the École Militaire, the Pantheon and the Place de la Concorde constructed.
1783	Ascent of the balloonists Pilâtre de Rozier (pp 242, 249), and Charles and Robert (p 52).
1784-1791	Erection of the Farmers General Wall (p 20) including the gateways and toll-houses by Ledoux.

The Revolution and the First Empire

14 July 1789	Taking of the Bastille *(p 236)*.
17 July 1789	Louis XVI at the Hôtel de Ville: adoption of the tricolour *(p 106)*.
14 July 1790	Festival of Federation *(p 65)*.
20 June 1792	The mob invades the Tuileries *(p 31)*.
10 Aug. 1792	Taking of the Tuileries and the fall of the monarchy *(p 32)*.
2-4 Sept. 1792	September Massacres *(p 177)*.
21 Sept. 1792	Proclamation of the Republic *(p 138)*.
21 Jan. 1793	Execution of Louis XVI *(pp 55, 242)*.
1793	Opening of the Louvre Museum.
1793-1794	The Terror *(pp 55, 120, 250)*.
8 June 1794	Festival of the Supreme Being *(pp 52, 65)*.
5 Oct. 1795	Royalist uprising suppressed by Napoleon *(p 139)*.
9-10 Nov. 1799	Fall of the Directory.
1800	Bonaparte creates the offices of Prefect of the Seine and of the Police.
2 Dec. 1804	Napoleon's coronation at Notre-Dame *(p 113)*.
1806-1814	Napoleon continues construction of the Louvre and erects the Arc de Triomphe and Vendôme Column. Stay at Malmaison.
31 March 1814	The Allies occupy Paris.

The Restoration

1815	Waterloo. Restoration of the Bourbons.
1821-1825	Construction of the Ourcq, St-Denis and St-Martin Canals.
1830	Fall of Charles X; flight to the Palace of Holyroodhouse.
1832	A cholera epidemic kills 19 000 Parisians.
1837	The first French railway line, Paris-St-Germain is opened.
1840	Return of Napoleon's body from St Helena *(p 70)*.
1841-1845	Construction of the Thiers fortifications *(p 20)*.
February 1848	Fall of Louis-Philippe *(p 82)*. Proclamation of the Second Republic *(p 106)*.

From 1848 to 1870

June 1848	The suppression of the national workshops creates disturbances in the Faubourg St-Antoine *(p 242)*.
1852-1870	Gigantic town planning undertakings by Baron Haussmann: the Halles, railway stations, Buttes-Chaumont, Bois de Boulogne and Vincennes, the Opera, the sewers, completion of the Louvre, laying of the boulevards through the old quarters of the city. Paris is divided into 20 *arrondissements*.
1855-1867	World Exhibitions.
4 Sept. 1870	The Third Republic is proclaimed at the Hôtel de Ville *(p 106)*.

The Third Republic

Winter 1870-1871	Paris is besieged by the Prussians and capitulates *(p 106)*. St-Cloud Château is burnt to the ground. Napoleon III goes into exile in England.
March-May 1871	The Paris Commune is finally suppressed by the Men of Versailles during the Bloody Week (21-28 May); fire, destruction (Tuileries, Old Auditor General's Office, Hôtel de Ville, Vendôme Column) and massacres *(p 252)*.
1885	State funeral of Victor Hugo.
1889	World Exhibition at the foot of the new Eiffel Tower *(p 66)*.
1900	First *métro* line opened: Maillot-Vincennes. Construction of the Grand and Petit Palais *(p 56)*; Cubism is born at the Bateau-Lavoir *(p 87)*. The Sacré-Cœur Basilica is erected on the Butte Montmartre *(p 88)*.
1914-1918	Paris under threat of German attack is saved by the Battle of the Marne. A shell hits the Church of St-Gervais/St-Protais *(p 105)*.
1920	Interment of the Unknown Soldier *(p 58)*.
February 1934	Rioting in the vicinity of the Chamber of Deputies.
June 1940	Paris is bombed then occupied by the Germans. Hostages and resistance fighters detained at Mount Valérien.
August 1944	Liberation of Paris: week of 19-26 *(pp 56, 138)*.

Since 1945

1950	Opening of the downstream port of Gennevilliers.
1958-1963	Construction of UNESCO *(p 67)*, CNIT *(p 230)*, and ORTF buildings (now Radio-France House *p 233*).
1964	Reorganization of departments of the Paris region: Nanterre, Créteil and Bobigny become prefectures.
1965	Paris region Town and Development Plan published.
May 1968	Strikes and demonstrations: Nanterre, Latin Quarter, the Boulevards, the Champs-Élysées.
1969	Transfer of the Halles Market to Rungis.
1970	Regional express *métro* system inaugurated. Thirteen autonomous universities created in the Paris Region.
1973	Completion of the ring road and Montparnasse Tower.
February 1974	Opening of the Paris Conference Centre *(p 250)*.
March 1977	Election of the first mayor of Paris since 1871 (1789-1871: 11 appointed mayors).
May-June 1980	Pope John Paul II on an official visit to Paris.

PARIS YESTERDAY

The capital's site was carved out of the limestone and Tertiary sands by the Seine at the centre of what is now the Paris Basin. At that time the river flowed at a level of 35m - 100ft — above its present course.

The Gallo-Roman Wall:🛈. — The Parisii, taking advantage of the *Pax romana*, emerged from Lutetia, built by the Gauls and defended by the river and surrounding swamps, to settle along the Left Bank of the river *(p 185)*. The Barbarians, however, forced them to retreat, in about 276, to the Cité. On the island, they built houses, fortifications and a rampart wall to defend themselves against future invasions.

The Philippe Auguste Wall:🛈. — Between the 6 and 10C, the swamps were drained and cultivated, monasteries founded and a river harbour established near the Place de Grève. Between 1180 and 1210 Philippe Auguste commanded that a massive wall be built *(pp 102, 191)* reinforced upstream by a chain barrage across the river and downstream by the Louvre Fortress and Nesle Tower.

The Charles V Rampart:🛈. — The Town, which was on the Right Bank (as opposed to the University on the Left Bank, and the Cité), prospered as roads were built connecting it with Montmartre, St-Denis, the Knights Templar Commandery, Vincennes Castle. By the end of the 14C, Charles V had erected new fortifications, supported in the east by the Bastille. The ramparts enclosed a Paris of just under 440ha — 1 3/4sq miles — and 150 000 inhabitants.

The Louis XIII Wall:🛈. — In the 16C the Catholic League, Wars of Religion, the siege by Henri of Navarre kept up the pressure on the city so that Charles IX and Louis XIII extended the 14C wall westward to include the Louvre Palace.

The Farmers General Wall:🛈. — The monarchy moved to Versailles. Paris now 500 000 strong, saw the erection of the Invalides, the Observatory, the Salpêtrière and the St-Denis and St-Martin Gates. The enclosed city was too small so a new wall (1784-1791) complete with 57 **toll-houses** by Ledoux was constructed *(pp 247, 254)*. "The wall, walling in Paris", it was said, however, "makes Parisians wail".

The Thiers Fortifications:🛈. — Under the Revolution properties were broken up but little was built; under the Empire, Paris began to know problems of overcrowding and supply; gas lighting appeared during the Restoration; industry, railways and economic development brought growth to outlying villages (Austerlitz, Montrouge, Vaugirard, Passy, Montmartre, Belleville) which Thiers had enclosed in a further wall (1841-45), reinforced at a cannonball's distance by 16 bastions — these became the capital's official limits from 1859. Twenty *arrondissements* were created in the 7 800ha - 30sq miles — as Haussmann began his transformation of the city (Population — 1846: 1 050 000; 1866: 1 800 000).

The present limits:🛈. — The forts remained intact (Mount Valérien, Romainville, Ivry, Bagneux...), but the walls after serving in the city's defense in 1871, were razed by the Third Republic in 1919.
Paris' limits were defined between 1925 and 1930 as including the Bois de Boulogne and Vincennes and not extending elsewhere beyond a narrow circular belt; the area equalled 10 540ha - 40 3/4sq miles — and the population, in 1945, 2 700 000.

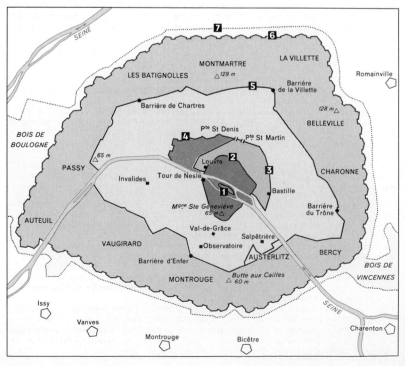

PARIS TODAY

Paris' centrifugal attraction dates from the First Empire; since then it has developed, pell mell, as the pivot of France's political, administrative, economic and cultural life. A century after Baron Haussmann's large-scale town planning works *(p 19)*, a plan was adopted in 1960 to resolve, at least, the capital's physical problems. 1965 saw the publication of a development plan.

Local government. — Since March 1977, the **Mairie de Paris** has had an elected mayor, chosen by the 163 councillors of the municipal council; the municipal elections are held every six years. With the exception of the police force, headed by a *préfet*, the mayor has the status and powers of mayors of other municipalities.

The municipal authority works closely with the primary units of Paris local government, the town halls of the 20 arrondissements, which are responsible for local problems. Paris being both a commune and a department its Council sits as a municipal authority and a general or departmental council.

The city's coat of arms features the boat motif from the armorial bearings of the watermen's guild whose members were appointed by St Louis *(p 106)* in 1260 to administer the township. In the 16C the device was complemented by the motto *Fluctuat nec mergitur* — she is buffetted by the waves but does not sink.

Seal of the Watermen's Guild (1210)

The **Ile-de-France Region** comprises eight departments (Paris, Seine-et-Marne, Yvelines, Essonne, Hauts-de-Seine, Seine-St-Denis, Val-de-Marne and Val-d'Oise), each with its own prefecture, and covers a total area of 12 011km^2 - 4 637sq miles with a total population of 10 073 053 (Paris: 105km^2 - 40 sq miles; 2 176 243). The Regional Council — drawn from local authorities — is paralleled by an Economic and Social Committee. Since the 1982 decentralisation act the Regional Council is no longer headed by the *Préfet*. The latter now known as Commissioner of the Republic also exercises the same role for the department of Paris.

Metamorphosis. — Paris' historic, architectural and archeological treasures stand out in all their glory once more thanks to the enlightened policy of André Malraux and his followers who instituted a programme of cleaning, restoration, revitalising even whole areas such as the Marais and preservation of archeological ruins.

Engineers and planners wrestle with today's problems — highways and transport (the ring road, expressway, RER), supply (Rungis, Garonor), cultural centre (Georges Pompidou Centre), sports facilities (Palais Omnisports de Bercy), office expansion (Défense, Front de Seine, Maine-Montparnasse), and urban renewal (Place d'Italie, Belleville, Bercy). The emphasis is now on the preservation and restoration of the historic heritage.

Major cultural projects include the City of Science and Industry and Music Centre at La Villette, the Museum of 19C Art in the Gare d'Orsay, the Grand Louvre project, a new Opera House at La Bastille and the International Foundation for the Rights of Man of La Défense.

The departure of the Halles to Rungis, the explosion of the University into thirteen autonomous universities, the decentralisation of the Higher Schools of learning, have contributed in relieving congestion at the centre. Modern hospitals, both public and private, have been erected. Green spaces (La Villette, Georges Brassens Park) have been created, aged parks and gardens refurbished...

Future prospects. — The future of the city is based on the revitalisation of run-down areas and the development of dynamic centres (La Défense, Bercy, La Villette) and on maintaining the level of population and employment in the city.

Population. — Paris which has over 2 million inhabitants is one of the most densely populated cities in the world.

The population of Paris proper is slightly decreasing but over the years Paris has become the home of men and women from Brittany to Corsica, of strangers from abroad who congregate in certain areas: Jews in the Marais, White Russians in Montparnasse, Spaniards in Passy, North Africans in Clignancourt, La Villette, Aubervilliers, Asians in the 13th arrondissement...

The true Parisian, however, remains easily identifiable among the cosmopolitan crowd: hurried, tense, protesting, frivolous, mocking, quick witted, punning — personified in the cabaret singer, the barrow boy, the urchin.

Paris quarters. — Some quarters have kept their association with a medieval craft or an age-old trade and retain something of the atmosphere of past centuries: Quai de la Mégisserie — seed merchants; the Odéon area — publishing houses and bookshops; the Rue du Faubourg St-Antoine — cabinet-makers; the Temple and Sentier quarters — secondhand dealers, particularly of clothes; the Rues Bonaparte and la Boëtie — antique dealers; Avenue Matignon and Rue du Faubourg St-Honoré — art galleries; Rue du Faubourg St-Honoré, Avenue Montaigne and Rue François-Ier — fashion houses; Opéra quarter — luxury shops; Rue de Rome — stringed instrument makers; Rue de Paradis — porcelain, crystal and glassware; Rue de la Paix and Place Vendôme — jewellers' shops.

There are, in addition, the streets lined with government offices (Rue de Grenelle, Chaillot), commercial organizations (Bourse, Opéra, Champs-Élysées, La Défense...), the big stores and schools. Between all these is a mosaic of workshops, warehouses and small shops which, with the many large undertakings, make up Paris' infinitely various economy.

PARIS AND THE ARTS

ARCHITECTURE

The Gallo-Roman style of architecture is virtually non-existent in Paris apart from a few cradle-vaulted arches still standing in the Roman baths at the Hôtel de Cluny and such heavily restored remains as the Lutetia arena.

Romanesque architecture. — This style, which is known in England as Norman, and is better represented elsewhere in France, can only be seen as features in a larger whole — the chancel columns and belfry-porch in St-Germain-des-Prés, the apse of St-Martin-des-Champs, and the capitals in St Peter's, Montmartre and St-Aignan Chapel.

Gothic architecture. — This is the true style of Paris' older buildings but it did not mark a clean break with Romanesque architecture. Gothic was born in the region, arising from the combined requirements of height and increased light. An ogival style evolved, characterized inside by broken arch-vaulting (St-Germain-des-Prés chancel) and outside by buttressing (St-Julien-le-Pauvre apse). These supports, it was soon discovered, could be hollowed out without diminishing their strength, and so appeared the flying buttress.

Early Gothic (12C). — The outstanding example of Gothic development between the 12 and early 14C is to be found in Paris' greatest monument Notre-Dame Cathedral: the vast chancel, the only slightly projecting transept, the sombre galleries at the back of the triforium are typical of early Gothic while firmly localizing the whole are the decorative carvings on the capitals of plants and flowers native to the Paris region. Light inside was very limited still, passing only through small narrow windows in the nave surmounted by equally small round windows or oculi, an arrangement still to be seen in the cathedral transept.

High or Rayonnant Gothic (13-14C). — Gothic skill reached its greatest heights in the reign of St Louis with the architect Pierre of Montreuil who, with awe-inspiring daring, replaced solid side walls by vast windows, letting the light pour in. Slender column walls only between the glass supported the roof, reinforced outside by unobtrusive buttresses or flying buttresses (the St-Martin-des-Champs refectory). The new lightness and window space inspired the glassmakers in their craft.

With the construction of its greatest masterpieces, the east end of Notre-Dame, the Sainte-Chapelle in the Cité, the Royal Chapel at Vincennes, the **High Gothic** style had, perhaps, reached its climax when building generally was interrupted by the outbreak of the unrest and fighting, known as the Hundred Years War (1337-1453). The rising provoked by Étienne Marcel, the civil strife between the Burgundians and the Armagnacs explain the reason for such architecture as existed in the period being massive and sombre, almost feudal in style (the Bastille and Men at Arms Hall in the Conciergerie).

Late or Flamboyant Gothic (15C). — Gothic continued into the 15C but was considerably marred by exaggerated interior decoration: purely decorative arches — liernes and tiercerons — segmented vaulting (St Merry transept, St-Germain-l'Auxerrois porch), window tracery with a flame motif, clerestory replacing the triforium, pillars, unadorned by capitals, rising in a single sweep to span out directly beneath the roof (St-Séverin ambulatory) from which hung monumental keystones (St-Étienne-du-Mont).

Examples of this Flamboyant Gothic style are the St-Jacques Tower, the Billettes Cloister and the contemporary Hôtel de Sens and Hôtel de Cluny. In these mansions, the defensive features — turrets, crenellations, wicket gates — are trimmed with richly sculptured decorations — balustrades, mullioned dormer windows — in the same way as the early châteaux of the Loire.

The Renaissance. — War with Italy introduced those who went there to the Antique style and the profane in decoration. Pointed arches gave place to cradle vaulting or coffered ceilings (St-Nicolas-des-Champs), rounded bays (St-Eustache) descended onto Ionic or Corinthian capitals topping fluted columns (St-Médard). The roodscreen at St-Étienne-du-Mont is the finest example of interior decoration which elsewhere included mythological or commonplace motifs (St-Gervais stalls).

Pierre Lescot adopted the Italian style of a uniform façade broken by advanced bays crowned by rounded pediments for the Cour Carrée in the Louvre and for the Hôtel Lamoignon. Statues decorated the niches between fluted columns; cornices and a frieze surmount the doors and each floor. Inside, the ceilings are frequently coffered and decorated as above the Henri II staircase in the Clock Pavilion again in the Louvre.

Classical architecture. — At the end of the Wars of Religion (1562-1589), the influence of Antiquity increased, the king once more asserted his power.

Religious architecture turned to the classical, a style which was to continue throughout the 17C and 18C and be characterized by a profusion of exterior columns, pediments, statues and cupolas reminiscent of the churches of Rome.

The Jesuit style of the Counter-Reformation produced a multiplicity of domes: the Sorbonne Church, the Val-de-Grâce and St-Paul-St-Louis. But this typically baroque feature was modified by the architects of Louis XIV and XV — Hardouin-Mansart (The Invalides), Libéral-Bruant (Salpêtrière), Le Vau (St-Louis-en-l'Ile), Soufflot (Pantheon). Contemporary civil constructions were characterized, in imitation of Versailles, by classical symmetry and simplification. The Place des Vosges and Place Dauphine are true Louis XIII with the alternating use of brick and stone while the Luxembourg Palace by Salomon de Brosse has a mixture of both French and Italian elements. Immediately after came the Mansarts, Androuet Du Cerceau, Delamair and Le Muet, evolving in the Marais, a new style of architecture with their designs for the town house.

Classical architecture reached its climax between 1650 and 1750 with the majestic constructions of Perrault in the Louvre Colonnade, Le Vau, the Institute, and Gabriel, the Place de la Concorde and École Militaire.

The antique simplicity of the Louis XVI style can be seen in the Palace of the Legion of Honour and the Farmers General Wall toll-houses by Ledoux (p 20).

The 19C. — The Empire and Restoration had little to show as regards architectural achievements: the Madeleine, Arc de Triomphe, and the Carrousel Arch are classical pastiches lacking any particular originality. The Second Empire, however, brought a fantastic new impetus to planning in the person of Baron Haussmann. A new style was rapidly imprinted on the capital — the iron and metalwork style exemplified by Baltard in St Augustine's and the Pavillon Baltard at Nogent-sur-Marne, Labrouste in the Bibliothèque Ste-Geneviève, Hittorff in the Gare du Nord and by Gustave Eiffel in the Eiffel Tower. While Garnier's Opera was being built, a construction in stone which was one of the most successful of the period, industrial development, the discovery of new materials and techniques and the ascendancy of domestic over monumental architecture, were inaugurating close collaboration between architects and civil engineers.

The 20C. — Just as the Grand and Petit Palais, the Alexandre III Bridge and Sacré-Cœur Basilica mark a certain attachment to the past, Baudot in St John's in Montmartre and the Perret brothers in the Champs-

A Tower at La Défense

Élysées Theatre, were discovering the possibilities of reinforced concrete which were demonstrated fully in 1937 in the Chaillot and Tokyo Palaces.
Since 1945, under the influence of Le Corbusier *(p 248)*, architectural design has undergone a fundamental reappraisal. The result is the wide variety of styles to be seen in the circular Radio-France House, the upraised UNESCO, the sweeping roof lines of the CNIT, the glass and aluminium façades at Orly, the new glass façades of the GAN and Manhattan Towers, the Georges Pompidou Centre and the Institute of the Arab World, whereas Charles de Gaulle airport, the Palais des Congrès and the Montparnasse tower illustrate the "concrete style". Currently architecture is viewed within the wider context of town planning; buildings are designed to fit into a scheme and sometimes as part of a plan for the renovation of an area (Maine-Montparnasse, Les Halles, La Villette), or the creation of a new area (La Défense). There are also large scale developments in progress such as the Bastille Opera House, the Ministry of Finance new offices in Bercy, Music City at La Villette and the Great Arch at La Défense.

SCULPTURE

The Gallo-Roman pillar of the Paris boatmen now at the Cluny Museum *(p 183)*, the capital's oldest sculpture, was followed 1 000 years later by low reliefs and statues carved by anonymous skilled craftsmen for Notre-Dame and other churches.
From the Renaissance and for the following three centuries, the monarchy decorated the city with sumptuous religious and civil constructions which were then adorned by the sculptors to the Court: Jean Goujon (Fountain of the Innocents), Germain Pilon (St-Paul-St-Louis), Girardon (Richelieu's tomb), Coysevox (Tuileries Gardens), Coustou (The Marly Horses), Robert Le Lorrain (Hôtel de Rohan), Bouchardon (Four Seasons Fountain), and Pigalle (St-Sulpice).
It was, however, during the mid and late 19C that Paris was gradually transformed into an open air museum with statues, particularly, multiplying in parks, gardens and streets: Carpeaux (Observatory Fountain) and Rude *(Marshal Ney, the Marseillaise)* were followed by Rodin *(Balzac, Victor Hugo)*, Dalou (Place de la Nation), Bourdelle (Tokyo Palace, Champs-Élysées Theatre), Maillol (Carrousel Gardens) and Landowski *(Ste-Geneviève)*.
Hector Guimard epitomized the style of 1900 in his famous wrought-iron *métro* entrances as Calder's mobile *(p 67)*, Louis Leygue, Agam (La Défense) and Arman's (St-Lazare Station) sculptures symbolize the work of the 20C abstractionists now appearing in parks and in new architectural schemes.

Métro station

PAINTING

Until the late 16C and the early 17C, Paris remained largely unrepresented pictorially apart from scenes depicted by miniaturists, painters, engravers and illuminators such as the Limbourg brothers, who included Paris backgrounds in the *Very Rich Hours* of the duc de Berry, and Jean Fouquet in the *Book of Hours* he painted for Étienne Chevalier. In the 17C landscape interest in the capital began to awaken, particularly in the Pont Neuf and the Louvre and the countryside surrounding the Invalides and the Observatory. J.-B. Raguenet, Hubert Robert, Antoine de Machy and later, Bouhot and Georges Michel, and finally Méryon with his deeply toned water colours, developed a descriptive tradition which bridges the period to the late 19C when the Impressionists emerged and made Paris the world art centre.

Corot, who painted the Paris quaysides and Ville d'Avray a few miles away, was followed by Jongkind, Lépine, Monet *(St-Germain-l'Auxerrois, Gare St-Lazare)*, Renoir, *(Moulin de la Galette, Moulin Rouge)*, Sisley *(Ile St-Louis, Auteuil Viaduct)* and Pissarro *(The Pont Neuf)* who depicted light effects in the capital at all hours and in all seasons.

Paris also played an important part in the work of Seurat *(The Eiffel Tower)*, Gauguin

Poulbot drawing

(The Seine by the Pont d'Iéna), Cézanne and Van Gogh (Montmartre scenes). Later, Vuillard painted the peace of Paris squares and gardens in a more poetic vein.

Toulouse-Lautrec, sketching with wit and intimacy cabaret artists before and behind the footlights, presented a totally different appreciation of the Paris scene. Equally keen of eye were André Gill, Forain, Willette and Poulbot *(p 88)* again portraying not Paris but the Parisian whether he be music-hall artist, politician, *pierrot* or street urchin.

At the beginning of the 20C Paris was at its height with the Paris School created by foreign artists working in here (Modigliani, Chagall, Soutine), the inspiration of all, and the Bateau-Lavoir *(p 87)* and the Ruche *(p 204)*, the centres of good talk, discussion and revolution. The painters of that time who devoted most of their work to the Paris scene were Marquet, who enjoyed a panoramic view of the city from his window, and Maurice Utrillo who painted the unfashionable areas, the grey skies and his favourite Montmartre district.

The modern lanscape of Paris has become familiar, particularly, through the widely reproduced paintings of the present-day artists, Yves Brayer and Bernard Buffet.

MUSIC

Yesterday. — Music, in France, as elsewhere, developed most elaborately first in the church: by the end of the 12C a school of polyphony had been established in Notre-Dame, expressing in harmony the deep religious faith of the period. The Hundred Years' War (1337-1453) interrupted its development and it was only with François I that attention turned once more to the art — this time in the form of court songs and airs accompanied on the lute. In 1571, the poet, Baïf founded the Academy of Music and Poetry, to re-establish the harmony of Antiquity in poetry and music.

"That most noble and gallant art" developed naturally at the royal court, first at the Louvre, and, later, at Versailles where sovereigns, their consorts and companions disported themselves in ballets, allegorical dances, recitals, opera and comedy. The Royal Academy of Music (1672), dominated by Lulli, encouraged sacred music to new heights in Notre-Dame (with Campra), St-Gervais and the Sainte-Chapelle (with the Couperins), St-Paul-St-Louis (Charpentier) and Notre-Dame-des-Victoires (Lulli).

The Regency saw the birth of comic opera and the revitalizing of opera proper by Rameau (1683-1764). Not long after, Gluck, Parisian by adoption, produced his mature operas: *Orpheus and Eurydice, Iphigenia in Aulis* and *Alcestis* (1774-1779).

Composition, since the Revolution, has centred round the National Conservatory, founded in 1795. It was there that the young Romantic school grew up with Cherubini, Auber and Berlioz who created his *Fantastic Symphony* while at the Conservatory in 1830. These were followed by César Franck, Massenet, Fauré. Paris became the international musical capital, drawing the Italians Rossini and Donizetti, the Polish Chopin *(p 84)*, the Hungarian Liszt and the Germans Wagner *(p 84)* and Offenbach, to come and stay, often for years.

1870 and the years that followed saw activity with Bizet, Saint-Saëns, Charpentier and Dukas, Parisians by birth or adoption, bringing new life to symphony and opera, d'Indy founding the Schola Cantorum *(p 201)* and Debussy and Ravel co-operating with Diaghilev's Russian Ballet *(p 211)*. Finally came the Group of Six (Honegger, Tailleferre, Auric, Milhaud, Poulenc, Durey) and the rival Arcueil School and Sauguet.

Today. — Today Paris' musical life is reflected in a plethora of performances of large orchestras in fine concert halls, chamber music and organ recitals.

Quite different are the clubs, cellars and *boîtes* or night-clubs scattered throughout the Latin Quarter, along the Champs-Élysées, in Montmartre and Montparnasse.

Among the best are the Trois Mailletz *(56 rue Galande, 5e)*, Le Caveau de la Huchette *(5 Rue de la Huchette, 5e)*, Le Slow Club *(130 Rue de Rivoli, 1er)* and La Louisiane *(18 Rue Buzelin, 18e)*.

LETTERS

Paris, the inspiration of poets and novelists and the setting for so many works, has occupied a central place in French literature since the 13C when the University was founded and the Parisian dialect was adopted as the language of the court.

The people of the streets appear, at this time, in epic poems and mystery plays *(p 109)*; individual characters and daily life in the poems of Rutebœuf and Villon (15C). Rabelais criticized Paris, but nevertheless sent Gargantua and Pantagruel to the Sorbonne and ended up living in the Marais (c1553 — *p 102)*.

As the capital grew and attracted men of letters amongst others, it inspired a devotion in many equal to their native soil: Montaigne, Guillaume Budé, who founded the Collège de France, Ronsard and the Pléiade poets *(p 187)* and Agrippa d'Aubigné who bore witness to the religious conflicts which engulfed Paris and the rest of the country at the end of the 16C.

The 17 and 18C. — As Paris underwent alternately embellishment, under Henri IV and Louis XIII, and disruption, by the Fronde at the time of Louis XIV's minority, writers, intellectuals, wits and lesser mortals developed what was to be a uniquely French cultural phenomenon, the cultivated philosophic conversation of the *salons*, first at the Hôtel de Rambouillet (17C) and later at the houses of the Marquise de Lambert, Madame du Deffand, Madame Geoffrin (18C).

In contrast to the exploration and discussion of new ideas in the *salons*, the French Academy, founded by Richelieu in 1635, sought to exert a restraining influence on all branches of literature — Saint-Amand was, meanwhile, writing satire, Boileau burlesque and Madame de Sévigné her *Letters* on daily life.

In the 18C cafés — Procope, La Régence... — developed as centres of discussion and debate; Marivaux and Beaumarchais were presenting light comedies on the capital's life style and the provincial, Rousseau, expressing his disdain of the "noisy, smoke-filled, muddy" city!

It is Voltaire, outstanding in story telling, history, correspondence and memoirs, however, who, many would say, epitomises the 18C and the Paris writer at his best, with his irony and wit, light touch and perfect turn of phrase.

The Encyclopaedists typified Paris in the Age of Enlightenment as clearly as Restif de la Bretonne's *Nights of Paris* and Sébastien Mercier's *Portrait of Paris* described the daily scene in the capital.

The 19 and 20C. — The two major writers on Paris, Hugo and Balzac, were, in fact, born in the provinces. Both, in *Les Misérables* and the *Human Comedy* respectively, portrayed Paris as a character in its own right, suffering moods, influencing others... Beside these two giants, Dumas the Younger, Musset, the song-writer Béranger, Eugène Sue *(Mysteries of Paris)*, Murger *(Scenes of Bohemian Life)*, Nerval and others, pale into the background.

To the new Paris of Baron Haussmann came Baudelaire and the Parnassian and Symbolist poets and Émile Zola.

Old Montmartre lives in the songs of Bruant (1851-1925), the novels of Carco (1886-1958) and Marcel Aymé (1902-1967), Montparnasse in the poems of Max Jacob (1870-1944) and Léon-Paul Fargue (1876-1947). More generally descriptive are the works of Colette and Cocteau, Simenon, Montherlant, Louise de Vilmorin, Aragon, Prévert, Sacha Guitry, Éluard, Sartre, Simone de Beauvoir...

PARIS AND THE ENGLISH

Paris conjures up an image in the mind of every man and woman in Britain — the association goes back so far, the distance is so small, the atmosphere so different, the streets so wide, the buildings so massive, the landmarks so familiar from posters, pictures and films. Political exchanges have been continuous, ending in agreements to differ or often in treaties — 1763, terminating the Seven Years' War, 1814 and 1815 ending the Napoleonic era, 1856 in alliance at the end of the Crimean War, 1904-1910 commercial treaties which concluded in the Entente Cordiale, 1919 the Treaty of Versailles.

From the time of William the Conqueror families have intermarried; since 1420 and the recognition of Henri V as King of England and France, the English have at times penetrated to the capital.

By the 17C, aristocrats and the wealthy were completing their education with the Grand Tour of Europe with Paris as the first stop; by the mid 19C, Thomas Cook was organizing group visits, since, as he stated in Cook's Excursionist and Advertiser of 15 May 1863, "We would have every class of British subjects visit Paris, that they may emulate its excellencies, and shun the vices and errors which detract from the glory of the French capital. In matters of taste and courtesy we have much to learn from Parisians..."

It was the Continental Sunday, above all, that shocked Thomas Cook, and later the Bohemianism of Montmartre and Montparnasse. But it was just this that attracted and has continued to attract many visitors from Britain ever since! A first visit to Paris for many, therefore, becomes a desire to get a kaleidoscopic view of the Eiffel Tower and the Moulin Rouge, to eat in a *bistro* and walk up the Champs-Élysées, to see the Bastille — which they can't! — and visit Versailles — which they can.

With second and third and later visits — for every Briton, once having been to Paris, surely desires to return — comes a growing interest.

Observation of what Lawrence Durrell has called "the national characteristics... the restless metaphysical curiosity, the tenderness of good living and the passionate individualism. This is the invisible constant in a place with which the ordinary tourist can get in touch just by sitting quite quietly over a glass of wine in a Paris bistro". Comparisons with London; how much is the same and, therefore, familiar — children and adults sailing model yachts on the ponds in the Tuileries and Kensington Gardens — and yet just different enough to make you feel on holiday, how much is unique. The following pages, we hope, will help you in your discoveries.

Key

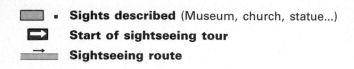

★★★ Highly recommended
★★ Recommended
★ Interesting

▭ ▪ **Sights described** (Museum, church, statue...)
⬛➡ **Start of sightseeing tour**
▭→ **Sightseeing route**

✠ ⚲	Church, chapel		Stadium	⬭
⚲	Protestant church		Water tower	🏛
▦	Synagogue		Windmill	✹
▪	Statue		Motorway	▬▬
▨	Gardens, parks		Dual carriageway	═══
✝✝✝	Cemetery		Town Hall	H
◎ ⊙	Basin — Fountain		Métro station nearest the start of a sightseeing tour	Ⓜ
⚘⚘	Panorama-View			

Michelin Paris Atlas No ▢▢

This Michelin publication contains a wealth of practical information.

A street index

A plan of the capital showing:
one-way streets, arrondissement boundaries, public buildings, museums, theatres, post offices, car parks, métro stations and taxi-ranks.

Useful adresses including:
government and municipal offices
embassies and other foreign representatives
churches, post offices, railway stations, department stores, etc.
museums, sports facilities, cinemas, theatres, etc.

Emergency telephone numbers

A public transport section: bus, métro and car.

Principal
Walks

The Obelisk and Mercury by Coysevox, Place de la Concorde

1

★★★

The Louvre

Michelin plan **11** - fold 31: H 13

Louvre-Rivoli métro station

♦

This walk is of great architectural, artistic and historical interest. The sheer size of France's and, in fact, the world's largest royal palace is most impressive, but it is the museum housed within its walls which has earned the Louvre international renown.

HISTORICAL NOTES

The original fortress. — The Louvre was constructed as a fortress on the banks of the Seine by Philippe Auguste in 1200 to protect the weakest point in his new city perimeter. It stood on less than a quarter of the space now occupied by the Cour Carrée and was used as treasure-house, arsenal and archive. In the 14C the fortress ceased its military function with the erection of a new perimeter and Charles V converted it into a residence, installing his famous library in one of the towers.

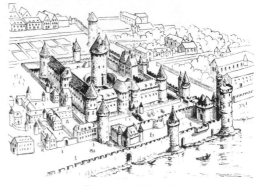

The Louvre of Charles V

A half Gothic, half Renaissance palace. — For 150 years after Charles V, France's kings chose to reside in their Paris mansions, the Hôtel St-Paul *(p 94)* and the Hôtel des Tournelles *(p 95)* which were better appointed and more easily accessible, or in their châteaux on the banks of the Loire, until, in 1527, François I, who was in need of funds, which he intended to raise from the local population, announced that he was going to take up residence in the Louvre. Rebuilding began with the razing of the keep, which obscured the courtyard, the knocking down of the advanced defences and the laying of a garden in their place. Only in 1546, was an architect, Pierre Lescot, commissioned to build a new royal palace on the site of the keep.

François I died the following year when the foundations were scarcely showing but building continued until the outbreak of the Wars of Religion. The west and south wings were built under the reigns of Henri II, Charles IX and Henri III by Lescot, who worked at the Louvre until his death in 1571, with the sculptural decoration entrusted to Jean Goujon. What came to be known as the Old Louvre consisted of the great Renaissance southwest façade of the Cour Carrée, and west and south wings with two Gothic and two Renaissance façades. These constructions were retained until the reign of Louis XIV.

Construction of the Tuileries. — On the tragic death of Henri II *(p 94)*, his widow, Catherine de' Medici decided to move, with the young king, François II, from the Hôtel des Tournelles to the Louvre. She did not wish to live in the palace itself, however, and in 1563 commissioned Philibert Delorme to build her a residence 500m-1/3 mile away in an area known as the Tuileries. Stone quarried at Vaugirard was brought to the site along the newly opened Rue du Bac and then ferried across the Seine; this was discontinued when the Pont Royal was built. Jean Bullant took over on Delorme's death in 1570. Suddenly, in 1572, all work stopped when an astrologer frightened the queen into believing she would die on the site. The Tuileries, nevertheless, remained empty of royalty until Louis XV.

The Waterside Gallery. — Catherine also planned a covered way, the Galerie du Bord de l'Eau (the Waterside Gallery), between the Louvre and the Tuileries affording private access between the two palaces and protection from the elements. The plan included a short passageway (Petite Galerie) starting from the old Louvre and at right angles to the quayside, a gallery parallel to the line of the Seine and a western section linking up with the Tuileries. Work started on the gallery but it, also, remained unfinished.

Extension of the Tuileries and Waterside Gallery. — On his arrival in Paris in 1594, Henri IV resumed the building work: he commissioned the internal decoration of the Tuileries, completed the Waterside Gallery with the addition of an upper storey, built the Flore Pavilion and another gallery at right angles to join up with the Tuileries. Work stopped on the king's death in 1610.

After years of neglect, in 1627 the palace was occupied by an assembly of dignitaries convened by Richelieu to raise money and that same year became the residence of Louis XIII's niece, Mlle de Montpensier, La Grande Mademoiselle *(qv)*.

Construction of the Cour Carrée. — Louis XIII decided to extend the old Louvre four-fold since the court had become horribly cramped. Le Mercier, architect of the Sorbonne, built the Clock Pavilion (Pavillon de l'Horloge) and extended it by an exact replica of Pierre Lescot's edifice. In 1659, Louis XIV commissioned Le Vau to work on the palace: the Apollo wing *(p 49)* was rebuilt, the houses and mansions surrounding the Louvre were pulled down to make way for the extended south wing and the north and east wings; the work was completed by 1664. Then the Sun King decided that his palace required a grand regal exterior and he summoned the greatest architect of the time, **Bernini**. The Italian's ideas, however, which began with the razing of the existing palace, proved unacceptable and alternative plans, therefore, were drawn up by a committee comprising Le Vau, Le Brun and Claude Perrault. The committee, and not Perrault alone, is thought to have created the

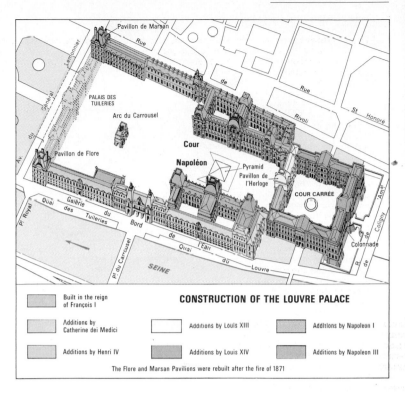

CONSTRUCTION OF THE LOUVRE PALACE

Built in the reign of François I

Additions by Catherine dei Medici

Additions by Henri IV

Additions by Louis XIII

Additions by Louis XIV

Additions by Napoleon I

Additions by Napoleon III

The Flore and Marsan Pavilions were rebuilt after the fire of 1871

Colonnade (1667-1670); they removed the Gothic wings from the Cour Carrée and replaced them with north and south façades in harmony with the colonnade. However, in 1682 the court left the Louvre for Versailles and building stopped once more.

Further extension of the Tuileries. — In 1652 Anne of Austria and Louis XIV moved from the Palais Royal (p 136) to the Louvre. Louis XIV built a theatre with a seating capacity of 5 000 (1659-61). The king then decided to adopt the Tuileries as his official Paris residence, and from 1664 to 1667 Le Vau remodelled the palace and built the Marsan Pavilion. After spending three winter seasons at the Tuileries, animated by festivities, ballets and spectacles, Louis XIV departed in 1671.

The Tuileries and the Louvre in the 18C. — After the death of the Sun King in 1715, the Regent brought the young Louis XV to the Tuileries, where he lived until 1722, when he returned to Versailles. After this the palace, except for the royal apartments, was taken over by various occupants; from 1725 to 1789 a room underneath the central dome was used as a public concert hall, which was visited by great European composers and musicians. The theatre was taken over by the Opera in 1763 and was occupied from 1770 to 1782 by the Comédie Française.

Years of neglect. — Louis XV was the last king of France to reside at the Louvre for a short period in 1719. The palace apartments, left empty by the departed court, were let to tenants: an artists' colony including Coustou, Bouchardon, Coypel, Boucher, settled in the galleries; the colonnade was divided into dwellings; stove chimneys stuck out in rows from the wonderful façade. Taverns and entertainers' shanties were built up against the walls until by 1750 the whole building had become so dilapidated it seemed in danger of being pulled down. Marigny, Minister to Louis XVI, came to its rescue.

Years of turmoil. — On 5 October 1789 the royal family was brought from Versailles to the Tuileries as the starving population rose in protest; on 20 June 1791 they fled from the palace, were arrested at Varennes-en-Argonne and returned, to be seized one year later to the day, by the Paris mob. Invading the palace the rabble pulled a red bonnet over the king's ears and made him pledge his loyalty to the nation in a toast. There followed the bloody 10 August when 600 of the Swiss Guard (p 242) were massacred by the mob before the palace was sacked.
The Convention and Directory installed themselves in the opera house and royal apartments.

Completion and destruction. — Bonaparte, the first consul, moved into the Tuileries in 1800 and remained in residence after his coronation as emperor. In 1810 Napoleon married Marie-Louise in the Salon Carré (Square Salon); in 1811 his son, the King of Rome, was born in the palace. All French sovereigns after Napoleon I resided in the palace. Louis XVIII, the only king to die in the Tuileries (1824) was succeeded by Charles X, Louis-Philippe and the Empress Eugenie who became regent during Napoleon III's captivity at Sedan; the last three were expelled by the Paris mob in 1830, 1848 and 1870 respectively. During Napoleon's reign building work resumed under the architect Fontaine, who also completed the Cour Carrée

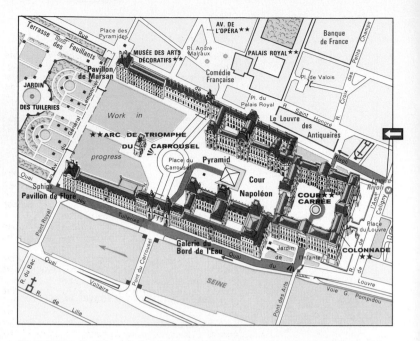

(Square Court): a triumphal arch was erected between the palace forecourt and the enlarged Carrousel Square, work began on the north gallery along Rue de Rivoli and a new theatre was built. Although the addition of an upper storey to the north, east and south wings caused unfortunate damage the harmony of the buildings remained unimpaired.

During the blood-soaked week of the Paris Commune of May 1871, the Tuileries was set on fire by the insurgents but the main building was saved. The Third Republic commissioned Lefuel to rebuild the Marsan and Flore Pavilions.

In 1965, the base of the Colonnade was cleared to give the columns their full height.

The museum through the centuries. — The dispersal of Charles V's rich library left the palace empty of treasure until François I began a new collection with twelve paintings by great masters including Titian, Raphaël, Leonardo da Vinci — the *Mona Lisa* — and antique casts brought back from Italy. By Louis XIII's reign the Cabinet du Roi contained some two hundred pictures. Colbert added generously to the collection as did others, so that by the death of Louis XIV, the king's paintings, scattered throughout the royal palaces, numbered 2 500. The Louvre, meanwhile, became the centre for the annual exhibition of the Academy of Painting and Sculpture.

The idea of a museum, which had been envisaged by Louis XVI, was finally realised by the Convention which, on 10 August 1793, opened the doors of the Great Gallery to the public.

Napoleon made the Louvre the world's richest museum by exacting a "tribute" in works of art from every country he conquered — but in 1815 the Allies took back what had been theirs.

Louis XVIII, Charles X and Louis-Philippe added to the Louvre collection, which already incorporated the Museum of French Monuments *(p 173)* created by Lenoir. The *Venus de Milo* had scarcely been rediscovered on the Island of Melos in 1820 before she was purchased by the French Government for 6 000F and brought to Paris; further Greek, Egyptian, Assyrian antiquities were collected and transported. In 1947, the Impressionist paintings were exhibited at the Jeu de Paume Museum *(p 54)* and transferred in 1986 to the Orsay Museum. Further gifts, legacies and acquisitions have augmented the collections so that the catalogue now lists nearly 300 000 entries.

The Great Louvre. — The Great Louvre Project adopted in 1981 by the French President provides for the restoration of the north Richelieu wing to the museum as the Ministry of Finance transfers to new premises in Bercy *(p 236)*. The architect Ieoh Ming Pei was commissioned to create more space for reception centres and services and to redevelop the outer public areas. In the Cour Napoléon, where car parking is no longer allowed, a glass pyramid gives light to the museum's main entrance and to the areas occupied by the information desks, reference centre, bookshop and auditorium.

Paris was not built in a day...

Unlike Rome and New York but like London, no one knows when Paris was founded. Julius Caesar sighted Lutetia in 53 BC and made the first written reference to the town in his Commentaries.

In 1951 Paris officially celebrated its second millennium.

TOUR OF THE EXTERIOR

Before starting along Rue de Rivoli, admire the Colonnade.

★★**Colonnade.** — Perrault produced in the Louvre colonnade a work of considerable grandeur and originality although it bears no relation to the rest of the building. Louis XIV's cypher of two coupled Ls marks the edifice; the central pediment, carved by Lemot at the time of the Empire, centred on a bust of Napoleon, replaced at the Restoration by one of the Sun King, thus crowned unusually by Minerva in imperial dress. Below, a winged Victory and quadriga stand between the columns. The true elevation and classical harmony of the structure can be fully admired now that the rusticated base has been cleared to a depth of 7m-23ft according to the original 17C plans.

Leave Rue de Rivoli to enter the Cour Carrée by the Marengo entrance.

★★**Square Court (Cour Carrée).** — The elegant and harmonious courtyard surrounded by four wings, about 112m-367ft long, is the most impressive part of the Old Louvre to remain.
On the right between the Clock Pavilion and the south wing is the Pierre Lescot façade, a Renaissance delight in proportion, balance and decoration.
The graceful and expressive decoration of the three projecting wings and the upper storey shows Jean Goujon's artistry: allegorical scenes in high relief, statues in niches and friezes of children and garlands.
In the centre of this west wing is the Clock Pavilion built during Louis XIII's reign by Lemercier who was also responsible for the north wing, a classical replica of Lescot's façade. The clock replaced a window during the Restoration.
The three remaining sides, although harmonising with the west wing, are not identical with it as in order to offset the difference in height between the latter and the Colonnade, Percier and Fontaine raised the upper storey of Le Vau's north façade and that of the south façade by Lescot (right half) and Le Vau (left half); the Italian-style terraced roof replaced the French-style sloping roof; the dome of the Clock Pavilion is a unique feature. The classical style of these wings contrasts with the Renaissance elegance of the west wing.
The period of each building is marked with emblazoned monograms: H interlaced with a double C and forming a D on the Lescot face are for Henri II, Catherine de' Medici and the king's favourite, Diane of Poitiers; K, H, HDB and HG on the south side, for Charles IX, Henri III, Henri IV (Henri of Bourbon) and Henri (IV) and Gabrielle d'Estrées; right of the Clock Pavilion, LA, LB, LMT for Louis XIII and Anne of Austria, Louis of Bourbon, Louis XIV and Marie-Thérèse.
The courtyard has been refurbished recently: four paved areas divided by bands of granite with a round basin in the centre de-signed by Duban, Na-poleon III's architect.

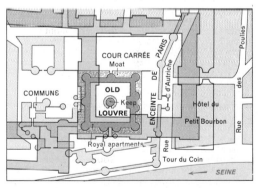

Old Louvre (in red, the Louvre today)

Old Louvre. — The ad-joining plan and the drawing of Charles V's palace (p 30) help to recreate the royal resi-dence: a massive keep, 32m-105ft high, and a fortified wall punctuat-ed by ten towers simi-lar to those of the Con-ciergerie (p 120), surrounded by a moat. The remains of Philippe Auguste's keep and Charles V's palace have been excavated (p 35). In the northwest tower (on the site of the Clock Pavilion), near a flower garden, Charles V kept his famous library consisting of 973 volumes. South of the tower was the Great Hall (now the Caryatid Gallery), the scene of royal receptions; further on the royal apartments overlooked the Seine.
To the east the Louvre's main gate opened between two towers (marked by setts) onto a bridge over the moat.

★**Embankment Façade.** — South of the Cour Carrée, there is a fine view of the Pont des Arts and of the dome of the Institute of France (p 173). From the embankment Perrault's majestic classical façade can be seen beyond the garden. The famous Apollo Gallery (p 49) is on the first floor of the building, from which runs the Waterside Gallery, restored under Napoleon III, with its frieze of cherubs mounted on monsters. The area west of the Carrousel gateways is the part rebuilt following the 1871 fire (p 32).
Cross to the Pont Royal to look below the great allegorical scene on the south wall at the high relief by Carpeaux, **Flora's Triumph★**, after which the corner pavilion is named.
On the site of the terrace in front of the palace overlooking the Tuileries Garden runs Avenue du General Lemonier (partly below ground). The flower beds (parterres) laid out in 1909, mark the site of of the Tuileries Palace which linked the Flore and Marsan Pavilions.

The Pyramid at the Louvre

The two arms of the Louvre. — Deriving from medieval tourneys and Italian war games, the tiltyard (**carrousel**) was a vast parade ground for horse shows and theatrical events, where, in the 17C, the nobility displayed its skill and wealth. The ground was named after brilliant celebrations for the Dauphin's birth in 1662. From the gardens the overall view of the palace is impressive but the architecture and decoration are unremarkable as Hector Lefuel copied the styles of earlier buildings.

There is an even grander **vista★★★** to be enjoyed through the line of the Carrousel Arch, across the Place de la Concorde and centring on the obelisk, up the Champs-Élysées to the Triumphal Arch at l'Étoile.

★★**The Carrousel Triumphal Arch.** — The Carrousel, a delightful pastiche of a Roman arch with eight rose marble columns, was erected between 1806 and 1808 in celebration of the Napoleonic victories of 1805. The decoration, at one time, included the four gilded bronze horses from St Mark's in Venice which Napoleon had brought back to France (returned 1815). The arch is now crowned by a goddess representing the Restoration of the Bourbons, attended by Victory, riding in a quadriga.

The Pyramid. — The Louvre façades framing the **Cour Napoléon** provide a majestic backdrop to the pure geometric form of the glass pyramid, 21m-69ft high and 33m-105ft wide at the base, built by **Ieoh Ming Pei**, using new techniques and materials: a fine mesh of steel tubes, cables and sheet glass. Surrounded by basins, fountains and three smaller pyramids, it serves as the museum's main entrance. An equestrian statue of Louis XIV (a copy of a Bernini statue) faces up the Champs-Élysées in line with the Old Louvre.

★★★ THE LOUVRE MUSEUM

Open 9am to 6pm (last admission 5.15pm); late opening on Mondays and Wednesdays to 9.45pm (last admission 9.30pm). The Napoleon Hall and the bookshop are open 9am to 10pm. Closed Tuesdays, 1 January, Easter Monday, 1 May, Whit Monday, 1 and 11 November and 25 December; 30F, Sundays 15F; ☎ 40 20 49 38.

There are guided lecture tours (23F extra) planned to include some of the most outstanding works of art. Other guided tours on a specific collection, school or period are also organized. For further details ☎ 40 20 51 77.

A pre-recorded commentary in English (self-guided audio tours) on the museum is available for hire.

For those with little time to spare we have short-listed the masterpieces of each department and their location is indicated on the accompanying plans.

*The Great Louvre as a building has been divided into three areas: the two wings, DENON and RICHELIEU and the ranges around the Cour Carrée, SULLY. To help visitors find their way around, each area has been subdivided into numbered districts. The signs in the museum use this system, eg the Oriental Antiquities are to be found in districts **1** to **5** of the SULLY area. This information is shown in red on the plans and in the text.*

Napoleon Hall. — Lit by Pei's glass pyramid, this vast (70m-230ft wide) reception area leads to the museum's three main areas: Denon, Richelieu and Sully. Additional services available to the public include a bookshop, chalcography gallery, cafeteria, guided tours, auditorium and workshop.

History of the Louvre Exhibition. — *Sully, start on the right.* On either side of the rotunda, adorned with low reliefs by Jean Goujon, two galleries present, in chronological order, the architectural and decorative evolution from a fortress, to a royal palace and its transformation into a museum. The documents, paintings, sculpture, and scale models evoke the sovereigns and architects associated with the Louvre.

Medieval Louvre. — *Sully crypt.* A black line on the floor shows the location of one of the ten towers belonging to Philippe Auguste's fortress as well as the library of Charles V *(see illustration p 30).*

Follow the moat of Philippe Auguste's 13C fortress round to the northern and eastern sections and note on the left the counterscarp wall, with visible signs of repairs, and on the right the stronghold's 2.60m-7ft thick curtain wall. The rectangular addition beyond the Taillerie Tower (or town gate, at the northeastern corner) locates the foundations of the residence added by Charles V in 1360.

The supporting pier of the drawbridge is framed by twin towers of the eastern gate. On these regularly placed rectangular stones putlog holes are visible as well as heart-shaped engravings carved by the stone masons.

Continue to the keep's moat, which, with an average width of 7.50m-25ft, was originally paved with enormous flagstones. The circular keep, also known as the Big Tower (Grosse Tour), was built 1190-1202 for Philippe Auguste; it measured 18m-59ft in diameter at its base and stood 31m-102ft tall. François I razed the keep in 1546, when he decided to transform the fortress into a royal palace.

The tour ends with a visit to two galleries. The first one displays pottery discovered during the excavation of the Cour Carrée; the second, the St Louis Gallery, with mid-13C vaulting, contains royal objects found at the bottom of the keep's well. Among the items displayed are the original fragments and a replica of Charles VI's parade casque.

Returning to the Napoleon Hall pass under the rusticated pier of the bridge built, during Louis XIV's reign, to cross the western section of the moat.

ORIENTAL ANTIQUITIES

Sully ground floor districts **1** to **5**.

The Far Eastern Art Collection is exhibited in the Guimet Museum (p 210). The Mesopotamian Antiquities wil be transferred to the Richelieu area in 1993. Major changes have been made in the first few rooms because of the reorganization in progress.

Major works displayed in this department

(see text and plan below)

Stele of the Vultures	Code of Hammurabi
Statue of the Intendant Ebih-Il	Frieze of the Archers
	Gold Hunting Cup
Stele of Naram-Sin	Vase of Amathus
Statues of Prince Gudea and his son Ur-Ningirsu	Assyrian low-reliefs

Mesopotamian civilizations. — The heartland of Mesopotamia, the Tigris and Euphrates river plains, was the cradle of a great civilization which saw the growth of cities. Its art is the complex expression of conflicting and successive trends.

Gallery I. — Pottery and other artifacts of Mesopotamian prehistory are presented in the display cases while large statues of Gudea, Prince of Lagash, and the obelisk of Manishtusu, King of Agade, stand in the centre.

Gallery II. — Sumerian antiquities from Telloh (formerly Girsu): the **Stele of the Vultures** (2450 BC) commemorating the victory of King Eannatum of Lagash over the neighbouring state of Umma; in a display case on the left King Entemena's silver vase (c2400 BC) and a votive cult low relief of Ur-Nanshe.

From Mari, on the Middle Euphrates, are the small statues of worshippers found in the Temple of Ishtar (goddess of war and love): the finest is the alabaster **statue of the Intendant Ehib-Il** (middle of 3rd millennium BC) wearing a furry skirt and staring out of inlaid blue eyes.

The Semitic Dynasty of Akkad (2340-2200 BC) is

ORIENTAL ANTIQUITIES (GROUND FLOOR)

highlighted by the admirable **Stele of Naram-Sin** (2250 BC) in pale rose-coloured sandstone. It shows the king climbing up the mountain over the bodies of enemy soldiers.

The impressive **statues of Prince Gudea and his son Ur-Ningirsu** (the latter is exhibited in rotation with the Metropolitan Museum of New York) carved at Lagash c2150 BC are masterpieces of Sumerian art.

THE DEPARTMENTS OF THE LOUVRE

Oriental Antiquities (p. 35)

Egyptian Antiquities (p. 39)

Greek Etruscan and Roman Antiquities (p. 41)

Sculpture (p. 43)

Paintings (p. 45)

Graphic Art (p. 49)

Art Objects (p. 49)

Public service areas

Closed to the Public

⇕ Lift

3 Numbered District

0   80 m

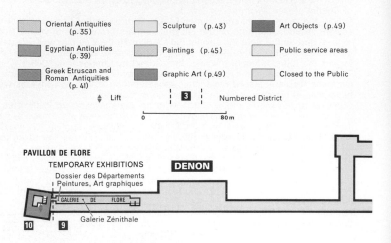

PAVILLON DE FLORE

TEMPORARY EXHIBITIONS

Dossier des Départements Peintures, Art graphiques

DENON

GALERIE DE FLORE

Galerie Zénithale

10   9

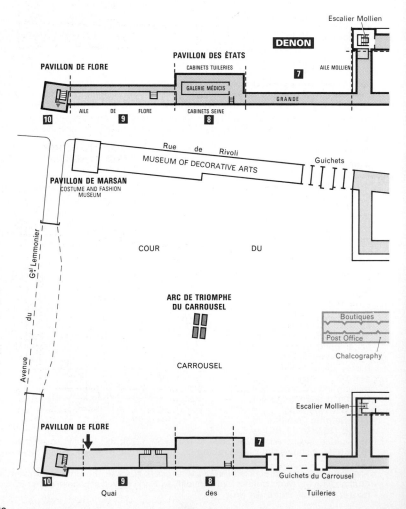

Escalier Mollien

DENON

PAVILLON DES ÉTATS

CABINETS TUILERIES

GALERIE MÉDICIS

AILE MOLLIEN

7

PAVILLON DE FLORE

AILE DE FLORE

CABINETS SEINE

GRANDE

10   9   8

Rue de Rivoli

MUSEUM OF DECORATIVE ARTS

Guichets

PAVILLON DE MARSAN
COSTUME AND FASHION MUSEUM

Gᵃˡ Lemmonier

Avenue du

COUR DU

ARC DE TRIOMPHE DU CARROUSEL

Boutiques

Post Office

Chalcography

CARROUSEL

Escalier Mollien

PAVILLON DE FLORE

7

Guichets du Carrousel

10   9   8

Quai   des   Tuileries

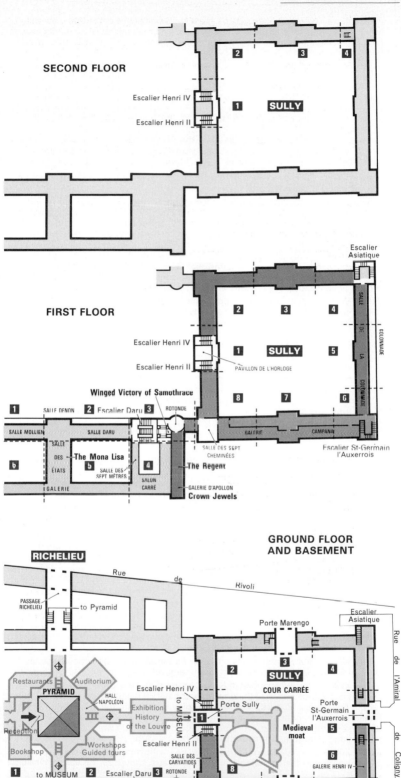

SECOND FLOOR

Escalier Henri IV
Escalier Henri II

2　3　4
1　SULLY

FIRST FLOOR

Escalier Asiatique

Escalier Henri IV
Escalier Henri II

2　3　4
1　SULLY　5
PAVILLON DE L'HORLOGE
8　7　6

SALLE DE LA COLONNADE

Winged Victory of Samothrace

1　SALLE DENON　2 Escalier Daru 3　ROTONDE
SALLE MOLLIEN　SALLE DARU
SALLE DES ÉTATS
b　**The Mona Lisa**
b　SALLE DES SEPT MÈTRES
GALERIE
4　SALON CARRÉ
SALLE DES SEPT CHEMINÉES
The Regent
GALERIE D'APOLLON
Crown Jewels
GALERIE　CAMPANA
Escalier St-Germain l'Auxerrois

GROUND FLOOR AND BASEMENT

RICHELIEU

Rue de Rivoli

PASSAGE RICHELIEU
to Pyramid

Porte Marengo

Escalier Asiatique
Rue de l'Amiral

Restaurants　Auditorium
PYRAMID
HALL NAPOLÉON
Exhibition History of the Louvre
Reception
Bookshop
Workshops Guided tours

2　3　SULLY　4
COUR CARRÉE

Escalier Henri IV
to MUSEUM
1　Porte Sully
Escalier Henri II
SALLE DES CARYATIDES
ROTONDE

Porte St-Germain l'Auxerrois

Medieval moat
5
6
GALERIE HENRI IV
de Coligny

1　to MUSEUM　2 Escalier Daru 3　ROTONDE
GALERIE MOLLIEN　GALERIE DARU
6
SALLE DU MANÈGE
5
COUR DU SPHINX
4
PAVILLON DES ARTS
8
Venus de Milo
7
Porte Champollion
Escalier St-Germain l'Auxerrois

DENON

Quai du Louvre

37

Gallery III. — Two models depict the great mud-brick palace from the city-state of Mari, which flourished at the beginning of the 2nd millennium BC. Exhibits include two wall paintings from the above palace, dating from the reign of Zimri-Lim, and a lion that guarded the Temple of Dagan.

Gallery IV. — At the beginning of the second millennium BC, the Babylonian Empire achieved supremacy: Mesopotamia was conquered and the city of Mari destroyed. The famous **Code of Hammurabi** (1792-1750) is a black basalt stele 2.50m-8ft high, inscribed with 282 laws in the Akkad language. The king, Hammurabi, is shown receiving the laws from the God of Justice. A partially gilded bronze statuette, shown in adoration, is exhibited in one of the display cases; he may be King Hammurabi.

The Babylonian Empire was followed by the Assyrian Empire *(see below)* in the 8 and 7C BC; and, after Nebuchadnezzar, in the 6C BC, by the Persian Empire, which extended from the eastern shores of the Mediterranean to India.

Iranian Art. — The art of the Iranian Plateau is expressed mainly in painted ceramics and metalwork.

Gallery V. — From the end of the fifth millennium BC, the finely decorated pottery is noteworthy. The Elamite civilization (ancient country of Elam, now southwestern Iran), produced delicate works as from the 4th millennium. From the 6 to 4C BC, Susa (the capital of Elam) was at the peak of its glory with the Achaemenid kings. The gold and silver plate was exceptionally fine. In the central glass case gold jewellery as well as other objects in gold and silver are on view.

Between these two galleries, one may see Bactrian art from the beginning of the second millennium BC. Bactria, an ancient country on the southern borders of central Asia, produced a brilliant civilization, influenced by Elam.

Gallery VI. — This gallery is devoted to the Elamite civilization of the 3rd and 2nd millennia. In the 13 and 12C BC, the art of bronze-making was at its zenith; there is a bronze statue of Queen Napir Asu and a basalt stele from Babylonia (end of the second millennium), usurped by a later Elamite king. After the fall of the Assyrians the province of Elam was incorporated into the Persian Empire.

Gallery VII. — Darius I the Great was the most famous of the Persian rulers of the Achaemenid dynasty and the two greatest centres of this civilization were Susa and Persepolis. The giant 6C BC capital gives some idea of the vast size of Darius' great Persian royal palace at Susa. In the central display cabinet are silver rhytons (drinking vessels). On the walls of the following galleries are the celebrated brick friezes from the palace in Susa.

Gallery VIII. — The **Frieze of the Archers** is an exquisite example of 6C BC Persian art. The archers belonged to Darius' elite guard as part of the Persian army which attempted to conquer Greece and was defeated at Marathon (490 BC).

Gallery IX. — Enamelled-brick friezes of griffins and lions from Darius's palace in Susa.

Gallery XI. — In the central display cabinet are examples of the delicately worked Luristan bronzes.

In **gallery XII**, at the top of the stairs, are the mosaics from Shapur's (king of the Sasanian Empire of Persia in 3C AD) palace, which mark the transition to Muslim Art.

Levantine Art. — In the Near East, at the confluence of the great civilizations, the various influences existed side by side or blended.

Marengo Crypt (Crypte Marengo) (**Galleries XIII-XV**). — Among the Phoenician tombs the mummiform sarcophagus of Eshmunazar II, King of Sidon (5C BC) (left side, second bay), testifies to the Egyptian influence in Syria. Beyond are marble statuettes (3rd bay) from a mithraeum in Sidon.

Gallery XVI. — Works from Phoenicia (Lebanese coast) include decorative ivory plaques once inlaid in royal palace furniture. Bronze statuettes of Jupiter from Heliopolis (present-day Baalbek) recall that this cult was prevalent in Syria during Roman rule.

Gallery XVII. — Biblical antiquities: model of a temple from the Israelite monarchy. Stele of Mesha, king of Moab, which commemorates his victory over the Israelites.

Gallery XVIII. — The excavations at Ugarit, modern-day Ras Shamra, has uncovered Phoenicia, the crossroads of the ancient world (tablet using the cuneiform alphabet for the first time, *c*1300 BC). In a large display cabinet, on the left, admire the **gold hunting bowl**, gold pendentives representing fertility symbols and lady with animals depicted on the cover of an ivory powder box. Against the wall stands the Stele of the Smiting Baal (the storm god) brandishing a club.

Gallery XIX. — Sculpture from Cyprus (7-3C BC): cult statues (Goddess of Tricomo), gilded bowls and the monolithic limestone cistern known as the **Vase of Amathus**.

Islamic Art. — Found in **Gallery XX** are the various aspects of Islamic art originating from Spain, Egypt, Iran, Syria and India. The objects include a pyx (sculpted ivory cylindrical box) belonging to the caliph Abd ar-Rahman III's son, a rock-crystal ewer and ceramics. The Barberini Vase and the St Louis Baptismal Bowl (1300) reveal the height of craftsmanship achieved in the decorative technique of gold and silver encrustation.

Assyrian Art. — Exhibited in **Gallery XXI** are the great **Assyrian low reliefs** from the palaces of Kings Ashurbanipal at Nineveh and Sargon at Khorsabad. In **Gallery XXII**, the giant sculptures (the five-legged winged bulls which guarded the palace entrance) proclaim Assyrian glory and ideal royal wisdom.

EGYPTIAN ANTIQUITIES

Sully ground floor **5** to **7** and first floor **6** to **8** — *cross the medieval Louvre to reach the Sphinx Crypt.*

Major works displayed in this department
(see text below and plan p 40)

Akhout-Hetep's Mastaba
Gebel-el-Arak's Knife
Seated Scribe
Low relief of King Sehi I
  and the goddess Hathor
Monastic church of St Apollo at
  Bawit
Bust of Amenophis IV
Jewellery
Statue of Karomama

Ground floor. — Sully districts **5** to **7**. In the **Sphinx Crypt** (Crypte du Sphinx), the great sphinx, in pink granite, discovered in Tanis, evokes the glory of ancient Egypt.
The next rooms are devoted to sober and powerful works from prehistory, the Thinite Period and the Old Kingdom.

Gallery 2: Akhout-Hetep's Mastaba, the upper chamber of a funeral chapel of a Fifth Dynasty (c 2350 BC) tomb, was used for the cult of the deceased; the inner walls are decorated with carved and painted scenes of everyday life.

THE DYNASTIES OF ANCIENT EGYPT

c 3100	Thinite Period	1st and 2nd dynasties
c 2700	OLD KINGDOM (Pyramids)	3rd to 6th dynasties
c 2200	First Intermediate Period	
2060	MIDDLE KINGDOM	End 11th and 12th dynasties
1785	Second Intermediate Period	
1555	NEW KINGDOM	18th to 20th dynasties
1080	Third Intermediate Period	21 st to 25 th dynasties
664	SAITE PERIOD	26th dynasty
525	Late Period	27th to 30th dynasties
332	CONQUEST OF ALEXANDER THE GREAT	
30	GRECO-ROMAN PERIOD	
Birth of Jesus-Christ	ROMAN PROVINCE Coptic Art	

Gallery 3: Gebel-el-Arak's knife, with its highly refined flint blade typical of the prehistoric period in Egypt, fitted with a finely carved ivory handle, demonstrates the emergence of low relief art. Opposite, the Serpent Kings' Stele, a masterpiece of the Thinite (Archaic) Period, commemorates one of the first pharaohs (King Djet), with a falcon symbolizing the god Horus.

Gallery 4: the Third Dynasty statues of Sepa and Nesa are early examples of civil statuary; its development can be traced in the Fourth Dynasty hieratic figures (head of King Didoufri), contemporary with the Great Pyramids.

Gallery 5: the famous **Seated Scribe** with his piercing gaze is a realistic work dating from the Fifth Dynasty. In the display cases are objects that the deceased took with him to the tomb.

Gallery 6: a poignant couple carved in wood (in bad condition) of a civil servant from Memphis and his wife, dating from the Sixth Dynasty are on display here.

Gallery 7: the central exhibit displays the silver and lapis-lazuli treasure found in a Temple at Tod. In the recess to the left stands a statue of Hapidjefaï, one of the largest wooden statues from the Middle Kingdom.
Also from the Middle Kingdom, stamped with a certain gravity, is the well-known lintel flanked by the highly expressive representations of Sesostris III.

The Henri IV Gallery is devoted to funerary monuments. Pass through two rows of statues of the lion-headed goddess Sekhmet; further on and to the right, is the group of four baboons worshipping the sun, carved from a single block of granite, which originally adorned the base of an obelisk still standing at Luxor. Two monuments originate from tombs in the Valley of the Kings: the great granite sarcophagus of Rameses III and the splendid **low relief** in painted limestone of **King Sethi I and the goddess Hathor.**
Flanking the stairs are two tabernacles, which were used to house the cult statue of the god who "lived" in the temple.
The **Osiris Crypt** (Crypte de l'Osiris), evokes the important role played by Osiris, God of the Dead, in all funerary rites. The Zodiac, dating from the Roman period, suspended from the ceiling, came from the temple at Dandarah. The sacred ram Chnoum is among the mummies of animals on exhibit.
Return to the Henri IV Gallery entrance: to the right is the **Coptic art** section. With the gradual spread of Christianity, Egyptian art drew its inspiration from both the Hellenistic Mediterranean world and Byzantium.
Gallery 1 traces the origins of Coptic art: an example being a mummy, painted with a portrait of the deceased from the Roman Period. In Gallery 2, a large collection of textiles and a fragment of an Annunciation show the development of Coptic art (5-7 C). Gallery 3 demonstrates the development of a more stylized form of art under Islamic influence, which prevailed until the 12C: reconstitued **monastic church of St Apollo in Bawit** and an icon of Christ and the Abbot Mena, the monastery's father superior.

Go back to the Henri IV Gallery, and climb the St-Germain-l'Auxerrois stairs framed by sphinxes from the Sarapeum in Memphis, a temple dedicated to the cult of Apis, the bull god.

At the top of the stairs, the **bust of Amenophis IV** (who changed his name to Akhenaton in deference to the symbol — solar disk — of Aton the sun god) is an exceptional work of art for its realism and refinement; it came from the temple of Aton at Karnak and was given to the French by the Egyptian government in thanks for France's help in saving the temples of Nubia.

First floor. — Sully districts ▣ to ▣. The exhibits are presented in chronological order ranging from the Middle Kingdom to the Roman Period.

Gallery A contains items found in the tombs of the Middle Kingdom and notably from the tomb of Chancellor Nakhti: models of a granary, boats, a bearer of votive offerings, blueglazed terracotta hippopotami and a large wooden statue of the Chancellor Nakhti in a rather rigid pose.

The items in **Gallery B** belong to the New Kingdom's most brilliant period, the Eighteenth Dynasty. During these settled and prosperous times art flourished as testified by the polychrome sandstone statue of the royal couple, Sennefer and Hatshepsut.

In a display cabinet are wooden spoons used for votive offerings decorated with swimming girls or delicate floral motifs. In another is the green enamelled statuette of Queen Tiy, wife of Amenophis III and a finely carved wooden statue of Touy, priestess of the god Min, showing the craftsman's skill as he depicted her hair in tight tresses and her garments draped around her figure.

Gallery C illustrates many aspects of daily life during the New Kingdom: furnishings, dress, toilet articles, games, music, hunting and fishing.

Art objects from the Amarna Period, a style which existed during the reign of Amenophis IV or Akhenaton in the Eighteenth Dynasty, are displayed in **Gallery D**. Akhenaton upset tradition and a more naturalistic style emerged.

The display cabinet on the right contains the head of a princess belonging to Akhenaton's family; the same person, in bust form, is treated in the central display cabinet; in another cabinet a small group of Akhenaton and his Queen Nefertiti can be viewed.

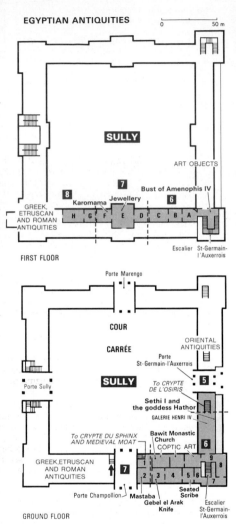

The Ramesside Period (**Gallery E**), during the rule of the Pharaohs Sethi and the many Rameses, is beautifully evoked by the *ostraca* (limestone fragments) carved by the workmen employed on the construction of the royal tombs in the Valley of the Kings. The stonemasons lived in the village of Deir-el-Medina, in western Thebes.

Exquisite **jewellery** and gold and silver plate spanning different periods can be admired in the display cabinet on the right.

During the Third Intermediate Period (**Gallery F**) bronze craftsmen produced such masterpieces as the **Statue of Karomama**, the divine worshipper of the god Amon, king of the gods (small central display cabinet); also on display are beautifully painted wooden coffins, blue ceramic funerary servants and the bronze statue of the god Horus.

The Saite Dynasty and the succeeding dynasties (**Gallery G**) were renowned for the quality of their statuary; the gods (Amon, Anubis, Apis, Bes, Horus, Isis...), ex-votoes of cats in bronze, representing the goddess Bastet, goddess of music and dance; other ex-votoes represent magic.

Egypt then fell under the Ptolemaic Dynasty, or post-Alexander period, before it became part of the Roman Empire (**Gallery H**). These influences can be seen in the pottery, sculpture, bronze craftsmanship and, especially, the portraits painted on wood which bring to mind those found in Pompeii (display cases on the left); objects connected to the burial cult (burial and embalming customs, scenes from the Book of the Dead) are found to the right. Towards the back of the gallery are writing-related items.

GREEK, ETRUSCAN AND ROMAN ANTIQUITIES

Sully ground floor districts **7** to **8**; Denon ground floor districts **2** to **3**

> ### Major works displayed in this department
> *(see text below and plans p 42)*
>
> | | |
> |---|---|
> | Lady of Auxerre | Venus de Milo |
> | Hera or Kore of Samos | The Cerveteri Sarcophagus |
> | Horseman Rampin | Winged Victory of Samothrace |
> | Apollo of Piombino | Tanagra Figurines |
> | The Parthenon Fragments | |

Greek Antiquities. — Ground floor Denon district **3** and Sully districts **7** and **8**. Go towards the Denon area and into the Manège Gallery (Salle du Manège): one may see sculpture and a pot-pourri of antiquities among which is the Dying Seneca, which was to inspire a work by Rubens.

Cross the Daru Gallery (Galerie Daru-15) full of 2 and 3C AD sarcophagi and 1 and 2C AD statues; bear left at the foot of the Victory of Samothrace stairs.

Gallery 16. — Orientalising Period and Archaic Period (7-6C BC). The **Lady of Auxerre** is one of the earliest examples of Greek sculpture and typical of the austere Dorian style: the kore stands rigid in a frontal pose (the face in line with the body). The **Hera** or **Kore of Samos**, from the Temple of Hera, is more Ionian in style, although dating only two generations later. From the mid-6C BC is an Attic work: the **Horseman Rampin**, his face lit by a delicate smile.

Gallery 17. — Early 5C BC. The transition between the Archaic and Classical Periods are treated in this gallery: a male torso from Miletus, **Apollo of Piombino**, a red-figured amphora from Mysia and the stele depicting the Exaltation of the Flower from Pharsalus.

Gallery 18. — *Reorganization in progress.* The Doric metopes (on the frieze; panels often carved in high relief alternating with triglyphs) from the Temple of Zeus will accompany the bronze and ceramic ware; they all date from the same period (*c*460BC).

Galleries 19 and 20. — Second half of 5C BC and early 4C BC. **Sculptural fragments from the Parthenon**, the Doric temple dedicated to Athena, which was built by Iktinos, under Pheidias's direction, is exhibited. This includes part of the frieze (a large part of it is in the British Museum) representing

The Lady of Auxerre

the Panathenaic procession (which took place every four years); it depicts a slow, noble procession of Athenians bearing an embroidered tunic to offer to Athena. To the right is a high relief representing a centaur and a woman; to the left the head of a woman, called the Laborde Head and the small head of an ephebus (a youth), known as Coulonché Head. On the opposite wall the figures of two maidens, one running towards the right and the other towards the left, are most likely acroterions from the Temple of Apollo at Bassae in southwest Arcadia. The builder Iktinos was also one of the designers of the Parthenon in Athens.

Galleries 21 and 22. — 4C BC. The majority of the works exhibited are funerary objects: lekythos (oil jugs), louthrophores and steles. Greek tombs were decorated with symbolic animal figures such as the lion, a gift from a French admiral to Charles X.

Gallery 23. — 3C BC. The portraits depict members of the Ptolemaic dynasty's royal family, who ruled Egypt following the death of Alexander the Great in 323.

Gallery 24. — 2C BC. The natural, serene beauty of the **Venus de Milo**, a balanced, graceful figure, is a masterpiece of ancient art. Alongside is a copy of Praxiteles's Cnidian Aphrodite (2C BC) known as the Kaufmann Head (after its former owner).

Gallery 25. — 2-1C BC. The fighting warrior, called the Borghese Gladiator (*c*100BC), exemplifies the new approach sought in attitude and expression.

Gallery 26. — Replicas of 5-4C BC. Several statues recall the severe style: Myron's Athena, the discus thrower... It is, however, the art of Polyclitus and Phidias that is treated here; from the former: Diadumenus and the Wounded Amazon (badly restored in the 17C); from the latter: a Kassel Apollo and a head of Athena Parthenos.

Classicism evolves towards a less conventional, freer style. The attitude of the Borghese Ares is severe and yet his facial expression is softer, more human.

At the end of the 5C, the Adonis or Narcissus is a precursor of Praxiteles's works (see gallery 27); the drapery covering the figure reveals the female form.

In the early 4C, the Discus Thrower by Naucydes and the Athena of Peace show a return to realism.

Gallery 27. — Replicas of 4C BC works. Apart from the muse Melpomene from the Pompeii theatre (1C BC) in Rome, all the sculpture displayed are copies of Praxiteles's works. The great sculptor, active from 370-330 BC, took marble and brought life to it: youths posed with the weight on one foot, feminity and modesty as in Artemis, known as the Diana of Gabies, or grace as in the Cnidian Aphrodite or the Venus of Arles.

Gallery 28. — This, the Caryatid Gallery (Salle des Cariatides), holds replicas of 4C BC works and Hellenistic period works. It was the former great hall of the old Louvre Palace and was built for Henri II by Pierre Lescot. Its name comes from the four monumental statues carved by Jean Goujon, which supported the minstrels' balcony.

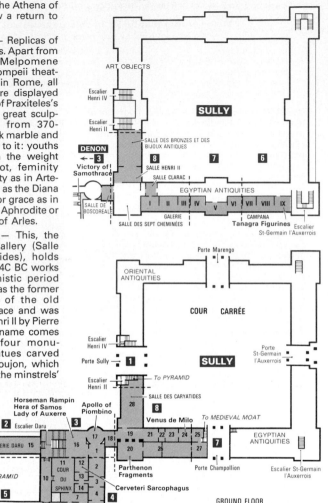

GREEK, ETRUSCAN AND ROMAN ANTIQUITIES

FIRST FLOOR

ART OBJECTS

SULLY

Escalier Henri IV

Escalier Henri II

DENON ◄─ 3

Victory of Samothrace

SALLE DES BRONZES ET DES BIJOUX ANTIQUES

8   7   6

SALLE HENRI II

SALLE CLARAC

SALLE DE BOSCOREALE

SALLE DES SEPT CHEMINÉES

EGYPTIAN ANTIQUITIES

I   II   III   IV   V   VI   VII   VIII   IX

GALERIE CAMPANA

Tanagra Figurines

Escalier St-Germain l'Auxerrois

Porte Marengo

ORIENTAL ANTIQUITIES

COUR   CARRÉE

Escalier Henri IV

Porte Sully — 1

SULLY

Escalier Henri II

To PYRAMID

Porte St-Germain l'Auxerrois

SALLE DES CARYATIDES

28   8

Venus de Milo

To MEDIEVAL MOAT

EGYPTIAN ANTIQUITIES

7

Horseman Rampin
Hera of Samos
Lady of Auxerre

Apollo of Piombino

DENON   2

Escalier Daru   3

GALERIE DARU   15   16   17   18   19   20   21   22   23   24   25   26   27

Porte Champollion

Escalier St-Germain l'Auxerrois

SALLE DU MANÈGE

To PYRAMID

10   11   12   13   14   7   9   8   6   5

COUR DU SPHINX

Parthenon Fragments

Cerveteri Sarcophagus   4

5

GROUND FLOOR

0   50 m

On display are copies of works by Lysippus, Alexander the Great's court sculptor; his works are full of power and movement as in his Hermes Fastening his Sandal. Sculpture then attempts to express personality and resemblance: the Three Graces, Artemis, or Diana of Versailles and the Sleeping Hermaphrodite. The Seated Venus from Vienne combines anatomical realism and harmonious proportions.

Etruscan Antiquities. — Denon ground floor, district 4. The Etruscans appeared in central Italy as early as the 7C BC; they then migrated to Campania and northern Italy. Their civilization reached its height in the 6C; their decline began in the 5C and continued until 265, when Etruria fell under the yoke of Rome.

Objects needed in their afterlife and the even rarer paintings, found in their monumental tombs, have revealed their burial customs. Etruscan art was strongly influenced by Oriental and Greek art, and in turn, greatly influenced Roman art. However, Etruscan art has retained a marked individuality.

Gallery 12. — Succeeding the Villanovan civilization, which is characterised by bronze or iron objects with geometric patterns (mid-7C throne in hammered-sheet bronze), comes the Etruscan civilization, represented by painted terracotta plaques (Campania plaques), refined versions of the Villanovan impasto-ware pottery and antefixes (ornamental end-tiles on roof eaves) in the shape of female heads.

In the centre of the room stands the famous 6C terracotta **Cerveteri sarcophagus**. Husband and wife are depicted side by side participating serenely in the divine banquet, a theme taken from Greek vase painting.

Gallery 13. — Bucchero-ware, Etruscan earthenware pottery, marked the Orientalizing period (mid-7C). Its characteristic black, often shiny texture was achieved by firing the clay in a reducing kiln. The simple shapes and carved motifs of the 7C tend to evolve into a more complicated style (heavy lines, relief decoration) in the 6C. Also on display are the Greek-inspired vases: the black-figure style (first half of the 6C) followed by the red-figure style (5-4C).

The Etruscans were reputed metalworkers. The sophisticated techniques of granulation and filigree (first display case in the passage on the right) culminated in the repoussé technique (display case opposite).

Gallery 14. — Etruscan art of the Classical and Hellenistic Periods. Note the alabaster cinerary urns, often with reclining figures on the lids, and the terracotta sarcophagi from Volterra and Chiusi. Bronze mirrors with wooden handles (display case on the right), sometimes decorated with Greek mythological scenes, were produced in vast quantities.

Roman Antiquities. — Denon ground floor, district ▣.

Galleries 1-5. — Exhibited in Anne of Austria's summer apartments are works which illustrate two of the most unique forms of expression: the portrait and historical relief carving. Among the portrait series (four effigies of Augustus, at different periods in his life and a bust in basalt of Livia Drusilla, Augustus's consort), which includes works from the Republican era and the Julio Claudian, Flavian, Antonine and Severan dynasties, there are historical relief carvings (altar of Domitius Ahenobarbus), funerary cippi and sarcophagi (The Nine Muses).

Gallery 6. — 3-4C AD. The decorated pillars are the remains of a Corinthian portico from the Incantada in Thessalonika.

Gallery 7. — Late Antiquity. The exquisite mosaic floor decorating the end wall comes from a small country church in Kabr Hiram (near Tyr in Lebanon).

Gallery 8. — Exhibited on these walls are mosaics which decorated the Christian places of worship in northern Africa. Architectural elements from the Tigzirt's basilica (in Algeria) are also on display.

Gallery 9. — On exhibit are a number of mosaics from Syria and objects and architectural elements in basalt related to the burial cult.

Gallery 10. — The opulence of the Roman villa is relived when admiring the Pompeian mosaics (Phoenix) and frescoes (seascapes).

Gallery 11. — In the old **Sphinx's Court**, the art of low relief is exemplified by the great frieze of the Temple of Artemis at Magnesia on the Maeander River. The magnificent mosaic depicting the seasons is from a villa at Antioch.

Take the Daru Stairway up to the first floor (on the right of the landing).

The **Winged Victory of Samothrace** (early 2C BC) seems to defy space; the wide, soaring movement in victory is striking. The statue's hand can be seen in a small display case.

Roman Antiquities contd. — Denon first floor, district ▣ and Sully districts ▣ to ▣. Beyond the Apollo rotunda is the **Boscoreale Room** (salle de Boscoréale) with frescoes from Herculaneum and silverware from Boscoreale.
Go through the Henri II Gallery (salle Henri II) — note the ceiling decorated by Braque in 1953 — to reach the Room of Antique Bronzes and Jewellery (salle des Bronzes et des Bijoux Antiques) *(reorganization in progress)* ranging from Greek Archaism (Case I), Classical and Hellenistic art (Case 3) to Roman specimens.
Figurative art (3rd case right) from the Gallo-Roman period includes the great gilded statue of Apollo from Lillebonne. Admire the precious gold jewels in the cases between the windows.

Greek Pottery. — Return to the Salle des Sept Cheminées to reach the **Clarac Gallery** (salle Clarac) which contains Minoan pottery and Cycladic idols in an abstract style, to reach the **Campana Gallery** (Galerie Campana) on the right. After the decline of Crete and Mycenae, the geometric style (10-8C) evolved towards a decorated frieze. Corinth and eastern Greece produced vases in new designs: figures in action (**Rooms I and III**). The same technique is used in the Master of Caere hydria (**Room II**) and by the artist of Amasis (**Room III**). About 530BC Andokides adopted a new style: figures in red against a glazed background (**Room IV**). Around 500BC Euphronios' pure style (**Room IV**) and Douris' graceful paintings (**Room V**), illustrated this art at its zenith. At the time of the building of the Parthenon (447-432), red-figured Classical pottery flourished (**Rooms VI-VII**). From the 4CBC (**Rooms VIII and Henri II**) painted scenes became very ornate: exhibits from Apulia and Lucania. The Myrina and **Tanagra figurines (Room IX)** are full of life, marvels of grace and delicacy.

SCULPTURE

Denon ground floor districts ▣ to ▣▣

Major works displayed in this department
(see text and plan p 44)

Virgin of Isenheim	Marly Horses (Coustou)
Diana of Anet	Busts by Houdon
The Three Graces (Pilon)	Psyche Revived by the Kiss of
Evangelists and Nymphs	Cupid (Canova)
(Jean Goujon)	The Slaves (Michelangelo)
Virgin and Child (Donatello)	

Access from Pavillon de Flore. Go up a staircase from the Medici Gallery in the Paintings Department — Start in Room 1

French Romanesque. — Room 1. With the development of Romanesque architecture, sculpture flourished and various local schools evolved. The Head of Christ from Lavaudieu (Haute-Loire) shows an advanced technique as early as the 12C. A capital from the old Church of Ste-Geneviève in Paris (Daniel in the lions' den), from

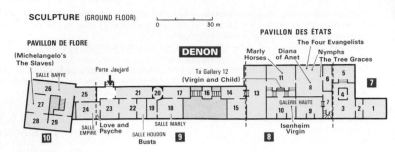

SCULPTURE (GROUND FLOOR)

PAVILLON DE FLORE

(Michelangelo's The Slaves)

DENON

PAVILLON DES ÉTATS

The Four Evangelists

Marly Horses   Diana of Anet   Nymphs The Tree Graces

an earlier period and in a rougher style is nonetheless very moving. Other outstanding works include St Michael and the Dragon, from Nevers — a remarkable triangular composition; the head of St Peter from Autun; a severe-looking Virgin from Auvergne; and a great Burgundian cross.

French Gothic. — Room 2. The rigid spirituality of the late Gothic period is evident in a retable from Carrières and statue-columns from Notre-Dame de Corbeil (right).

Room 3. In the 13-14C, Gothic art flourished with faces illustrating regional characteristics: fragments from Rheims (head of a woman), Chartres (St Matthew) and Paris. There are also the recumbent figures of Charles IV and Jeanne d'Evreux by Jean de Liège; statues of Charles V and Jeanne de Bourbon; and several Madonnas and Child dating from the 14C.

Upper Gallery (9). The Virgin of Javernant reflects the artificiality of 14C art (first alcove). The smiling angels from the second half of the 13C are characteristic of Rheims (second alcove). In the third alcove are mourning figures (15C). A dignified St John from Loché illustrates the elegant style of Touraine.

German and Dutch Gothic. — Upper Gallery (10). The intricate drapery of the **Virgin of Isenheim** is characteristic of German sculpture (mainly in painted wood) in the late Middle Ages. Swabian artists developed a simpler style as in the Mary Magdalene by Gregor Erhart. A delicate marble Virgin of the Annunciation opposite reveals the artistry of the Franconian master Tilman Riemenschneider.

The altarpiece from Coligny, Marne (third alcove) is a good example of the carved works made up of picturesque small reliefs in painted wood which were produced in large quantities in the Netherlands and exported far and wide.

French — Late Gothic and Renaissance (15-16C). — Room 4 contains two recumbent figures in marble portraying Pierre d'Evreux-Navarre and Catherine d'Alençon. In **Room 5**, at the back, great 15C masterpieces are exhibited at the foot of mutilated carvings from the rood-screen of Bourges Cathedral (mid-13C); they include the striking tomb of Philippe Pot, the seneschal of Burgundy, surrounded by hooded mourning figures; the recumbent figure of Anne of Burgundy; against the far wall a Mary Magdalene from Champagne and a Virgin from Montigny in pure Burgundian style. In **Room 6** is displayed a famous low relief of St George fighting the dragon by Michel Colombe, marking the transition to the Renaissance.

In **Room 8** the **Diana of Anet** stands in the midst of Renaissance masterpieces, expressing the sensitivity and aesthetic sense of the period and combining Classical Antiquity, Italian art and French tradition seen in the strength and antique poses of Pierre Bontemps (Admiral Chabot to the left along the wall); the power and mastery of Germain Pilon (along the far wall, a Resurrection, a funerary monument for the heart of Henri II, and **The Three Graces**); the grace and refinement of Jean Goujon's low relief (**The Evangelists** and **Nymphs** from the Fountain of the Innocents in Paris); and the elegance of the funeral monuments of the Montmorency family by Barthélemy Prieur. The monuments are characteristic of Renaissance humanism in France, as the spiritual quest of the Middle Ages gave way to the anatomical study of Classical Antiquity.

Italian Sculpture. — In the 13C, Italian sculpture had become stereotyped as evidenced by the Virgin from Ravenna to the right of the stairway (**Lower gallery 12**). In the 14C, Pisa witnessed a new awakening (graceful Virgin by Nino Pisano), which peaked at the beginning of the 15C in Siena with Jacopo della Quercia (seated Madonna at the far end of the gallery) and especially in Florence with the incomparable Donatello (low relief of the **Virgin and Child** in the fourth alcove next to two delightful small angels by Verrocchio). In the fifth alcove the painted, gilded bust of a woman is a remarkable example of Florentine art; to the left is a lovely, delicate medallion by Desiderio da Settignano. Displayed in the sixth alcove is the bust of the Princess of Aragon by Francesco Laurana.

At the end of the 15C, Florentine art developed a more mannered style, which is illustrated by a low relief by Agostino di Duccio (left wall of gallery) and great enamelled terracottas by the Della Robbias.

On the ground floor (**Room 11**) note above the doorway the Nymph of Fontainebleau, a bronze low relief by Benvenuto Cellini. Provisionally on display in this room are Coustou's **Marly Horses** and Coysevox' Winged Horses, which were previously in Place de la Concorde.

17C. — Rooms 13, 14 and 15. Under Henri IV and Louis XIII French sculpture came to a standstill: note the mannerism of Francheville *(The Slave, Orpheus playing the Viol)* and the early classical style of Sarrazin *(Cardinal de Bérule at Prayer)*. On the other hand, the reign of Louix XIV saw the advent of several master sculptors including Puget *(Milo of Crotone)*, Girardon, Coysevox and Anguier.

18C. — **Room 17** contains examples of garden statuary from royal and princely palaces such as Versailles, Marly and Petit-Bourg *(Louis as Jupiter and Maria Leczinska as Juno* by the Coustou brothers).
The Regence period is represented by works by artists such as J.B. Lemoyne, P.A. Slodtz and G. Coustou.

Room 18. There are several allegorical and mythological statues by Antoine Coysevox *(The Seine, The Marne)* and Nicolas Coustou *(Nymph with a Dove)* from the magnificent Grande Cascade in the park at Marly.

Room 19. In contrast with the pompous official statues (models by Lemoyne, Pigalle) a more flexible style evolved: busts (G. Coustou and Lemoyne) and smaller pieces for interior decoration (graceful *Bather* by Falconet).
Statuary reached a turning point with Bouchardon: *Cupid Cutting his Bow from Hercules' Club* **(Rotunda 20)**.

Room 21. The monumental sculptures from the old châteaux of Bellevue, Choisy and Louveciennes enhance the charm of the small allegories by Falconet *(The Threatening Cupid)*, the expressiveness of the statue of Voltaire by Pigalle and the nobility of works inspired from Antiquity *(Psyche Abandoned* by Pajou).

Room 22 (to the left, works by **Houdon**). Displayed around the statue of Diana, in a slightly rigid stance although portrayed in action, are an outstanding series of lifelike **busts** of the Encyclopaedists and other contemporaries ranging from Voltaire's ugly smiling face to the youthful countenance of the Brongniart children, which illustrate Houdon's sense of observation.
The realism of Julien's *Dying Gladiator* and the delicate busts by Caffiéri and terracottas by Clodion are also noteworthy.

19C. — **Room 24 (Empire)**. The classical severity of the effigies of Napoleon (statue by Ramey and bust by Chaudet) makes a striking contrast with the languid poses of Pradier's mythological figures and the tenderness of feeling of the group **Psyche Revived by the Kiss of Cupid** by Canova. *Peace* by Chaudet is a monumental work carved in silver.

Room 25. The neo-classical style of Bosio and Pradier contrasts with the vigour of the medallions of David d'Angers, the force and energy of *The Marseillaise* by Rude and the charm of his *Young Neapolitan Fisherman* and of the *Dancing Fisherman* by Duret.

Room 26 (Barye). Bronzes, sketches and models of monuments illustrate Barye's wide-ranging style, showing great realism and vitality. His enormous knowledge of the animal kingdom is evident in his groups of animals in combat.

Foreign Sculpture. — **Rooms 27 and 28. The Slaves** by Michelangelo, masterpieces of controlled strength and profound emotion were carved between 1513 and 1520 and were intended for the tomb of Pope Julius II. Also on display are works by 15 and 16C Italian artists (Vittoria, Rustica).

Room 29. Collection of baroque sculptures from Italy and the Netherlands. Bernini's mastery ranges from a delicate model of an angel to the large-scale expressive bust of Richelieu in marble.

PAINTINGS

The location of a painting may change as work on the Great Louvre progresses. Numbers in red identify the paintings on the plan pp 46-47.

How to find the different schools of painting

French	14C	Sully 2nd floor ■
	15-17C	Sully 2nd floor ■ to ■
	18-19C	Denon 1st floor ■ to ■
	19C	Denon 1st floor ■, ■ and ■
	Beistegui Collection	Denon 1st floor ■
Italian	Primitives	Denon 1st floor ■
	16C	Denon 1st floor ■
	17C	Denon 1st floor ■
	17-18C	Denon 1st floor ■
Flemish and Dutch	Primitives	Denon 1st floor ■
	16-17C	Denon 1st floor ■
	17C	Denon 1st floor ■
Spanish	14-18C	Denon 1st floor ■■
German	15-16C	Denon 1st floor ■
English	17-19C	Denon 2nd floor ■

French School Sully second floor districts ■ to ■

14C. — **Gallery 1.** In a period when religious subjects were the rule — as is the case with the altarcloth of Narbonne with its fine Gothic decorations on silk — the painting of Jean II le Bon, against a traditional gold background, is the first real portrait (1360) of a French king. The two panels from the Thouzon altarpiece are of a later period.

15C. — Gallery 2. The Avignon Pietà (1), a masterpiece of early French painting, is a composition of great simplicity and poignancy. The composition centres on Christ's broken body framed by heads bowed in sorrow. Jean Fouquet, the greatest contemporary painter, executed miniatures and lifelike portraits *(Charles VII, Guillaume Jouvenel des Ursins)*.

16C. — Galleries 3 and 5. As Renaissance humanism expanded its influence, religion and nature were superseded by man as the main theme in art. The numerous portraits, fascinating in their lifelike quality and meticulousness, painted by Jean Clouet **(François I-2)**, his son, François Clouet, *(Pierre Quthe)* and François Quesnel *(Henri III)* attest to this.

Gallery 4 presents a rich collection of small portraits by François Clouet *(Elizabeth of Austria, Henri II, Charles IX)* and Corneille de Lyon *(Pierre Aymeric)*.

François I, during the building of Fontainebleau Palace, hired numerous artisans, crafts-

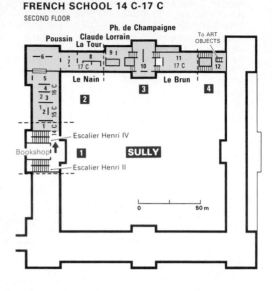

FRENCH SCHOOL 14 C-17 C
SECOND FLOOR

men, painters... from Italy; these artists brought mannerism and a new style of decoration, in which both stucco and painting were incorporated. This was the beginning of the First Fontainebleau School as illustrated by *Diana the Huntress*. When work on the palace was taken up again by Henri IV, a new school of painting was born, the Second Fontainebleau School. The portrait evolved towards a more idealized style with a taste for allegory and symbolism *(Gabrielle d'Estrées and One of Her Sisters)*.

17C. — French painters resided in Rome, the art centre of Europe, and reacted against the exaggerations preponderant in the mannerist style; they painted in the same line as Caravaggio **(Gallery 6)** with a return to reality and the effect of chiaroscuro (Le Valentin: *The Fortune Teller*). The room also contains Parisian painting under Louis XIII: Simon Vouet's *Presentation at the Temple*, a composition of cool colours and Philippe de Champaigne's *Cardinal Richelieu*.

Nicolas Poussin **(Gallery 7)** is one of the great French classical painters. He directed his attention to religious painting (a number of Holy Families) and sought inspiration from mythology *(Orpheus and Eurydice)*.

Gallery 8. With Georges de La Tour *(St Irene Lamenting over St Sebastian, The Cheat)*, who was known for his studies of light and shadow similar to Caravaggio's, painting comes to grips with reality. A social message is conveyed by the Le Nain brothers and their scenes of peasant life *(Dinner, The Cart, The Forge)*. A number of small still-lifes were painted by lesser-known painters influenced by Flemish artists, who had come to Paris to work *(Still-life with a Chessboard* by Lubin Baugin).

Gallery 9. The soft, warm hues of Claude Lorrain's compositions *(Seaport at Sunset, Landing of Cleopatra at Tarsus)* contrast with the cold tonality of Nicolas Poussin's series of paintings depicting the seasons.

Gallery 10. The Royal Academy of Painting and Sculpture founded in 1648 assembled artists who specialized in large religious compositions. Among the works commissioned for Parisian churches are the "Mays" *(p 115)*; these works (Le Sueur's *St Paul's Sermon at Ephesus,* May 1649) were offered to Notre-Dame every year in May from 1630 to 1707 by the goldsmiths' guild. Philippe de Champaigne's works demonstrate a close observation of people and scenes: *Portrait of Robert d'Andilly* and, especially, the well-known *Ex-voto of 1662*, both the result of his contact with Jansenist circle of Port-Royal.

Gallery 11. Le Brun, Louis XIV's official court painter, was the author of these immense compositions (1661-73) recounting the history of Alexander the Great. The portrait of Le Brun is by Nicolas de Largillière.

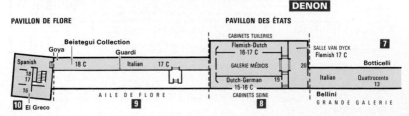

18C. — Denon first floor districts 🄵 and 🄶. Under the Regency and Louis XV's reign, a reaction against the rigidity of classicism appeared in the arts as well as the morals. The atmosphere of the Age of Enlightenment is reflected in Watteau's ethereal, dream-like works; colours light up and contours soften, as in his **Pilgrimage for Cythera (3)**, where the figures are placed harmoniously in a pastoral landscape.

The indulgent way of life prevalent in the 18C transpires in the light-hearted scenes by Lancret *(Music Lesson, Innocence)* and the comic scenes by Watteau (the wistful **Gilles-4**). Realism appears with Chardin in his still-lifes *(The Skate)* and domestic scenes *(Child with Top)*.

Boucher sought inspiration in mythology; his compositions were full of grace and

Gilles by Antoine Watteau

sensuality as in *Venus and Vulcan*, and especially *Diana Resting after her Bath*, painted in fresh colours with a hint of affectation. Genre scenes such as *Lunch* reveal a period in his artistic production when he was influenced by the Dutch masters. He stressed the decorative quality of the landscape in *The Mill* and *The Bridge*.

The *joie de vivre* apparent in the works of this period found its foremost exponent in Fragonard. His *Women Bathing* shows the originality of his style: the opulent nudes, warm tones, sense of movement all combine to form a blithesome painting. This spontaneity is brought out in his *Music*. Still using gallant themes, and yet expressed in a more formal manner, under the influence of David and neoclassicism, *The Lock* marked a turning point in his career.

With Greuze a new genre, a moral tone, appeared: the family, placed in a rustic setting, is extolled as the perpetuator of virtues *(The Father's Curse: Punished Son, Ungrateful Son)*. Mme Vigée-Lebrun, Marie-Antoinette's official painter and a Greuze admirer, continued this genre with the emphasis on maternal and filial love, as in the famous portrait of *The Artist and Her Daughter*.

Landscapes, which up to then provided the backdrop, became the central theme in Vernet's works *(View of Naples, Toulon Roadstead)*.

Prior to the Revolution, Hubert Robert, with his series commissioned for Louis XVI's apartments in Fontainebleau, brought into fashion Roman ruins placed in idealized surroundings, although he was not particularly faithful to their correct location *(Le Pont du Gard)*. Two works by Robert represent the Louvre's Grande Galerie.

19C. — The stiff neo-classical style of the Empire is best seen in the vast historic canvas by David of the **Coronation of Napoleon (6)**, which is opposite his portrait of *Madame Récamier* in a classic pose on the couch which bears her name, the récamier. His nude antique scenes celebrating the human form were a prelude to Girodet *(The Deluge)* and Ingres's **(Grande Odalisque —7, Turkish Bath —5)** academicism. The latter attached great importance to line and draughtsmanship and was totally opposed to the Romantic Movement, which evolved with Géricault and Delacroix's experiments with colour and light effects.

Stormy skies, violent death and colourful war scenes (Delacroix: **Massacres at Chios —8**, *The Death of Sardanapalus, Liberty leading the People*) reached a climax with Géricault's poignant shipwreck scene **Raft of Medusa (9)**, where only one of the victims is depicted full face.

PAINTINGS (FIRST FLOOR)

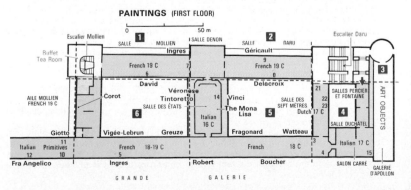

Italian School Denon first floor districts **4**, **5**, **7** and **9**

Primitives. — The works of the Italian schools of the 14C (Trecento) and 15C (Quattrocento), the precursors of the Renaissance, are displayed in the Grande Galerie. Cimbue's **Virgin and Angels (10)** (c1280) faces Giotto's **St Francis of Assisi (11)**, which is one of the first paintings to include an authentic landscape and a living person.

At a time when art drew its themes from religion, the vivid colours on the traditional gold background are striking. Note the predominance of blue in Fra Angelico's **Coronation of the Virgin (12)** and the pink of St John's vestment in Sassetta's triptych. Then the themes, expressions and attitudes became freer. The Virgin and Child remained a favourite subject (Fra Filippo Lippi, Botticelli and Perugino) but portraits became more expressive: *Sigismondo Malatesta* by Piero della Francesca, **Saint Sebastian (13)** by Mantegna, *Christ in Benediction* by Bellini, *Portrait of an Old Man* and *The Visitation* by Ghirlandaio.

16C. — Denon first floor district **6** *Salle des États*. There was a smooth transition to the Renaissance as the Holy Family and Venus, studies of Christ and contemporary portraits were painted alternately. The **Mona Lisa** with her rather melancholic expression, the most famous work of art in the world, holds pride of place. The enigmatic smile of the Mona Lisa, the wife of a rich Florentine, del Giocondo, is to be found in the next group, **Virgin and Infant Jesus with Saint Anne (14)**.

In addition to careful modelling, the Venetians added a profusion of colour and life to their works: Titian's *Open Air Concert,* and Veronese's vast painting, **Wedding at Cana** *(restoration in progress)*. In this evangelical scene the artist depicts the golden age of Venice, its luminous skies, its majestic architecture and its splendid life style. Most of the 130 portraits are of contemporary figures: Christ appears beside the Emperor Charles V, Suleiman the Magnificent, the 16C Venetian high society and the artist as a cello player.

17C. — Denon first floor district **5** *Salon Carré*. The artists of the baroque style experimented with subtle lighting: Guido Reni's light and shade effects, Giordano's supernatural glow in his *Adoration of the Shepherds,* the intense luminosity of Piazzetta's *Assumption of the Virgin* and the contrasts of Caravaggio (**The Death of the Virgin** — 15), which anticipate the chiaroscuro technique.

17 and 18C. — Denon first floor district **9** *Aile de Flore.* On display are works by Guido Reni *(St Sebastian)*, Caravaggio *(The Fortune Teller)* and Carraci. Domenichino's landscapes *(Flight into Egypt)* are reminiscent of Poussin's classical scenes. The lavishness of the Age of Enlightenment is illustrated by Pannini *(Concert* illustrating the concert given at the wedding of the Dauphin, Louis XV's son) and principally in Venice by Guardi (a series of paintings commemorating the festivities held during the Doge's coronation) and Tiepolo, whose bright mythological and religious scenes are not as evocative as his street scenes *(Carnival Scene, The Charlatan)*. The canvas, *Woman with a Flea,* by the Bolognese artist G.M. Crespi, recalls the Dutch school.

Spanish School Denon first floor district 10

The golden age of Spanish painting, which encompasses many contrasting styles, is preceded by the work of some 15C primitive artists including Martorell and his *Martyrdom of St Georges*.

Ribera's *St Paul the Hermit*, the face ravaged and the body worn, stands out amid the livid, almost transfigured portraits of El Greco (**Crucifixion** —16)

The realism of Ribera's **The Club Foot (17)** with the subject's sad smile, and of Murillo's **Young Beggar (18)** with its effective indirect lighting, contrasts with the mystical works of Zurbaran *(St Bonaventura's Funeral)* the baroque exaltation of Carreno de Miranda *(The Foundation of the Trinitarian Order)* and the stiff portraits of the Spanish Court by Velasquez. The delightful Madonnas by Murillo painted in muted colours have a pastel-like quality. The Beistegui Collection (Aile de Flore) contains Goya's masterpiece of portraiture, *The Marquesa de la Solana*.

Dutch and Flemish Schools Denon first floor districts 4 and 8

15, 16 and 17C. — Denon first floor district **8** *Cabinets Seine and Tuileries*. The works of the Flemish primitives are characterised by an oval face, carefully draped garments and familiar details: Van der Weyden *(Greeting of the Angel)*, Jan Van Eyck (**Madonna with Chancellor Rolin** — 19) — outstanding for the candid expressions, the detailed backcloth and crown), Memling, Quentin Massys *(The Moneylender and his Wife)*. A certain realism appears in the works of Hieronymus Bosch *(The Ship of Fools)* and Bruegel the Elder *(The Beggars)*.

The peaceful paintings *(Earth, Air)* of Jan Bruegel, son of the above and known as Velvet Bruegel, precede the small genre canvases of bourgeois life of the period by Teniers, Terborch and Vermeer (the exquisite *Lacemaker)*.

Flanders 17C. — Denon first floor districts **9** *Salle Van Dyck.* While Jordaens achieved a vigorous style bursting with realism and colour *(The Four Evangelists)*, Van Dyck dominated the period with his extremely elegant paintings (**King Charles I** — 20, *Madonna with Donors)*.

Even in his religious works, Rubens expressed his celebration of life with rich colours *(Adoration of the Magi, The Village Fair)*, intensity of expression (charming *Portrait of Hélène Fourment,* his second wife), sensual human forms and luxurious garments as in the twenty-one vast formal paintings of the **Life of Marie de' Medici** (Galerie Médicis).

Holland 17C. — Denon first floor district **4** *Salle des Sept Mètres.* The dark still-lifes by Snyders and the sombre portraits by Frans Hals, in which a white collar is the only bright note (*The Gypsy* — **21** — full of life and spontaneity is the only exception) make a striking contrast with Van Honthorst's riot of colour *(The Concert)*. Fine landscapes by Jacob van Ruisdael *(The Ray of Sunlight)*.

In his four celebrated **Self-Portraits** (**22**) and the two portraits of his companion, Rembrandt, the master of the chiaroscuro technique, uses a limited colour range with great mastery. His paintings are bathed in an ethereal golden glow which exudes intense feeling (**Pilgrims at Emmaüs** — **23**).

Aile de Flore, second floor, Galerie Zénithale. Works by minor artists include the charming *Five Senses* by Palamedesz, *Skating Scenes* by Van Goyen and *The Slippers* by S. van Hoogstraten.

German School Denon first floor district **8** *Cabinets Seine I*

The German Renaissance is represented by a few important works: a fine, solemn *Self-Portrait* of Dürer as a young man holding a thistle; a colourful allegory, *A Knight, A Young Woman and Death*, by Hans Baldung Grien; a *Venus* by Lucas Cranach; and a remarkable portrait of the humanist *Erasmus* by Holbein the Younger.

English School Denon second floor district **9** *Aile de Flore, second floor, Galerie Zénithale*

Apart from Hans Holbein and Van Dyck, who were official painters to the English Court, the English School is represented by 18C works in the great tradition of English portrait and landscape painting: Lawrence *(Sir Thomas Bell)*, Reynolds (the delightful *Master Hare)* and Gainsborough *(Lady Alston, Conversation in a Park)*.

GRAPHIC ARTS

Denon second floor district **10**

Gallery. — *Pavillon de Flore, second floor, and in a gallery off the Napoleon Hall.* The 140 000 drawings, engravings and pastels are shown in rotation by school, period and theme.

ART OBJECTS

Sully first floor districts **1** to **6** and Denon first floor district **4**

Major works displayed in this department
(see text, plan p 37 and plan p 50)

Crown Jewels (The Regent)	The Boulle Cabinets
Harbaville Triptych	Monkey Commode by Crescent
Ivory Virgin from the Ste-Chapelle	« Loves of the Gods » Tapestries
The Maximilian Tapestries	

★★★**Apollo Gallery** (Galerie d'Apollon). — *First floor (plan p 37).* Built in the reign of Henri IV and remodelled after a fire in 1661, this state room is royal both in its dimensions and decoration. Le Brun worked here before leaving to paint the Hall of Mirrors at Versailles. Delacroix then took over and the decoration was completed during the Second Empire. The wrought-iron grille (1650) is from Maisons-Lafitte. The gallery provides a Grand Siècle setting for all that remains of the royal treasures.

Besides the priceless **Crown Jewels** which include the **Regent diamond** (140 carats, purchased by the Duke of Orleans in 1717 from England) and the Côte de Bretagne ruby (107 carats), the display cases contain the most precious mementoes of the French monarchy, especially the Coronation ornaments, gold and silver ware (including the porphyry vase mounted in silver gilt as an eagle presented by Abbot Suger), chased reliquaries, jasper vessels, rock-crystal ewers, finely mounted gems. Go through the Egyptian galleries to the right to reach the St-Germain l'Auxerrois stairway.

★★**Colonnade Galleries** (Salles de la Colonnade). — The Vestibule has splendid panelling taken from the Château Neuf of Vincennes and contains four ceremonial mantles of the Order of the Holy Spirit. The King's Bedchamber, in the Louvre, is reconstructed in a room with an alcove next to the State Chamber, with its panelling and carved ceiling.

Middle Ages. — In **Gallery 4** works from Christian Rome (porphyry columns from the original Basilica of St Peter, Barberini Ivory) are shown alongside those from Byzantium (10C **Harbaville ivory triptych**) and Carolingian objets d'art (ivories, bronze statuette of Charlemagne), offset by Romanesque items (*champlevé* enamels). The shrine of St Polentin is a later work from the Rhineland.

Gallery 5: The religious inspiration of 13C Parisian artists is apparent in the Gothic treasures: precious **Ivory Virgin from the Ste-Chapelle**, moving Descent from the Cross. The mastery of the Limousin enamellers can be admired in the reliquaries, shrines, crosses, pyxes and the admirable ciborium by the master enameller Alpais. A stained-glass window illustrates the art of the master-glaziers. In the 14 and 15C Gothic art works became more expressive and more skilled (Embriachi retable in wood and ivory).

Renaissance. — Decorators and artists in all fields were imbued with the humanist spirit.

Gallery 6: Bronzes from Padua by Riccio *(The Poet Arion holding a Lyre)*, Florence and Venice and fine medals by Pisanello illustrates the new trend which originated in Italy.

Gallery 7: Examples of Limousin enamels made famous by the Limosin brothers *(Portrait of the Constable Anne de Montmorency* — central display cabinet), Reymond and Pénicaud). The masterpieces of Italian potters are note-worthy: ornate decoration from Faenza, warm hues of Urbino, reddish highlights from Deruta and glazed faience from

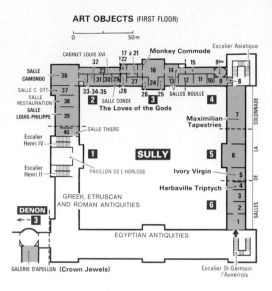

ART OBJECTS (FIRST FLOOR)

Gubbio. In France, Bernard Palissy produced elaborately coloured pottery (plate from Isabella d'Este's dinner service). The walls are hung with a magnificent set of twelve tapestries of **The Hunts of Maximilian**, woven *c*1540 for the Emperor Charles V by the Brussels workshops at the height of their fame.

Gallery 10: Original jewellery from Spain and Italy, watches and clocks from France and Germany show the refinement of European life.

The Golden Age. — Marshal d'Effiat's room (**Gallery 12**) gives a perfect example of the severe Louis XIII style of furniture. The tapestry *Moses in the Bulrushes* (**Gallery 11**) is from the Louvre workshop which preceded the Gobelins, their work including the famous series on Fable Themes (*Coronation of Psyche* — **Gallery 16**). From 1660 onwards the majesty of Louis XIV's reign influenced the decorative arts. At the time when Le Vau and Le Brun decorated the Apollo Gallery, the royal cabinetmaker **Boulle** created his first pieces of furniture in ebony (splendid **cabinets** and desk belonging to the Elector of Bavaria) inlaid with pewter, tortoiseshell and copper and ornamented with gilded bronze mounts (**Galleries 13 and 14**).

The Age of Enlightenment. — The Regency signalled a relaxation in art and morals. Fantasy reigned, decoration became daintier with the curvilinear forms of the rococo style. **Cressent** was a brilliant exponent of this trend: cabinets, the famous **Monkey Commode** in bronze, clocks, a bureau (**Gallery 16**). After 1750 a purer style evolved with simpler forms.

Gallery 9 bis and 15: displayed in the David Weil Rotunda and the Niarchos Gallery are the magnificent pieces by French gold and silversmiths; among them are works by Roettiers (the Prince de Condé's table-centre) and Germain.

The Seasons' rotunda (**Gallery 17**), rooms devoted to Rouen and Moustiers faiences (**Galleries 18-19**) precede the porcelain room (**Gallery 20**) with its fine panelling displaying a Sèvres collection, and the snuff-box section (**Gallery 23**) which includes ivories and silverware.

There are examples of the works of the greatest cabinetmakers including Cressent, Carel (lacquer commode), B. Van Risen Burgh, Dubois, Migeon (**Galleries 24 to 27**). Oeben's distinctive marquetry design (desk and chiffonier in **Gallery 28**) and Leleu's elegant commodes with straight lines (**Gallery 29**) are noteworthy. A roll-top desk by Riesener stands next to Benneman's splendid bureau (**Gallery 30**) used by Napoleon at the Tuileries. Marie-Antoinette's desk (**Gallery 31**) is also by Riesener. Chairs by Jacob and lacquered furniture by Carlin are displayed in the Chinese room (**Gallery 32**). Marie-Antoinette's travelling-case (**Gallery 35**) is beautifully decorated.

Gobelins tapestries on a rose background — **The Loves of the Gods** after Boucher (**Gallery 29**), a Chinese wall hanging (**Gallery 30**), torches, clocks, consoles, escritoires and occasional furniture reflect the creativity and refinement of this elegant period.

19C. — Exquisite pieces evoke the Empire: silver-gilt nécessaire by Biennais, a great Medici vase in Sèvres porcelain and biscuit ware with bronzes by Thomire (**Room 36**), a silver-gilt tea set made for Napoleon by Biennais and a jewel case by Jacob Desmalter (**Room 37**). The Louis-Philippe gallery contains furniture, gold and silver ware and porcelain of that period. The collection assembled by Thiers (**Room 40**) displays 18C porcelain, small bronzes and Japanese laquerware.

2

★★★

The
Champs-Élysées

Michelin plan **11** - folds 16, 17, 29
and 30: from F 8 to H 12

Total distance: 6.5km-4 miles — Time: 5 1/2 hours
Start from the Tuileries métro station

*The Paris vista known the world over extending
up the Champs-Élysées to the Arc de Triomphe,
silhouetted against the sky, is known to Parisians
as the Voie Triomphale or Triumphal Way.
It begins at the Louvre, passes through
the Tuileries Gardens, across the Place de
la Concorde and up the Champs-Élysées
to the Arc de Triomphe.*

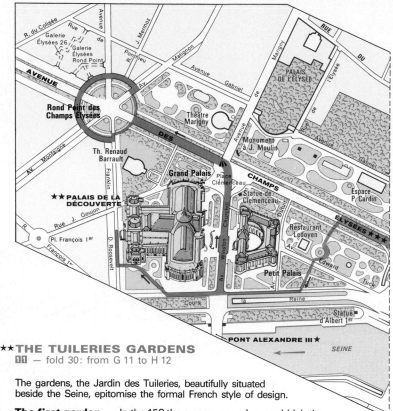

★★THE TUILERIES GARDENS
☐☐ — fold 30: from G 11 to H 12

The gardens, the Jardin des Tuileries, beautifully situated beside the Seine, epitomise the formal French style of design.

The first garden. — In the 15C the area was used as a rubbish tip by butchers and tawers of the Châtelet district. The clay soil was used for making tiles — *tuiles* — hence the name: Tuileries.
When, in 1563, the Queen Mother, Catherine de' Medici, decided to build a château next to the Louvre *(p 30)*, she bought land from the Tuileries for an Italian-style park. This included fountains, a maze, a grotto, decorated with terracotta figures by Bernard Palissy, and a menagerie. East of the octagonal basin stood a semicircular screen of trees famous for its echo; Henri II added an orangery and a silkworm farm. The park became the fashionable airing place and as such broke new ground, for hitherto fashion and elegance had always been displayed indoors.

Le Nôtre French Garden. — By 1664 the gardens required attention: Colbert entrusted the embellishment to Le Nôtre, born near the Marsan Pavilion and a gardener at the Tuileries, like his father and grandfather before him. He raised two terraces lengthways and of unequal height to level the sloping ground; created the magnificent central alley vista; hollowed out the pools; designed the formal flowerbeds, quincunxes and slopes.
Colbert was so delighted that he wanted the gardens kept for the royal family but was persuaded by the author, Charles Perrault, to allow the public to enjoy them also.
In the 18C the garden's appeal was increased by such attractions as chairs being available for hire and toilets being built. Part of the gardens was reserved for the royal family in the reign of Louis-Philippe.
In 1783 the physicist, Charles, and the engineer, Robert, made an early balloon flight from the gardens.

The Revolution. — On 10 August 1792, Louis XVI and his family fled the Tuileries Palace, crossed the gardens and sought refuge with the Legislative Assembly. The Swiss Guards also tried to escape but two thirds of them were slaughtered in the gardens by the mob.
The Festival of the Supreme Being, organised by the painter David on 8 June 1794, opened in the gardens before proceeding to the Champ-de-Mars *(p 65)*.

The Tuileries today. — The part of the Tuileries designed by Le Nôtre remains unaltered, although the effect of his positioning of occasional statues has been jeopardized by less satisfactory additions, apart from those by Maillol (dotted around the gardens) which are outstanding.

During the season, it is difficult to find hotel accommodation in Paris.
It is wise to book your hotel in advance by letter or by telephone.

Or, apply to **Accueil de France**
127, Champs-Élysées, 75008 Paris — ☎ 47 23 61 72.

TOUR

The modern area of the Tuileries, between the wings of the Louvre and the Carrousel Arch, is described on p 34. Start from the Flore Pavilion, where Avenue du Général-Lemonnier meets the quay and two sphinxes, brought back after the capture of Sebastopol in 1855, stand guard.

The Waterside Terrace. — Walk up the steps to the Terrasse du Bord de l'Eau from which there is a **view★★** overlooking the gardens, the Seine and, in the background, the Louvre. This was the playground of royal princes and the sons of Napoleon I and III.

An underground passage beneath the terrace, communicating with the Place de la Concorde, enabled Louis-Philippe to escape from the palace in 1848. The bronze group *The Sons of Cain* is by Landowski.
Walk towards the formal gardens.

★The Parterres. — The small grille, marked by a ditch, formerly divided the royal garden from the public area. The paths are lined with copies of statues from Antiquity and decorative vases. Towards the eastern end are works by Le Pautre, Auguste Cain and Rodin.

Quincunxes (Quinconces). — The central alley affords a magnificent **vista★★★**. On either side are areas of greenery with 19 and 20C statues: Autumn, Winter and Night.
The large, voluptuous **statues★** by Maillol *(Pomona, Action in Chains, Venus...)* on the lawns have been moved from their site between the two wings of the Louvre until the completion of the works.

The Octagonal Basin (Bassin octogonal) and Terraces (terrasses). — The huge octagonal basin and the adjoining statues, terraces, slopes, stairways were designed as a single architectural composition. Numbers correspond with numbers on the plan above.

1) The Seasons (N. Coustou and Van Clève)
2) Arches from the Tuileries Palace
3) Bust of Le Nôtre (Coysevox). The original is in St-Roch *(p 139)*
4) The Tiber in the Antique manner
5) The Seine and the Marne (G. Coustou)
6) The Nile in the Antique manner
7) The Loire and the Loiret (Van Clève)
8) Commemorative tablet of the balloon ascent of Robert and Charles in 1783 *(p 48)*
9) Fame on a winged horse (after Coysevox)
10) Mercury on a winged horse (after Coysevox). Originals in the Louvre.

Until 1716 there was no exit from this end of the Tuileries, the moat at the foot of the Louis XIII wall cutting it off from the Esplanade or future Place de la Concorde. A swing bridge was constructed over the moat and ornamented in 1719 by Coysevox' Winged Horses (Chevaux Ailés) which were brought for the purpose from Marly. The bridge disappeared when Louis-Philippe had Place de la Concorde redesigned.

Steps and ramps afford access at several points to the terraces (the Feuillants on the north side, the Bord de l'Eau on the south, which run the length of the gardens and culminate in the Jeu de Paume and Orangery Museums.

The two pavilions, the **Orangery** (Orangerie) and the **Jeu de Paume** were built during the Second Empire and have served as art galleries since the beginning of the 20C. The latter, now known as the **Galerie National du Jeu de Paume**, has been soberly refurbished to display to best advantage the most advanced elements in contemporary art *(temporary exhibitions; ☎ 47 03 12 50)*.

★ORANGERY ⃞⃞ — fold 30: H 11

Open 9.45am to 5.15pm; closed Tuesdays; 1 January, 1 May, 25 December; 25F, 13F Sundays; ☎ 42 97 48 16 Ext. 406.

The horseshoe staircase with wrought ironwork by Raymond Subes leads to the first floor galleries, where the Walter-Guillaume Collection (Impressionists to 1930) is on display.

There are good examples of canvases by several artists: Soutine's portraits and still-lifes *(Young Pastrycook)* reflect a tortured mind; like Picasso *(Nude with a Red Back Drop)* and Modigliani *(Antonia)* he belonged to a group of foreign artists working in Paris; Cézanne (1839-1906) concentrated on still lifes *(Apples and Biscuits)*; Renoir (1841-1919) showed special interest in portraiture *(Bather with Long Hair, Woman with a Letter)*; Derain (1880-1954) used brown tones in his severe compositions *(A Blond Model)*; Matisse (1869-1954) experimented with colour *(Three Sisters)*; Henri Rousseau (le Douanier, 1844-1910) achieved special light effects in his naive compositions *(Old Junier's Cart)*.

The two oval rooms on the ground floor are the setting for the series of paintings made by Monet in the garden of his house at Giverny, Normandy (he lived there: 1883-1926) of water-lilies and known as the **Nymphéas★**.

★★★THE PLACE DE LA CONCORDE ⃞⃞ — fold 30: G 11

Everything — the site, the size, the general elegance of the square — combines to impress.

Paris aldermen, wanting to find favour with Louis XV, commissioned Bouchardon to sculpt an equestrian statue of the Well Beloved, as he was known, and organised a competition to find an architect for the square. Servandoni, Soufflot, Gabriel and others all submitted plans. The winner was Gabriel who designed an octagon bordered by a dry moat and balustrade. Eight massive pedestals, in pairs and intended later to support statues, were to mark the oblique corners. Twin edifices with fine colonnades were to be constructed to flank the opening of the Rue Royale. Work began in 1755 and continued until 1775.

In 1770, at a firework display to celebrate the marriage of the Dauphin and Marie-Antoinette, the crowd panicked and 133 people were crushed to death in the moat. In 1792 the royal statue was toppled and Louis XV Square became the Square of the Revolution.

On Sunday 21 January 1793 a guillotine was erected near where the Brest statue now stands, to perform the execution of Louis XVI. Beginning on 13 May, the « nation's razor », by now installed near the grille to the Tuileries, claimed a further 1 343 victims including Marie-Antoinette, Mme du Barry, Charlotte Corday, the Girondins, Danton and his friends, Mme Roland, Robespierre and his confederates *(p 120)*. The executions ceased in 1795. The Directory, in hope of a better future, renamed the blood-soaked area, Concorde.

The Concorde Bridge was opened in 1790 and the square's decoration completed in the reign of Louis-Philippe by the architect Hittorff. The king decided against a central statue which all too easily might become an object of contention with any change in regime and selected, instead, an entirely non-political monument, an obelisk. Two fountains were added, similar to those in St Peter's Square in Rome. The north fountain represents fluvial navigation and the south fountain maritime navigation.

Eight statues of towns of France were commissioned for the pedestals provided by Gabriel. Cortot sculpted Brest and Rouen, Pradier Lille and Strasbourg. It was at the foot of this last figure, that the poet-politician, Déroulède, rallied patriots after 1870 when the town of Strasbourg was under German rule. Lyons and Marseilles are by Petitot and Bordeaux and Nantes by Caillouette.

★**Obelisk (Obélisque).** — The obelisk comes from the ruins of the temple at Luxor. It was offered by Mohammed Ali, Viceroy of Egypt, to Charles X in 1829, when seeking French support, but only reached Paris four years later, in the reign of Louis-Philippe. The monument in pink granite, 3 300 years old, is covered in hieroglyphics; it is 23m-75ft tall — and weighs more than 220 tons. The base depicts the apparatus and stratagems used in its transport and erection on the square *(Maritime Museum p 64)* — Cleopatra's Needle in London, offered by the same ruler to Queen Victoria, comes from Heliopolis and is 2m-6ft 6 shorter.

★★★**Views.** — The best point from which to get a view of the Champs-Élysées — Triumphal Way — is the obelisk. The view is framed by the Marly Horses as you look up the avenue towards the Arc de Triomphe, and by the Winged Horses of the Tuileries towards the Louvre. Both sets are replicas. There are good vistas also, north to the Madeleine and, south, to the Palais-Bourbon.

★★**The two mansions.** — Gabriel's colossal mansions on either side of the opening to Rue Royale are impressive without being overbearing; the colonnades inspired by that at the Louvre are even more elegant than the original and the mansions themselves, among the finest examples of the early Louis XVI style.

The right pavilion, the **Hôtel de la Marine**, was originally the royal store, until 1792 when it became the Admiralty Office. Today it houses the Navy Headquarters.

The pavilion, across the street, was at first occupied by four noblemen. It is now divided between the French Automobile Club and the **Hôtel Crillon**, a world famous luxury hotel. It was in this building on 6 February 1778 that the *Treaty of Friendship and Trade* between the King, Louis XVI and the 13 independent States of America was signed. Benjamin Franklin was among the signatories for the States. On Rue Royale side, a plaque in English and French commemorates this treaty by which France officially recognised the independence of the U.S.A.

The two mansions on their far sides from Rue Royale are bordered respectively by the American Embassy *(left)* and the Hôtel Talleyrand, designed in the 18C by Chalgrin for the Duc de la Vrillière, and where the statesman and diplomat Talleyrand died in 1838.

★★★THE CHAMPS-ÉLYSÉES 🔲🔲 — folds 16, 17, 29 and 30: from F 8 to G 11

The Champs-Élysées, the most famous thoroughfare in Paris, is at once an avenue with a spectacular view, a place of entertainment and a street of luxurious and smart shops.

Origin. — In the time of Henri IV there were only fields and marshlands in the area; in 1616 Marie de' Medici created the Cours-la-Reine, a long avenue which began at the Tuileries and followed the line of the Seine to the present Alma Square. The tree-lined route, in time, became the fashionable carriage ride.

In 1667 Le Nôtre extended the Tuileries vista by planting trees in rows on the plain known as the Grand Cours. The calm shades were renamed the Elysian Fields — Champs-Élysées — in 1709. In 1724 the Duke of Antin, Director of the Royal Gardens, extended the avenue to the Chaillot Mound — the present Étoile; his successor, the Marquis of Marigny, prolonged it in 1772 to the Neuilly Bridge. Two years later Soufflot, reduced the road gradient by lopping the mound by more than 5m-16ft — the surplus rubble being dumped, producing the still apparent rise in the Rue Balzac.

The fashion. — At the end of the 18C the Champs-Élysées were still wild, deserted, unknown and only six private mansions had been built within their precincts. Of these, one, the Hôtel Massa, was later transported stone by stone and re-erected near the Observatory *(p 202)*. The Allies, who occupied Paris in 1814, allotted the green area in the centre of the capital, the English and the Prussians camping in the Tuileries and Place de la Concorde, the Russians beneath the trees on the Champs-Élysées. The ensuing dilapidation took two years to clean up.

The avenue, by 1828 in the City's care, was embellished by fountains, footpaths, gas lighting. During the time of the Second Empire it became a favourite meeting place and the curious, seated on either side of the thoroughfare, might see cavaliers and their escorts riding side-saddle, tilburies and broughams, eight abreast in a cloud of dust. Café orchestras (the Alcazar rebuilt by Hittorff in 1840), restaurants, panoramas, circuses atttracted the elegant who swelled in number when there were race meetings at Longchamp or the great world exhibitions (1844, 1855, 1867, 1900...). In the gallant Widows' Alley, now Avenue Montaigne, crowds gathered to dance beneath the three thousand blinding gas flares as Olivier Metra conducted polkas and mazurkas with gay abandon or in the nearby Winter Garden, to listen to Sax, the musician playing his new instrument, the saxophone.

The heart of the nation. — Today there is little that is aristocratic about the avenue, but it still sparkles, it still appeals to all.

On 14 July, military processions with bands playing draw immense crowds. At times of great national emotion, the triumphal avenue is the spontaneous rallying point for the people of Paris: the procession of the Liberation (26 August 1944), the demonstration of 30 May 1968, the silent march in honour of General de Gaulle on 12 November 1970, the bicentennial parade in 1989.

From Place de la Concorde to the Rond Point
see plan pp 52 and 53

The Champs-Élysées, in this area, is planted with trees, landscaped, bordered with grand old chestnut alleys, dotted with occasional pavilions and even a small children's funfair.

The Marly Horses (Chevaux de Marly). — Replicas now replace the two original marble groups *(Africans Mastering the Numidian Horses)*, which were commissioned from Guillaume Coustou for Marly, Louis XIV's superb château near Versailles, to replace Coysevox's *Winged Horses* which had been moved to the Tuileries. Following Marly's destruction during the Revolution a special trailer drawn by sixteen horses brought the marbles to their present site in 1795. The originals are now in the Louvre.

Go through the gardens to the left to Cours-la-Reine. In Louis XVI's time the Ledoyen Restaurant was a modest country inn where passers-by paused to drink fresh milk drawn from the cows grazing outside.

To the south, the **Alexandre III Bridge★** was built for the 1900 World Exhibition and is an example of the popular steel architecture and ornate style of the period. It has a splendid single-span, surbased arch; it affords a fine view of the Invalides.

The Petit Palais and the Grand Palais. — The halls were also built for the 1900 World Exhibition. The palaces' stone, steel and skylight architecture and very varied exterior decoration have always had critics as well as admirers but the constructions, nevertheless, have gradually become part of the Paris urban scene.

The **Petit Palais** houses the **Museum of the Petit Palais★** *(open 10am to 5.40pm; closed Mondays and holidays; 15F, free on Sundays; special admission times and charges during temporary exhibitions; 28F; ☎ 42 65 12 73)*.

The museum is divided into the Dutuit (antiques, medieval and Renaissance art objects, paintings, drawings, books, enamels, porcelain), Tuck (18C furniture and art objects) and the city of Paris's 19C collections (Ingres, Delacroix, Courbet, Dalou, Barbizon school, Impressionists). The south gallery displays large historical and religious canvases (Gustave Doré) and the north gallery contains works by Carpeaux.

An Ionic colonnade before a mosaic frieze forms the façade of the **Grand Palais** along its entire length. Enormous quadrigae crown the corners; elsewhere the decoration is turn-of-the-century Art Deco. Inside, the single hall space in covered by a flat glass dome.

The Grand Palais, long the home of annual exhibitions and shows (cars, domestic equipment, etc), has been entirely remodelled. It now comprises conference rooms with attendant facilities, a library, closed-circuit television, an exhibition area of nearly 5 000m²-6 000sq yds — known as the Galleries of the Grand Palais *(entrance: Avenue du Général Eisenhower)* and is now a cultural centre where temporary exhibitions are held.

An area on the west side has been given over to the Palais de la Découverte and a further area on the south side to the Paris IV University.

The statue on the left is of La Fayette.

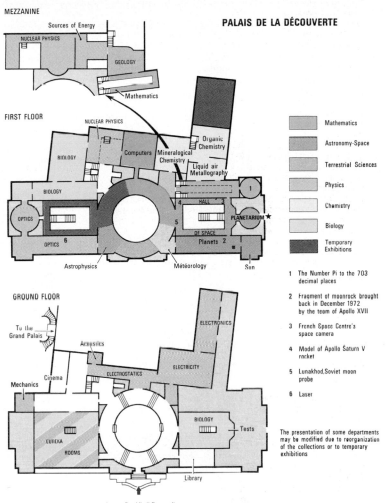

MEZZANINE

Sources of Energy

NUCLEAR PHYSICS

GEOLOGY

Mathematics

PALAIS DE LA DÉCOUVERTE

FIRST FLOOR

NUCLEAR PHYSICS

BIOLOGY

Computers — Mineralogical Chemistry

Organic Chemistry

Liquid air Metallography

BIOLOGY

OPTICS

HALL

PLANETARIUM ★

OPTICS

OF SPACE

Planets

Astrophysics — Météorology — Sun

	Mathematics
	Astronomy-Space
	Terrestrial Sciences
	Physics
	Chemistry
	Biology
	Temporary Exhibitions

1 The Number Pi to the 703 decimal places

2 Fragment of moonrock brought back in December 1972 by the team of Apollo XVII

3 French Space Centre's space camera

4 Model of Apollo Saturn V rocket

5 Lunakhod, Soviet moon probe

6 Laser

GROUND FLOOR

ELECTRONICS

To the Grand Palais

Acoustics

ELECTRICITY

Cinema — ELECTROSTATICS

Mechanics

BIOLOGY — Tests

EUREKA ROOMS

Library

Avenue Franklin D. Roosevelt

The presentation of some departments may be modified due to reorganization of the collections or to temporary exhibitions

★★**Palais de la Découverte.** — *Avenue Franklin-Roosevelt. Open 10am to 6pm; 4 planetarium shows (time: 3/4) daily on weekdays, 5 at weekends and during school holidays; closed Mondays, 1 January, 1 May, 14 July, 15 August, 25 December; 20F (13F for the planetarium); ☎ 40 74 80 00; Minitel: ☎ 45 63 18 07.*

This museum of scientific discoveries, founded in 1937, is a centre both for higher scientific study and for popular enlightenment. Diagrams, lectures and demonstrations, experiments, documentary films and temporary exhibitions illustrate progressive stages and the most recent discoveries in the sciences. The domed **planetarium★** presents a clear and fascinating introduction to the heavens including the course of the planets in the solar system.

In Place Clemenceau stands a bronze statue of the statesman Clemenceau, *The Father of Victory*, by François Cogné (1932). The monument on the far side of the Champs-Élysées is to the Resistance leader, Jean Moulin: the five steles bear heads with anguished expressions symbolising pain and suffering.

Cross Avenue Winston Churchill. From the centre of the avenue there is a good **view★★** towards the Invalides. Further along, the former Panorama, later a skating-rink, is now the Théâtre du Rond-Point, the home of the Renaud-Barrault Theatre Company.

The Rond-Point. — Designed by Le Nôtre, it has retained the surrounding Second Empire buildings: on the right the former premises of the *Figaro* newspaper, with its original façade now a shopping arcade.

From the Rond-Point to the Arc de Triomphe
see plan pp 54 and 55

This section is the second widest thoroughfare in Paris, it measures 71m-233ft overall. (Avenue Foch: 120m-394ft).

The Second Empire private houses and amusement halls which once lined it have vanished so the avenue appears without historical memories. The only exception is No **25**, a mansion built by La Païva, a Polish adventuress, whose house was famous for the dinners attended by the philosophers Renan and Taine and the Goncourt brothers, and for its probably unique onyx staircase. The Coliseum (Le Colisée), an amphitheatre built in 1770 to hold 40 000 spectators, has left its name to a street, a café and a cinema.

Along the Champs-Élysées today airline and tourist offices, motorcar showrooms and banks alternate with cinemas and big cafés. The dress and fashion houses of the shopping arcades provide attractive and elegant window displays. Point Show at No **68** and Les Champs at No **84** are examples of a new style of multi-purpose centres where restaurants, cinemas and shops are to be found under one roof.

★★★THE ARC DE TRIOMPHE ⊞⊞ — fold 16: F 8

The arch and the **Place Charles-de-Gaulle**★★★ which surrounds it, together form one of Paris' most famous landmarks. Twelve avenues radiate from the arch which explains why it is also called Place de l'Étoile (*étoile* = star).

The arch commemorates Napoleon's victories, evoking at the same time, imperial glory and the fate of the Unknown Soldier, whose tomb lies beneath.

A Remembrance Ceremony is held on 11 November.

Historical notes. — By the end of the 18C the square was already star-shaped although only five roads so far led off it. At the centre was a semicircular lawn.

1806: Napoleon commissioned the construction of a giant arch in honour of the French fighting services. Chalgrin was appointed architect.

1810: With the Empress Marie-Louise due to make her triumphal entry along the Champs-Élysées and the arch only a few feet above ground, as it took two years to lay the foundations, Chalgrin had to erect a dummy arch of painted canvas mounted on scaffolding, to preserve appearances.

Arc de Triomphe

1832-1836: Construction, abandoned during the Restoration, was completed under Louis-Philippe.

1840: The chariot bearing the Emperor's body passed beneath the arch.

1854: Haussmann redesigned the square, creating a further seven radiating avenues, while Hittorff planned the uniform façades which surround it.

1885: Victor Hugo's body lay in state for a night beneath the arch, draped in crape for the occasion, before being transported in a pauper's hearse to the Pantheon.

1919: On 14 July victorious Allied armies, led by the marshals, marched in procession through the arch.

1920: 11 November, the Unknown Soldier began his vigil.

1923: 11 November, the flame of remembrance was kindled for the first time over the tomb of the Unknown Soldier.

1944: 26 August, Paris, liberated from German occupation, acclaimed General de Gaulle.

Circling the Arch. — It is suggested that first you walk round the square to see from a distance the arch's proportions and the relative scale of the sculpture. Chalgrin's undertaking, inspired by Antiquity, is truly colossal, measuring 50m high by 45m wide-164 × 148ft, with massive high reliefs. Unfortunately, Etex and Cortot used influence with President Thiers against their fellow artist Rude and succeeded in cornering three of the four groups of sculpture — Rude's is the only group with a hint of inspiration. Pradier filled the cornerstones of the principal faces with four figures sounding trumpets. A frieze of hundreds of figures, each 2m tall-6ft encircles the arch in a remarkable crowded composition; above, a line of shields rings the coping.

Facing the Champs-Élysées: 1) The Departure of the Volunteers in 1792, commonly called the Marseillaise, Rude's sublime masterpiece. 2) General Marceau's funeral. — 3) The Triumph of 1810 (by Cortot) in celebration of the *Treaty of Vienna.* 4) The Battle of Aboukir.

Facing Avenue de Wagram: 5) The Battle of Austerlitz.

Facing Avenue de la Grande-Armée: 6) Resistance (by Etex). 7) The Passage of the Bridge of Arcola. 8) Peace (by Etex). 9) The Capture of Alexandria.

Facing Avenue Kléber: 10) The Battle of Jemmapes.

On reaching the Champs-Élysées once more, take the underground passage, which starts from the right pavement to the arch.

The names of the greatest victories won during the Revolution and the Empire appear upon the shields at the summit. Beneath the monument, the Unknown Soldier rests under a plain slab; the flame of remembrance in rekindled each evening at 6.30pm.

Lesser victories are engraved on the arch's inner walls together with the names of 558 generals — the names of those who died in the field are underlined.

The Arch platform. — *Access: 10am to 5.30pm (5pm 1 October to 31 March); closed 1 January, 1 and 8 May, 14 July, 1 and 11 November, 25 December; 31F; children 6F; lift available.*

There is an excellent **view**★★★ of the capital generally from the platform and, in the foreground, of the twelve avenues radiating from the square. The arch stands halfway between the Louvre and the La Défense Quarter *(p 227)*, at the apex of the Champs-Élysées — Triumphal Way.

Assembled in a small museum in the arch are mementos of its construction and the celebratory and funerary ceremonies with which it has been associated. A documentary film traces the monument's highlights.

Place de la Concorde

The **Eiffel Tower**

Michelin plan **11** - folds 28 and 29: from H 7 to K 9

Distance: 3.5km-2 miles – Time: 2 1/2 hours
(without visiting the museums)
Start from the Trocadero métro station

The Chaillot Palace, Trocadero Gardens,
Champ-de-Mars and Eiffel Tower together form
Paris' most striking early 20C architectural
group. Closing the view to the southwest is
the École Militaire, a handsome reminder
of the 18C.

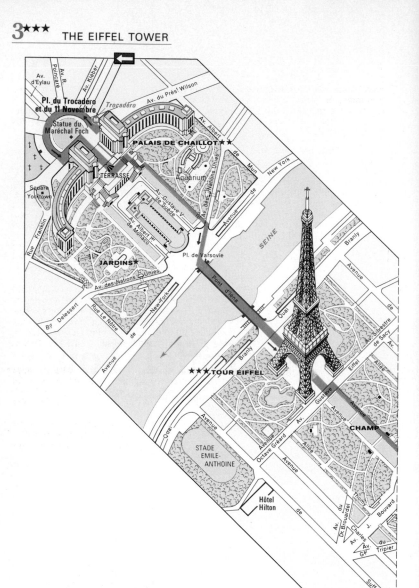

←

★★ CHAILLOT PALACE ⅡⅠ — fold 28: H 7

The Bassompierre Mansion. — In the second half of the 16C, Catherine de' Medici built herself a country house on Chaillot Hill, then a rural area some distance from the city. This was bought, in due course, by Marshal Bassompierre, a companion in arms of Henri IV. Handsome, witty, valiant in the field, he lived life to the full and was also a reckless gambler. He eventually offended Cardinal Richelieu and in 1631 was sent to the Bastille — first gallantly burning 6 000 love letters it was said.

The Convent of the Visitation. — Queen Henrietta of England, wife of Philip of Orleans, took over the mansion on Bassompierre's death, and founded a Convent of the Visitation of Holy Mary — Parisians happily referred to the nuns as the Sisters of Bassompierre!

The convent became known for great preachers: Bossuet, Bourdaloue and Massillon, and as a place of retreat for great ladies of the court: Marie Mancini, Cardinal Mazarin's niece, Mlle de La Vallière — for both of whom it seemed politic to withdraw from the attentions of Louis XIV.

Grandiose projects. — Napoleon chose Chaillot as the site for a palace for his son, the King of Rome. Stupendous plans were drawn up by Percier and Fontaine; the convent was razed; the top of the hill levelled; the slope lessened; the Iéna Bridge built — then the Empire fell. Marshal Blücher demanded that the bridge be destroyed since it commemorated a Prussian defeat but Louis XVIII interposed, saying that he would sit in the centre in his sedan and be blown up with it.

The Trocadero. — The name Trocadero was given to the area in 1827 after a military tournament on the site had re-enacted the French capture four years previously of Fort Trocadero, near Cadiz.

The square, Place du Trocadéro, was laid out in 1858; twenty years later, at the time of the 1878 Exhibition an edifice, said to be Moorish inspired, was erected upon it. In 1937 this was replaced by the present Chaillot Palace.

TOUR

The Place du Trocadéro-et-du-11-Novembre. — The semi-circular square, dominated by an equestrian statue of Marshal Foch, is a centre point from which major roads radiate to the Alma Bridge, the Étoile, the Bois de Boulogne and the Passy quarter — the wall at the corner of Avenue Georges-Mandel marks the boundary of Passy cemetery *(p 252)*

Chaillot Palace (Palais de Chaillot). — The spectacular, low-lying palace of white stone, consisting of twin pavilions linked by a portico and extended by wings curving to frame the wide terrace, was the design of architects Carlu, Boileau and Azéma. The palace's horizontal lines along the brow of the hill make a splendid foil to the vertical sweep of the Eiffel Tower, when seen from the Champ-de-Mars or from almost any of the capital's viewpoints. The pavilion copings, back and front, bear inscriptions in letters of gold by the poet Paul Valéry. Low reliefs and sculptures by forty artists adorn the wings and steps to the gardens, a monumental bronze of Apollo by H. Bouchard *(p 240)* stands on the terrace.

Looking across to the Champ-de-Mars, you get a wonderful **view★★★**, in the foreground, of the Seine and the Left Bank, and beyond dominating all, the Eiffel Tower. Beyond again, in the far distance is the École Militaire.

Beneath the palace terrace is one of the capital's largest theatres *(access through the hall in the left pavilion)*. Under skilled directors and talented actors, it became the home of the People's National Theatre — Théâtre National Populaire, the T.N.P. Known now as the **Chaillot National Theatre** this modernised theatre serves as a multi-purpose cultural centre, seating 1 200. On the left, below the steps to the gardens, is the small Gémier Theatre (salle Gémier), erected in 1966 as an experimental playhouse.

★The Gardens (Jardins). — Beyond the walls on either side of the long rectangular pool in direct line with the Iéna Bridge, the final slopes of Chaillot Hill lead down, beneath flowering trees, to the banks of the Seine.

The pool, bordered by stone and bronze gilt statues, is at its most **spectacular★★** at night when the powerful fountains are floodlit.

The maps and plans are orientated with north at the top.

THE MUSEUMS

★★Maritime Museum. — *Open 10am to 6pm; closed Tuesdays and 1 May; 22F.* ☎ *45 53 31 70.*
The museum, founded in 1827 by order of Charles X, displays scale models and artifacts originating mostly from the naval dockyards. Figureheads, pictures, dioramas, and mementoes of naval heroes add interest to the displays.
The great hall is devoted to naval art and maritime history from the 17C. The side gallery overlooking the Trocadero gardens deals with the scientific, technical and traditional aspects of the evolution of navigation.

1) **Ocean** — late 18C ship.
2) 17 and 18C vessels: the **Louis XV** (an educational toy for the young king), **The Royale** and the **Louis le Grand**. Fine group of galleys dominated by **The Reale** (its decoration is attributed to Puget).
3) The Ports of France, a series of canvases by the 18C artist, Joseph Vernet. The **Royal Louis**, a rare model from the Louis XV period; remains of the vessel, **Le Juste**, lost in 1759. Stern and bow of Marie-Antoinette's barge at Versailles.
4) The Revolution and the First Empire. The **Emperor's Barge** (1811). **The Belle Poule** in which Napoleon's body was returned from St Helena in 1840.
5) The Restoration, the Second Empire and the Third Republic, **The Valmy**, modelled in ebony, ivory and silver, the Navy's last sailing ship. **The Gloire**, the first armour-plated vessel in the world (1859). Dioramas of the dismantling, transportation and erection of the Luxor obelisk (1831).
   Mementoes of great naval heroes: F. de Lesseps, Brazza, Charcot.
6) The modern navy. Reconstruction of a gun-boat bridge.
7) Underwater exploration, hydrography, life saving and diving.
8) Fishing and maritime traditions.
9) Model of an early steamship (Jouffroy d'Abbans). Restoration of models.
10) History of merchant shipping.
11) Wooden boats (18-19C). The great explorations. The **Astrolabe**, the sloop of the 19C navigator and Antarctic explorer, Dumont d'Urville. Wreckage from the ships of the 18C navigator La Pérouse.
12) Maritime maps and navigation instruments.
13) Temporary exhibitions.

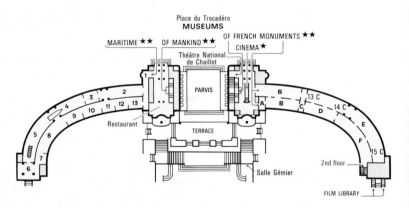

★★Museum of French Monuments. — *Open 9am to 6pm; closed Tuesdays; 16F, Sundays: 8F, under 18s: free;* ☎ *47 27 35 74.*
This museum of France's monumental art and mural painting, comprising casts and replicas, was the brainchild of the Gothic Revival architect and restorer of medieval monuments Viollet-le-Duc. It was opened in 1880.
The exhibits are grouped by geographical region, by school and by period, making evolutions of style, themes, geographical and other influences, easy to follow.

Sculpture *(left) double gallery on the ground floor: Room 1* **A**. Early Romanesque art — *Rooms 2 to 6* — **B**. Romanesque sculpture and tympana from Moissac, Vézelay, Autun — *Room 7* — **C**. Military architecture of the Crusade Campaigns: knights' fortress in Syria. — *Rooms 8 to 11* — **D**. Gothic cathedral statuary (Chartres, Amiens, Rheims, Notre-Dame). — *Rooms 12 to 18* — **E**. Sculpture of the 13 and 14C (recumbent figures from the St-Denis Basilica and other churches) and 15C (palace ornaments, fountains, calvaries). *Rooms 19 to 21* — **F**. The Renaissance (tombs from Tours and Nantes).
2nd floor: Rooms 22 to 24: works by Jean Goujon, Ligier Richier, Germain Pilon. *Room 25:* Sculpture from the Versailles park. *Rooms 26 to 28:* Busts and small works of the 18 and 19C (Pigalle, Houdon, Rude, Barye, Carpeaux...). *Rooms 29:* models.

Mural painting *(right) pavilion's upper floors:* the most important Romanesque and Gothic frescoes are reproduced on lifesize architectural replicas: the crypt of St-Germain Abbey, Auxerre (featuring the oldest frescoes in France), the vault, porch and gallery of St-Savin-sur-Gartempe, the chancel of St Martin's at Vic, the apse of Berzé-la-Ville, the dome of Cahors Cathedral, The Dance of Death of La Chaise-Dieu Abbey Church, etc. The richness of the colours and the vitality of the figures are amazing when examined closely.

★★**Museum of Mankind (Musée de l'Homme).** — *Open 9.45am to 5.15pm, closed Tuesdays and holidays; 25F.* ☎ 45 53 70 60.
The subject of the museum is the races of man and his way of life.
On the first floor are an anthropological gallery, explaining the origin of the species and the palaeontological gallery where human characteristics are compared by means of fossils (examples include the mammoth ivory Lespugue Venus and the neolithic Grossgartach burial from the Yonne Valley).
From Africa, there are fine collections on prehistory (frescoes from the Ahaggar area in the Sahara), ethnography (costumes, tools, arms) and art (medieval Abyssinian art, Central African sculpture). The European Gallery is at the end.
On the 2nd floor are displays from the Arctic regions (Eskimo crafts, masks from Greenland) and the Near and Far East and the Pacific (Easter Island, New Guinea). The Continental America galleries are rich in pre-Columbian, Maya and Aztec art (beautiful rock crystal skull and statues of the god Quetzalcóatl).

★**Henri Langlois Cinema Museum.** — *Guided tours (time: 1 1/2 hours) at 10 and 11am, 2, 3 and 4pm; closed Tuesdays and 1 May; 22F.* ☎ 45 53 74 39.
The history of motion pictures, from the very beginning of photography, is traced in sixty galleries. Reynaud's *théâtre optique* (1888), Marey's photographic rifle, Edison's kinetoscope (1894); the Lumière brothers' kinematograph and photorama, posters, models (some on them were executed by the Russian director Eisenstein), settings (the robot of Fritz Lang's *Metropolis*), film studios (Méliès, Pathé), costumes and dresses worn by film stars (Rudolph Valentino, Greta Garbo) illustrate the film world.
Over 5 000 objects show the evolution of the technical aspects of filming: shooting, staging, projection and evoke the magical world of cinema.

Film Library (Cinémathèque). — *Trocadero Gardens, Albert-de-Mun side.* This film library is one of the richest in the world. As many as 3 to 4 films are shown daily. It is a meeting place for the professionals and amateurs of the film world. *Programmes at the box office and In the press; closed Mondays; 20F.* ☎ 47 04 24 24.

★**THE CHAMP-DE-MARS** ▯▯ — fold 28: J 8

The Champ-de-Mars is now a vast formal garden closed at one end by the École Militaire and at the other by Chaillot Hill. Bestriding it is the Eiffel Tower.

The parade ground. — When Gabriel had completed the École Militaire, he replaced the surrounding market gardens, which ran down to the Seine, by a parade ground or Champ-de-Mars — Field of Mars (1765-67). The public was first admitted in 1780.
In 1783 the physicist, Charles, launched the first hydrogen-filled balloon from the ground, which came down 20 miles away near Le Bourget. Blanchard, a year later, launched a balloon complete with basket and ailerons... in which he landed on the far side of Paris at Billancourt.

The Festival of Federation. — It was decided to commemorate the 14 July 1790, the first anniversary of the taking of the Bastille, by a Festival of Federation on the Champ-de-Mars. Stands were erected; mass was celebrated by Talleyrand, Bishop of Autun, assisted by 300 priests. La Fayette, at the altar, swore an oath of loyalty to the nation and the constitution which was repeated by the listening crowd of 300 000 and, finally, by Louis XVI, in the midst of the general enthusiasm.

Festival of the Supreme Being. — In 1794, Robespierre had the Convention decree a state religion recognising the existence of a Supreme Being and the immortality of the soul. These hypotheses were solemnly affirmed on 8 June at a mammoth festival presided over by Robespierre, the Incorruptible, as he was known. The procession began in the Tuileries and ended on the Champs-de-Mars.

The capital's fairground. — From time to time the ground has been given over to exhibitions; on 22 September 1798 the Directory commemorated the anniversary of the Republic with an Industrial Exhibition destined to replace the old Saint-Germain and Saint-Laurent Fairs — an innovation was the payment of exhibitors.
World exhibitions were held in 1867, 1878, 1889, 1900 and 1937 — the Eiffel Tower remains as a souvenir of the Exhibition of 1889. In the same year, the army exchanged the ground with the City of Paris for a terrain at Issy-les-Moulineaux. The latter has now become Paris' heliport.

The gardens. — The present gardens, laid out by J.C.Formigé, were begun in 1908 and completed in 1928. Part is landscaped with grottoes, arbors, cascades and a small pool at the foot of the tower and part is formal. Wide strips on either side, along Avenue de Suffren and Avenue de La Bourdonnais, were sold for building and are now lined by large private houses and blocks of luxury flats.

In general buses run from 7am to 8.30pm. To find out about:

the route operated by city lines
the fare stages
the services extended to midnight
night buses or Sunday and holiday services...

Consult the **Michelin Paris Atlas No** ▯▯*.*

★★★THE EIFFEL TOWER ▯▯ — fold 28: J 7 and J 8

The tower is the capital's look out and Paris' best known monument. When it was erected it was the tallest construction the world had ever known but since then its 300m-984ft have been topped by skyscrapers and telecommunication towers elsewhere. The additions made for television transmission have increased its height by another 20.75m-67ft to 320.75m-1 051ft.

Historical notes. — The idea of a tower came to Eiffel as a natural consequence of his study of the use of high metal piles for viaducts. The first project dates from 1884; between 1887 and 1889 three hundred skyjacks put the tower together with the aid of two and a half million rivets. Eiffel, in his enthusiasm, remarked "France will be the only country in the world with a 300m flagpole".

Artists and writers, however, were appalled; among the 300 who signed a protest were Charles Garnier, architect of the Opera, the composer, Gounod, and the poets and writers François Coppée, Leconte de Lisle, Dumas the Younger, Maupassant... Equally the tower's very boldness and incredible novelty brought it great acclaim and by the beginning of the century it had become a subject of celebration by other poets and dramatists, Apollinaire, Cocteau... and painters such as Pissarro, Dufy, Utrillo, Seurat, Marquet, Delaunay... Since then its form, appearing in millions of souvenirs, has become familiar everywhere.

Eiffel Tower

In 1909, when the concession expired, the tower was nearly pulled down — it was saved through the importance of its huge antennae to French radio telegraphy; from 1910 it also became part of the International Time Service.

In 1916 it was made the terminal for the first radio telephone service across the Atlantic. French radio has used it as a transmitter since 1918 and television since 1957. The top platform served as the base for a revolving light beacon (replaced in 1975 by a fixed red light) and as a meteorological and aircraft navigation station.

Nobody now questions the tower's aesthetic appeal or its utility — it has taken its place on the capital's skyline and beckons a welcome to all who come to Paris. It is often the venue for artistic and publicity events.

The tensile masterpiece. — The tower's weight is 7 000 tons; the deadweight of 4kg per cm^2-57lbs per sq inch — is about that of a man sitting in a chair. A scale model made of steel 30cm high-11.8 inches — would weigh 7 grams or 1/4oz; 50 tons of paint are used every seven years when it is repainted. The sway at the top in the highest winds has never been more than 12cm-4 1/2 inches — but the height can vary by as much as 15cm-6 inches — depending on the temperature.

The visitor looking upwards through the interesting latticework of pig iron, gets an incredible feeling of the stupendous: there are three platforms: the 1st is at 57m-187ft; the 2nd at 115m-377ft; the 3rd at 276m-899ft. The bold will climb the 1 652 steps to the top; others will take the lifts which have had to have special brake attachments fitted because of the variation in the angle of ascent.

Ascent. — *1 July to 9 September 9.30am to midnight; 10am to 11pm the rest of the year. Fare by lift including the museum: stage 1 — 17F, stage 2 — 32F, stage 3 — 49F; by the steps (south pillar): stages 1 and 2 — 8F.* ☎ 45 55 91 11.

The view★★★ for the visitor to the 3rd platform may extend 67km-42 miles if the atmosphere is really clear — but that is rare. Paris and its suburbs appear as on a giant map *(viewing tables)* — the best light is usually one hour before sunset. From the open terrace (stage 3), Eiffel's sitting room can be seen through a window. On the first floor there is an audio-visual museum which presents the tower's history *(20min)*.

Beneath the tower, by the north pillar, is a bust by Bourdelle of the engineer, Eiffel, who presented the country with one of the most frequented French monuments. At night the illuminated tower has a jewel-like quality.

★★THE ÉCOLE MILITAIRE ⬛⬛ — fold 29: K 9

The French Military Academy, one of the finest examples of French 18C architecture, was perfectly sited by its architect at the end of the Champ-de-Mars.

Construction. — Thanks to Mme de Pompadour, Louis XV's favourite, the financier and supplier to the army, Pâris-Duverney, obtained, in 1751, permission to found and to personally supervise the building of a Royal Military Academy where young gentlemen without means would be trained to become accomplished officers. The parade ground was given the name Champ-de-Mars.

Jacques-Ange Gabriel, architect of the Petit Trianon at Versailles and of Place de la Concorde, produced grandiose plans, which the financier duly modified. The final construction, nevertheless, remains incredibly magnificent when one remembers that it was designed as barracks.

The king took no further interest in the future school and, in fact, money to pay for the building was raised from a tax imposed on playing cards and a lottery. The academy numbered 500 students; the course lasted three years. In 1769 Louis XV agreed to lay the foundation stone for the chapel; by 1772 the buildings were complete.

Bonaparte, the Military Cadet. — In 1777 the Royal Academy became the Higher Officers' School. In 1784 Bonaparte, who had been to the lesser military academy at Brienne and was then 15, was admitted on the recommendation that he would "make an excellent sailor". He passed as a lieutenant in the artillery with the mention that he would "go far in favourable circumstances".

The military tradition. — The institution was suppressed by the Revolution, but the buildings, which had been enlarged in the 18C, have retained their military tradition both as quarters and instruction centre. The Swiss Guards of the Ancien Régime, the National Guard of 1848, have been replaced by French and foreign officers attending the School of Advanced War Studies, and the Higher School of National Defence.

THE EXTERIOR

The impressive **central pavilion** which you see as you walk up from the Champ-de-Mars, is ornamented with ten superb Corinthian columns, each two storeys high; completing the decoration are a carved pediment, trophies, allegorical figures and a crowning quadrangular dome. Low lying wings frame the main building. The barracks on either side are 19C. Facing the central pavilion, is the equestrian statue of Marshal Joffre by Real del Sarte (1939).

Leave the **Village Suisse** (antique and second-hand dealers' shops — open 11am to 7pm, closed Tuesdays and Wednesdays) on the right, to circle the academy by way of Avenue de Suffren and Avenue de Lowendal to Place Fontenoy. (Lowendal commanded part of the French army, which defeated the British and Dutch at Fontenoy in 1745).

From the semicircular square, look across the sports ground to the **main courtyard★★**, lined on either side by beautiful porticoes with paired columns. At the back is the central pavilion, flanked by colonnaded buildings ending in advanced wings. Inside, the chapel, the main staircase, the Marshals' Saloon and the guardroom on the first floor are remarkably decorated (not open to the public).

Place de Fontenoy has entirely lost its 18C character. The huge blocks on its east side include the Ministries of Health, Merchant Navy and Post Office, on its south side lies UNESCO.

★UNESCO HOUSE ⬛⬛ — fold 41: K 9

Open Mondays to Fridays 9am to 12.30pm and 2 to 6pm; guided tours, debates, film shows for groups on application: ☎ 45.68.03.71.

The home of UNESCO (United Nations Educational, Scientific and Cultural Organization) was opened in 1958 and is the most truly international undertaking in Paris, the membership by 158 states and construction of the buildings jointly by Breuer, Nervi and Zehrfuss, American, Italian and French architects respectively, demonstrate unique cooperation.

The buildings. — The main building, in the form of a Y supported on piles, houses the secretariat (sales counters in the entrance hall with souvenirs, newspapers, periodicals, coins and stamps). A second building with fluted concrete walls and an accordion-pleat designed roof contains the conference halls and committee rooms. The small cubic construction four storeys high beside the Japanese garden, is a secretariat annexe. Additional accomodation was provided in 1965, by means of two floors being constructed underground and lit naturally by six low level patios and since 1970, at No 1 Rue Miollis, and No 31, Rue François-Bovin.

Decoration. — The decoration is also the result of international artistic cooperation. There are frescoes by the Spaniard, Picasso, and the Mexican, Tamayo, walls by the Spanish ceramic artists, Miro and Artigas, mosaics by the French, Bazaine and Herzell, a mosaic from El Jem in Tunisia (2C), a relief by Jean Arp, tapestries by Lurçat, and the French-Swiss, Le Corbusier, a Japanese fountain by Noguchi and an angel's head from a Nagasaki church destroyed by the bomb in 1945. A monumental statue (Figure in Repose) by Henry Moore and a black steel mobile by the American Calder, can be viewed from Avenue de Suffren. In and around the later annexes are works by the Italian, Giacometti, the Spanish, Chillida, the Venezuelan, Soto and the American, Kelly.

The overall impression is a remarkable synthesis of mid-20C art.

4

★★★

The Invalides

Michelin plan **11** - fold 29: from H 10 to K 10

*Distance 2.5km-1 1/2 miles — Time: 4 to 5 hours
(including visits to the museums)
Start from the Invalides métro station*

*This is the most outstanding single
monumental group in Paris which attracts
large numbers of visitors.
The adjacent Army Museum is rich
and spectacular.*

Barracks for 4 000 men.

Before Louis XIV's reign, old soldiers, invalided out of the service, were, in theory, looked after in convent hospitals. In fact, most were reduced to beggary.

In 1670 the Sun King founded the Invalides on the edge of what was then the Grenelle Plain. Funds were raised in part by a levy on acting soldiers' pay over a period of five years. Construction of the vast edifice capable of providing quarters for 4 000 began in 1671 to plans by Libéral Bruant and was completed only five years later. A dome, added to the original undertaking by Jules Hardouin-Mansart in 1706, lifted the project out of the utilitarian into the monumentally inspired.

Pillage.

On the morning of 14 July 1789 rebels advanced on the Invalides in search of arms. They crossed the moat, disarmed the sentries and entered the underground rifle stores. As further crowds blocked the stairs fierce fighting broke out in the half darkness. The mob finally made off with 28 000 rifles towards the Bastille.

Napoleon's return.

The major event in the history of the Invalides was the return of Napoleon's body in 1840. After seven years of negotiation with the British Government, the French King, Louis-Philippe, was able to dispatch his son, the Prince of Joinville, to St Helena in the frigate, *The Belle Poule* *(model in the Maritime Museum; p 64)* to collect the Emperor's remains. On the prince's arrival on 8 October, the coffin was exhumed and opened for two minutes during which it was seen that the body of the Emperor who had been dead nineteen years, had remained in a state of perfect preservation; those present, including the generals Gourgaud and Bertrand, the 19C historian Las Cases and Napoleon's valet, Marchand, viewed the Emperor once more in his guardsman's uniform.

The coffin, after its long sea voyage, was disembarked at Le Havre and brought up the Seine to Paris where it was landed at Courbevoie *(p 231)*. The funeral was held on 15 December 1840. A snowstorm enveloped the city as the hearse passed beneath the Arc de Triomphe, down the Champs-Élysées and across Place de la Concorde to the Esplanade.

The coffin lay under the cupola and in St Jerome's Chapel until the tomb, designed by Visconti, was completed. The transferring took place on 3 April 1861.

The institution's revival.

After the two world wars the institution is used as originally intended: to provide shelter and care for the war wounded in modernised hospital facilities. The buildings today are occupied by the military services and the Army Museum.

To choose a hotel or restaurant, use the small MICHELIN Red Guide:
PARIS, Hotels and restaurants,
an extract from the current MICHELIN Guide FRANCE.

★★★ THE INVALIDES (HÔTEL DES INVALIDES) ▣▣ — fold 29: J 10

From the Alexandre III Bridge, there is a superb **overall view** of Libéral Bruant's classical style buildings and Mansart's crowning dome.

Esplanade. — The Esplanade, designed and constructed between 1704-20 by Robert de Cotte, Mansart's brother-in-law, affords a spectacular vista 500m-1/3 mile long and more than 250m-820ft wide, ending of course in the classically balanced Invalides buildings. The expanses of green lawns are bordered by avenues of limes. On the left beside the quay is the air terminal, Aérogare des Invalides.

Garden. — Preceding the Invalides are a garden, bordered by a wide dry moat, ramparts lined by 17 and 18C bronze cannon and an 18 piece triumphal battery used to fire salutes on such occasions as the 1918 Armistice and 14 July 1919 Victory March. The battery, removed by the Germans in 1940 and returned in 1946, now stands disposed on either side of the entrance.

★★**Façade.** — The façade is majestic, in style and line, in proportion and size — it is 196m-645ft long. At the centre is a magnificent doorway, flanked at either end by pavilions. Decoration appears in the form of trophies surrounding the dormer windows and in the equestrian statue of Louis XIV supported by Prudence and Justice in the rounded arch above the entrance.

The first statue by Guillaume Coustou (1735), damaged during the Revolution, was replaced by the present figure by Cartelier in 1815.

Restoration work on the **lateral walls★** has uncovered noble buildings on the right side, along Boulevard des Invalides and on the left, alongside Boulevard de Latour-Maubourg, the fine proportions of Robert de Cotte's Order of Liberation Chancellery and the original trench.

★**Main courtyard (Cour d'honneur).** — Go through the entrance to the main courtyard, lined on all sides by two superimposed arcades.

Four central pavilions with carved pediments break the even architectural lines as do the sculptured horses, trampling the attributes of war, at the corner angles of the roof. The dormer windows are decorated, like those on the façade, with trophies. The fifth window to the right of the east central pavilion *(left on entering)* has a peculiar history: Louvois had been in charge of the construction of the Invalides and a mason thought up the idea of encircling a window with the paws of a wolf, making a play on the intendant's name and surveillance; *loup voit* — the wolf sees all. The end pavilion, which is the most ornate, serves as the façade to the Church of St-Louis-des-Invalides. At the centre is the Seurre statue of Napoleon, known as the Little Corporal, which stood for some years at the top of the column in Place Vendôme.

In the perfectly proportioned classical courtyard with its steeply pitched slate roofs and cobbled paving, there is an impressive series of cannon lined up along the walls: note the "Catherine" (1407) bearing the name of Sigismund of Austria, the "Württemberg culverin" (16C) with its chiselled breech and its barrel entwined by a snake.

On either side of the church stand a tank and a cannon (1) and a 1914 taxicab (2).

★**Church of St-Louis-des-Invalides.** — *Open 10am to 6pm (5pm 1 October to 31 March); closed 1 January, 1 May, 1 November, 25 December and during services.*

The church, also known as the Soldiers' Church, was designed by Libéral Bruant and built by Mansart, who later added the dome to the group. Its architectural plan is cold and functional. The only decoration derives from the captured enemy banners overhanging the upper galleries. A window behind the high altar enables one to see through to the baldachin in the Dome Church.

The organ, enclosed in a loft designed by Hardouin-Mansart, is a magnificent 17C instrument on which Berlioz's *Requiem* was played for the first time in 1837.

The banners were more numerous at the end of the Empire but when the Allies entered Paris in March 1814, the Invalides governor burnt 1 417 of them in the courtyard; the history of each is commemorated on the church pillars.

In the crypt *(not open)* lie former governors of the Invalides and 19 and 20C marshals and generals of the field, including Leclerc, Giraud and Juin.

Conserved in an urn is the heart of Mademoiselle de Sombreuil, daughter of the Governor in 1789. During the massacres of September 1792, her filial love moved the murderers to spare her father.

★★★ THE ARMY MUSEUM (MUSÉE DE L'ARMÉE) ▣▣ — fold 29: J 10

Open 10am to 6pm, 1 April to 30 September (5pm the rest of the year). Closed 1 January, 1 May, 1 November and 25 December. Ground floor, east: films shown on the two World Wars; 27F (ticket valid two consecutive days, to allow a thorough visit of the museum, the Dome Church, the exhibition of models and for films shown). ☎ 45 55 37 70.

The galleries, of one of the world's richest army museums, lie on either side of the main courtyard.

EAST SIDE

Ground floor

These galleries, two of the former four refectories situated on either side of the courtyard, are decorated with frescoes of Louis XIV's campaign in Flanders in 1672 by Martin des Batailles.

Turenne Gallery (Salle Turenne). — It contains banners dating from 1619 to 1945. Napoleon's flag of farewell flown at Fontainebleau on his abdication in 1814 is displayed underneath Ingres' painting of Napoleon in his coronation robes. In the centre stands a model of the Invalides at a scale of 1 to 160. 19C trophies.

Vauban Gallery (Salle Vauban). — It is devoted to the history of the cavalry from 1800 to 1940 and to regulation firearms from 1717 to 1979.

2nd floor

These rooms are devoted to **military history** from the Ancienne Monarchie (1618-1782) to the Second Republic. Among the countless souvenirs of French military history are the cannon ball that killed Turenne (1675) (Louis XIV Gallery), mementoes of Napoleon: his coat, hat, sword and medals (Boulogne Gallery) and charming souvenirs of the King of Rome (Montmirail Gallery).

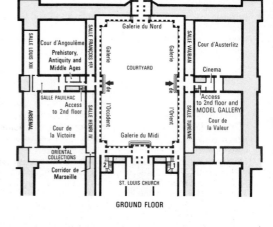

GROUND FLOOR

The **Restoration Gallery** recalls Napoleon's removal to Elba, the Hundred Days, Waterloo and his exile to St Helena. The room in which he died, on the island, is movingly reconstructed.

The **La Fayette Gallery** displays mementoes of General La Fayette, the national guard and the 1830 Revolution.

The **Bugeaud Gallery** (1830-1852) features the conquest of Algeria.

3rd floor

The **Pelissier Gallery** is devoted to the early part of the Second Empire (1852-1860): the Imperial Guard and the Crimean (photographs) and Italian campaigns.

The **Chanzy Gallery** deals with the end of the Second Empire (overseas expeditions) and the 1870-1871 Franco-Prussian War: two animated maps show troop movements. The models displayed in these two galleries trace the evolution of regimental uniforms, equipment and arms. The cooks' costumes are unusual.

WEST SIDE

Ground floor

The number and diversity of arms and armour attractively displayed illustrate the evolution of methods of defense and attack from prehistorical times.

François I Gallery (Salle François Ier). — This former refectory is adorned with paintings depicting Louis XIV's battles and victories in the 1672-78 Dutch war. On display are royal arms and armour.

Prehistory, Antiquity and Middle Ages. — This gallery contains arms dating from the dawn of history to the 9C.

Pauilhac Gallery (Salle Pauilhac). — Renaissance swords and daggers. The firearms collection includes Charles V's pistol, a wheel-lock gun and Philippe V's gun. Fine Spanish armour.

Louis XIII Gallery (Salle Louis XIII). — Splendid royal chased harnesses. Louis XIII's arms collection.

Arsenal. — About 40 complete suits of armour, 1 000 helmets and half suits, 400 pikes and spears, 500 swords and rapiers, 250 projectiles and firearms are on display on shelves and racks.

Oriental Gallery. — Arms and armour from Persia, India, Japan. Among the helmets are those of the Ottoman sultan Bajazet II and of a Slav ruler (Russia, 16C).

Marseilles Gallery (Corridor de Marseille). — 19C saddle cloth.

Henri IV Gallery (Salle Henri IV). — This former refectory is decorated with frescoes commemorating the taking of Flemish towns during the Dutch war. Armour for jousting and foot combat, finely decorated helmets and shields.

2nd floor

The **gallery devoted to the First World War** (1914-18) traces three stages of the conflict; maps showing troop movements, model of Verdun, Marshal Foch's military map and 1918 Armistice bugle.

The **gallery devoted to the Second World War** (1939-45) contains documents, mementoes, photographs and animated map relating to the military aspect (model of the invasion) as well as civilian life and the Resistance movement.

3rd floor

The gallery devoted to the period 1871 to 1914 and the **Gribeauval Gallery** (artillery models) are closed for restoration.

MODELS GALLERY ▢▢ — fold 29: J 10

Fourth floor: west side. Open 10am to 5.45pm (4.45pm 1 October to 31 March); closed 1 January, 1 May, 1 and 11 November and 25 December; 27 F; ☎ 47 05 11 07.

Audio-visual presentation (10 min) of the history and manufacture of models.
A collection of models of towns, harbours and fortresses at a scale of 1: 600 from the time of Vauban (17C) to the present illustrates the evolution of fortifications in France over the last three hundred years. The large scale model of Perpignan (1686) and of Strasbourg (1836), Trompette Castle in Bordeaux made of separate pieces, the model of Briançon, the highest fortified town in Europe *(son et lumière)* are particularly interesting.

The Nîmes Gallery overlooks a courtyard where stone slabs from Napoleon's tomb in St Helena can be seen.

★★★DOME CHURCH (ÉGLISE DU DÔME) ▢▢ — fold 29: J 10

From the front courtyard there is a **general view** of the Dome Church. On the left, behind Mansart's original trench, the Intendant's Garden has been replanted in formal style.
The church is one of major masterpieces of the age of Louis XIV. With this building, Hardouin-Mansart perfected the French classical style, which had first appeared in the Carmelite Church, St-Joseph des Carmes and been developed in St-Paul-St-Louis *(p 94)*, the Sorbonne *(p 188)* and the Val-de-Grâce *(p 200)*. To complete the baroque effect, the original plan envisaged the creation before the south face of a colonnaded esplanade in the manner of Bernini before St-Peter's in Rome. Instead, to afford a good vista, a wide avenue was cut through the then open countryside, Avenue de Breteuil.

The Dome arose when Louis XIV commissioned Hardouin-Mansart to build a church to complement the Invalides buildings of Libéral Bruant and to epitomise the splendour of his reign. In 1677, therefore, work began on the Dome Church, oriented towards the north and joined to the Soldiers' Church by a common sanctuary. It was completed by Robert de Cotte in 1735. The Dome Church stands, finally, as the greatest example of the French 17C or *Grand Siècle* religious architecture, just as Versailles does of the civil architecture of the same period.
In 1793, the Revolution transformed the two churches, which were still united, into a Temple to Mars. It was also decided to transfer to the Temple Tower the captured enemy standards, until then hung in Notre-Dame. With Napo-

The Invalides

leon's interment of Marshal Turenne (d 1675) in the church in 1800, it became a military mausoleum, receiving also countless trophies from the imperial campaigns. It was guarded by the old soldiers, known as the *grognards* or grumblers, billeted in the Invalides barracks. In 1842, two years after the return of Napoleon's body *(p 70)*, Visconti enlarged the central altar, replaced the original baldachin and had the crypt dug to receive the coffin. The big window was constructed only in 1873. These alterations disturbed the inner balance, but the grandeur remains.

Façade. — The façade consists, in the usual Jesuit style, of a projecting central section flanked by outer wings. All are the same height, thus avoiding heavy connecting areas. Between the Doric columns at ground level are statues of St Louis (Louis IX) by Nicolas Coustou and Charlemagne by Coysevox; above a projecting entablature are Corinthian columns, statues of the four Virtues and a pediment carved by Coysevox.

Dome. — Hardouin-Mansart's masterpiece captures the imagination both by its sweeping lines and its dignity; it has a beauty all its own whether standing out against a clear summer sky or rising, almost invisibly, a deeper shadow, against the darkness of the night. The design was based on a prodigious knowledge of balance and proportion which enabled it to rise in a single thrust without buttressing. Forty columns separate the windows round the drum; the cupola base, pierced by round-arched windows, is ornamented with consoles while above, divided into twelve sections, rises the massive gilded dome, decorated with trophies, garlands and other ornaments. Windows in the form of helmets provide air and light inside. Crowning all is an elegant lantern, once again decorated with four statues of the virtues, removed during the Revolution, and a spire which rises 107m-35ft into the sky.

The dome's covering of lead sheeting, attached by copper nails to the wood frame was gilded for the first time in 1715 and has been restored several times since, notably in 1989.

Interior. — *Same times as for the Army Museum (p 71) but closed at 7pm in June, July and August.* The decoration is sumptuous: painted cupolas, walls adorned with columns and pilasters and low reliefs· by the greatest contemporary artists.

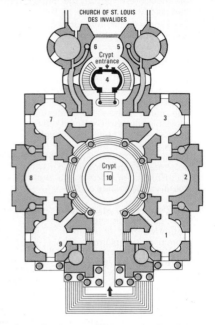

1) Tomb of Joseph Bonaparte, elder brother of Napoleon, King of Spain.
2) Monument to Vauban by Etex. The Emperor himself commanded that the military architect's heart be brought to the Invalides.
3) Marshal Foch's tomb by Landowsky.
4) Ornate high altar surrounded by twisted columns and covered by a baldachin by Visconti. Vaulting decoration by Coypel.
5) General Duroc's tomb.
6) General Bertrand's tomb.
7) At the back — the heart of La Tour d'Auvergne, first grenadier of the Republic; in the centre, the tomb of Marshal Lyautey.
8) Marshal Turenne's tomb by Tuby.
9) St Jerome's Chapel (carvings by Nicolas Coustou). The tomb at the foot of the wall is Jerome Bonaparte's, Napoleon's younger brother and King of Westphalia.
10) The Emperor's tomb.

Cupola. — The cupola is an impressive sight resting on its four massive piers of masonry. The corner chapels are visible through openings in the piers. Painted on the pendentives are the four Evangelists by Charles de la Fosse and then, in ascending order, the kings of France (in medallions) and the Twelve Apostles by Jouvenet. On the cupola itself a vast composition by La Fosse of St Louis presenting Christ with the sword with which he conquered the infidels.

★★★ **Napoleon's tomb.** — The majesty of the setting perfectly befits the Emperor's image. Visconti designed a circular crypt in which to stand the red porphyry sarcophagus upon a base of green granite from the Vosges. It was completed in 1861.

The Emperor's body is placed in six coffins, each contained inside the other: the innermost is of tin-plate; the second of mahogany; the third and fourth of lead; the fifth of ebony; the last of oak.

Napoleon's Tomb

Crypt. — At the base of the stairs, behind the baldachin, two massive bronze statues stand guard at the crypt entrance, one bearing an orb, the other the Imperial sceptre and crown. Low reliefs around the gallery depict institutions founded by the Emperor.

The sarcophagus stands at the centre of the inlaid marble pavement, designed as a star while, against the pillars circling the crypt, are twelve colossal statues by Pradier symbolising Napoleon's campaigns from the Italian victories of 1797 to Waterloo in 1815.

In the *cella*, before a statue of the Emperor in his coronation robes, lies the King of Rome. He died in Vienna in 1832 and remained in the crypt of the Hapsburgs before being transferred to Paris on 15 December 1940 exactly one century after his father; he was finally entombed in 1969.

★★MUSEUM OF THE ORDER OF LIBERATION ⅅⅅ — fold 29: J 10

Pavillon Robert-de-Cotte, 51 bis, Boulevard de Latour-Maubourg. Open 2 to 5pm; closed Sundays and holidays; 10F; ☎ 47 05 04 10; audio-guides available in English
The Order of Liberation, created by General de Gaulle at Brazzaville in 1940, honoured as "companions", those who made an outstanding contribution to the final victory. The list, which was closed in 1946, consists of service personnel and civilians, a few overseas leaders including King George VI, Winston Churchill and General Eisenhower, and several French localities (Paris, Nantes, Grenoble, Vassieux-en-Vercors, Sein Island). The memory is also perpetuated of French heroes, major operations of the Resistance and the concentration camps: documents, trophies and relics.

From the Invalides to St Francis Xavier

Walk from the Place Vauban along Avenue de Breteuil to No 46.

The Michelin Tourist Services. — In France in 1900 there were 3 000 vehicles on the road — phenomena which threw country folk into a panic. Car owners bought petrol at the local grocer and it was for these car owners and drivers that André Michelin, brother of Édouard, who manufactured tyres, compiled a little red book: the Guide FRANCE. This, with its selection of hotels and restaurants and pages of practical information, has grown in size and fame until it is now known to seasoned travellers the world over complete with its star rating system for restaurants.

The young André Michelin next created in Paris, in 1908, a Car Travellers' Information Bureau which provided enquirers with itineraries and road information. He went on to supply the local authorities with name plates for towns and villages, to undertake, in 1910, the mapping of France to a scale of 1: 200 000 — 1 inch: 3 miles — the numbering of all roads (1913) and the production, from locally quarried pumicestone near Clermont-Ferrand, of large square milestones covered in distinctive vitreous enamel. After the 1914-1918 War, guides were published to the Battlefields and in 1926, the Regional Guide Brittany, the first tourist guide in the series now known as the Michelin Green Tourist Guides.

Michelin, formerly located at No 97 Boulevard Pereire with nearly three quarters of a century of experience, and still at work producing and improving maps and guides for the motorist and the tourist, is to be found at No 46 Avenue de Breteuil.

Retrace your steps along Avenue de Breteuil for a good view of the Invalides Dome. St Francis Xavier Church, on the right is a late-19C Romanesque pastiche.

5

★ ★ ★

The Faubourg St-Honoré

Michelin plan **11** - folds 17, 18 and 30: F 10, F 11 – G 10, G 11

Distance: 4km-2 1/2 miles – Time: 1 1/2 hours
Start from the Concorde métro station

After visiting the Madeleine,
stroll along the Faubourg St-Honoré,
famous for its luxury shops and former
town houses.

Rue Royale. — The street running between the two great mansions built by the architect Gabriel *(p 55)* who designed Place de la Concorde, has a double vista: ahead to the Madeleine, its immense pediment raised high on its line of columns, and backwards to the white mass of the Palais-Bourbon.

Luxury shops add a quiet opulence to this select quarter: Villeroy and Boch, Lalique and **Bouilhet-Christofle** which has an exhibition celebrating 150 years of gold and silver craftsmanship on the mezzanine *(visit by appointment only; closed Mondays, Sundays and holidays);* ☎ 49 33 43 00). The famous restaurant Maxim's, at no 3, was formerly the Hôtel de Richelieu. At the end of the 18C the writer, Mme de Staël lived in no **6**, and Gabriel in no **8**.

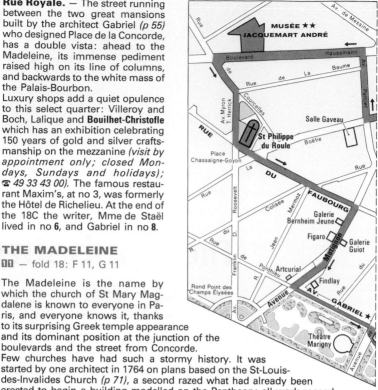

★★THE MADELEINE

🮰🮰 — fold 18: F 11, G 11

The Madeleine is the name by which the church of St Mary Magdalene is known to everyone in Paris, and everyone knows it, thanks to its surprising Greek temple appearance and its dominant position at the junction of the boulevards and the street from Concorde.

Few churches have had such a stormy history. It was started by one architect in 1764 on plans based on the St-Louis-des-Invalides Church *(p 71)*, a second razed what had already been erected to begin a building modelled on the Pantheon; all work ceased between 1790 and 1806 as various projects were considered. Napoleon announced that on this spot should be erected a temple to the glory of the Great Army and gave the commission to Vignon. Once more the existing structure was razed and building started on the Greek temple; work proceeded slowly. In 1814 Louis XVIII confirmed that the Madeleine should indeed be a church. In the reign of Charles X it was still surrounded by waste land. In 1837 the building was nearly selected for use as Paris' first railway terminal. The church's vicissitudes ended with its consecration in 1842 although its priest was shot by the Commune in 1871.

Tour. — *Closed Sundays and holidays 1.30 to 3.30pm.* A majestic colonnade of Corinthian columns — 52 in all, each 20m-66ft tall — frames the church on all sides and supports a sculptured frieze. A monumental flight of steps (28) leads to the imposing peristyle giving on to Place de la Madeleine and affords a splendid view down Rue Royale, beyond the obelisk to the Palais-Bourbon and the Invalides dome. The gigantic pediment is adorned with a sculpture by Lemaire of the Last Judgement and the reliefs on the bronze door are inspired from the Ten Commandments.

The single nave church has a vestibule and a semicircular chancel. In the dark vestibule note at the far end on the right a *Marriage of the Virgin* by Pradier and on the far left a *Baptism of Christ* by Rude. The nave is crowned by three domes; on the pendentives statues of the Apostles have been carved by Rude, Foyatier and Pradier. A group featuring St Mary Magdalene ascending to Heaven dominates the high altar.

Next to the church is a flower market. Place de la Madeleine is also famous for its superb provision stores.

★★RUE DU FAUBOURG ST-HONORÉ

The superstitious Empress Eugénie had no 13 suppressed, which it remains to this day. The street imparts a leisured elegance with its luxury shops, art galleries, antique shops and fashion houses particularly around Rue Royale and Rue de l'Élysée.

The Élysée Palace (Palais de l'Élysée). — *Not open to the public.* The mansion was constructed in 1718 for the Count of Évreux. It was acquired for a short time by the Marquise de Pompadour and then by the financier Beaujon who enlarged it; during the Revolution it became a dance hall. Caroline Murat, Napoleon's sister, then the Empress Josephine both lived in and redecorated it. It was in this palace that, after Waterloo, Napoleon signed his second abdication on 22 June 1815 and that the future Napoleon III lived and planned his successful *coup d'état* of 1851.

Since 1873 the Élysée Palace has been the Paris residence of France's presidents. The Council of Ministers meets on Wednesdays in the Murat Salon.

In Place Beauvau (1836), a fine wrought-iron gate marks the entrance to the Ministry of Home Affairs installed since 1861 in the 18C mansion built for the Prince of Beauvau.

Jacquemart-André Museum★★ **(Musée Jacquemart-André).** — *Open 1.30 to 5.30pm; closed Mondays, Tuesdays, holidays and in August; 15F;* ☎ *45 62 39 94.*

This elegant late-19C house contains outstanding European and Italian Renaissance art.

On the ground floor the Louis XV period is vividly recalled with paintings and drawings by Boucher, Greuze, Chardin, Watteau; sculpture

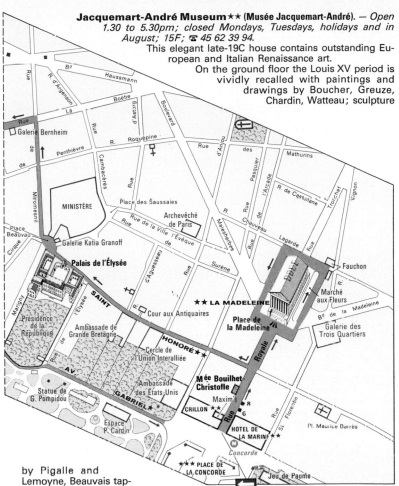

by Pigalle and Lemoyne, Beauvais tapestries, furniture and objets d'art. The 17 and 18C schools of painting are represented by Rembrandt, Van Dyck, Canaletto, Reynolds and frescoes by Tiepolo (ceilings in rooms 4, 5, 13 and over the stairs). There are also beautiful 16C Limoges enamels and ceramics by Palissy.

In the Italian rooms are displayed a remarkable collection of Tuscan Primitives, works from the Florentine Quattrocento (Botticelli paintings, Della Robbia terracottas, Donatello sculptures), the Venetian Renaissance (Mantegna, Tintoretto, Titian). Uccello's famous *St George Slaying the Dragon* and a fine bronze bust by Bernini are noteworthy.

From the Jacquemart-André Museum to Place de la Concorde

Take Rue de Courcelles and Avenue Myron-T.-Herrick to Place Chassaigne-Goyon.

Church of St-Philippe-du-Roule. — *Closed holidays and 12noon to 4pm at weekends.* The church designed by Chalgrin in imitation of a Roman basilica, was erected between 1774 and 1784. The semicircular chancel was added in 1845. A fresco over the chancel of the Descent from the Cross is by Chassériau.

On leaving the church turn left into Rue du Faubourg St-Honoré. There are several art galleries, notably Artcurial *(open 10.30am to 7.15pm; closed Sundays, Mondays and in August)* which also includes a specialist bookshop, in the **Avenue Matignon** to the right.

★**Avenue Gabriel.** — It runs between the Rond-Point and the Concorde along the landscaped garden area of the Champs-Élysées *(p 56)*. Beside the Marigny Theatre, the Stamp Market is open on Thursdays, Saturdays and Sundays. On the right is a landscaped garden with a statue of President Pompidou by Louis Derbré.

At the corner of the Avenue de Marigny, on the left, the gardens of the Élysée Palace (fine Cock iron grille wrought in 1905) form an enclave. The avenue then runs along the back of the shaded gardens of the mansions on Faubourg St-Honoré: the British Embassy, the Interallied Union Circle.

The Espace Pierre Cardin, formerly the Théâtre des Ambassadeurs, is the venue for exhibitions, concerts, cinema, theatre and dance shows. Near Place de la Concorde stands the American Embassy (once the house of the gastronome Grimod de La Reynière, whose culinary judgment was absolute).

6

★★★

The Opéra Quarter

Michelin plan **11** - folds 18 and 30: from F 12 to G 11

Distance: 2.5km-1 1/2 miles – Time: 1 1/2 hours
Start from the Madeleine métro station

This walk, stretching from Boulevard de la Madeleine to Place de la Concorde by way of the Opera and Place Vendôme, takes the visitor through some of the most elegant streets in Paris. In the evening the pavements are thronged with lively crowds attracted by the many theatres.

From the Madeleine to the Opera

Boulevard de la Madeleine. — Immediately on your left as you start to walk towards the Opera from the Place de la Madeleine *(p 78)* is the flower market. no **11** is where Alphonsine Plessis died. She was celebrated in *The Lady of the Camelias* by Alexandre Dumas the Younger and in Verdi's *Traviata.*

Boulevard des Capucines. — It was named after a Capuchin monastery which stood between the Place Vendôme and the boulevard.
In Rue des Capucines there is a fine house (1726) at no **19** which is now occupied by a bank. The writer Stendhal collapsed and died on the pavement opposite in 1842.
The boulevard was the scene of the call to arms, barricades and street fighting throughout the night of 23 February 1848 which was followed by the abdication of Louis-Philippe.
On the left, the Olympia music-hall at no 28 is a popular venue for entertainers and at no **14** a tablet commemorates the first public showing of 16m-52ft films by the Lumière brothers on 28 December 1895.
At no 27 the old Samaritaine department store has a splendid and sober façade built in 1917 by Frantz Jourdain, the master of the Art Nouveau style. Beside it was the site of the Cognacq-Jay Museum, now installed in the Hôtel Donon *(p 97)*, wich was founded by the owners of the Samaritaine, Ernest Cognacq and his spouse Louise Jay.

Place de l'Opéra. — Haussmann did not see Place de l'Opéra simply as a setting for the National Music Academy but as a circus from which a number of roads should radiate and he constructed his boulevards accordingly. Public opinion, at the time, was divided as to whether the square was not altogether too vast; today it barely copes with the milling traffic.
The square is lined with luxury shops which invite window shoppers to gaze at the elegant displays of leather goods, gifts (Lancel) and jewellery (Clerc) while the Café de la Paix terraces provide an international meeting place. Behind the Opera are the popular Printemps, Galeries Lafayette, and Marks and Spencer stores.

★★THE OPERA

⬛⬛ — fold 18: F 12

The Opera Staircase

The celebrity of France's first home of opera, the prestige of its ballet company, the architectural magnificence of the great staircase and foyer, the sumptuous decoration of the auditorium, invite the tourist to treat himself to an enjoyable evening.

Construction. — The site of Garnier's Opera House was determined by Haussmann's town planning project. In 1820 the idea developed of building a new opera house, forty years later a competition was held to find an architect. Charles Garnier, a 35-year old architect, winner of the Rome prize in 1848 but otherwise unknown, was chosen from the 171 contestants. Within a year Garnier had solved the problem raised by an underground spring and building started but subsequently the work was interrupted for several years and the opera was finally opened in 1875.
Garnier dreamed of creating a Napoleon III style of architecture, but the opera house created no new school, having insufficient originality. It is, nevertheless, remarkable and, in its way, is the most successful monument of the Second Empire.
It is a large theatre with a total area of 11 000m²-118 404sq ft and a vast stage for up to 450 artists. But the offices and exits are so extensive that the auditorium seats only 2 200. The central chandelier weighs over six tons.

Opera moves ballet stays. — Glittering performances of classical opera were held here until 1990 when the French opera company moved to its futuristic and functional new home, the Opera-Bastille *(p 236)*. The ballet company (Ballet de l'Opéra), under the direction of leading dancer Patrick Dupond has remained in its historic home and pursues its dynamic programme of classical and contemporary ballet.

Exterior. — The main façade overlooks Place de l'Opéra. At the top of a flight of steps and preceding the arcades to the theatre are statues by various sculptors, including a Paul Belmondo copy of Carpeaux' **Dance** (the original which was showing signs of wear is now in the Orsay Museum *(p 128)*.

A majestic balcony fronts the foyer. Above are the dome over the auditorium and a triangular pediment marking the stagefront. Go round the building starting from the right. The projecting wing was originally for subscribers who could drive in their carriages into the courtyard lit by lamp-posts decorated with statues of women by Cartier-Belleuse. At the back is the stage door. The so-called Emperor's Pavilion, on Rue Scribe, had a double ramp to enable the sovereign to ride straight to the royal box in his carriage.

The pavilion is now occupied by the Opera's Library and Museum *(see below)*.

Interior. — *Enter by the main door. Open 11am to 4.30pm; closed holidays, during August and on days when there is a matinée performance; 25F.* ☎ *40 17 33 33.* An original feature is the use by Garnier of marble of every hue — white, blue, pink, red and green — from all the quarries of France. The **Great Staircase** and the **main foyer** are remarkable and at their best on state occasions. A false ceiling inspired by opera and ballet painted by Chagall in 1964 adorns the **auditorium** which can be visited when rehearsals are not in progress.

The recently refurbished **Library Museum** displays models of stage sets, drawings of costumes and scenery, busts and mementoes of famous artists connected with the operas and ballets performed in the glorious setting of Garnier's opera house. The Library *(not open to the general public)* houses all the scores performed by the company since 1669, relevant documents and 80 000 books and etchings on dance, choral music, art, theatre...

From the Opera to Place Vendôme

Rue de la Paix, laid in 1806 over the site of a Capuchin monastery, was originally known as Rue Napoléon. Napoleon, on his column, can be seen with his back towards it. The beautiful jewellers' shops, Cartier (no **11**) among others, which line the street have made its name a synonym for elegance and luxury throughout the world.

★★PLACE VENDÔME ⅡⅡ — fold 30: G 12

Place Vendôme is a superb display of the majesty of French 17C architecture. In c1680, Louvois, Superintendent of Buildings, conceived the idea of building upon the land to the north of Rue St-Honoré, a square which would serve as a setting for a monumental statue of Louis XIV and be surrounded by suitable buildings housing academics, the National Library, the Mint and the Residence for Ambassadors Extraordinary. It would be even grander than Place des Victoires *(p 154)*. In 1685, the Duke of Vendôme's mansion and the neighbouring Capuchin convent were purchased.

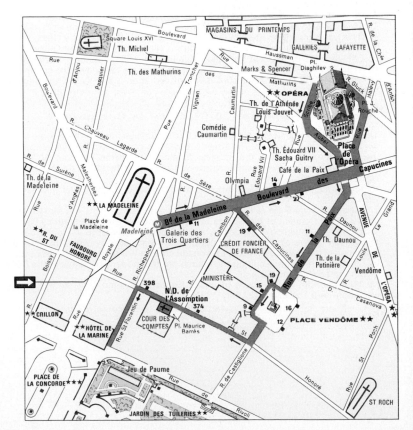

Hardouin-Mansart was commissioned to design the square which was originally known as the Place des Conquêtes but soon renamed Place de Vendôme or Louis-le-Grand. In 1699 the equestrian statue of the king by Girardon was unveiled. But the square was just a beautiful façade, only gradually were the lots at the back taken up. The first building was completed in 1702, the last in 1720. The royal statue was destroyed during the Revolution and the square temporarily renamed Place des Piques.

In 1810 Napoleon placed the Austerlitz column at its centre.

Place Vendôme

The Square. — Arcades at ground level, pilasters rising two floors above and finally steeply pitched roofs with dormer windows, surround the square. The pedimented façades of the principal buildings and of those standing obliquely at each of the square's four corners add variety.

As you walk round the square (224 × 213m - 245 x 233yds) by the right, every house evokes a memory or a name: no **19** is the former Hôtel d'Évreux (1710); no **15** is now the Ritz Hotel; nos **13** and **11**, now the Ministry of Justice, were formerly the Royal Chancellery — the official measure for the metre was inlaid in the façade in 1848; no **9** was the house of the military governor of Paris at the end of the 19C. Chopin died at no **12** in 1849; no **16** was the home of the German, Dr. Mesmer, founder of the theory of mesmerism.

The square with its surrounding area is the place for great names among jewellers: Van Cleef & Arpels, Boucheron, Mauboussin...

The Column. — The column's stone core, 44m-132ft high, is entwined in a spiral made from the bronze from 1 250 cannon captured at the Battle of Austerlitz (1805) and decorated with military scenes similar to Trajan's column in Rome.

The first statue to be placed at the top of the column was of Napoleon as Caesar; in 1814 he was replaced by Henri IV, who was removed for the 100 Days (1815) when Napoleon attempted to regain power. Louis XVIII hoisted a colossal fleur-de-lys; Louis-Philippe re-established Napoleon, this time in military uniform. Napoleon III substituted a copy of the original statue. The Commune tore down the column in 1871; the Third Republic re-erected it and placed upon it a replica of the original statue.

From Place Vendôme to Place de la Concorde

The windows of Rue St-Honoré between Rue de Castiglione and Rue Royale are a window-shopper's paradise. The street's reputation goes back many years: before the Revolution, the court, the nobility, financiers, all came to shop. At No **374** Mme Geoffrin established a salon which was frequented by all the great names of Louis XV's reign.

In Rue Cambon, is the house from which Coco Chanel reigned over the fashion world for half a century.

The **Church of Notre-Dame de l'Assomption**, now the Polish Church, was formerly the chapel of the Convent of the Sisters of the Assumption on Place Maurice-Barrès. This round 17C building is capped by a disproportionately large dome. Inside are respectively at the altar and to its right, an Annunciation by Vien (18C) and an Adoration of the Magi by Van Loo, and on the dome a 17C fresco of the Assumption by Charles de la Fosse. Abutting the church are the modern buildings of the Cour des Comptes (Auditor General's Office, 1912).

No **398** is the site of the house in which Robespierre lived until the eve of his execution on 9 Thermidor (27 July 1794).

Turn left into Rue St-Florentin towards Place de la Concorde *(p 54)*.

Montmartre

Michelin plan **11** - folds 6, 7 and 19: from C 12 to D 14

Distance: 5km-3 miles — Time: 4 hours
Start from Place de Clichy métro station

*The « Butte », as it is known locally, is the part
of Paris most full of contrasts — anonymous
boulevards run close to delightful village
streets and courts, steep stone steps lead
to open terraces, Sacré-Cœur pilgrims
tread the streets beside nightclub revellers.*

Martyrs' Mound. — Although it is known that the name Montmartre derives from the Mound of Mercury, a local legend dating from the 8C prefers ascription to the local martyrs, St Denis, first Bishop of Lutetia *(p 18)*, the priest, Rusticus, and the deacon, Eleutherius. These are said, in about 250 AD, to have been tortured on the grill in the Cité and decapitated, whereupon Denis picked up his blood-covered head and walked north to the place known as St-Denis *(see Michelin Green Guide to Ile-de-France).*

A powerful abbey. — Rue des Abbesses perpetuates the memory of the forty-three mother superiors of the Benedictine convent established on the hill

The Sacré-Cœur by S. Valadon

in the 12C and which was used by the King of Navarre, the future Henri IV as his headquarters four centuries later when he laid siege to Paris in 1589. He failed to take the city before his next campaign, his only conquest it is said, being that of the 17-year-old abbess, Claude de Beauvilliers.

In the reign of Louis XIV the ruined "upper" convent and its chapel, St Peter's, at the top of the hill, were abandoned in favour of the "lower" convent on the hillside below. 1794 saw the name of the hill changed, provisionally, to Mont-Marat, the last abbess guillotined and the convent buildings razed. Shortly afterwards the gypsum quarries were abandoned and the thirty flint and grain mills were closed.

The early days of the Commune. — In 1871, after the fall of Paris, the people of Montmartre collected 171 cannon on the hill to prevent their capture by the Prussians. Forces sent by the government seized the cannon on 18 March but were unable to remove them, the generals being taken prisoner and shot by the crowd — a bloody episode which was to mark the beginning of the Commune. Montmartre remained under Federal control until 23 May.

Bohemian Life. — Throughout the 19C, artists and men of letters were drawn to the free and easy, picturesque way of life as lived on the Butte. The composer Berlioz and the writers and poets, Nerval, Murger and Heine, were the precursors of the great 1871-1914 generation; young painters sought inspiration on Place Pigalle, artists' models and seamstresses led a free, Bohemian existence. The early poets' circles transformed themselves into café groups from which flowed songs (Aristide Bruant), poems, humour, drawings (Caran d'Ache, André Gill, Toulouse-Lautrec). Everyone went to the newly opened Moulin-Rouge (1889) to applaud the singers, clowns and dancers — Yvette Guilbert, Valentin le Désossé, Jane Avril, La Goulue. The Butte, thanks to the Lapin Agile café and Bateau-Lavoir studios, remained, until 1914, the capital's literary and artistic centre, then inspiration moved to Montparnasse *(p 204)* and Montmartre abandoned itself to night life.

From Place de Clichy to Place du Tertre

Boulevard de Clichy. — The bustling Place de Clichy was the site of one of Ledoux's toll-houses *(p 20)*, where in March 1814 Marshal Moncey's troops put up a spirited defence against the Allied army.

Walk along Boulevard de Clichy, laid along the line of the Farmers General wall. Restaurants, cinemas, theatres and nightclubs make it a centre of the Paris night life. The **Deux-Anes Theatre** at no 100 maintains the Parisian cabaret tradition.

Further along, **Place Blanche**, which owes its name to the quarries beneath the hill, is dominated by the sails of the famous **Moulin Rouge**, the French music-hall, which was the cult of Paris at the time of the Belle Époque and which has been immortalized in Toulouse-Lautrec's drawings.

The next square, **Place Pigalle** and the adjoining streets were at the end of the 19C, lined with artists' studios and literary cafés, of which the most famous was the Nouvelle Athènes. Today the quarter is as brilliantly lit and populous as ever.

Boulevard de Rochechouart. — Places of entertainment continue: at no **118** the former Belle-en-Cuisses cabaret. It was at no **84**, that Rodolphe Salis opened the Chat-Noir cabaret night-club made famous in a song by Aristide Bruant:

Je cherche fortune

Autour du Chat Noir

Au clair de la lune

A Montmartre le soir.

Belle Époque façade (no **72**) on the former Élysée-Montmartre music-hall.

The Abbesses' Quarter. — Walk left up Rue de Steinkerque.

At the foot of the mound on the right, the **St-Pierre Hall** *(open 10am to 6pm; closed 1 January, 1 May, 25 December; children's museum: 30F, children: 20F; Museum of Naive Art: 22F; ☎ 42 58 74 12)*, a fine 19C cast-iron building houses two small museums.

The **children's museum** (Musée en Herbe), on the ground floor holds temporary year-long exhibitions.

The **Museum of Naive Art** (Musée d'Art naif Max Fourny), on the first floor, displays modern paintings and sculpture by artists from some thirty countries.

Walk back and turn right into Rue Orsel to reach the quiet little Place Charles-Dullin. On the square is the small **Atelier Theatre** (Théâtre de l'Atelier), founded in the early 19C, which grew to fame between the wars.

Bear left from Rue des Trois-Frères into Rue Yvonne-Le-Tac where, at no **11**, stands a chapel on the site of a medieval sanctuary marking the **Martyrium** *(to visit phone in advance ☎ 40 22 07 07)*, the place where St Denis and his companions are presumed to have been decapitated. It was in the former crypt that on 15 August 1534 Ignatius Loyola, Francis Xavier and their six companions made apostolic vows in the service of the Church from which was born the Society of Jesus. Six years later the order was recognised by Pope Paul III.

Continue to Place des Abbesses. On the right is Square Jehan-Rictus, on the site of the former town hall of Montmartre. Opposite is the **Church of St John the Evangelist** (St-Jean-l'Évangéliste) designed by Baudot and the first to be built of reinforced concrete. The building is still interesting in the bold use made of its structural material, the slenderness of its pillars and beams, particularly as it was completed as long ago as 1904. The church's rose facing has earned it the local nickname of the Brick St John.

To the right of the west face steps lead up to Rue André Antoine. At the bottom of the steps, at no **37** a modest hall, which has been pulled down, saw the amateur beginnings of the free theatre, Antoine Theatre.

The Bateau-Lavoir. — This world-renowned artistic and literary Mecca, which disappeared in a fire in 1970, preceded, in the evolution of art, the no less outstanding Ruche of Montparnasse *(p 204)*. Now rebuilt as artist studios and apartments and located at no 13 in the delightful **Place Émile-Goudeau ★**, this small wooden building saw the birth in 1900 of modern painting and modern French poetry. It was here that Picasso, Van Dongen, Braque, and Juan Gris, created **cubism** — with Picasso's famous *Demoiselles d'Avignon* — and Max Jacob, Apollinaire and Mac Orlan broke away from traditional poetic form and expression.

★**A few old streets.** — Rue Ravignan ends at Place J.-B. Clément (at the end of the street, on the left is a former water tower) which you cross to take Rue Norvins on the right. The **crossroads ★** formed by the meeting of Rue Norvins, Rue des Saules and Rue St-Rustique was painted many times by Utrillo. Even today it is typical of the old Montmartre.

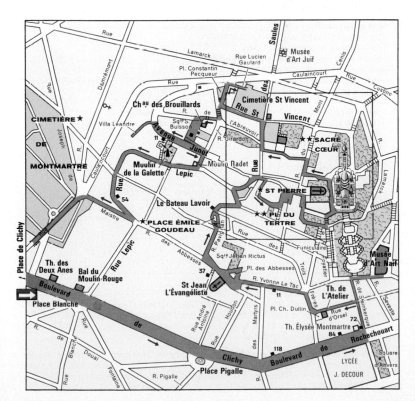

The Bonne-Franquette night-club was very famous around 1890. The narrow and often deserted Rue St-Rustique marks the highest point of the Butte and of Paris (129.37m-427ft). Nearby, in Rue Poulbot on the right, the **Montmartre Cultural Centre** (Espace Montmartre) illustrates by means of sculptures, prints and engravings, the fantastic world of the Catalan Surrealist, Salvador Dali (1904-89) *(open daily 10am to 10pm; 35F; audiovisual presentation)*.

Place du Calvaire commands an exceptional view of Paris.

★★**Place du Tertre.** — This long-standing meeting place has an almost village atmosphere at times, particularly in the morning. At other times, however, it is transformed into the tourist centre of Montmartre as crowds wander under the flaring lights, pause before the restaurants and glance at the paintings of unknown artists.

Rue Foyatier

No 21 (formerly no **19 bis**) is the seat of the Free Commune founded in 1920 by Jules Dépaquit to preserve the imaginative and humorous traditions of the Butte and houses the tourist information centre. No **3**, once the local town hall, is now Poulbot House to commemorate local children (P'tits Poulbots), popularised in the artist's delightful line drawings *(illustration p 24)* in the early 20C.

★ST PETER'S CHURCH ⬜⬜ — fold 7: C 14, D 14

The church, Église St-Pierre, the only remaining building of the great Abbey of Montmartre and, with St-Germain-des-Prés and St-Martin-des-Champs, one of the oldest churches in the capital, was begun on the site of an earlier Merovingian church in 1134 and completed before the end of the century. The nave vaulting was reconstructed in the 15C; the banal west façade in the 18C. The three bronze west doors, depicting St Denis, St Peter and the Virgin, are the work of the Italian sculptor, Gismondi (1980).

Interior. — Four marble columns with capitals said to have come from a Roman temple which crowned the mound, have been placed in pairs, against the west wall in line with the columns of the nave and in the chancel, where the oldest pointed arches in Paris (1147), their tori very roughly hewn, meet above the single bay. In the north aisle is the tombstone of Queen Adélaïde of Savoy, wife of Louis VI the Big, who spent her last days in the abbey, which she had founded in 1133. The Romanesque-style capitals are worn originals or replacements. The apse and aisles are

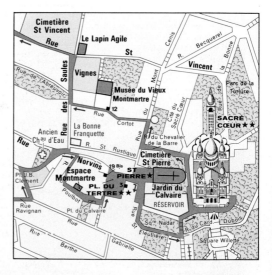

lit by modern stained glass designed by Max Ingrand (1953). The four sides of the high altar are adorned with enamelled plaques depicting the Butte Montmartre with its vineyard, the Virgin, St Peter and St Dominic by Froidevaux (1977). The Way of the Cross is also by Gismondi.

Calvary Garden (Jardin du Calvaire). — *Not open.* The garden is on the site of the old Benedictine abbey. In 1794 the Convention used the church apse as a suitable site for the new invention by the engineer, Chappe, of a telegraph station linking Paris and Lille.

St Peter's Cemetery (Cimetière St-Pierre). — *Open only 1 November.* North of the church lies the very old and minute church cemetery, in which are the tombs of the explorer, Bougainville (only his heart is interred here), the brothers Debray, original owners of the Moulin de la Galette and Montmartre's first Mayor, Félix Desportes. The bronze door by Gismondi features the Resurrection.

Bear left round the vast Montmartre reservoir towards the Sacré-Cœur terrace. This overlooks the Square Willette laid out in 1929 and approached by steps and slopes and also a funicular. The square commands a magnificent **view**★★ of Paris *(viewing table)*.

Note how the simple grace of St Peter's belfry contrasts sharply with the rounded mass of the Sacré-Cœur.

★★THE SACRÉ-COEUR BASILICA ▢▢ — fold 7: C 14, D 14

After the disastrous Franco-Prussian War of 1870, some Catholics vowed to raise money by public subscription to erect a church to the Sacred Heart on Montmartre hill. The proposal was declared a state undertaking by the National Assembly in 1873.
Abadie, who had become known for his restoration of St-Front Cathedral in Périgueux *(see Michelin Green Guide to Dordogne)*, recalled the old church's design as he drew Romano-Byzantine plans for the new basilica. It was begun in 1876 (Abadie died in 1884, when only the foundations had been laid), completed only in 1914 and consecrated in 1919; it cost 40 million francs. For over a century worship has continued, without interruption, within its walls.

The edifice. — The tall white outline is very much a part of the Paris skyline. The basilica's many cupolas are dominated by the dome and 80m-262ft high campanile. The interior of this pilgrim church is decorated with mosaics. On the chancel vaulting Luc-Olivier Merson has evoked France's devotion to the Sacred Heart. The stained-glass windows, shattered during 1944, have now been replaced.
From the dome *(access via the steps down into the moat to the left of the church, open 9am to 7pm 1 April to 30 September, 9am to 6pm in winter; 15F; crypt and dome 25F)* there is a bird's-eye view of the interior and, from the gallery outside on a clear day, a **panorama**★★★ extending over 30km-18 1/2 miles.
The crypt *(in season same access and times; 15F)* contains the treasure and presents an audio-visual history of the basilica.
In the belfry hangs the Savoyarde, the bell cast in 1895 at Annecy, which was given by the Savoy dioceses and, at 19 tons, is one of the world's heaviest bells.

From the Sacré Cœur to Montmartre Cemetery

Walk along Rue Chevalier-de-La-Barre and turn right into Rue du Mont-Cenis.

Round the vineyard. — No 12 in the Rue Cortot had as tenants over the years Renoir, Othon Friesz, Utter, Dufy, Émile Bernard, Suzanne Valadon and her son, Utrillo. It is the entrance to the **Museum of Old Montmartre** (Musée du Vieux Montmartre) *(open 11am to 6pm; closed Mondays, 1 January, 1 May and 25 December; 25F; ☎ 46 06 61 11)*, which is rich in mementoes of Bohemian life in the quarter with its nightclubs and artists, and features interesting temporary exhibitions. The house itself was the country residence of the actor Rosimond (d 1686). The museum contains a reconstruction of the Café de l'Abreuvoir where Utrillo was a frequent visitor, and another of the composer Charpentier's studio; documents relating to the statesman Clemenceau who was the local mayor in 1870, and a collection of porcelain made in 1870 for the Count of Provence by the Clignancourt factory.

Lapin Agile

Walk round the famous Montmartre vineyard where on the first Saturday in October, the start of the grape harvest, is always a great festive event.
The **crossroads**★ where Rue des Saules meets Rue St-Vincent is one of the most delightful corners of the Butte: small steps leading away mysteriously, the road rising steeply beside the cemetery, a leafy vista of the Sacré-Cœur, all add to the rustic charm, which is further enhanced by the famous **Lapin Agile**, half-hidden by an acacia. This former Cabaret des Assassins, later called "A ma compagne" by a new owner and rechristened when André Gill painted it a new sign, was, between 1900 and 1914, the haunt of writers and artists. Among those who began the tradition of literary evenings, which continue to this day *(every evening, except Mondays, at 9pm)* were Francis Carco, Roland Dorgelès, Pierre Mac Orlan, Picasso, Vlaminck...

Continue down Rue St-Vincent on the left, immortalised by Bruant. On the far side of Place Constantin-Pecqueur you will find Rue Lucien-Gaulard and on the far right, the modest **St-Vincent cemetery** where the musician Honegger, the painter Utrillo, the writer Marcel Aymé and many others lie buried.

Château des Brouillards. — Walk up the steps from Place Constantin-Pecqueur. On the left is Rue de l'Abreuvoir, named after the water trough once used by the cattle which grazed the mound. Turn right into the shaded alley skirting the **Château des Brouillards**, an 18C folly, later a dance hall. Its grounds have become Square Suzanne-Buisson. The statue of St Denis stands on the spot where he is said to have washed his decapitated head.

Avenue Junot. — Opened in 1910, this wide peaceful thoroughfare gave onto the Montmartre maquis, an open space of ill repute where mills still turned their sails to the wind. Amidst the artists' studios and private houses are at no **11** the Hameau des Artistes, and at no 25 the Villa Léandre. Walk back until level with no 10; from here there is a view of the windmill.

Moulin de la Galette. — The former dance hall, the Moulin de la Galette, which was the rage at the turn of the century, inspired many painters including Renoir, Van Gogh, Willette... The windmill which has topped the hill for more than six centuries, is the old Blute-fin defended against the Cossacks in 1814 by the heroic mill-owner Debray whose corpse was finally crucified upon the sails. Close by stands the 1736 Paris north bearing *(plan p 202)*. The Radet mill *(p 138)* stands at the corner of Rue Lepic.

Walk down the steeply winding **Rue Lepic**, an old quarry road, and the scene each autumn of a veteran car rally. Van Gogh lived with his brother at no **54**.

Take Rue Joseph-de-Maistre, then turn right into Rue Caulaincourt; on the left a steel bridge spans the Montmartre Cemetery (1795).

★**Montmartre Cemetery**
(Cimetière de Montmartre). —
Access by the stairs on the left.

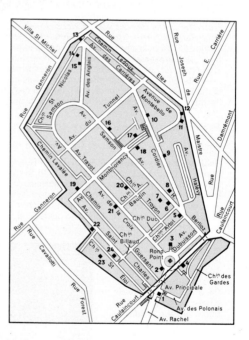

1) Lucien and Sacha Guitry (playwrights and actors).
2) The Cavaignac family (statue by Rude).
3) Émile Zola (novelist).
4) E. Labiche (playwright).
5) Hector Berlioz (composer).
6) Greuze (painter).
7) Heinrich Heine (poet and writer).
8) François Truffaut (film producer).
9) Th. Gautier (poet and critic).
10) Henri Murger (writer — *p 204*).
11) Hittorff (architect).
12) Edgar Degas (Impressionist painter — *p 130*).
13) Leo Delibes (composer).
14) Poulbot (cartoonist).
15) J. Offenbach (composer).
16) Nijinsky (dancer).
17) Ernest Renan and Ary Scheffer (philosopher; painter)
18) Alexandre Dumas the Younger (novelist).
19) Edmond and Jules de Goncourt (novelists).
20) Charcot (explorer).
21) Stendhal (H. Beyle) (novelist).
22) Alfred de Vigny (poet, dramatist).
23) Louis Jouvet (actor).
24) Alphonsine Plessis, the Lady of the Camelias *(p 82)*.

The Marais

Michelin plan **11** - folds 32 and 33: H 16, H 17 – J 16, J 17

Distance 3km-2 miles – Time: one day
Start from the St-Paul métro station

Visitors should tour the area on a weekday
when it is possible to gain access to
the buildings.
A tour of the Marais quarter which has
undergone careful restoration is a very
rewarding experience. A Drama and Music
Festival is held in June and July every year.

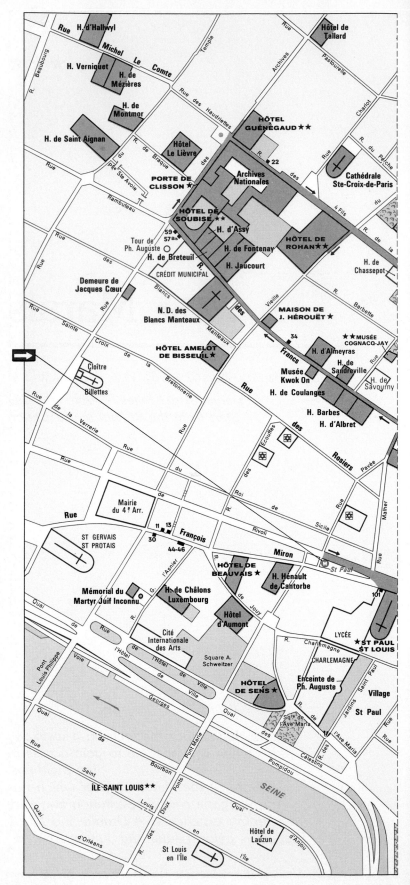

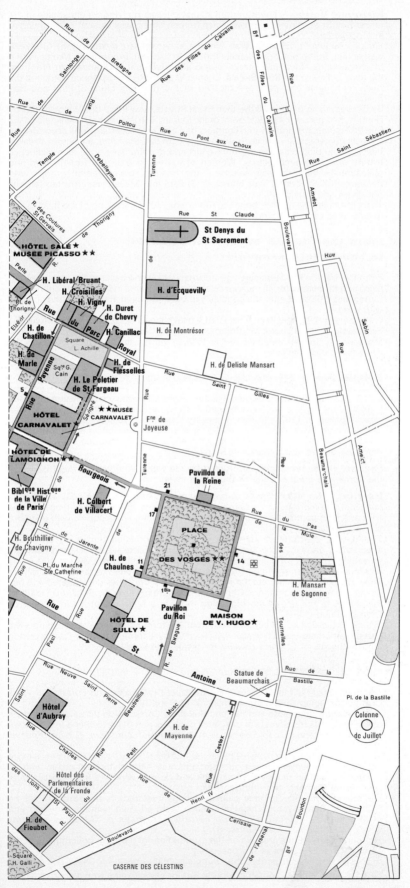

Historical Notes. — It was in the 13C that the swamp lying on either side of the raised Rue St-Antoine, a highway since Roman times, was cleared and converted into arable land.

Philippe Auguste's defensive wall, which also served as a dyke, and the Charles V wall ending in the powerful Bastille fortress in the east, brought the Marais within the city bounds. Royal patronnage began after the flight of Charles V *(p 118)* from the royal palace to the **Hôtel St-Paul**. Charles VI also took up residence there and the royal menagerie and park are recalled in the Rue des Lions-St-Paul and Rue Beautreillis.

By the beginning of the 17C the then Place Royale, now Place des Vosges, built by Henri IV, had become the focal point of the Marais. The Jesuits had settled along the Rue St-Antoine, the nobility and courtiers had built splendid mansions decorated by the best contemporary artists. It was at this time that the *hôtel*, a discreet classical building, standing between entrance court and garden, developed as a distinctive feature in French architecture. Women of the world attracted free-thinkers and philosophers through their *salons* — the brilliant conversational groups who frequented their houses. Two churches, St-Paul and St-Gervais, attracted famous preachers and musicians.

Then, gradually the nobility began to move west. After the taking of the Bastille, the quarter was virtually abandoned.

From the Church of St-Paul-St-Louis to the Hôtel Carnavalet

From the 14C the **Rue St-Antoine** was unusually wide and became the local meeting place and the setting for all popular celebrations. The area in front of the church was turned into a tilt-yard after the cobbles had been removed and the ground covered with sand.

It was here that in 1559 **Henri II** received a fatal blow to his eye in a tourney with his Scots captain of the guard, Montgomery. The king died in the Hôtel des Tournelles. Montgomery fled but was executed in 1574. In the 17C the Rue St-Antoine was the city's finest thoroughfare.

★CHURCH OF ST-PAUL-ST-LOUIS ▯▯ — fold 32: J 16

In 1627, on land donated by Louis XIII, the Jesuits adding to the monastery founded in 1580, built a new church (completed in 1641) dedicated to St Louis. The Jesuits were expelled in 1763 and the monastery reverted to secular use. After the old St-Paul church was razed, the edifice in Rue St-Antoine became known as the Church of St-Paul-St-Louis (1796). It is the second oldest baroque church in Paris modelled on the Gesù church in Rome.

Façade. — The tall classically ordered façade with superimposed columns hides the dome, the great novelty of the Jesuit style.

Interior. — *No visits allowed during church services; closed Sunday afternoons until 3pm and mornings on weekdays from 30 June to 15 September.* It has a single aisle and inter-communicating chapels, cradle vaulting and a cupola with a lantern above the transept crossing. Tall Corinthian pillars line the walls.

This well-lit, spacious church with its ornate decoration and sculptures, was attended by an elegant congregation drawn by musical excellence and eloquent preaching. The rich furnishings were lost at the Revolution. The twin stoups at the entrance were given by Victor Hugo who lived in Place des Vosges. In the transept three 17C paintings illustrate the life of St Louis. A fourth has disappeared and has been replaced by a painting of Christ on the Mount of Olives by Delacroix (1826). In the chapel to the left of the high altar there is a Mater Dolorosa in marble by Germain Pilon (1586).

In the courtyard of no **101** (left of the church), the former Jesuit convent and now the Lycée Charlemagne, is a fine **stairwell** crowned by a dome in *trompe-l'œil* depicting the Apotheosis of St Louis *(closed for restoration work).*

★HÔTEL DE SULLY *(62, Rue St-Antoine)* ▯▯ — fold 33: J 17

The house was built in 1625 by Jean Androuet Du Cerceau and bought ten years later by the aging Sully, former minister of Henri IV.

The Ancient Monuments and Historic Buildings Commission (la Caisse Nationale des Monuments Historiques et des Sites) occupies part of the building *(information centre: open Mondays to Fridays 9am to 1pm and 2 to 6pm, 5.30pm Fridays,* ☎ *44 61 20 00)*.

The main gate, between massive pavilions, has been restored and opens once more into the inner **courtyard**★★, an outstanding Louis XIII architectural group with an ordered decoration of carved pediments and dormer windows and figures representing the Elements and the Seasons.

The main bulding has original painted ceilings (restored). In the garden wing the Duchess of Sully's rooms have also been restored: fine painted panelling and ceilings (1661) *(guided tours on certain Saturdays or Sundays at 3pm;* ☎ *44 61 21 70; time: 1 1/2 hours; 31F)*.

Temporary exhibitions are held on the ground floor of the main building and of the garden wing as well as in the basement.

At the far end of the garden, the Orangery (1625) opens into Place des Vosges.

Turn left into Rue de Birague (formerly Rue Royale) leading to Place des Vosges.

★★PLACE DES VOSGES ⅠⅠ — fold 33: J 17

This is Paris' oldest square.

Hôtel des Tournelles. — The house, acquired by the crown in 1407 on the assassination of the Duke of Orléans *(p 100)*, was the residence of Charles VII where Louis XII ended his days and Henri II died *(p 94)*. Catherine de' Medici had it pulled down.

Place Royale. — In 1605, Henri IV determined to transform the Marais into a splendid quarter with a vast square at its centre in which all the houses would be "built to a like symmetry". On its completion in 1612, the Royal Square became the centre of elegance, courtly parades and festivities. Duels were also fought there in spite of Cardinal Richelieu's ban on duelling.

At the Revolution the square lost its central statue of Louis XIII (replaced in 1818) and was named Place de l'Indivisibilité.

From 1800 it took the name of Place des Vosges after the Vosges department, the first to pay its taxes.

The square today. — The 36 houses retain their original symmetrical appearance with arcades, two storeys with alternate stone and brick facings and steeply pitched slate roofs pierced by dormer windows, and with courts and hidden gardens.

The soberly decorated **King's Pavilion** (Pavillon du Roi) on the south side and the largest house in the square, is balanced by the Queen's Pavilion (Pavillon de la Reine) to the north.

No 9, the **Hôtel de Chaulnes** is the Academy of Architecture *(not open)*. The ceilings from the Hôtel de la Rivière (no **14**) by Lebrun are in the Carnavalet Museum.

Also of interest around the square: no **1 bis** where Madame de Sevigné was born; no **11** occupied by the courtesan Marion Delorme in 1639-1648; no **17** where Bossuet lived; no **21** where Richelieu lived (1615-1627) and no 6 Victor Hugo's residence.

★**Victor Hugo's House** (Maison de Victor Hugo). — *Open 10am to 5.40pm; closed Mondays and holidays; 12F, free on Sundays;* ☎ 42 72 10 16.

A museum opened in 1903 in the former Hôtel de Rohan-Guéménée (early 17C) which was the home of the poet from 1832 to 1848. Drawings by Hugo himself are shown in rotation as part of temporary exhibitions on the first floor. On the second floor the displays evoke Hugo's various residences. The Chinese salon and the furniture from his house on Guernsey illustrate his talent as a decorator. There are also portraits, busts, photographs and mementoes of the poet and his family.

Leave Place des Vosges by Rue des Francs-Bourgeois, cross Rue de Turenne and turn right into Rue de Sévigné.

★**HÔTEL CARNAVALET** *(23, Rue de Sévigné)*
ⅠⅠ — folds 32 and 33: J 16, J 17

The Renaissance mansion, whose construction was started in 1548 for Jacques des Ligneris, president of Parlement, was given its present appearance by Mansart in c1660. Marie de Rabutin, the Marquise de Sevigné, who wrote the famous *Letters* which, with a light touch and quick wit give a lucid picture of day to day events, lived in the house from 1677 to 1696. The buildings surrounding the three garden courts are 19C.

Exterior. — Jean Goujon carved the lions at the main entrance which is 16C, and the keystone cornucopia. The supporting globe was later recarved into a carnival mask in allusion to the mansion's name.

Place des Vosges

The **statue**★ of Louis XIV in the courtyard by Coysevox was originally at the Hôtel de Ville. The building at the end is Gothic; only the four statues of the Seasons are Renaissance. The large figures on the wings are 17C; the cherubs with torches decorating the end of the wing are again by Jean Goujon. The Nazarene arch in Rue des Francs-Bourgeois is 16C.

★★Carnavalet Museum. —

Open Tuesdays to Sundays 10am to 5.40pm; closed Mondays and holidays; 15F, free on Sundays; shop and bookshop; ☎ 42 72 21 13.

The collections illustrating the history of Paris are presented chronologically in two separate mansions, linked by a first-floor gallery. The Hôtel Carnavalet covers the period up to 1789 while the Hôtel Le-Peletier-St-Fargeau continues the story from the Revolution to the present.

The Hôtel Carnavalet is currently being refurbished and rearranged.

The three rooms on the ground floor with monumental chimneypieces are typical of a Renaissance dwelling. One of the rooms **(21)** presents mementoes of Mme de Sévigné, who lived in the house for almost 20 years. The staircase **(32)** leading to the first floor is decorated with paintings by Brunetti, a *trompe l'œil* specialist during Louis XV's reign. The paintings originally came from a staircase in the now demolished Hôtel de Luynes in Boulevard St-Germain.

The delicately worked panelling from other Parisian *hôtels* provide attractive settings for fine pieces of period furniture of Louis XIV, Regence, Louis XV and Louis XVI styles.

On the second floor of the Hôtel Le-Peletier-de-St-Fargeau, the Revolutionary period and the better known personalities of the time are evoked by paintings, sculpture, engravings, varied objects and canvases by such famous artists as Hubert Robert, David, Boilly and Chinard or by lesser-known ones (portrait of Robespierre). Note the large painting by Charles Thévenin depicting the *Festival of Federation (p 65)* (Fête de la Fédération) **(103)**, the furniture of the royal family during their captivity in the Temple **(106)** and a selection of watercolours by Le Sueur **(112)**.

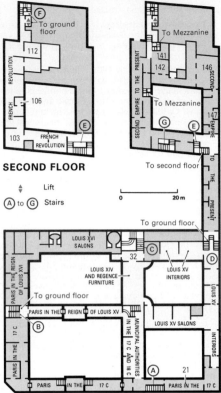

CARNAVALET MUSEUM

SECOND FLOOR

▲▼ Lift

(A) to (G) Stairs

0   20 m

FIRST FLOOR

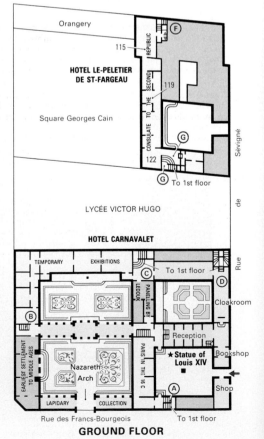

GROUND FLOOR

The larger rooms on the ground and first floors present the successive political regimes and some of the most notable events: the Empire, the Restoration, the Three Glorious Days or Trois Glorieuses of 1830 (a model shows the Duke of Orléans' arrival at the Hôtel de Ville) **(119)**, the July Monarchy, the events of February and June 1848, the Second Empire and the Commune of 1871. Paintings and mementoes illustrate how the artistic life in the capital flourished during this period. Look for the portrait of Mme Récamier by François Gérard **(115)**, one of the musician Franz Liszt by Henri Lehmann **(122)** as well as numerous street scenes including those by Béraud depicting Paris during the Belle Époque. The bedchambers of both Marcel Proust and Anna de Noailles **(147)** have been recreated. Beyond are the salon from the Café de Paris by the architect Sauvage **(141)**, the workshop of the goldsmith Fouquet by Mucha **(142)** and the ballroom decorated by Sert **(146)** from the Hôtel de Wendel.

In the connecting gallery are some very personal visions of Paris by 20C artists.

From the Hôtel Carnavalet to the Hôtel Salé

Rue de Sévigné. — Walk past the façade of the **Hôtel Carnavalet** and the **Hôtel Le-Peletier-de-Saint-Fargeau** (no 29) built by Pierre Bullet between 1686-90 and named after its owner who was responsible for Louis XVI's death sentence. no 52, the much restored **Hôtel de Flesselles**, bears the name of Paris' last provost.

Rue du Parc-Royal. — The 17C mansions lining the street opposite Léopold-Achille Square form a remarkable architectural group notwithstanding remodelling: **Canillac** (no 4), **Duret-de-Chevry** (no 8, extensively restored), **Vigny** (no 10, a National Documentation Centre) and **Croisilles** (no 12) which houses the library and archives of France's historic buildings commission.

Rue Payenne. — The Square Georges-Cain, lined by the orangery and façade of the Hôtel St-Fargeau, is a stone garden. The **Hôtel de Châtillon** (no 13) has a paved courtyard and an interesting staircase. The neighbouring **Hôtel de Marle** or **de Polastron-Polignac** (no 11) has a fine mask above the entrance and a keel-shaped roof attributed to Philibert Delorme. The mansion which once belonged to the Countess of Polignac, the governess of Marie-Antoinette's children, is now a Swedish Cultural Centre. It was at no **5** that François Mansart died. The old gateway was uncovered during restoration.

★★**Hôtel de Lamoignon.** — The Hôtel d'Angoulême, which was built around 1585 for Diane of France, the legitimized daughter of Henri II, was bought in 1658 by Lamoignon, president of the first parliament to sit in Paris. There he entertained Racine, Mme de Sévigné, the Jesuit preacher, Bourdaloue, and the poet and critic, Boileau. Another member of the Lamoignon family who was born here was the jurist and royal administrator, Malesherbes, who conducted Louis XVI's defence before the Convention.

An unusual square turret overlooks the street. On the far side of the courtyard the majestic building is divided by six Corinthian pilasters which rise unbroken to the cornice — the first example in Paris of the colossal order. Two rudimentary wings are crowned with curved pediments adorned with attributes of the chase and crescent moons (allusions to the goddess Diana).

Historical Library of the City of Paris (Bibliothèque Historique de la Ville de Paris). — *Open 9.30am to 6pm; closed Sundays, holidays and 1 to 15 August,* ☎ *42 74 44 44.* Founded in 1763, the library is rich in French Revolution documents and has precious collections of books, journals, manuscripts, maps, posters, photographs and cuttings...

The **reading room** with its painted ceiling is one of the finest in Paris.

Turn right into Rue Elvézir. The Hôtel Savourny at no 4 has an attractive courtyard while the Hôtel Donon is the new home of the Cognacq-Jay Museum.

★★**Cognacq-Jay Museum.** — *Open Tuesdays to Sundays 10am to 5.40pm; closed Mondays and holidays; 12 F;* ☎ *40 27 07 21.*

This collection of 18C European art was bequeathed to the city of Paris by Ernest Cognacq (1839-1928), founder of Samaritaine department store. The Hôtel Donon has been refurbished to provide a worthy setting for the collection. The late-16C main part of the building with its tall roof is typical of Philibert Delorme's syle. The harmony and taste of both the mansion and the collection give a good impression of the gallant and sophisticated lifestyle of the Age of Enlightenment.

In the panelled ground floor rooms is a selection of drawings by Watteau and paintings by Rembrandt, Ruisdael, Largillière and Chardin. Portraits bring to life some of the personalities of Louis XV's court: his Queen, Marie Leczinska; their daughter Madame Henriette; and Alexandrine, the daughter of Louis XV's mistress, Madame de Pompadour.

On the second floor watercolours by Mallet illustrate the spartan but elegant lifestyle of the bourgeois during the reign of Louis XVI. In the Oval Room Fragonard's fantasy and portrayals of children contrast with the terracottas of Lemoyen, the master of the art, and the canvases of Greuze. The sculpture gallery with works showing a strong Italian influence, by Falconet, Houdon and Clodion, also includes paintings by Hubert Robert and Boucher.

The third floor has sections on Mme Vigée-Lebrun and her period, pastels including a self-portrait by La Tour and English paintings. In the carved oak-panelled salon are an oval table and commode signed by Roger Vandercruse, better known as Lacroix (stamp: RVLC) and a pair of commodes by Martin Carlin. The cabinet is hung with a selection of Venetian scenes, including Guardi's *St Mark's Square*. The showcases display Meissen and Sèvres porcelain, snuffboxes and bonbonnières.

Rue des Francs-Bourgeois. — This old street was originally known as Rue des Poulies after the pulleys *(poulies)* on the looms of the local weavers' shops. It took its present name in 1334 when almshouses were built in it for the poor who were known as "the men who pay no tax" or *francs bourgeois*.

Hôtel d'Albret. — Nos 29 bis and 31. The house built in the 16C for the Duke of Montmorency, Constable of France, and was remodelled in the 17C. It was in this house that the widow of the playwright Scarron, the future Marquise de Maintenon, became acquainted with Mme de Montespan to whose children Louis XIV appointed her governess in 1669; she later became the king's mistress. The façade was interestingly reordered in the 18C. The restored mansion houses the city's Cultural Affairs Department.

The **Hôtel Barbes** (no 33, *go into the courtyard*) was built around 1634. The **Hôtel de Coulanges** (nos 35-37), now Europe House, is 18C. The **Hôtel de Sandreville** (no 26) opposite dates from 1586.

At no 30, the brick and stone façade of the **Hôtel d'Almeyras** is hidden behind a gateway featuring curious rams' heads. No 41 houses the **Kwok On Museum** *(p 102)*. No **34**, the former Hôtel Poussepin, now serves as the Swiss Cultural Centre.

On the corner of Rue Vieille-du-Temple, at no 54, stands the **House of Jean Hérouët**★, treasurer to Louis XII. Built around 1510, it still has its mullioned windows and an elegant corbelled turret. Nearby, stood in the 15C the **Hôtel Barbette**, the discreet residence of Queen Isabella of Bavaria who began the fashion for masked balls, while the King, Charles VI, was living at the Hôtel St-Paul.

Opposite the Crédit Municipal Bank, a former pawnbroker's, are the Hôtels **de Jaucourt** (no 54), **de Fontenay** (no 56), **de Breteuil** (no 58), **d'Assy** (no 58 bis), annexes to the French Archives.

Behind the gateway of no **57 bis** rises one of the towers of Philippe Auguste's perimeter wall. At no **59**, against the wall, is a fragment of the façade of a 1638 hôtel.

★★HÔTEL DE SOUBISE *(60 Rue des Francs-Bourgeois)*

□□ — fold 32: H 16

In about 1375 the Constable of France, Olivier de Clisson, companion in arms of the great French hero Du Guesclin, began to build a manorhouse on the site of the present buildings. Only the **gateway**★ remains, flanked by a pair of corbelled turrets *(58 Rue des Archives)*.

In 1553 the manor passed into the Guise family, who made it their headquarters during the Wars of Religion. In 1700 François de Rohan, Prince of Soubise, acquired the house thanks to generous gifts from Louis XIV to the prince's wife. From 1705 to 1709 the mansion was remodelled into an elegant palace.

The palace. — The plans were entrusted to an unknown architect, Delamair, who retained the Guise mansion, built the main façade at right angles to the mansion and created a majestic **courtyard**★★. Between 1735 and 1740 the most gifted painters (Boucher, Natoire, Van Loo) and sculptors of the period worked with Boffrand, a pupil of Mansart, on the magnificent **interior decoration**★★. Delamair's classical architectural style, typical of Louis XIV's reign (simple façade, vast courtyard and suites of rooms), contrasts with Boffrand's extravagant rococo decoration under Louis XV, when formal decor gave way to intimate settings.

On the ground floor are the apartments of the Prince of Rohan-Soubise. The princess' apartments on the first floor house an historical museum.

The Archives. — The National Archives, established under the National Assembly in 1789, have been housed in the Soubise Palace since 1808 where the millions of government and legal papers and personal archives occupy nearly 350km-217 miles of shelving. The Hôtel de Rohan *(87 Rue Vieille-du-Temple)*, converted into the imperial printing house under Napoleon, was taken over as an annexe in 1927. Four adjoining mansions (54-58 Rue des Francs-Bourgeois) as well as a modern building at 11 Rue des Quatre-Fils also serve as annexes.

★★**Historical Museum of France.** — *Open 1.45 to 5.45pm; closed Tuesdays and holidays; 12F.*

Among the great historical documents dating from the 7C to the 20C on display in the former guardroom are the Edict of Nantes (1598) and its Revocation (1685), the wills of Louis XIV and Napoleon and the Declaration of Human Rights. Also on view is a model of the Bastille carved from a stone from the fortress. The oval room is decorated with paintings of the Legend of Psyche by Natoire. The next two rooms are devoted to the French Revolution: Louis XVI's diary, the Oath of the Jeu de Paume (20 June 1789) and the French Constitution.

★★HÔTEL GUÉNÉGAUD *(60 Rue des Archives)* **□□** — fold 32: H 16

This mansion, built *c*1650 by Mansart, was minimally remodelled in the 18C and has been beautifully restored in the 20C. With its plain harmonious lines, its majestic staircase and its small formal garden, it is one of the finest houses of the Marais.

★★**Museum of the Chase and of Nature.** — *Open 10am to 12.30pm and 1.30 to 5.30pm; closed Tuesdays and holidays; 25F;* ☎ 42 72 86 43.

The collection includes arms from prehistory to the 19C *(first floor)* and trophies and souvenirs from Mr. Sommer's (who restored the Hôtel) own big game expeditions *(2nd floor)*. On the stairs and in the red, green and blue salons are pictures by Desportes, Oudry, Chardin and Carle Vernet. There are also tapestries, ceramics and sculptures on the theme of the hunt in the museum.

Walk left in Rue des Quatre-Fils to see the garden and rear façade of the mansion. At no **22** Mme du Deffand held a famous salon in the 18C.

★★HÔTEL DE ROHAN

(87 Rue Vieille-du-Temple)
▥ — fold 32: H 16

Open for temporary exhibitions.

In 1705 Delamair started work on the mansion simultaneously with the Hôtel de Soubise, for the Soubise's son, the Bishop of Strasbourg who later became Cardinal de Rohan. It was successively the residence of four cardinals of the Rohan family, all of whom were Bishops of Strasbourg. The last one lived there in grand style until his disgrace in the affair of the queen's necklace (1785). It

Horses of Apollo

was occupied by the state press (Imprimerie Nationale) under Napoleon and later in 1927 by the national archives.

The courtyard bears no comparison with that of the Soubise mansion as the main façade gives onto the garden which serves both properties.

On the right the former stables are crowned by the wonderful **Horses of Apollo**★★ by Robert Le Lorrain. The quivering horses are depicted at the drinking trough.

A staircase leads to the Cardinals' **apartments**★. Gobelins tapestries hang in the entrance hall. The first salons are adorned with Beauvais tapestries after cartoons attributed to Boucher. Also of interest are the Gold Salon and the amusing small Monkey Room with animal decorations by Christophe Huet, and the delicate panelling and wall hangings of the smaller rooms (Fable Room).

Turn right into Rue de la Perle. The Hôtel de Chassepot is at nos 3 and 5.

HÔTEL LIBÉRAL BRUANT *(1 Rue de la Perle)* ▥ — fold 32: H 16

Built in 1685 by the architect of the Invalides for himself, this elegant mansion has been restored to its original appearance and now houses a lock museum.

★**Bricard Museum.** — *Open 10am to 12 noon and 2 to 5pm; closed Sundays, Mondays, and between Christmas and New Year's Day; 10F;* ☎ 42 77 79 62.
In five well-lit rooms the art of the locksmith is traced from the Roman era to the Empire: collections of iron and bronze keys, wrought-iron Gothic locks; Venetian door knockers; gilded bronze locks from the Tuileries and Palais-Royal, combination lock, etc., as well as 20C ironwork and pieces from the Bricard workshops. To the right of the courtyard is a reconstruction of a locksmith's workshop.

★HÔTEL SALÉ *(5 Rue de Thorigny)* ▥ — fold 33: H 17

The house was built from 1656 to 1659 for a salt tax collector, hence its name, Hôtel Salé or Salted. In the 18C it passed to the de Juigné family, then became the École Centrale (1829-84) and subsequently the École des Métiers d'Art (1944-69). Recently restored and refurbished the mansion now houses the Picasso Museum. Inside the main **staircase**★ with its spacious stairwell and splendid wrought ironwork, rises majestically to the first floor and the profusely sculptured ceiling.

★★**Picasso Museum.** — *Open 9.15am to 5.15pm (10pm Wednesdays); closed Tuesdays; 23F, 12 F on Sundays, free for those under 18 and art students;* ☎ 42 71 25 21.

One of the dominant figures of 20C art, Pablo Ruiz Picasso (1881-1973) was born in Malaga. The young Picasso took courses in art at both Barcelona, where his father was a teacher, and Madrid. Aged only 23 he left his native country to settle in France, where he pursued his long and active career.

Following his death at Mougins in 1973, Picasso's heirs donated an outstanding collection of the artist's works in lieu of estate duties. The collection comprises over 200 paintings, an excellent group of sculptures, 3-dimensional pictures, more than 3 000 drawings and engravings, 88 ceramics as well as illustrated books and manuscripts.

To follow the chronological order of the different phases *(explanatory notices)* of Picasso's prodigiously productive and long painting career, start on the first floor with his *Self Portrait* from the Blue Period. All the artist's styles and techniques are represented from his sketches for *Les Demoiselles d'Avignon, Still Life with Cane Chair* and *Pipes of Pan*. Some of Picasso's favourite themes were nudes, travelling acrobats and portraits of couples and the family (portrait of his son, *Paul as Harlequin*).

Also included in the holding *(first and second floors)* is Picasso's private collection known as the Picasso Donation with works by Braque, Cézanne, Rousseau... Films on the artist, his life and work are shown on the third floor.

The Rue des Coutures St-Gervais and Rue Vieille-du-Temple skirt the gardens and afford glimpses of the imposing garden front. There is an unusual fountain by Simounet in the formal public garden beyond the museum's garden.

ADDITIONAL SIGHTS

★**Hôtel Amelot-de-Bisseuil** (or **Hôtel des Ambassadeurs de Hollande**). — *47 Rue Vieille-du-Temple.* The present mansion replaced an earlier building in 1655, the medieval residence of the Marshals de Rieux, companions in arms of Du Guesclin and Joan of Arc. In 1407, Duke Louis d'Orléans, after visiting Queen Isabella at the Hôtel Barbette *(p 98)*, was assassinated nearby by the supporters of John the Fearless. This led to civil war during which Paris was occupied by the English (1420-1435) and besieged by Charles VII and Joan of Arc *(p 140)*.

The 17C house, which has been remodelled at various periods, was at one time let to the Dutch ambassador's chaplain, hence its name. By 1776 the house, by now the home of the playwright Beaumarchais, who wrote the *Marriage of Figaro* here, had become a depot for arms to be dispatched to the American rebels; it was later a poor home.

The **gateway★**, decorated with masks and allegories, is one of the Marais' most outstanding. *(Ring to see the courtyard — the house is not open to the public.)* The house and wings are ornamented with sculptured motifs and four monochrome sundials.

Hôtel d'Aubray (or **de la Brinvilliers**). — *12 Rue Charles-V. Closed to the public.* There is a fine wrought-iron banister in the left wing. In the 17C it belonged to the notorious poisoner, the Marquise de Brinvilliers *(p 233)*.

Hôtel d'Aumont. — *7 Rue de Jouy.* The house was built in the early 17C by Le Vau; it was later remodelled and enlarged by Mansart and decorated by Le Brun and Simon Vouet. The formal garden is attributed to Le Nôtre. Until 1742 the house was the residence of the Dukes of Aumont who built up several collections and gave lavish parties. The inner court and façades are almost severe in line. A large garden has been created between the house and the river. During the 19C the mansion suffered considerable damage but it has now been restored and serves as the Paris administrative court.

★**Hôtel de Beauvais.** — *68 Rue François-Miron. Closed to the public.* In the 13C the Abbot of Chaalis, near Senlis, had his town house on this site.

In 1654 Catherine Bellier, known as One-Eyed Kate, first woman of the bedchamber to Anne of Austria, bestowed her favours on the sixteen-year-old Louis XIV and was rewarded with a fortune. In addition, for her services, her husband, Pierre Beauvais, and she were ennobled and acquired the site of the former town house of the Abbots of Chaalis. They commissioned the architect, Lepautre, to build them a splendid mansion. Anne of Austria, the Queen of England, Cardinal Mazarin and dignitaries watched the triumphal entry of Louis XIV and Marie-Thérèse into Paris in 1660 from its balcony.

When Mozart came to Paris at the age of seven in 1763, accompanied by his father and sister, he stayed in this house, which was then the residence of the Bavarian ambassador, and gave several concerts.

Hôtel de Châlons-Luxembourg. — *26 Rue Geoffroy-l'Asnier. Closed to the public.* Built in 1610 it has a carved main gate and an interesting stone and brick façade.

Hôtel Colbert-de-Villacerf. — *23 Rue de Turenne.* Its fine salon decorated with painted panelling is now in the Carnavalet Museum *(p 95)*.

Hôtel d'Ecquevilly (or **du Grand Veneur**). — *60 Rue de Turenne.* The house has a fine façade decorated with emblems of the chase and a magnificent **great staircase★** adorned with hunting trophies and a wrought-iron balustrade.

Hôtel Fieubet. — *Square Henri-Galli.* The house was built by Jules Hardouin-Mansart in 1680 for Gaspard Fieubet, Queen Anne of Austria's chancellor. An ornate decoration was added to the plain façade around 1850 and since 1877 it has been a school.

Hôtel Le Lièvre. — *4 and 6 Rue de Braque.* It was built in 1663 and has interesting twin doorways and balconies. There is a formal grand staircase at no 4.

Hôtel de Montmor. — *79 Rue du Temple.* The house, erected in the reign of Louis XIII for his treasurer Montmor, was remodelled in the 18C. Montmor's son invited the great physicians and doctors of the day to join Abbot Gassendi, who lived there for many years; these meetings heralded the founding of the Academy of Science (1666).

A fine balcony with a carved pediment adorns the façade pierced with tall windows overlooking the first court. The wrought-iron banister of the stairway is outstanding.

Hôtel de Saint-Aignan. — *71 Rue du Temple.* This house built in 1650 by Le Muet was acquired in 1680 by the Duke of Saint-Aignan, Colbert's son-in-law and joint tutor with Fénelon of Louis XIV's three grandsons. A monumental gateway decorated with fantastic masks precedes the main façade with its colossal order. The left side of the courtyard, in fact, is a facing (windows in *trompe-l'œil*) applied by Le Muet to the Philippe Auguste wall.

The house was greatly disfigured during the Revolution when it became a town hall (1795-1823). The outbuildings house a section of the Paris Archives' reading room. The stables (no 75) have attractive pointed vaulting.

★**Hôtel de Sens.** — *1 Rue du Figuier.* The Hôtel de Sens, the Hôtel de Cluny and Jacques Cœur's house are the only great medieval private residences to remain in Paris.

The mansion was constructed between 1475 and 1507 as a residence for the archbishops of Sens of which Paris was a dependency until 1622. During the period of the Catholic League in the 16C it became a centre of intrigue conducted by the Cardinal of Guise. In 1594 Monsignor de Pellevé died of apoplexy within its walls while a Te Deum was being sung in Notre-Dame to celebrate Henri IV's entry into Paris.
In 1605 Queen Margot, Henri IV's first wife, came to live in the mansion.
From 1689 to 1743 the house was occupied by the office of the Lyons stage coach which made a journey reputed to be so unsafe that passengers made their wills before setting out.

The mansion. — The old houses which originally surrounded the mansion have been pulled down. Its façade is ornamented with corner turrets and a tall dormer window with a stone finial. A large and a small door each with basket-handle arches are surmounted by pointed arches.
Walk through the Flamboyant Gothic porch into the courtyard where there is a square tower, cut by a machicolated balcony and enclosing a spiral staircase. Turrets and beautiful dormer windows adorn the façades.
The **Forney Library** *(open 1.30pm to 10am; Saturdays to 8.30pm; closed Sundays, Mondays, 1 and 8 May, Easter and Whit Saturdays; 15F; ☎ 42 78 14 00; temporary exhibitions Tuesdays to Saturdays 1.30pm to 8pm)* is devoted to decorative and fine arts and industrial techniques. It has a large collection of posters and wall paper.

Hôtel de Tallard. — *78 Rue des Archives.* Since its restoration it has regained the classical aspect Bullet gave it and recovered the medallions on the garden side.

Rue François-Miron. — This road, once a Roman highway through the marshes, still bears the name of a local magistrate of the time of Henri IV. In the Middle Ages it began on the low St-Gervais hill *(p 105)* and was lined with the town houses of several abbots of Ile-de-France. The half-timbered and much restored nos **11** and **13** date back to the reign of Louis XI in the 15C. The beautiful Marie Touchet, mistress of Charles IX, is said to have lived at no **30**.
The association for the preservation of Paris' historic buildings has uncovered in the basements of nos **44-46**, fine Gothic **cellars**★ from the town house belonging to Ourscamp Abbey, north of Compiègne. *Open 2 to 6pm; closed Sundays and holidays;* ☎ 48 87 74 31.

★**Hôtel de Beauvais.** — *See opposite.*

There are 17C and 18C façades (nos 72 to 80) between the Hôtel de Beauvais and Hôtel Hénault-de-Cantorbe named after one of the farmers general. Fine ironwork at no 74.

No 82, the **Hôtel Hénault-de-Cantorbe** has attractive balconies and a pleasant inner courtyard.

Rue Michel-le-Comte. — In this street are the ruined **Hôtel de Mézières** (no 19) and the **Hôtel Verniquet** (no 21), named after the geometrician who at the end of the 18C completed the first detailed maps of Paris *(p 184)*.
The **Hôtel d'Hallwyl** (no 28), where the writer Mme de Staël was born in 1766, was built in the late 17C and remodelled by Ledoux, architect to Louis XVI.

Rue des Rosiers. — This street, together with the adjoining Rue des Écouffes, which derives its name from a pawnbroker's shop sign, is typical of the **Jewish quarter** which has grown up in Paris' 4th arrondissement.

Church of Notre-Dame-des-Blancs-Manteaux. — *Rue des Blancs-Manteaux. Closed 12 noon to 4pm and on Mondays.* ☎ 42 72 09 37. The Crédit Municipal bank stands on the site of a monastery founded by Louis IX for the mendicant order of the Serfs of the Virgin whose members wore white cloaks *(blancs manteaux)*. In 1695, the Benedictines of St William, the Guillemites, who had replaced the earlier order at the end of the 13C, rebuilt the old monastery chapel. At the time of Baron Haussmann's transformation of Paris, during the Second Empire, the architect Baltard took the 18C façade of the Church of St-Éloi to incorporate it into this building.
The interior has remarkable woodwork — an inner door, organ loft, communion table and a magnificent Flemish **pulpit**★ in which marquetry panels are inlaid with ivory and pewter and framed in gilded and fretted woodwork in the rococo style of 1749. Concerts of organ music are held in the church, especially during the Marais Festival.

Church of St-Denys-du-St-Sacrement. — *Rue de Turenne. Closed Saturdays and Sundays 1 to 4pm.* The church, built in the form of a Roman basilica at the time of the Restoration, contains a remarkable **Deposition**★ by Delacroix (1844) at the back of the chapel to the right of the entrance *(lighting)*, a grisaille painting of St Denis preaching in the chancel and the Pilgrims of Emmaüs in wax (1840).

Church of Ste-Croix-de-Paris. — *Open Sundays 10.30am to 1pm.* This much-restored church was erected in 1624 as a Capuchin monastery chapel and was attended by Mme de Sévigné. It is now the Armenian church.
The chancel is adorned with 18C gilded panelling from the former Billettes church. To the left stands a remarkable **statue**★ of St Francis of Assisi by Germain Pilon (16C), and to the right St Denis by J. Sarazin.

Jacques Cœur's House (Maison de Jacques Cœur). — *40 Rue des Archives.* Resurfacing work on a building in 1971 uncovered a façade decorated with brick panels in a red and black lattice pattern. This led to its identification as the 15C house of Jacques Cœur, Chancellor of the Exchequer to Charles VII. It is one of the oldest buildings in Paris.

St-Paul Village (Village St-Paul). — The area bordered by the Rues des Jardins-St-Paul, Charlemagne, St-Paul and Ave-Maria has been restored. Houses and antique shops crowd around the inner courts.

A long section of the **Philippe Auguste Wall** (Enceinte de Philippe Auguste), intersected by two towers, which once skirted the city, can still be seen in the Rue des Jardins St-Paul. It linked the **Barbeau Tower** (Tour Barbeau) at 32 Quai des Célestins to the St-Paul postern and is the largest fragment still in existence.

Rabelais died in this street in 1553.

At the far end there is a view of the east end and dome of the St-Paul-St-Louis Church.

Memorial to the Unknown Jew (Mémorial du Martyr Juif Inconnu). — *17 Rue Geoffroy-l'Asnier. Open 10am to 1pm and 2 to 5pm; closed Sundays (except afternoons 1 October to 30 June), Saturdays, Jewish holidays and 1 May; 12F,* ☎ *42 06 00 17.*

In the crypt burns the eternal flame to the Jewish victims of National Socialism. There is also a museum devoted to the Jewish struggle against Hitlerism.

Kwok-On Museum (Oriental Theatre Museum). — *41 Rue des Francs-Bourgeois. Open 10am to 5.30pm; closed Saturdays, Sundays and holidays; 10F;* ☎ *42 72 99 42.*

This museum, named after its patron, is devoted to oriental theatrical traditions. There is a large collection of theatrical costumes, masks, musical instruments, glove, string and wand puppets and shadow theatre from Asia presented in temporary exhibitions.

The Quays

Michelin plan **11** - folds 31 and 32: J 14 to K 16

Distance: 5km-3 miles – Time: 3 hours
Start from the St-Michel métro station

*A tour of the Cité and Ile St-Louis along
the quays and bridges over the Seine,
affords the most magnificent **views**★★★ that Paris
has to offer.
Trees shade the banks of the river which
remains, even today, Paris' greatest
thoroughfare; fourteen bridges span its
course of a little over a mile through the
capital; **booksellers' stalls** garnish
the parapets and offer early editions and
etchings, but bargains are rare.*

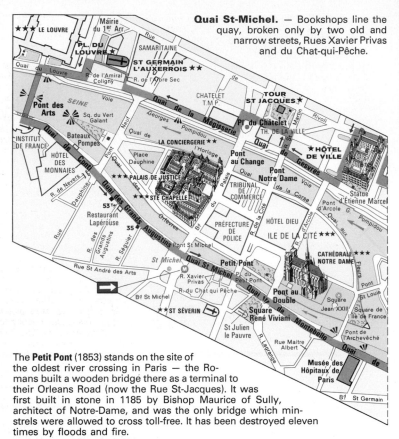

Quai St-Michel. — Bookshops line the quay, broken only by two old and narrow streets, Rues Xavier Privas and du Chat-qui-Pêche.

The **Petit Pont** (1853) stands on the site of the oldest river crossing in Paris — the Romans built a wooden bridge there as a terminal to their Orleans Road (now the Rue St-Jacques). It was first built in stone in 1185 by Bishop Maurice of Sully, architect of Notre-Dame, and was the only bridge which minstrels were allowed to cross toll-free. It has been destroyed eleven times by floods and fire.

Quai de Montebello. — In the Middle Ages, wood for building and heating was floated on rafts down to Paris and was stored at the Port-aux-Bûches between the Petit Pont and the Pont au Double.

In the 17C the two hospital buildings, the Hôtel-Dieu, on the river bank and the Cité respectively, were linked by a bridge, the **Pont au Double**, so named because the toll levied by the hospital was a *double tournois* or a doubloon struck in Tours (coin minted in Tours — until the 13C — which had only 75% of the value of Parisian coin). The present bridge was built in 1885.

Square René-Viviani. — The small church close was enlarged in 1928 to its present size, care being taken to preserve the Robinia or false acacia planted in 1680, one of the two oldest acacias in Paris, and now supported with a prop. (The species was introduced from the United States by the botanist, Robin, and called after him.)

Booksellers' stalls

The **view**★★★ is remarkable: St-Julien itself stands out clear and white behind a curtain of trees; the street St-Julien-le-Pauvre bustles with life beneath the picturesque jumble of roofs; the Ile de la Cité; and finally, and above all, Notre-Dame seen from an angle in all its mass, its delicacy and its grandeur.

Quai de la Tournelle. — Among the old houses lining the Tournelle Quay which lies just before the Archevêché Bridge (1828) is no 47, the Hôtel Martin (1630), variously a private house, a community of young girls, a bayonet forge — during the Revolution — a hospital pharmacy — during the Empire — and now a **Paris Hospitals' Museum** (Musée des Hôpitaux de Paris). *Open 10am to 5pm; closed Mondays, Tuesdays, in August and holidays; 14F;* ☎ *46 33 01 43.* The museum traces the history of the hospital system from the earliest religious institutions and almshouses through documents, paintings, engravings and artefacts. On the ground floor are reconstructions of a physicians' room, a dispensary with a fine collection of pots and vases and a hospital ward.

No 15, opposite the Tournelle Bridge, is the very old Tour d'Argent restaurant where Henri IV is said to have discovered the use of a fork *(a small museum is open to restaurant patrons).*

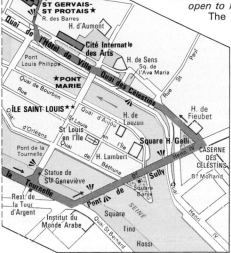

The Tournelle Bridge was first built in wood in 1370 and has been reconstructed several times since. A statue of St Genevieve by Landowski marks it out from its neighbours. At this point stood the St-Bernard gate of the Philippe Auguste perimeter wall. In the Middle Ages a chain curtain, to stop attacks from the river, was suspended from a tower in the 14C **Tournelle Castle** (destroyed 1787) across the Seine to the Barbeau Tower *(qv)* on the right bank. Splendid **view**★★★ of Notre-Dame from the bridge. The modern building on the right houses the Institute of the Arab World *(qv).*

Sully Bridge (Pont de Sully). — This bridge, which dates from 1876, rests on the tip of the Ile St-Louis as a pendant to the Pont-Neuf on the Ile de la Cité. From the first section there is a good **view**★ of Notre-Dame, the Cité and the Ile St-Louis. Upstream the river with its ports and quays is more industrial. On the right the Quai St-Bernard is bordered by the Pierre and Marie Curie University *(p 239).*

In the 17C there was a bathing beach here which was popular with the Court and the aristocracy. Henri IV and his son are said to have been frequent visitors. At the centre of the bridge, on the Ile St-Louis, is a formal garden, all that remains of the terraced gardens belonging to Bretonvilliers Mansion *(qv).*

The **view** from the bridge's second section is delightfully unspectacular — the Anjou Quay and Lambert Mansion, Célestins Quay, Marie Bridge and St-Gervais belfry.

Square Henri-Galli. — The square at the end of Sully Bridge contains stones from the Bastille. In the Middle Ages the area between the Hôtel Fieubet *(qv)* and the Arsenal Library was occupied by the Celestine Monastery *(p 233)*; while on your right, that between the Boulevard Morland and the river bank was **Louviers Island** which served as practice ground for crossbowmen and later as a wood depot. It was joined to the mainland in 1843.

Quais des Célestins and de l'Hôtel de Ville. — Walk left, along Quai des Célestins from where there in an attractive **view**★ of part of the Ile St-Louis and the Marie Bridge. By the Square de l'Ave Maria on the right you can catch a glimpse of the Hôtel de Sens.

The **Marie Bridge**★ with its alcoves and projecting piles, was named after one of the contractors who sold off land on the Ile St-Louis and marks the start of Quai de l'Hôtel de Ville.

The **International City of the Arts** (1965), to the right, provides studios and lodgings for a year for both French and foreign artists, musicians, architects and sculptors.

In line with the Louis-Philippe Bridge on the left, which replaced a suspension bridge during the reign of Louis-Philippe, are the Pantheon and St-Etienne-du-Mont. Take Rue des Barres for a clear view of the east end of St-Gervais church and its original buttresses. At no 15 is the fine balcony of a former charnel-house.

Walk down Rue François-Miron on the left. In the **St-Gervais precincts**, note the uniform façades of the 18C houses with wrought iron balconies featuring an elm.

★**Church of St-Gervais-St-Protais.** — *Closed on Mondays.* The church stands on a low mound emphasized by steps leading up to the façade and from Rue François-Miron. A basilica dedicated to the saints, Gervase and Protase, Roman officers martyred by Nero, has stood on the site since the 6C. The main part of the present building, in Flamboyant Gothic, was completed in 1657.

Exterior. — The imposing façade (1616-1621) with superimposed Doric, Ionic and Corinthian orders was the first to be built in the classical style in Paris and is attributed to Métezeau or Salomon de Brosse. The elm in the square was, according to medieval custom, a place where justice was dispensed as well as a place for transactions.

Interior. — There remain the Flamboyant vaulting, 16C windows and 16C and 17C finely carved stalls. The organ built in 1601 and enlarged in the 18C is the oldest in Paris. Eight members of the Couperin family held the position of organist from 1656 to 1826.

In the north aisle, near the font, is a model of the church façade carved by du Hancy who executed the large panels in the main door. The altar front in the third chapel is a 13C low relief of the Death of the Virgin. To the left of the arm of the transept is a beautiful 16C Flemish painting of the Passion on wood and, left of the crossing, against a pillar, a Gothic stone statue of the Virgin and Child. A wooden Christ by Préault (1840) and a fine 17C wrought iron grille adorn the sacristy exterior. In the Lady Chapel there is a remarkable Flamboyant keystone, hanging 1.5m-5ft below the vault and forming a circlet 2.5m-8ft in diameter. The adjoining chapel contains the tomb of Chancellor Michel Le Tellier (d 1685).

★HÔTEL DE VILLE ⬛⬛ — fold 32: J 15

The Hôtel de Ville is Paris' official reception and city government building.

Place de Grève. — The Place de l'Hôtel de Ville which shelved gently down to the Seine, was known, until 1830, as the Place de Grève. In the Middle Ages, the foreshore — *grève* — became a meeting place for those out of work, hence the expression « *faire la grève* ». During the Ancien Régime, it was a place of punishment for wrongdoers.

Pillared House (Maison aux Piliers). — Municipal government was introduced in the 13C. Until that time Paris was administered by the king's representative. The powerful watermen's guild held the monopoly of and regulated river traffic on the Seine, Oise, Marne and Yonne, and fixed the levies. In 1260, Louis IX appointed leading men of the guild to administer the township.

The municipal assembly headed by a merchant provost and four aldermen elected by the notables, who nominated the town councillors, moved from the Place du Châtelet to the Pillared House on the Place de Grève in 1357, at the instigation of Étienne Marcel.

Étienne Marcel. — This rich draper who was a merchant provost, became leader of the States General in 1357 and came out in open revolt against royal power *(p 118)*. He held Paris, attempted to make the whole of France rise up in arms, made an alliance with the peasants in revolt, let the English into the city. But Charles V who had taken refuge in the Hôtel St-Paul *(qv)* was victorious and Marcel died miserably at the hands of the Parisians in 1358 as he opened the gates of the city to Charles the Bad.

The Hôtel de Ville. — Under François I, the Pillared House fell into ruin. The king, intent on building a large town hall, had plans drawn up by Il Boccadoro, and the first stone was laid in 1533. The building was completed, however, early in the 17C. The middle part of the present façade is a copy of the original.

Until the Revolution the municipal authority was weak, the king making his own appointments, although those selected had to be citizens of Paris.

July 1789. — After the fall of the Bastille, the rioters took over the town hall. On 17 July 1789 Louis XVI appeared in the hall to kiss the newly adopted tricolour cockade. Red and blue had been the city colours since the provostship of Etienne Marcel in the 14C. La Fayette introduced the royal white.

The Commune. — Throughout the Revolution the town hall was in the hands of the Commune. The popular insurrection of 10 August 1792, which was led by Danton, Robespierre and Marat forced the king to flee the Tuileries Palace and take refuge with the Legislative Assembly. The Montagnard faction, or deputies of the extreme left, was an offshoot of the Commune and dominated the National Convention (1793-4).

The 9 Thermidor (27 July 1794) the National Convention tired of Robespierre's tyrannical behaviour and had him taken to the Luxembourg prison. Released by the Commune he was given refuge in the town hall where he was injured in the jaw by a pistol shot. Robespierre was guillotined the next day (10 Thermidor).

In 1848 when Louis-Philippe was dismissed, it was in the Hôtel de Ville that the provisional government was set up and from there that the Second Republic was proclaimed on 24 February 1848.

The Second Empire and Commune of 1871. — Napoleon proclaimed himself emperor in 1851 and it was at this time that Baron Haussmann, as Prefect of the Seine, undertook the work of replanning the area around the Hôtel de Ville. He razed the adjoining streets, enlarged the square and built the two barracks in Rue de Lobau. On 4 September 1870, after the defeat of the French Army at the Battle of Sedan, Gambetta, Jules Favre and Jules Ferry proclaimed the Third Republic from the Hôtel de Ville and instituted a National Defence Government. The capitulation of Paris on 28 January 1871, however, roused the citizens and in their anger they removed the government, installing in its place the Paris Commune of 1871. In May during its final overthrow, the Hôtel de Ville, the Tuileries and several other buildings were set on fire by the Federalists.

TOUR

Guided tour of the Reception Rooms, Mondays 10.30am. Visitors should go to the Bureau d'Accueil, 29 rue de Rivoli (☎ 42 76 50 49) where temporary exhibitions are held. It is always advisable to phone in advance.

The Hôtel de Ville was entirely rebuilt between 1874 and 1882 in the neo-Renaissance style by Ballu and Deperthes, complete with 146 statues of the illustrious and of French towns to adorn the building's façades.

Inside, the sumptuous main staircase leads to a ballroom and reception rooms. Ornate **decoration★**, part Renaissance, part Belle Époque, reveals the official style in the early years of the Third Republic. Amid the caryatids and rostra, coffered ceilings and crystal chandeliers are panels by Laurens depicting Louis XVI's reception at the Hôtel de Ville and mural paintings by Puvis de Chavannes (*The Seasons*). Note the unusual architecture of the triple chambers of the Arcade Room (Salon des Arcades).

The Place de l'Hôtel de Ville adorned with a fountain on either side, is paved in granite with the boat motif, the coat of arms of the 13C watermen's guild *(p 21)*, at the centre.

Quai de Gesvres. — Along this quay which begins at the Arcole Bridge (rebuilt 1888) with its bird and grain merchants, Haussmann's monumental creations — the Hôtel-Dieu, police headquarters, commercial courts, and Law Courts — can be admired on the Ile de la Cité.

The **Notre-Dame Bridge** (Pont Notre-Dame — 1913) was the Great Bridge in Roman times, as opposed to the Small Bridge (Petit Pont) on the far side of the island. Burnt down by the Normans and rebuilt on piles in 1413, it was the first to be given an official name, and the houses built on it were the first to be numbered in Paris. It fell down in Louis XII's reign (1499), but was rebuilt and lined with identical houses with richly decorated façades, since it was on the royal route of solemn entries into Paris. One of the houses belonged to the art collector Gersaint who befriended Watteau. The gallery figures in Watteau's famous picture *L'Enseigne de Gersaint* which now hangs in the Charlottenburg Museum in Berlin.

★St-Jacques Tower (Tour St-Jacques). — The tower is the former belfry of the church of St-Jacques-la-Boucherie, built in the 16C and one of the starting points for pilgrims making the journey to Santiago de Compostela in Spain. The church was pulled down in 1802. A meteorological station has been installed at the top of the 52m-171ft tower. When Rue de Rivoli was constructed the tower had to be consolidated as the mound on which it stood previously was razed.

The statue of the physicist and philosopher, Pascal, recalls his experiments into the weight of air carried out on this spot in 1648.

Place du Châtelet. — The Square gets its name from the Grand Châtelet or Great Barbican which commanded the Pont au Change. It was lined with the halls of powerful guilds. The Châtelet or Palm Fountain (1808) commemorates Napoleon's victories; the base was decorated with sphinxes in 1858.

The two theatres on either side were built by the architect Davioud in 1862. The Châtelet, after extensive renovation, is now the Théâtre Musical de Paris. Opposite, the Théâtre de la Ville, formerly the Sarah Bernhardt Theatre, is a centre of popular culture.

Quai de la Mégisserie. — The **Pont au Change** or Money Changers' Bridge in front of Châtelet Square, established in the 9C by Charles the Bald, was closely occupied all through the Middle Ages by jewellers and money-changers. It was to this bridge that all foreigners and visitors to Paris had to come to change their money. The present bridge dates from the Second Empire.

Walk along Mégisserie Quay, so called because until the Revolution, the quayside was the public slaughterhouse *(mégisserie: tawing)*. Now there are pet shops and seed merchants. An attractive **view★★** extends over the Law Courts, Conciergerie, and the old houses along Horloge Quay and Pont-Neuf.

At the end of the Pont-Neuf stands the Samaritaine department store — from the terrace of Samaritaine shop no 2 there is an excellent **view★★** over the whole of Paris.

★★ST-GERMAIN L'AUXERROIS ⬚⬚ — fold 31: H 14

The church is named after St Germanus who was Bishop of Auxerre in the 5C. The present church, on the site of an 8C sanctuary demolished by the Normans and a later one built by Robert the Pious, combines five centuries of architectural design with a Romanesque belfry, High Gothic chancel, Flamboyant porch and nave and Renaissance doorway. The tympanum and pier and the magnificent roodscreen by Lescot and Jean Goujon were removed in the 18C to allow the passage of processions.

When the Valois moved into the Louvre in the 14C, St-Germain became the royal parish church and the receptacle for gifts and decoration.

It was from this tower that the bells rang on the night of 24 August 1572 giving the signal for the Massacre of St Bartholomew when thousands of Huguenots, invited to celebrate the marriage of Henri of Navarre to his cousin, Marguerite of Valois, were slaughtered in accordance with a plan laid by the Cardinal Duke of Guise, Catherine de' Medici, Charles IX and the future Henri III.

During the Revolution, it became a barn; in 1831 it was further desecrated. Finally, however, it was restored (1838-1855) by Baltard and Lassus, which explains its composite style.

Many poets: Jodelle, Malherbe; painters: Coypel, Boucher, Nattier, Chardin, Van Loo; sculptors: Coysevox, the two Coustous; architects: Le Vau, Robert de Cotte, Gabriel the Elder, Soufflot and others associated with the court, are buried in the church.

Since 1926, following a vow by the painter and illustrator Adolphe Willette (1857-1926) artists come to St Germain on the first Sunday in Lent to receive ashes and to pray for those artists who will die in the year.

Exterior. — From the Samaritaine pavement there is a good view of the east end and Romanesque belfry which abuts on the transept.

The chancel aisles are covered by a series of small attic-like structures in which the bones taken from tombs in the cloisters, which at one time surrounded the church, were heaped. The apsidal chapel given by the Tronson family is decorated with a frieze of carp.

Porch. — The porch, which is the building's most original feature, was built between 1435 and 1439. The statues at the pillars are modern. The outer bays which are also the lowest, are surmounted by small chambers, covered with slate, in which the chapter placed the church archives and treasure.

The three central bays have multi-ribbed Flamboyant vaulting, while the other two are plain Gothic. The centre doorway, the most interesting, is 13C. The figure in the right embrasure is St Genevieve with a candle which a small devil is trying to snuff out and an angel *(next niche)* stands ready to relight.

Interior. — The nave is flanked by double aisles which continue round the chancel to the flat apse. The restored 17C organ **(1)** comes from the Sainte-Chapelle *(qv)*. The **churchwarden's pew (2)**, dating from 1684, is thought to have been used by successive kings and their families. In the fourth chapel is a fine early 16C, Flemish **altarpiece (3**-*light switch)*.

The **stained glass** in the transept and the two rose windows are late 15C. The much compartmented vaulting above the south arm of the transept is a good example of the Flamboyant style.

The chancel is surrounded by an 18C grille before which stand 15C polychrome statues of St Germanus **(4)** and St Vincent **(5)**. In the 18C, when the roodscreen was removed (the low reliefs are in the Louvre), the columns were fluted and their Gothic capitals transformed into garlanded torri.

The Chapel of the Holy Sacrament contains a 14C polychrome stone statue of the Virgin **(6)**; a 14C Crucifixion **(7)**; one of the original statues from the main doorway, St Mary the Egyptian **(8)**; a Last Supper **(9)** by Theo Van Elsen (1954) and a 13C statue of St Germanus **(10)**.

Place du Louvre

★**Place du Louvre.** — The square was the site on which the Roman, Labienus, pitched his camp when he crushed the Parisii in 52 BC, and the Normans when they besieged Paris in 885 *(p 112)*. Until the Second Empire, between the Louvre and St Germain-l'Auxerrois church stood fine mansions *(plan p 33)* including the Petit Bourbon (demolished 1660) where the States General met in 1614, Molière performed his plays in 1658 and the young Louis XIV danced before the court.

In 1854 Haussmann transformed the narrow Rue des Poulies into the wide Rue du Louvre (this part is now Rue de l'Amiral-de-Coligny), demolishing in the process the last of the 17C houses. These were replaced by a neo-Renaissance building by Hittorff and a neo-Gothic belfry by Ballu with a 38-bell carillon *(Wednesdays, 1.30 to 2pm)*.

Pass along Quai du Louvre. The view extends over the tip of the Vert-Galant Square, the Mint and the Institute of France. By the Louvre walk up to the Pont des Arts.

Pont des Arts. — The « academic » bridge faces the Institut de France *(qv)*. In 1803 the bridge was novel on two counts: it was the first to be built of iron and it was for pedestrians only — there were chairs to sit on and glasshouses with rare plants to shelter in, in case of rain. It was a toll bridge and on the day it was opened 65 000 Parisians paid to walk upon it. It has been rebuilt in steel with only seven arches instead of the original eight.

The **view★★★** is outstanding encompassing the Pont-Neuf and the Vert Galant Square *(qv)*. Behind the Square are the Law Courts, the Sainte-Chapelle spire and the towers and spire of Notre-Dame; visible beyond a screen of plane trees are the two theatres on Place du Châtelet, the top of the St-Jacques Tower, the Hôtel de Ville and the St-Gervais belfry; downstream the Louvre, the Grand Palais and the Carrousel Bridge.

Quai de Conti. — The quay is overlooked by the impressive buildings of the Institute of France *(qv)* and the Mint *(qv)* and runs past the fire boats on the Seine to the Pont-Neuf. In 1906, the scientist Pierre Curie, was run over by a horse-drawn carriage and killed near the Pont-Neuf.

Quai des Grands-Augustins. — This quay is the oldest in Paris. It was built in 1313 by Philip the Fair and in 1670 was named after the Great Augustine Monastery *(p 172)* which stood on the site extending from Rue Dauphine to Rue des Grands-Augustins. Its fine Gothic chapel was razed to make way for a game and poultry market. In 1869 the premises were then taken over by the Omnibus Company to serve as a depot with its headquarters at no **53** ter. The building is now the head office of the Paris Transport Authority which has a tourist office at no 53 bis.

Further on are two 17C mansions: no 51 at the corner of the Rue des Grands-Augustins, now the famous Lapérouse Restaurant, and no **35** at the corner of Rue Séguier.

Place St-Michel, which dates from the reign of Napoleon III, was the scene of student fighting against the Germans in August 1944. The fountain is by Davioud. The Pont St-Michel built in the 14C was remodelled at the same period as the square.

10

★★★

The Cité

Michelin plan 11 - folds 31 and 32: from J 14 to K 16

Distance: 3.5km-2 miles – Time: 1 day
Start from the Cité métro station

The Ile de la Cité is the heart of Paris and,
together with the neighbouring Ile St-Louis,
forms an area of outstanding beauty. Its history,
architecture and remarkable setting make it one
of the city's principal attractions.

Lutetia. — Between 250 and 200 BC Gaulish fishermen and boatmen of the Parisii tribe discovered and set up their huts on the largest island in the Seine — Lutetia was born. The township, whose Celtic name meant « habitation surrounded by water », was conquered by Labienus' Roman legions in 52 BC. The Gallo-Roman town prospered on river transport *(p 186)*, so that the vessel which was later incorporated in the capital's coat of arms *(p 21)* is a reminder both of the shape of the island and of the way of life of its earliest inhabitants. The boatmen's existence has been confirmed by the discovery of one of their pagan altars beneath Notre-Dame *(p 183)*.

In the 4C the Roman prefect, Julian the Apostate, was proclaimed emperor here by his legions and at the same period the name Lutetia was changed to that of its inhabitants and thus became Paris.

St Geneviève. — In 451 Attila crossed the Rhine at the head of 700 000 men; the Parisians began to flee at his approach until Geneviève, a young girl from Nanterre who had consecrated her life to God, calmed them assuring them that the town would be saved by heavenly intervention. The Huns arrived, hesitated, and turned, to advance on Orléans. Parisians adopted the girl as their protector and patron. Ten years later the island was besieged by the Franks and suffered famine; Geneviève escaped the enemy watch, loaded boats with victuals in Champagne and returned, again miraculously avoiding detection. She died in 512 and was buried at King Clovis' side *(p 191)*.

The Count of Paris becomes King. — In 885, for the fifth time in forty years, the Normans sailed up the Seine. The Cité — the island took the name in 506 when Clovis made it his capital — was confronted by 700 ships and 30 000 warriors bent on advancing into Burgundy. Assault and siege proving unsuccessful, the Normans took their boats out of the water, mounted them on logs and rolled them on land round Paris. Eudes, Count of Paris and the leader of the resistance, was thereupon elected king.

Cathedral and Parliament. — During the Middle Ages the population spread from the island along both banks of the river. But while the episcopal see remained under Sens (Paris did not have its own archbishop until 1622), schools were established within the cathedral's shadow which were to become famous throughout Europe. Among the teachers were Alexander of Paris, inventor of the poetic alexandrine line and, at the beginning of the 12C, the philosopher Abelard, whose moving romance with Heloise began in the cloister of Notre-Dame. Chapels and convents multiplied on the island: St-Denis-du-Pas (where St Denis' martyrdom is said to have begun), St-Pierre-aux-Bœufs (the porch is now the St-Séverin porch), St-Aignan *(p 117)*, St-Jean-le-Rond (where unwanted children were abandoned), were but a few of the belfried edifices which by the end of the 13C numbered at least twenty-two.

The Cité, the seat of parliament, the highest judiciary in the kingdom was, inevitably, involved in revolutions and uprisings such as that attempted by Étienne Marcel *(p 106)* in the 14C and the Fronde in the 17C. During the Terror of 1793-94 the Conciergerie prisons were crowded, while next door, the Revolutionary Tribunal continued to sit in the Law Courts, endlessly pronouncing merciless sentences.

Transformation. — Under Louis-Philippe and to an even greater extent, under Napoleon III, the entire centre of the island was demolished: 25 000 people were evacuated. Enormous administrative buildings were erected: the Hôtel-Dieu, barracks (now the police prefecture), the commercial courts. The Law Courts were doubled in size; the Place du Parvis before the cathedral was quadrupled in size; the Boulevard du Palais was built ten times wider than before.

In August 1944 the Paris police barricaded themselves in the prefecture and hoisted the tricolour. For three days they held the Germans at bay until relieved by the arrival of the French Army Division under General Leclerc.

East end of Notre-Dame

★★★NOTRE-DAME CATHEDRAL ⬛⬛ — fold 32: K 15

The cathedral of Paris, which can be seen in all its radiant glory from the parvis or Viviani Square, stands in an admirable setting. Notre-Dame has a perfection all its own, with balanced proportions and a façade in which solid and void, horizontal and vertical, combine in total harmony. It is a beautiful religious edifice and one of the supreme masterpieces of French art.

Construction. — For 2 000 years prayers have been offered from this spot: a Gallo-Roman temple, a Christian basilica, a Romanesque church preceded the present sanctuary founded by Bishop Maurice of Sully. A man of humble origin, he had become a canon at the cathedral and supervisor of the diocese by 1159 and, shortly afterwards, undertook to provide the capital with a worthy cathedral to rival the basilica built at St-Denis by Abbot Suger.
Construction began in 1163, during the reign of Louis VII. To the resources of the church and royal gifts, were added the toil and skill of the common people: stone masons, carpenters, iron smiths, sculptors, glaziers, moved with religious fervour, worked with ardour under Jean of Chelles and Pierre of Montreuil, architect of the Sainte-Chapelle. By about 1345 the building was complete — the original plans had not been modified in any way.

Ceremonial Occasions. — Long before it was completed, Notre-Dame had become the setting for major religious and political occasions: St Louis placed the Crown of Thorns in the cathedral in 1239 until the Sainte-Chapelle was ready to receive it; in 1302 Philip the Fair went to the cathedral solemnly to open the first States General; ceremonies, thanksgiving, state funerals, the Te Deum, processions, have followed down the centuries; the young Henri VI of England was crowned there in 1430; Mary Stuart was crowned there on becoming Queen of France by her marriage to François II; and Marguerite of Valois stood alone in the chancel while the Huguenot, Henri of Navarre, waited at the door as their marriage ceremony was performed in 1572 — although he came later to agree that « Paris is well worth a mass » and attended subsequent ceremonies inside the cathedral! With the Revolution, the Church of Our Lady was dedicated to the cult of Reason and then of the Supreme Being. All but the great bell were melted down and the church interior was used to store forage and food.
On 2 December 1804 the church was decked with hangings and ornaments to receive Pope Pius VII for the coronation of the Emperor (see the picture by David in the Louvre: p 47). After the anointing, however, Napoleon seized the crown from the pontiff and crowned first himself and then Josephine.

Restoration. — Gradually the building began to fall into disrepair, until in 1841, in accordance with popular feeling roused by the Romantic Movement and Victor Hugo's novel The Hunchback of Notre-Dame, the July Monarchy ordered that the cathedral be restored. A team of men under Viollet-le-Duc worked for twenty-three years on the statuary and glass, on removing additions, repairing the roof and upper parts, re-ordering the doors and chancel and erecting the spire and the sacristy. Notre-Dame emerged virtually unscathed from the Commune of 1871 and the Liberation of 1944 and remains the focal point for great occasions in Paris' history: the magnificent Te Deum of 26 August 1944, the Requiem Mass for General de Gaulle on 12 November 1970 and the Magnificat of 31 May 1980, followed by Mass on the parvis celebrated by Pope John Paul II.

PLACE DU PARVIS

The square is dominated by the grandiose façade of Notre-Dame, somewhat diminished by the parvis having been quadrupled in size and the surroundings opened out by Haussmann in the 19C.
In the Middle Ages, when mysteries were played before churches and cathedrals, the porch represented paradise from which the word parvis evolved.
A bronze plaque in the centre of the square marks the zero point from which all road distances are measured.

Hôtel-Dieu. — The Hôtel-Dieu hospice, founded in the 7C had, by the 17C, been enlarged to two buildings linked by the Pont au Double (p 104). In about 1880 these buildings were replaced on the island by the present Hôtel-Dieu and a square laid on the old site with, at the centre, a statue of Charlemagne. The hall and inner court are of architectural interest.

★**Archaeological Crypt.** — Open 10am to 6pm (5pm 1 October to 31 March); closed 1 January, 1 May, 1 and 11 November, 25 December. 25F. ☎ 43 29 83 51. Excavations beneath the parvis — the layout is marked on the parvis pavement — have uncovered 3C to 19C vestiges. Included are two Gallo-Roman rooms heated by hypocaust (to the left on entering), fragments of the Late Roman Empire rampart, medieval cellars and foundations of a children's home and of a church.

THE NOTRE-DAME FAÇADE

The façade's overall design is majestic and perfectly balanced. The central portal is taller and wider than the others; that on the left is surmounted by a gable. It was a medieval practice to avoid monotony by dissymmetry.

West Front Portals. — In the Middle Ages the portals looked completely different: the multicoloured statues stoods out against a gilt background affording a bible in stone from which those who could not read could learn the scriptures and the legends of the saints.

The six panels of the portals are adorned with splendid wrought-iron strap hinges. According to legend the side portals were carved by the devil himself to whom the ironsmith, Biscornet, had forfeited his soul, but it proved impossible for him to decorate the central one through which the Host was carried in procession. Its hinges are 19C replicas.
The three portals remain worthy of examination in detail:

Portal to the Virgin. — The beautiful tympanum **(1)**, a model to sculptors throughout the Middle Ages, shows below, the Ark of the Covenant, prophets and kings, above, a moving Dormition of the Virgin in the presence of Christ and the Apostles, and at the apex, the Coronation of the Virgin: in an attitude full of nobility, Christ gives a sceptre to his mother who is crowned by an angel.

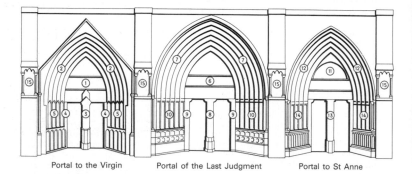

Portal to the Virgin   Portal of the Last Judgment   Portal to St Anne

The arching **(2)**, is delicately beaded, leaves, flowers and fruit framing angels, patriarchs, kings and prophets of the celestial court. The Virgin and Child at the pier **(3)** are modern. The small low-reliefs on the side walls and arch shafts **(4)** show the labours of the months and the signs of the Zodiac.
The statues in the embrasures **(5)**, were added by Viollet-le-Duc and include St Denis framed by two angels, St John the Baptist and St Stephen.

Portal of the Last Judgment. — The tympanum **(6)** was breached by Soufflot in 1771 to allow the processional dais through. Viollet-le-Duc restored the two lower lintels. Below is illustrated the Resurrection and, above, the Weighing of the Souls, the good being led to heaven by angels, the damned to hell by demons. At the apex, Christ sits in Majesty with the Virgin and St John interceding for the sinners.
The six archivolts **(7)** show the celestial court. Below, heaven and hell are symbolised by Abraham receiving the souls (left) and grimacing demons (right). The statue of Christ at the pier **(8)** is 19C; the Wise and Foolish Virgins, beneath open (left) and shut (right) doors to Paradise on the archway shafts **(9)** are modern. In the embrasures **(10)**, the Apostles by Viollet-le-Duc rise above medallions depicting the Vices (lower tier) and the Virtues (upper tier).

Portal to St Anne. — The cathedral's oldest statues, carved in about 1170 some sixty years before the portal was erected, and intended for a narrower door, fill the two upper levels of the typanum **(11)**. At the apex is a Virgin in Majesty with the Christ Child in the Romanesque tradition; she is surrounded by two angels with Bishop Maurice of Sully (standing, left) and Louis VII (kneeling, right) consecrating the cathedral. The 12C central lintel shows scenes from the Life of the Virgin, the lower depicts St Anne and St Joachim (13C).
Framing the tympanum, the four archivolts **(12)** illustrate a celestial court of angels, kings and patriarchs; the pier **(13)** supports a long and slender statue of St Marcel, Bishop of Paris in the 5C when he is said to have delivered the capital from a dragon — he is sticking his crozier down the monster's throat. It is very similar to the Romanesque statue-columns. The original statue is in the north tower chapel. In the embrasures **(14)** on either side of the portal are statues of kings, queens and saints.
The buttresses between the portals are adorned with modern statues **(15)** of St Stephen, the Church, the Synagogue (with a blindfold) and St Denis.

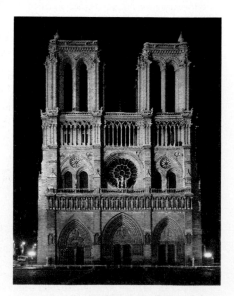

Kings' Gallery. — *Above the portails.* The 28 statues are of the Kings of Judea and Israel, Christ's forebears. In 1793 the Commune took them for the Kings of France and shattered them on the parvis *(see p 183, The Baths)*; Viollet-le-Duc restored them.

Rose Window Level. — The design of the great rose window, nearly 10m-30ft across, is so perfect that it has never shifted in over 700 years and was used as a model by all master-builders. It forms a halo to the statue of the Virgin and Child, supported by two angels, before it. In the lateral bays, surmounted by relief arches, are statues of Adam (left) and Eve (right). The ensemble portrays the Redemption after the Banishment (restored by Viollet-le-Duc).

Great Gallery. — The gallery is a superb line of ornately carved arches linking the towers. At the balustrade's buttress corners Viollet-le-Duc placed fantastic birds, monsters and demons which although large, are scarcely visible from below as they are partly obscured by the projecting balustrade.

Towers. — The majestic and graceful twin towers, 69m-226ft high, are pierced by slender lancets more than 16m-50ft in height. Emmanuel, the great bell in the south tower, tolled only on solemn occasions, weighs 13 tons and its clapper nearly 500kg-9 3/4cwts. It is said that when it was recast in the 17C, women threw gold and silver jewellery into the heated bronze, which is why the tone is so pure.

Ascent. — *Open 10am to 6pm (5pm from 1 October to 31 March); last admission 1/2 hour before closing time; closed 1 January, 1 May, 1 and 11 November, 25 December. Access at the foot of the north tower; 386 steps; 31F.* Steep steps lead to the south tower platform: splendid **view**★★★ of the spire and flying buttresses; the Cité and Paris generally. At the level of the great gallery note the monsters and great bell. In the south tower upper chapel, a video-museum traces the highlights of Notre-Dame *(time: 1/4 hour).*

THE CATHEDRAL INTERIOR

Notre-Dame impresses immediately by its size, its lighting, the noble uplift of its lines. A congregation of 6 500 can be accommodated within its 130m length, 48m width and 35m height - 427 × 158 × 115ft. The plan is the prototype of all large Gothic cathedrals. In the 13C the upper windows and galleries were enlarged and lowered respectively to increase the light reaching the chapels off the outer aisles. Flying buttresses were then added to support the roofing. Part of the 12C architecture can still be seen at the transept crossing in the small rose and tall windows. The massive pillars (1) supporting the towers measure 5m-16ft across.

The stained glass of the Middle Ages was replaced by clear glass with *fleur-de-lys* design in the 18C and grisaille glass in the 19C; the modern glass by Le Chevalier, installed in 1965, returned to medieval manufacturing processes and colours. The organ which was remodelled in 1868, has 110 stops *(concerts: Sundays at 5.45pm).*

Chapels. — Notre-Dame is entirely surrounded by chapels. They were built between the buttresses in response to the great number of foundations made by guilds and the rich in the 13 and 14C. This called for a lengthening of the transepts, which would have otherwise lost their profile.

In accordance with a tradition renewed in 1949, the goldsmiths of Paris offer a work of art to the cathedral every year in May — the most beautiful are by Le Brun (**2, 3**) and Le Sueur (**4**). On the left are the tombstones of a 15C canon (**5**), and of Cardinal Amette (**6**).

Transept. — The diameter — 13m-42 1/2ft and lightness of the rose **windows** are brilliant evidence of the advances made in architecture in the Gothic period. The north rose (**7**) which has remained practically intact since the 13C, shows Old Testament figures around the Virgin; in the restored south rose (**8**) Christ sits surrounded by saints and angels.

Ambulatory
18
20
21
19
14 12 13
22
CHANCEL   TREASURY
23
17
24
15   16
Sacristy
Red Door
4   9   10   11
St Stephen's Portal
Cloister Portal
7   8
TRANSEPT
5
NAVE
6
3
2
Access to the towers
1   1

Portal to   Portal of   Portal to
the Virgin   the Last Judgment   St Anne
Place du Parvis Notre-Dame

■ 12 C   ▨ 13 C   ▫ 14 C

The statue of St Denis (9) by Nicolas Coustou makes a pair, against the transept pillars at the entrance to the chancel, with the beautiful 14C **Virgin and Child (10)** — Our Lady of Paris, previously in St-Aignan *(p 117)*. A pavement inscription recalls the conversion of the 20C poet Paul Claudel (11).

Chancel. — Louis XIII, childless after twenty-three years of marriage, consecrated France in 1638 to the Virgin — a vow materialised in the redecoration of the chancel by Robert de Cotte. Of this there remain the stalls, and a *pietà* by Coysevox (12), flanked by statues of Louis XIII (13) by Guillaume Coustou and Louis XIV (14) by Coysevox.

It was at this time that the stone chancel screen was cut back leaving, of the remarkable 14C **low reliefs**, only scenes from the Life of Christ (15) and His Apparitions (16) which were restored by Viollet-le-Duc.

Mausoleums of bishops of Paris, who are buried in the crypt, line the ambulatory (17-24).

Treasury. — *Open 9.30am to 6pm; closed Sundays, Ascension Day, 15 August, 1 November, 25 December; 15F.*

The former sacristy built by Viollet-le-Duc contains 19C manuscripts, ornaments and church plate. The Crown of Thorns, the Holy Nail and a fragment of the True Cross are displayed on Fridays during Lent and on Good Friday in the main area of the cathedral.

EXTERIOR

Notre Dame's lovely exterior presents an excellent summary of 13C architecture. There are fine vistas of the soaring towers silhouetted against the sky.

North Face. — A canons' cloister, now destroyed, gave its name to the street and north transept face.

The magnificent **Cloister Portal** erected in about 1250 by Jean of Chelles, on the experience acquired at the Sainte-Chapelle which was completed in 1248, served as a model throughout the Gothic period. The great and finely worked transept rose rests on a clerestory with which it forms an unprecedented and delicate opening 18m-58ft high. It is slightly bigger — 13m-43ft in diameter — but as perfectly designed as the west façade rose on which it is modelled. Below the rose is the many-gabled carved doorway, richly decorated by comparison with the thirty-years-older doors of the main west face. On the lower level of the tympanum are events from the Life of the Virgin and above, scenes from a mystery play which was performed on the parvis.

The portal's jewel is the figure at the pier, a superb **Virgin** (the Child was lost at the Restoration) with a gentle smile and the infinite nobility of a 13C masterpiece. It is more expressive than the Romanesque Virgin of the St Anne portal and has a nobler mien than the 14C transept statue.

Opposite, at no **10**, is the **Cathedral Museum** *(open Wednesdays, Saturdays, Sundays, except at Easter, Whitsun and Christmas, 2.30 to 6pm; 10F)* which evokes the cathedral's re-modellings and restoration and the major historical moments since the 17C, and displays pottery uncovered underneath the parvis.

Chimeras of Notre-Dame

Further along, the **Red Door**, built by Pierre of Montreuil and used only by members of the cathedral chapter, has, on the tympanum, the Virgin being coronated by her Son between St Louis and his Queen, Margaret of Provence, and on the archivolts, scenes from the Life of St Marcel.

Seven 14C **low-reliefs** inlaid into the chancel chapels' foundations depict the Death and Assumption of the Virgin.

John XXIII Square. — Until the beginning of the 19C, the area between Notre-Dame and the tip of the island was crowded with houses, chapels and also the Archbishop's Palace built in the reign of Louis XIII (1610-1643) after Paris had been made an episcopal see in 1622, between the chevet and the Seine. On 2 November 1789, the clergy's possessions were nationalised and in 1831 the buildings were severely damaged in a riot and later razed to the ground. The square opened as a formal garden with a neo-Gothic fountain in 1844.

From this spot there is an outstanding view of the **east end** of the cathedral with its intricate decoration of balustrades, gables, pinnacles, gargoyles and the 14C flying buttresses rising 15m-50ft into the air to form the boldest medieval crown of all. If you take a few steps back you can see the 13C roof which retains the original timberwork. Viollet-le-Duc reconstructed the **spire**, destroyed during the Revolution, above the transept crossing using at least 500 tons of oak and 250 tons of lead, so that it could rise once more to 90m-295ft. He included himself among the decorative copper figures of Evangelists and Apostles!

Beyond the 19C sacristy is the magnificent **St Stephen's portal**, a pair with the cloister door but even richer in sculpture. A railing prevents close approach. Begun in 1258 by Jean of Chelles and completed by Pierre of Montreuil, it has a remarkable tympanum comprising three tiers and illustrating the life and stoning of St Stephen to whom the church preceding the cathedral had been dedicated. The statue of St Stephen at the pier and that of St Marcel on the gable and most of the coving carvings were executed in the 19C. At the base of the buttresses, eight small 13C low-reliefs depict street and university scenes.

Splendid vistas of Notre Dame and the Seine can be enjoyed from the small, verdant, southfacing John XXIII Square which is always very crowded.

Cross Place du Parvis and make for Place Louis-Lépine.

★THE NOTRE-DAME QUARTER

Place Louis-Lépine. — A colourful **flower market** lights up the cold administrative blocks of the Hôtel-Dieu, the police headquarters and the commercial court which have surrounded the square on three sides since the Second Empire. On Sundays birds replace the flowers for sale in the square named after the popular prefect who, in addition to many reforms, gave the Paris police their white truncheons and whistles.

★**The Ancien Cloître Quarter.** — By Quai de la Corse and Quai aux Fleurs, from Rue d'Arcole. The area between the north face of Notre-Dame and the Seine was the property of the cathedral chapter. Students boarded with the canons. Although considerably restored, the quarter is the only reminder of what the Cité looked like in the 11C and 12C when students such as Abelard *(p 112)*, St Bonaventure and St Dominic built up the reputation of the cathedral school which was later to merge with the Sorbonne.

In the middle of the Quai aux Fleurs, which affords a vast panorama of St-Gervais and of the tip of the Ile St-Louis, is the picturesque corner of Rue des Ursins and Rue des Chantres on which stands a medieval mansion. Go down some steps to admire the Notre-Dame spire in the perspective along Rue des Chantres.

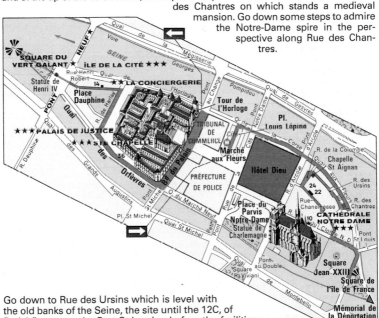

Go down to Rue des Ursins which is level with the old banks of the Seine, the site until the 12C, of Paris' first quay, the Port St-Landry, before the facilities on the Hôtel de Ville foreshore were established. At the end of the narrow street stand the remains of the Cité's last medieval chapel, St-Aignan, where priests celebrated mass secretly during the Revolution.

Turn left into Rue de la Colombe where there is a curious tavern at the top of some steps and traces of the Lutetian Gallo-Roman wall in the pavement. Take on the left Rue Chanoinesse, the main thoroughfare of the former cloister, now blighted by an annexe of the police headquarters. Nos **24** and **22** are the last two medieval canons' houses; note the stone posts in the courtyard.

Ile-de-France Square. — This ancient upstream point of the island now bears, at its tip, the **Deportation Memorial** *(open 10am to 11.30 and 2 to 5.30pm, 7pm 1 April to 30 September)*; sculpture by Desserprit, funeral urns and the tomb of the Unknown Deportee. The **view** of the cathedral from the square includes the majestic east end.

The construction of Notre-Dame, which began after that of St-Denis and Sens in about 1140, heralded the age of great Gothic cathedrals in France: Strasbourg (c1176), Bourges (c1185), Chartres (c1194), Rouen (1200), Rheims (1211), Amiens (1220), Beauvais (1247).

★★★ LAW COURTS (PALAIS DE JUSTICE) ⊡⊡ — fold 31 : J 14

On the Ile de la Cité stands not only the Gothic splendour of Notre-Dame but the seat of the civil and judicial system — the Law Courts. It forms with the Sainte-Chapelle and the Conciergerie an architectural ensemble of great historical interest.

The King's Palace. — The Roman governors, the Merovingian kings, the early Capetian kings, lived in turn on the Cité, establishing administrative quarters, building a dwelling of the finest stone for royal use, inaugurating a mint and, lastly, constructing a chapel and keep.

In the 13C St Louis (Louis IX) lived in the Upper Chamber (today the First Civil Court), dispensed justice in the courtyard and built the Sainte-Chapelle; Philip the Fair constructed the Conciergerie, a sumptuous palace «more beautiful than anyone in France had ever seen ». The Hall of the Men-at-Arms was the largest ever built in Europe. The former St-Michel Chapel which gave its name to the bridge and boulevard on the left bank, was razed to the ground in the 18C.

On 22 February 1358, the mob under Étienne Marcel *(p 106)* entered the apartments of the Dauphin, the future Charles V, whose father John the Good had been taken prisoner by the Black Prince at Poitiers and held in England, and slew his counsellors before his eyes. On regaining control, Charles V left the palace, preferring to live at the Louvre, the Hôtel St-Paul or at Vincennes outside Paris — an example followed by Charles VII, Henri IV and Louis XIV who all subdued Paris; Louis XVI, Charles X and Louis-Philippe, who refused to abandon the palace, all lost their thrones.

Parliament's Palace. — Parliament, installed in the former royal residence by Charles V, was the kingdom's supreme court of justice. Originally its members were nominated by the king, but in 1522 François I sold the rights which thus became hereditary. The highest dignitaries in the land were members by right or privilege. Conflicts between the officers of state and the king were settled by courts presided over by the monarch, and offenders were sometimes sentenced to exile or imprisonment.

Judges, barristers, clerks and others thronged the lesser courts in the palace. Fires were frequent: the Great Hall was badly damaged in 1618, the Sainte-Chapelle spire in 1630, the Debtors' Court in 1737, the Marchande Gallery in 1776. In 1788 Parliament demanded the convocation of the States General — not a good idea — as the General Assembly announced its suppression and the Convention sent the members to the guillotine.

Palace of Justice. — The Revolution overturned the judicial system. New courts were installed in the old building which took the name of Palace of Justice. Restoration began in 1840 and continued until 1914, interrupted only by the Commune fire, after which the building was given the façade which now overlooks Place Dauphine and the wing on the Orfèvres Quay.

TOUR

The palace is open from 9am to 6pm except on Saturdays, Sundays and holidays and all the courts, galleries and halls may be entered with the exception of the Busts Gallery, and the Juvenile Court (Galerie des Bustes, Tribunal pour Enfants).

May Courtyard (Cour du Mai). — The courtyard, which overlooks Boulevard du Palais is separated from it by a fine Louis XVI wrought-iron railings. The name of this forecourt was due to a very old custom by which the clerks of the court — an important corporation — planted a tree on the 1 May in this courtyard. The tree used in these celebrations, which were similar to the traditional English festivities, came from one of the Royal Forests.

The imposing buildings round the courtyard were erected after the fire of 1776. A small yard to the right abuts on the old Conciergerie wicket gate *(guichet plan p 121)* through which the victims of the Terror passed on their way to the tumbrils beneath the watchful eyes of the curious and the *tricoteuses* — the women knitting — perched upon the steps.

From the Marchande Gallery to the Harlay Vestibule. — Turn left in the Marchande Gallery (Galerie Marchande) formerly the most animated part of the building, bustling with plaintiffs, lawyers, clerks, court officials and hangers-on, then left again to walk down the Sainte-Chapelle Gallery. Turn right, up the Procureur de la République's Corridor and right again up a passageway which skirts the lively petty court area (Chambres Correctionnelles). Turn right at the end into the Duc Gallery, getting an open **view**★ of the Sainte-Chapelle from the corner.

Turn left beyond the ornate Chamber of the Civil Court of Appeal, into the Première Présidence Gallery and leave on the left the **C.I.D.** (Police Judiciaire) known to all admirers of Inspector Maigret. From the vast and empty Harlay Vestibule steps lead to the Assize Court *(open only when in session)* on the right. At the end is the Chamber of the Court of Cassation (frescoes and tapestries — *but not often open*).

From the Harlay Vestibule to the May Courtyard. — Walk down to the right the Lamoignon Gallery (glance at the St-Louis Gallery in passing, on your left) and the following Prisoners' Gallery.

Enter the **Lobby** (Salle des Pas-Perdus), formerly the Gothic Great Hall of Philip the Fair, twice destroyed and reconstructed most recently after the Commune of 1871. The two classical aisles, crowded with plaintiffs, barristers in their gowns but without the English distinctive wig, clerks and officials, are now the busiest place in the building — Balzac called it « the cathedral of chicanery ».

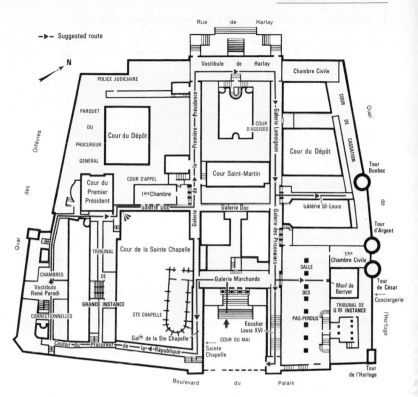

Rue de Harlay

--▶-- Suggested route

N

POLICE JUDICIAIRE

Vestibule de Harlay

Chambre Civile

PARQUET

DU

PROCUREUR

GÉNÉRAL

Cour du Dépôt

COUR D'ASSISES

Galerie Lamoignon

COUR DE CASSATION

Quai

Cour du Dépôt

Tour Bonbec

Orfèvres

COUR D'APPEL

Cour Saint-Martin

Cour du Premier Président

1ère Chambre

Galerie Duc

Galerie Duc

Galerie St-Louis

Tour d'Argent

des

Galerie de la Première Présidence

Galerie des Prisonniers

Quai

TRIBUNAL

Cour de la Sainte Chapelle

1ère Chambre Civile

Tour de César

CHAMBRES

DE

SALLE

Conciergerie

Vestibule René Parodi

Galerie Marchande

DES

Mont de Berryer

GRANDE INSTANCE

TRIBUNAL DE Gde INSTANCE

l'Horloge

CORRECTIONNELLES

STE CHAPELLE

PAS-PERDUS

Escalier Louis XVI

Galie de la Ste Chapelle

Couloir du Procureur de la République

Sainte Chapelle

COUR DU MAI

Tour de l'Horloge

Boulevard du Palais

Notice the tortoise — a malicious dig at the delays in the law — in the monument, on the right, of the 19C barrister, Berryer. At the end on the left is the former apartment of St Louis, later the Parliamentary Grand Chamber, when Louis XII had it decorated with a fine ceiling, then the Revolutionary Tribunal under Fouquier-Tinville (1793-94 — *p 120*) and now the **First Civil Court**.

Walk down the grand Louis XVI staircase built by the architect Jacques Antoine, noting the old shop names.

★★★SAINTE-CHAPELLE ⬛⬛ — fold 31: J 14

The chapel is a Gothic marvel — the deep glow of its windows one of the great joys of a visit to Paris.

Baudouin, a French nobleman and Emperor of Constantinople, when in need of money, pledged the Crown of Thorns. **St Louis** (Louis IX) redeemed the Crown from the Venetians in 1239. For additional relics and the shrine made to contain them, he paid two and a half times the amount spent subsequently on the Sainte-Chapelle building, which was erected to shelter them.

Pierre of Montreuil (known also as Pierre of Montereau) was probably the architect of the building which was completed in record time — less than thirty-three months — and consecrated in 1248.

Originally the chapel stood in the centre of the court, linked at the upper level of the porch to St Louis' apartments by a small gallery.

When the palace was remodelled in the 18C, parliament, unfortunately, built a wing of the May Courtyard abutting on the chapel.

Services, when the chapel was in use, were elaborate; in the 17C the organ was played by the Couperins — the instrument is now at St-Germain-l'Auxerrois.

Window of the Ste-Chapelle

During the Revolution, although some of the relics were saved and are now in Notre-Dame *(p 116)*, the reliquary shrine was melted down. From 1802 to 1837 the building became the judiciary archive; restoration, when it came, took from 1841 to 1867.

Exterior. — The Sainte-Chapelle made a great impression when it was built: for the first time a building was seen to possess practically no walls — its roof being supported on slender pillars and buttresses between which were windows nearly 15m-50ft high. It was a feat of balance — balance so perfect that no crack has appeared in seven centuries.

The spire rises 75m-246ft — into the sky. Its lead covered wooden frame has three times been destroyed by fire and rebuilt, the last time in 1854. The lead angel above the apse used to turn so as to show the Cross in his hands to all points of the compass. The small adjunct to the fourth bay was constructed by Louis XI and comprises a chapel at ground level with an oratory above.

Interior. — *Open 9.30am to 6.30pm 1 April to 30 September; the rest of the year 10am to 4.30pm; closed 1 January, 1 May, 1 and 11 November, 25 December; 25F.* ☎ *43 54 30 09.*

Enter through the **lower chapel** which was intended for the palace servants. The chamber is 17m wide and only 7m high-56 × 23ft. Columns, garishly decorated in the 19C, uphold the central vault, and are supported, in their turn, by elegantly pierced flying buttresses. The pavement is made up of the tombstones of canons buried beneath it.

A spiral staircase to the left leads to the **upper chapel**, a wondrous jewel, which attracts even the faintest ray of sunlight. The **stained-glass windows** are the oldest in Paris and amongst the finest to be produced in the 13C in their vividness of colour and the vitality of the thousands of small characters they portray; the 1 134 scenes on glass spread over an area of 618m²-6 672sq ft — form a veritable illustrated bible. The mid - 19C restorations are hard to detect.

The windows which illustrate scenes from the Old and New Testaments, should each be read from bottom to top and left to right. Nos **6, 7, 9** and **11** must be read lancet by lancet.

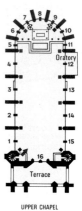

UPPER CHAPEL

1) Genesis — Adam and Eve — Noah — Jacob.

2) Exodus — Moses and Mount Sinai. — 3) Exodus — The Law of Moses.

4) Deuteronomy — Joshua — Ruth and Boaz.

5) Judges — Gideon — Samson. — 6) Isaiah — The Tree of Jesse.

7) St John the Evangelist — Life of the Virgin — The Childhood of Christ.

8) Christ's Passion. — 9) John the Baptist — Daniel. — 10) Ezekiel.

11) Jeremiah — Tobias. — 12) Judith — Job. — 13) Esther.

14) Kings: Samuel, David, Solomon.

15) St Helena and the True Cross — St Louis and the relics of the Passion.

16) 15C Flamboyant rose window: the Apocalypse.

The vessel is encircled by blind arcades with capitals delicately carved with leaf motifs; against each pillar stands a statue of an apostle holding one of the Church's twelve crosses of consecration — six of the figures are old *(red on the plan)* and in spite of their modern colouring, are very lifelike (others are in the Cluny Museum: *p 182*). Two small niches in the third bay were reserved for the king. In the next bay, on the right, is the door to the oratory built by Louis XI: a grille enabled him to follow the service.

The reliquary shrine stood at the centre of the apse in a gallery *(no access)* covered by a wooden baldachin and reached by twin circular staircases enclosed in openwork turrets. The original staircase on the left was often mounted by St Louis who then, himself, opened the door to the shrine, inlaid with sparkling jewels.

The porch onto the terrace is a reconstruction with a 19C tympanum and pier.

★★CONCIERGERIE ▫▫ — fold 31: J 14

The Conciergerie includes three superb Gothic halls built by Philip the Fair in the 14C, revolutionary prisons and mementoes of its tragic history.

A noble keeper. — The name Conciergerie was given in the old palace to the part controlled by a person of high degree: the *concierge* or keeper of the king's mansion — a remunerative office involving the licensing of the many shops within the palace walls. Among pre-Revolutionary prisoners were several who had made successful or unsuccessful attempts on successive kings' lives: Montgomery on Henri II; Ravaillac on Henri IV...

The guillotine's antechamber. — At the Revolution as many as 1 200 men and women were held at one time in the Conciergerie; during the Terror the building became the antechamber to the Tribunal, which in nine cases out of ten meant the guillotine. Among those locked in the cells were: Queen Marie-Antoinette; Madame Elisabeth, sister to Louis XVI; Charlotte Corday who stabbed Marat; Mme du Barry, the favourite of Louis XV; the poet André Chénier; Philippe-Égalité; the chemist, Lavoisier; the twenty-two Girondins condemned by Danton who, with fifteen of his companions, was in turn condemned by Robespierre, who was himself condemned with twenty of his followers by the Thermidor Convention, and finally the public prosecutor Fouquier-Tinville, and the judges of the Revolutionary Tribunal. In all nearly 2 600 prisoners left the Conciergerie between January 1793 and July 1794 for the guillotine.

Exterior. — The best **view** is from Mégisserie Quay on the right bank from where can also seen the four towers reflected in the Seine which originally flowed right up to their base. It is the oldest part of the palace built by the Capetian kings. The ground level was raised appreciably at the end of the 16C when Quai de l'Horloge was built.

The crenellated Bonbec Tower (Tour Bonbec), on the right, which is the oldest, got its name babbler, because it was used as a torture chamber.

The twin towers in the centre of the 19C neo-Gothic façade commanded the palace entrance and the bridge of Charles the Bald. The White Tower (Tour d'Argent) on the right contained the royal treasure. In the César Tower (Tour César), to the left, were the apartments of the Public Prosecutor, Fouquier-Tinville, during the Terror.

The 14C **Clock Tower** (Tour de l'Horloge) has since 1370 housed the first public clock installed in Paris. The carvings on the face are by Germain Pilon (16C-restored). The silver bell, having chimed the hours for the monarchy, was melted down in 1793.

Interior. — *No 1 Quai de l'Horloge. Go through the porch, cross the courtyard and go down on the right to the Guardroom. Open 9.30am to 6.30pm 1 April to 31 August; 10am to 5pm in winter; closed 1 January, 1 May, 1 and 11 November and 25 December; 25F.*
☎ *43 54 30 06.*

Guardroom (Salle des Gardes). — Stout pillars with interesting capitals support the Gothic vaulting in this dark room which now lies some 7m-23ft below the level of the 16C quay.

Hall of the Men-at-Arms (Salle des Gens d'Armes). — This magnificent four aisled Gothic hall covers an area of 1 800m² - 19 375sq ft, unfortunately

THE CONCIERGERIE DURING THE TERROR

Existing areas   Areas now disappeared
• • • Route to the scaffold

obscured by the 18C building erected in the May courtyard. Exactly above were the palace's Great Hall and the royal apartments. Additional supporting pillars were added in the 19C by Viollet-le-Duc.

Kitchens (Cuisines). — The four huge chimneys and fires in the kitchens were each intended for a separate purpose — spit roasting, boiling cauldrons, etc. — and between them, could serve the royal family and 2 000 to 3 000 others. The canopies are supported by unusual buttresses.

« Rue de Paris ». — The Rue de Paris was the name given to the last bay, closed by a grille from the Hall of the Men-at-Arms, as it led to the quarters of the executioner, known traditionally as Monsieur de Paris. During the Terror, penniless prisoners slept in it on the ground while the rich paid for their own cell and better food.

Prison. — The Galerie des Prisonniers was the busiest part of the building, with prisoners arriving and departing, lawyers, police and gaolers.

From the 1st floor, the police escorted the prisoner down the spiral staircase, situated in one of the turrets of the Bonbec Tower, and into the gallery (through a door on the right which has since been walled up). This room gave onto the council room which on one side served as antechamber (parloir) to the men's prison yard (Préau des Hommes) and on the other side it opened onto a staircase (1), which led to the Tribunal. The prisoners were most likely herded into the room, which is now used as the kitchens for the Law Courts restaurant and from there, one by one, they were taken to a neighbouring room where they were sat on a stool and their last toilet was performed.

Then they walked through the wicket gate *(guichet)* to the clerk of the court (register office — *greffe*) — abutting on the May Courtyard — and out to the tumbrils.

The history of the prison and important prisoners of state are the subject of the exhibitions on the first floor. These included the Scots captain of the guard Montgomery who inflicted a fatal blow to Henri II's eye during a tourney, Châtel who wounded Henri IV and Ravaillac who killed him, Louvel the assassin of the Duc de Berry and Fieschi who set in motion the infernal machine against Louis-Philippe and then Robespierre.

The Girondins' Chapel (Chapelle des Girondins). — **Ground floor**. The chapel was transformed into a collective prison where prisoners heard mass through the grille on the upper storey. Twenty-two Girondins were held there together in 1793.

Having visited the chapel the tourist should then visit the cell occupied by Marie-Antoinette from 2 August to 16 October 1793. In 1863 it was transformed into an expiatory chapel (2).

The Women's Courtyard (Cour des Femmes). — In the centre, as in earlier times, is a pathetic patch of grass and a tree. During the day the prisoners were allowed out into the courtyard. Only the first floor of the surrounding buildings is old; the rest was added in the 19C.

In the corridor is the Place of the Twelve (3) where men and women prisoners could talk and where the twelve selected daily for the guillotine said their farewells.

Once back in the prison corridor a door on the right leads to a re-creation of Marie-Antoinette's cell (4). The furniture consisted of a cot, a chair and a table. A screen separated the queen from the day and night watch.

Danton spent time in the adjacent cell, while Robespierre spent the night prior to his execution.

★LAW COURTS QUARTER

For a long time the Cité ended in the west in a sort of river level archipelago, separated from the main island by the arms of the Seine. It was on one of the islets that Philip the Fair had the stake erected in 1314 for the Grand Master of the Order of Templars, Jacques de Molay, watching him burn from his palace window. The King's Garden (Jardin du Roi) which extended from the islands to the Conciergerie became the first botanical garden under Marie de' Medici.

At the end of the 16C Henri III decided to re-order the Cité point: the mud-filled ditches were drained, the islets joined (the Vert-Galant Square is at the old ground level), the central earth terrace of the future Pont Neuf built up and the south bank raised by some 6m-20ft. By about 1580 the new terrain was ready for the builders. Start from the Quai de l'Horloge. The Commercial Law Courts (Tribunal de Commerce) opposite were built in 1865 on the site of the former St Bartholomew's the royal parish church from the 9C to the Revolution. Cross the vestibule to look at the dome which rises majestically to a height of 42m-141ft.

Opposite the May Courtyard, the construction of the Boulevard du Palais by Haussmann did away with a punishment area where prisoners were publicly branded. Further on a tablet marks the site of the former St-Michel chapel, the palatine chapel until the reign of St Louis (13C). On the Quai du Marché Neuf nearby lived the Huguenot **Theophraste Renaudot**, physician to Louis XIII and founder of the first French periodical, the *Gazette de France*.

Quai des Orfèvres. — The Quai des Orfèvres — literally the gold and silversmiths quay — was the jewellers' centre of 17C and 18C Paris: Strass, inventor of the synthetic diamond, Boehmer and Bassenge who fashioned Marie-Antoinette's celebrated necklace, had their shops in the Place Dauphine and on the quay. No **36** is today well known as the headquarters of the C.I.D. (Police Judiciaire).

Place Dauphine. — In 1607 Henri IV ceded the land between the palace and the Pont-Neuf for the development of a triangular square to be surrounded by a series of houses constructed of brick,

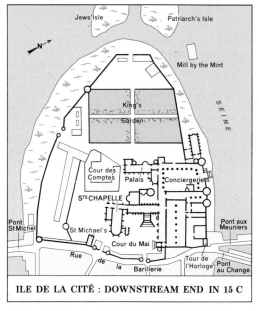

ILE DE LA CITÉ : DOWNSTREAM END IN 15 C

white stone and slate to a uniform design. The square was named in honour of the Dauphin, the future Louis XIII. In the 18C the square was the scene, each spring, of the Exhibition of Youth, when young painters presented their works in the open air. Only a few façades such as no **14** in the square, look as they did originally. Further on, the side on the square facing the palace was razed in 1874 to make way for a monumental staircase.

Pass between two houses dating from 1608 and extensively restored to reach the Pont Neuf.

★Pont-Neuf. — The Pont-Neuf is the oldest of the Paris bridges. The two halves begun in 1578 to the designs of Androuet Du Cerceau and completed in 1604 are not strictly in line. The twelve rounded arches are decorated with humourous grotesques, the half circles resting on each pile with carvings of open-air shops, tooth drawers at work, comic characters such as Tabarin and the Italian Pantaloon and a host of gapers and pickpockets. The Pont-Neuf's other attributes included the view down river — the first unencumbered by houses and other buildings — and the first pavements in Paris to be properly separated from the hurtling traffic in the roadway. A pump beneath an arch, which drew water from the river to supply the Louvre until 1813 and was decorated with a figure of the woman of Samaria giving Jesus water at the well, became known as the *Samaritaine* — a name later adopted by a department store nearby *(p 107)*.

It was also decided to place the first statue to be erected on a public highway in France on the bridge. The figure chosen was an equestrian bronze of Henri IV. This was melted down by the Revolution in 1792 but replaced at the Restoration by the present figure, cast in bronze from the Vendôme Column's first statue and another from the Place des Victoires, by a Bonapartist who is said to have included in the monument a copy of Voltaire's epic poem *La Henriade* (on the League and Henri IV), a statuette of Napoleon and various written articles glorifying the Emperor!

The bridge has been restored many times but the basic construction remains unchanged.

★**Vert-Galant Square.** — Walk down the steps behind the Henri IV statue. The Vert-Galant Square — the nickname given to Henri IV, meaning gay old spark — at the extreme tip of the island, is a peaceful spot from which to enjoy a **view★★** of the Pont-Neuf, the Louvre and the Mint.

★★ILE ST-LOUIS ▫▫ — fold 32: K 15, K 16

Calm quays and unpretentious classical architecture make the Island of St-Louis one of the most attractive places in Paris.

Originally there were two islands, the Ile aux Vaches and the Ile Notre-Dame, where in the Middle Ages judicial duels were held known as the Judgments of God. The contractor, Marie, early in the reign of Louis XIII, together with two financiers, Poulletier

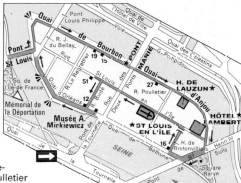

and Le Regrattier, obtained permission from the king and chapter of Notre-Dame to join the islets and to construct two stones bridges linking the new island to the mainland. In return they were to be allowed to sell the land for building. The work began in 1627 and was completed by 1664. The Ile St-Louis, therefore, like the nearby Marais *(p 91)*, is classical in style. But what makes the island unique is its atmosphere of old world charm and provincial calm. Writers, artists and those who love Old Paris have taken up their abode in its peaceful setting.

On the island you see a 17C house at almost every step: nobly proportioned façades, most bearing historical or anecdotal tablets, wrought iron balconies and tall brick chimneys. Behind massive panelled doors, studded with bosses and great nails, are inner courts where the stone sets and mounting blocks have not changed since the days of horse-drawn carriage.

Quais de Bourbon and Anjou. — At the end of the new St-Louis Bridge turn left and follow the Bourbon Quay round the picturesque tip of the island where chain linked stone posts, canted 18C medallions and the view of St-Gervais Church combine to make an altogether delightful **scene★**. A little further on are two magnificent mansions (nos **19** and **15**) which once belonged to parliamentarians — steep mansard roofs, mascarons, spacious stairwells encircled by wrought iron balusters, indicate their former splendour. A plaque on no **19** recalls that the sculptress Camille Claudel lived and worked here between 1899 and 1913, after her break with Rodin.

The Anjou Quay, beyond the **Marie Bridge★** (Pont Marie), is lined by some of the island's finest mansions. The Marquise de Lambert, hostess of a famous literary salon, lived at no **27** *(Hôtel de Nevers, p 137)*.

★**Hôtel de Lauzun.** — *No 17 Quai d'Anjou; not open to the public.*
The mansion, erected in 1657 by Le Vau for the caterer to the army, Gruyn, who was imprisoned shortly afterwards for corruption, belonged for only three years to the Duke of Lauzun, Saint-Simon's brother-in-law, who nevertheless left it his name. The poet, Théophile Gautier, lived there in the 1840's, also Baudelaire, Rilke, Sickert and Wagner. The house now belongs to the City of Paris.

★**Hôtel Lambert ou Le Vau.** — *No 2 Rue St-Louis-en-l'Ile; not open.* The mansion of President Lambert de Thorigny, known as Lambert the Rich, was built in 1640 by Le Vau and decorated by Le Sueur (whose designs may be seen at the Louvre) and Le Brun.

From the Hôtel Lambert to St-Louis-en-l'Ile. — Square Barye has been laid out at the tip of the island — last trace of the terraced gardens of the financier, Bretonvilliers.

No **16** Quai de Béthune, previously known as Quai des Balcons from the number of overhanging balconies, was the house of the Duke of Richelieu (great nephew of the cardinal). Turn right into Rue de Bretonvilliers which ends beneath an arcade, part of the former mansion of the same name, then left into Rue St-Louis-en-l'Ile, the island's main street.

★**St-Louis-en-l'Ile Church.** — *Closed between 12noon and 3pm except on Sundays.* ☎ *46 34 11 60.*
The church is marked outside (no 21) by an unusual iron clock and an original pierced spire. Building began in 1664 to plans by Le Vau, who lived on the island, but was only completed in 1726. The interior, in the Jesuit style, is ornately decorated, with woodwork, gilding and marble of the Grand Siècle (17C), statuettes and enamels. A plaque presented in 1926 in the north aisle bears the inscription: « In grateful memory of St Louis in whose honor the City of Saint Louis, Missouri, USA is named ».

From the Church to St-Louis Bridge. — Continue along Rue St-Louis-en-l'Ile to no **51** which, in the middle of the 19C, was the archbishopric and where there is a very fine doorway surmounted by a faun mask, also a majestic balcony.
The Rue Budé, on the left, comes out onto the Orléans Quay. A 17C building at no 6 houses the Polish Library and the small **Adam-Mickiewicz Museum**: portraits, mementoes, manuscripts, documents relating to the poet and his family and busts by Bourdelle and David d'Angers. *Guided tours Thursdays 3 to 6pm; closed during July and 10 days at Easter and Christmas;* ☎ *43 54 35 61.* At no **12** a medallion marks the birthplace of the poet Arvers.
From the Orléans Quay there is a splendid **view**★★ of the east end of Notre-Dame and the Left Bank.

11
★★★

The Orsay Museum

Michelin plan **11** - fold 30: H 12

Solférino métro station or Musée d'Orsay RER station (line C)
Main entrance: 1 Rue de Bellechasse
Entrance for special exhibitions: Quai Anatole France

From rail station to museum. — *At the end of the 19C the Orléans rail company acquired the site of the ruined Orsay Palace, formerly occupied by the Auditors' Office and the State Council and set ablaze in 1871 during the Commune (p 106), on which to build a new rail terminus.*

Orsay Station

The company commissioned Victor Laloux (1850-1937), the winner of the Prix de Rome in 1878 and professor of architecture at the Fine Arts School, to design a station which would harmonize in style with the buildings of this elegant quarter facing the Louvre and the Tuileries across the Seine. He designed an iron and glass structure screened on the outside by a monumental façade modelled on the Louvre and on the inside by a coffered ceiling with stucco decoration. He also planned an adjoining hotel. The work lasted two years and the building was inaugurated on 14 July 1900.

For nearly forty years Orsay station, the terminus for the southwest region and the first station purpose-built for electric traction, handled about 200 trains daily. As electrification spread to the rest of the network, longer trains came into service and the platforms at Orsay station soon proved inadequate. In 1939 progress put an end to its use as a main line station and after serving as a suburban station it was finally closed down. The building then suffered a varied fate: as reception centre for prisoners at the Liberation, the setting for Kafka's *The Trial* filmed by Orson Welles in 1962, theatre for the Renaud-Barrault Company in 1973, temporary auction-rooms during the refurbishment of the Hôtel Drouot in 1974.

The hotel which closed down on 1 January 1973, witnessed a momentous event: here on 19 May 1958 General de Gaulle agreed to serve as president thus ending the crisis brought about by the Algerian war of independence. That same year (1973) a plan was mooted to convert Orsay station, which had been saved from demolition, into a museum of 19C art. The final decision was made in 1977 by President V. Giscard d'Estaing and the architects P. Colboc, R. Bardou and J.P. Philippon won the commission to remodel the building. Gae Aulenti, the architect who had carried out the renovation of the National Museum of Modern Art in Paris and of the Palazzo Grassi in Venice, was entrusted with the museum's interior design and decoration. The rebuilding took six years and on 1 December 1986 the museum was inaugurated by President F. Mitterrand.

TOUR *allow one day*

Open 9am (10am on weekdays from 20 September to 20 June) to 5.30pm (9pm Thursdays); closed Mondays, January, 1 May and 25 December; 30F. ☎ 40 49 48 84.; recorded general information ☎ 45 49 11 11.
Guided tours daily at 11am and 1pm and at 7pm on Thursday. A single work of art "A work to see" is presented every day at 12.30pm. The meeting point is at the groups' counter 15 minutes before the start. Short guides on a particular theme enable the visitor to do a quick tour of the museum. A yearly membership card (Carte Blanche, 250F) gives free admission to all parts of the museum and a reduction on the price of admission to cultural events (concerts, cinema, lectures, discussion groups...).
Facilities: coffeeshop, restaurant, bookshop, telephones, bureau de change, audioguides. Special facilities and activities for young visitors (5-15 years old).

Documentary exhibitions (dossiers). — Throughout the museum small exhibitions which are changed at frequent intervals, feature a theme or artist in the fields of painting, sculpture, architecture, literature, opera...

Permanent exhibitions. — The collections presented in chronological order on three floors (ground floor, middle and upper levels) comprise all forms of artistic expression (painting, sculpture, architecture, decorative arts, cinema, photography, graphic art, music, literature, history) to illustrate the profusion of artistic talent between 1848 and 1914. The Orsay museum bridges the gap between the Louvre and the museum of modern art at the Pompidou Centre.

To the right of the square stand six large statues of the continents (2 statues of America), to the left a horse and a rhino and further on is a young elephant caught in a trap by Frémiet.

After visiting the ground floor which covers the period 1840 to 1870, go up to the upper level which displays the works of the Impressionists, the Post-Impressionists, the Pont-Aven school and the Nabis group and finally down to the middle level which features works from the late 19C and early 20C (Art Nouveau and sculpture between 1870 to 1914).

The expressive *Spirit of the Fatherland* (1), a fragment of the high relief of the Arc de Triomphe, by Rude (1784-1855) which is displayed on the right of the ticket desk, is a fitting introduction to the museum.

GROUND FLOOR

The central gallery is devoted to sculpture while the side galleries feature on the right classicism, romanticism and academism and on the left realism, landscape painting and pre-impressionism. *The Lion* (2), a realistic composition by Barye, stands guard at the entrance to the central gallery.

Sculpture *central gallery*

The romantic movement, which derived its inspiration from Antiquity and the Renaissance, was born in 1830 and flourished between 1850 and 1870.

GROUND FLOOR

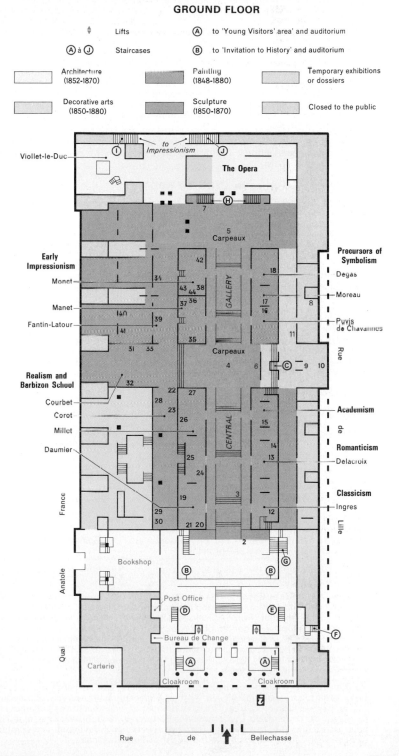

⇕ Lifts	Ⓐ	to 'Young Visitors' area' and auditorium
Ⓐ à Ⓙ Staircases	Ⓑ	to 'Invitation to History' and auditorium

Architecture (1852-1870)

Painting (1848-1880)

Temporary exhibitions or dossiers

Decorative arts (1850-1880)

Sculpture (1850-1870)

Closed to the public

Pradier (1790-1852). — His style, although classical in essence, is tinged with romanticism.	*Sappho* **(3)**

Carpeaux (1827-1875). — His work reveals the influence of Rude and Michelangelo. He was appointed as the official sculptor and carved fine busts. In collaboration with other artists he worked on official commissions including four figures representing the four corners of the world for the Observatory fountain *(p 198)*.	*Ugolin* **(4)** *Fountain of the Observatory* **(5)**

The *Romans in the Period of Decadence* **(6)** by T. Couture (1815-1879) who specialized in vast historical compositions, holds pride of place in the middle of the central gallery.

The architecture of the Second Empire (1852-1870)

Model of the Opera quarter. — *Far end of central gallery.*
A model at a scale of 1: 100 displayed under glass shows the lay-out of the Opera quarter. Garnier's successful design for the new Opera combines curved lines, a riot of multicoloured decoration in marble, bronze, copper and prophyry and a multitude of statues. A transverse section reveals the foyer, stage, auditorium, machines as well as the grandiose internal decoration. Carpeaux's original sculpture *The Dance* **(7)** (replaced by a Paul Belmondo copy on the façade) is noteworthy.

Viollet-le-Duc (1814-1879). — *First floor of the Pavillon Amont.*
The architecture and writer, Viollet-le-Duc, is famous for the restoration of great Gothic monuments and was keenly interested in decorative painting (murals of Notre-Dame's chapels).

The decorative arts (1850-1880)

Access to this section at the far right of the central gallery is from the far end or middle of the gallery behind Couture's painting.
The exhibits illustrate the versatility of the period between 1850 and 1880 which was influenced by colonisation, foreign travel, the universal exhibitions, in particular that of 1867 which revealed Japanese art (fine Japanese-style **porcelain service (8)** made by the painter-engraver Bracquemont for E. Rousseau).
The new industrial firms employed artists who combining business and pleasure produced unique specimens as well as mass-produced objects. **Christofle** expanded considerably as the introduction of electro-plating brought about mass production in silver plate while maintaining traditional craftsmanship in solid silver. Some items like the **Vase depicting the Education of Achilles (9)** were manufactured for the universal exhibitions. The cabinet-maker **Diehl**, famous for his boxes in different styles and materials and occasional furniture, also made ornate show pieces. The **medal cabinet (10)**, one of the most original pieces of the 1867 exhibition, is decorated with scenes from Merovingian history (low-relief in bronze and silver by Frémiet). **Jules Desfossé** commissioned artists to paint landscapes as decorative wall hangings: **Armide's garden (11)** is the central panel of a decor by Müller.

Painting (1848-1880)

Classicism, romanticism and academism. — *Right gallery near decorative arts. Walk down some steps.*
In the 1850s Ingres and Delacroix were the leading figures in the conflict between classicism and romanticism. The major part of their works are still in the Louvre and only some late works are on view in the museum.

Classicism: Ingres (1780-1867). — His works emphasize sinuous line.	*The Spring* **(12)**

Romanticism: Delacroix (1798-1863). — He experimented with colour and light effects.	*The lion hunt* **(13)**

Academism

Chassériau (1819-1856). — He combines draughtsmanship and the use of colour.	*Tepidarium* **(14)**

Cabanel (1808-1879). — He won great acclaim at the Salon of 1863.	*The Birth of Venus* **(15)**

The dawn of symbolism. — *Right gallery.* Ingres had a great influence on Puvis de Chavannes and G. Moreau among others. **Puvis de Chavannes** (1824-1898) drew inspiration for his murals from biblical subjects. His flat colours and simplified lines evoke an atmosphere of contemplation as in *The Poor Fisherman* **(16)**. **Gustave Moreau** (1826-1898), influenced by Chassériau, painted mythological fantasies in delicate colours and with a wealth of detail. (*Orpheus* — **17**). **Edgar Degas** (1834-1917) is represented by his early works prior to the 1870 war: portraits of the Bellelli family — **18** and contemporary scenes.

Realism and the Barbizon school. — *Left gallery, first part of central gallery.*
Some artists, who were influenced by their observations of everyday life and of nature, painted life size figures. The development of industrial towns led others to rediscover the countryside. Corot moved to Barbizon in 1830; he was later joined by other artists and they founded the Barbizon school which favoured dark colours, half-light and found inspiration in the forest of Fontainebleau.

Realism

Daumier (1808-1879). — He was primarily a lithographer and illustrator and he casts a sharp satirical eye on the social and political life of the period.

Busts of Parliamentarians (19)
The Republic (20)
The laundress (21)

The Barbizon school

Theodore Rousseau (1812-1867). — He was the leader of the group and his fleeting light effects are admirable.

An avenue in the forest of l'Isle Adam (24)

Millet (1814-1875). — He came from a peasant background and remained attached to the land and to country life.

The Angelus (25)
The gleaners (26)
Spring (27)

Troyon (1810-1865). — He specialized in scenes featuring cattle.

Oxen driven to the fields (29)

Rosa Bonheur (1822-1899). — Her main themes were the countryside and animals.

Ploughing in the Nivernais (30)

Corot (1796-1875). — He studied the play of light in woods and ponds.

The glade (22)
The catalpa (23)

Daubigny (1817-1878). — He was attracted to simple things, the shimmering waters of rivers and the silence of forests.

The harvest (28)

Courbet (1819-1877). — The scenery of his native Ornans was the inspiration for many of his paintings.

Burial at Ornans (31)
Painter in his studio (32)
Self-portrait (33)

Early impressionism. — *Left gallery, 2nd half of central gallery.*
The new generation of artists rejected the dark tones of their predecessors and endeavoured to render on canvas the vibration of light, the colours of impression. They studied the play of light which was of primary importance; their favourite themes were sunlit gardens, snow, mist and flesh tints. They were susceptible to the charm of the forest of Fontainebleau but they chose to settle at Chailly and although they did not join the Barbizon group, they welcomed their advice.

Manet (1832-1883). — His bold experiments with composition and colour broke new ground.

Le déjeuner sur l'herbe (34)
Olympia (35) - *The balcony* (36)
The fife player (37)

Fantin-Latour (1836-1904). — He admired Manet and was on good terms with the Batignolles group. He specialized in portraits and flower compositions.

Studio in the Batignolles (39)
The corner of the table (40)

Whistler (1834-1903). — His style is characterized by simplified lines and neutral colours.

The mother (41)

Bazille (1841-1870). — He was fascinated by contrasting light effects.

A family reunion (38)

Monet (1840-1926). — The true founder of the Impressionist movement *(see below)*.

The magpie (42)
Women in a garden (43)
Le déjeuner sur l'herbe (44)

UPPER LEVEL

Access from the tower housing architectural exhibitions or by the escalator behind the tower.

Impressionism from 1872

Gallery overlooking the Seine.
After the 1870 war which prompted artists to disperse, they gathered together in the Ile-de-France region: Pontoise, Auvers-sur-Oise... As the official Salons repeatedly rejected their paintings, they decided to form a group and show their work independently. The first exhibition was held in 1874 at the studio of the photographer Nadar where the term "impressionists" was first coined after Monet's celebrated canvas, *Impression-Sunrise,* (property of the Marmottan Museum). Six more exhibitions took place.

Monet (1840-1926). — He was the leading exponent of impressionism. His paintings reveal an original approach to the places he visited. After 1883 he painted numerous studies of water-lilies at Giverny.

Saint-Lazare station (45)
Rouen cathedral (46)
Blue water-lilies (47)

Renoir (1841-1919). — He was introduced to impressionism by Monet in 1875 and his canvases celebrate the joy of living. His female nudes exude sensual charm.

Le Moulin de la Galette (48)
Nude in the Sunlight (49) -
Young girls at the piano (50) -
Dance in the City and Dance in the Country (51)

UPPER LEVEL

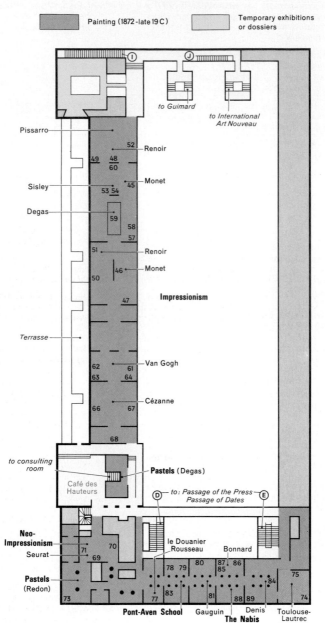

| | Painting (1872-late 19 C) | | Temporary exhibitions or dossiers |

Pissarro (1830-1903). — His main themes were fields, hills, streets, hamlets peopled with ideal peasant women.

Red roofs (52)

Sisley (1839-1899). — He was fascinated by the light of the Ile-de-France and lived at Moret-sur-Loing. He concentrated on landscapes depicting flowing waters and scudding clouds.

Flooding at Port-Marly (53)
Snow scene at Louveciennes (54)

Degas (1834-1917). — Originally a follower of Ingres, he remained aloof from the group until the end of the Second Empire. He was more interested in movement than light and his favourite themes were from the world of theatre and dance and racing.

Blue dancers (57)
The glass of absinth (58)
Sculptures (59)

Caillebotte (1848-1894). — His canvases were shown at several impressionist exhibitions but he is better known as a patron of the arts: the Caillebotte bequest is part of the museum's impressionist collections.

Planing the floor (60)

Van Gogh (1853-1890). — This Dutch artist took up painting in 1880 after visiting the Borinage countryside. The influence of the Impressionists led him to use brighter colours and he discovered the special quality of light in Provence. His disturbed mind led him to take his own life at Auvers-sur-Oise *(see the Michelin Green Guide to Ile-de-France)* in spite of the care and friendship of Dr. Gachet and a passionate correspondance with his brother Theo.

Self-portrait (61)
A woman of Arles (62)
A room at Arles (63)
The church at Auvers-sur-Oise (64)

Cézanne (1839-1906). — He returned to Aix-en-Provence after spending several years with Pissarro at Auvers. His broad strokes of bright colours emphasize the relief and contour of his simplified figures.

L'Estaque (66)
The House of the Hanged Man (67)
Woman with a coffee-pot (68)

Post-impressionism (late 19C)

Neo-impressionism. — The impressionists' technique which involved quick dabs of colour is refined into small dots of pure colour intermingled to evoke shimmering light. This new technique was given the name "divisionism".

Pastels. — This technique was rediscovered by many great artists including Degas, Redon, Manet who created landscapes, portraits, still-lifes and genre scenes.

The Pont-Aven school. — Gauguin, Emile Bernard, Serusier and Lacombe were among the artists attracted to the charming Breton village of Pont-Aven. They advocated elimination of detail, simplified forms and flat, bright colours.

The Nabis. — This movement was started in 1880 at Pont-Aven. On Gauguin's advice, Serusier painted *The Talisman* which fired his friends'enthusiasm and they formed the Nabis group (the name comes from the Hebrew word nabis meaning prophet).

Neo-impressionism

Seurat (1859-1891). — He evolved the theory of divisionism.

The circus (69)

Signac (1863-1935). — He aimed for greater luminosity.

The red buoy (70)

Cross (1856-1910). — He developed a more assured and vigorous technique.

Evening (71)

Redon's pastels (1840-1916). — He chose this technique to portray his world of fantasy.

The Buddha (73)

Toulouse-Lautrec (1864-1901). — A keen observer of Montmartre's night life. His portraits, theatre and circus scenes show great insight.

Jane Avril dancing (74)
The clown Cha-U-kao (75)

Henri (Douanier) Rousseau (1844-1910). — His naive and allegorical paintings place him in a class of his own in the history of art.

War (77)

The Pont-Aven school

Gauguin (1848-1903). — After making several visits to Pont-Aven, he travelled to the South Seas where he was captivated by the beauty of the landscape and the charm of the people.

Les Alyscamps (78)
La belle Angèle (79)
Tahitian women (80)
The white horse (81)

Emile Bernard (1868-1941). — He abandoned detail to concentrate on form.

Madeleine au Bois d'Amour (83)

The Nabis

Maurice Denis (1870-1943). — He was the group's principal theorist and he created mystical frescoes from everyday events.

The Muses (84)
A sunlit terrace (85)

Bonnard (1867-1947). — The influence of Japanese etchings is evident in his decorative themes and sinuous lines.

A game of croquet (86)
Women in a garden (87)

Vuillard (1868-1940). — His interior and street scenes evoke a quiet charm.

A public park (88)

Vallotton (1865-1925). — His strong realism and flat swathes of colour herald expressionism.

The ball (89)

Passage of the Press. — It presents a selection of contemporary newspapers. A more democratic press evolved with the introduction of advertising and broadsheets. More changes later occurred with articles, features on sports and gastronomy, serialization of novels and more illustrations.

Passage of Dates. — *Below the Passage of the Press.*
Panels trace the historical events arising from a particular date, event or painting.

Photography and cinema. — About 13 000 photographs testify to the wealth of talented photographers which existed in France and abroad from the invention of the daguerrotype in 1839 to the First World War. The early days of the cinema are represented by the praxinoscope, the photochronograph, Edison's praxinoscope and public film shows.

MIDDLE LEVEL late 19C to 1914

Painting and sculpture
after the proclamation of the Third Republic

Left wing, first half beyond the reception hall.

The hotel's reception hall and dining-room now used as the museum's restaurant have retained their decorative paintings, sculpture and gilding.

Naturalism, history painting and symbolism. — The official style adopted by the **Third Republic** was naturalism: all works of art were based on true facts and events from daily life.
In contrast to realism and impressionism, this was followed by symbolism in which reality gave way to fantasy, reflection, poetic and religious inspiration. This movement which started in Britain with Burne-Jones, flourished mainly in France.

Bouguereau (1825-1905). — *Hall*. The fine draughtsmanship and mastery of form of his allegorical and mythological compositions reveal Raphael's influence.	*The Birth of Venus* **(90)**
Gérôme (1824-1904). — *Hall.* He was primarily a painter but he took up sculpture at the end of his life and remained faithful to the academic style.	*Tanagra* **(93)**
Bastien-Lepage (1848-1884). — He painted country life and occupations.	*Haymaking* **(91)**
Cormon (1845-1924). — He specialized in scenes of prehistory and of religious history.	*Cain* **(92)**
Detaille (1848-1912). — He concentrated on military paintings.	*The dream* **(94)**

The works of foreign artists illustrating these trends are also on display:

Böcklin (1827-1901). — His mythological paintings evoke his love of Italy.	*Diana the huntress* **(95)**
Burne-Jones (1833-1898). — He was a great admirer of Botticelli and Michelangelo and his themes are inspired from medieval legends.	*The wheel of fortune* **(96)**
Breitner (1857-1923). — He painted historical scenes and scenes of Old Amsterdam.	*Two white horses drawing a load in Amsterdam* **(97)**
Homer (1836-1910). — This naturalist painter was famous for his country scenes and for his colourful and powerful paintings of the sea.	*Summer evening* **(98)**

Monumental sculpture. — After the proclamation of the Third Republic on 4 September 1870, artists were commissioned for the decoration of new buildings and for commemmorative busts and statues. Some turned to history and mythology while others found inspiration in daily life. Exaggerated movement and expression mark a return to baroque style.

Frémiet (1824-1910). — He stresses historical accuracy.	*St Michael* **(99)**
Meunier (1831-1905). — He portrays life at work: at sea, in the factory and especially in the mines.	*Docker at Antwerp* **(100)**
Dalou (1838-1902). — A great 19C naturalist sculptor.	*Peasant* **(101)**

Art Nouveau *left wing, 2nd half and part of right wing*

Art Nouveau in France and Belgium. — The need to make a clean break with the past and to find a new form of expression prompted the creation of the principal movement which developed in Europe around 1890 especially in the fields of architecture and applied arts: Art Nouveau or Modern Style. This movement which is linked to industrial progress is characterized by sinuous lines and plant motifs. Art Nouveau's fundamental concept of total art with no distinction made between major and minor forms of art led artists of various disciplines to join forces.
In France Art Nouveau was launched by the Nancy School, an association of artists and craftsmen founded by Emile Gallé.

MIDDLE LEVEL

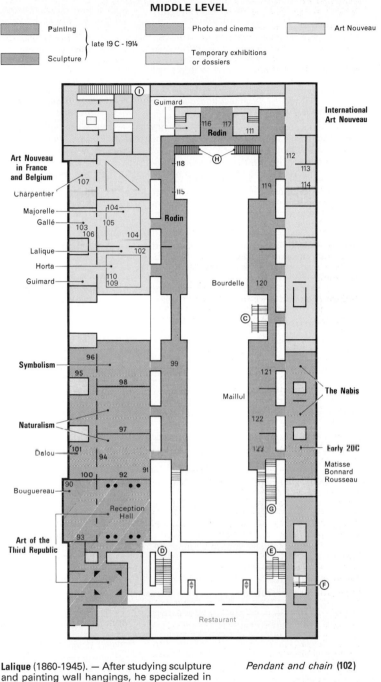

Painting
Sculpture
} late 19 C - 1914

Photo and cinema

Temporary exhibitions or dossiers

Art Nouveau

Lalique (1860-1945). — After studying sculpture and painting wall hangings, he specialized in moulded glass and jewellery.	*Pendant and chain* **(102)**
Gallé (1846-1904). — He worked as a master glazier, ceramist and cabinet-maker-decorator and started the fashion of flower-decorated ceramics.	*Vases* *Cabinet with dragonfly motif* **(103)**
Majorelle (1859-1926). — His mahogany furniture is decorated with orchids or his favourite water-lilies in gilded bronze.	*Writing desk and bookcase* **(104)** *Bed* **(104)**
Gruber (1870-1930). — He worked in various fields before specializing in stained glass.	*Door of Nancy fitting-room* **(105)**
Carabin (1862-1932). — His furniture can be classed as sculpture.	*Bookcase* **(106)**
Charpentier (1856-1909). — Sculptor and medal maker.	*Dining-room* **(107)**

Guimard (1867-1942). — He is famous for the decoration of métro station entrances.	*Cast iron motifs, Castel Béranger, Rue La Fontaine*
Belgium: Van de Velde (1863-1957). — He designed functional houses and furniture while remaining true to the principle of continuity of line and plan. He created chairs with a great purity of line.	*Writing desk and armchair* **(109)**
Horta (1861-1947). — Architect and decorator whose work shows great fantasy.	*Panelling (Hotel Aubecq, Brussels)* **(110)**

International Art Nouveau. — From 1880 the first examples of Art Nouveau appeared in England and soon spread to other parts of Europe (Vienna, Glasgow) and to the United States.

Michael Thonet (1796-1871). — His Vienna factory manufactured furniture in stained beech.	*Bentwood furniture (in the tower)* **(111)**
Glasgow: Mackintosh (1868-1928). — Architect and decorator famous for decorating interiors with white walls and furniture and public places (Argyle Street).	*High back chair Chest of drawers and mirror* **(112)**
Chicago: Wright (1867-1959). — He reinstated detached housing with his "prairie" houses. Seating is an important feature of the rooms.	*Chair* **(113)**
Vienna: Loos (1870-1933). — He favoured straight lines and stark masses.	*Bedroom suite* **(114)**

Rodin and his followers

2nd part of terrace.

Rodin (1840-1917). — The turn of the century was dominated by Rodin's strong personality which is evident in the works on display. From 1880 he created busts of famous artists *(Laurens, Victor Hugo)* and a symbolic portrait of Camille Claudel, *Thought* **(115)**. *The Gates of Hell* **(116)** comprises elements cast as separate pieces: *The Thinker, the Kiss, Fugit Amor* and *Ugolin* and his children, a moving composition full of anguish. The proud statue of *Balzac* **(117)** which evokes the writer's creative power is one of his masterpieces.

Rodin's successors. — The Italian sculptor, Medardo Rosso, who experimented with the vibration of light like the impressionists, also made his mark at the same period.
Many of Rodin's followers, like Desbois, remained faithful to the master's style while others such as Bartholomé and Bourdelle broke away and tried to recapture the balance and clarity of antiquity.

Camille Claudel (1864-1943). — Rodin's collaborator and muse.	*Old age* **(118)**
Rosso (1858-1928). — Wax was his favourite medium. His sculptures capture fleeting impressions.	*Ecce Puer* **(119)**
Bourdelle (1861-1929). — His themes are often derived from Antiquity.	*Hercules with a bow* **(120)**
Maillol (1861-1944). — He created strong, harmonious female figures.	*The Mediterranean* **(121)** *Monument to Cézanne* **(122)**
Joseph Bernard (1866-1931). — He returned to the technique of carving directly from blocks of wood and stone for greater realism.	*Dancing woman and child* **(123)**

Painting at the beginning of the 20C

Nabis. — After 1900 the style of the Nabis group evolved into softer colours and more complex design as in the large canvases by Bonnard *(In a boat)* and Vuillard *(The library)*.

Great international modern trends. — The last gallery is devoted to the principal artistic trends in Europe at the beginning of the century: the early stages of Fauvism in France (Braque, Derain, Marquet, Van Dongen); the development of independent artists in France (Bonnard, *The Bernheim brothers;* Douanier Rousseau, *The Snake-charmer*) and on the international scene (Munch, Holder, Klimt).

12
★★

The **Palais-Royal**

Michelin plan 11 - folds 19, 30 and 31: G 12, G 13 – H 13

Distance: 3km-2 miles – Time: 3 hours
Start from the Palais-Royal-Musée du Louvre métro
station

In this part of Paris the Palais-Royal,
the Bibliothèque Nationale and St-Roch
Church remind one vividly of the city's past in
contrast to the Avenue de l'Opéra and the Rue
de Rivoli which seem to epitomize the present.

To the right of the métro station is the **Louvre des Antiquaires** *(open Tuesdays to Sundays 11am to 7pm; closed Mondays, 1 January, 14 July, 25 December and Sundays from early July to early September. ☎ 42 97 27 00.)* a building containing 250 art galleries and antique shops.

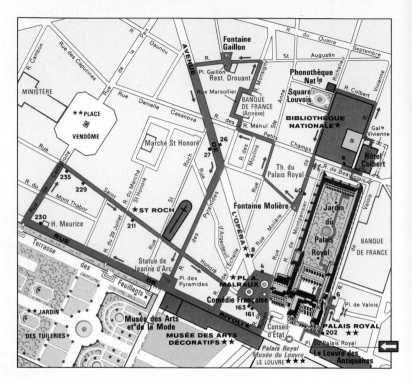

★★PALAIS-ROYAL ▯▯ — fold 31: H 13

The façades of Richelieu's palace, now the office of the Council of State can be seen though not entered. The quiet garden has retained its 18C atmosphere.

The Cardinal's Palace. — In 1624, Richelieu, who was Prime Minister, acquired a mansion near the Louvre with ground extending to the Charles V perimeter wall. In 1632 he commissioned the architect Jacques Le Mercier to build the huge edifice known as the Cardinal's Palace.

The Royal Palace. — The Cardinal on his deathbed in 1642 left his mansion to Louis XIII who soon followed him to the grave. His widow, Anne of Austria, with her son, the young Louis XIV, then quit the Louvre for the smaller and more beautiful mansion which henceforth became known as the Royal Palace. The Fronde in 1648 forced their hasty departure. When Louis XIV returned to Paris he went to live in the Louvre and lodged Queen Henrietta Maria, widow of Charles I of England, and then her daughter, Henrietta in the palace.

The Orléans. — After a lightning illness had carried off Henrietta, the palace was given in apanage to her husband Philippe of Orléans, brother of Louis XIV and subsequently to his son, appointed Regent during the minority of Louis XV. Philippe II of Orléans was highly gifted and also highly dissolute — palace suppers at that period were notorious.

In 1780 the palace passed to Louis-Philippe of Orléans, who being short of money, undertook the construction round three sides of the garden, of apartment houses with ground level shopping arcades and uniform façades. The three new streets skirting the frontages were called after the younger Orléans brothers: Valois, Montpensier and Beaujolais. The palace precinct became the favourite idling place for Parisians. Between 1786 and 1790 the same architect, Louis, was commissioned by Philippe-Égalité to build the Théâtre-Français, now the Comédie-Française *(p 140)* and the Palais-Royal Theatre at the corner of Rues de Montpensier and Beaujolais; it is now a vaudeville theatre.

After the Revolution, the palace became a gambling house until, in 1801, Napoleon converted it into offices, and in 1807, into the Exchange and Commercial Court. Louis XVIII returned the mansion to the Orléans and it was from there that Louis-Philippe set out for the Hôtel de Ville, in 1830, to be proclaimed king.

The garden formerly. — During the Revolution, the garden became a popular meeting-place. In the 18C it was the setting for cafés which attracted a varied clientele, a circus, a riding school, a dance hall, a theatre until this went up in flames, a wax museum, funfair attractions and gambling houses. The July monarchy closed the gaming houses in 1838 and the popularity of the arcade shops began to decline. The Commune set the buildings on fire but they have been restored.

THE PALACE AND THE GARDEN

The palace. The façade overlooking the square consists of a central building and two receding wings decorated with 18C carvings of military trophies and allegorical figures by Pajou.

The east wing now stands on the site of the theatre built by Richelieu and in which Molière created his major plays between 1661 and 1673 (when he collapsed on stage while acting out *Le Malade Imaginaire*; he died at no **40** Rue de Richelieu). It later became an opera house where Lulli's works continued to be performed until it was burnt down in 1763.

At no **6**, Rue de Valois (beautiful balcony), in 1638 Richelieu conducted the early sessions of his new foundation, the French Academy. Nearby is the quiet Place de Valois which is on the site of the palace's former outbuildings.

★**Main courtyard.** — Enter by the covered passage. Enclosed by projecting wings lined with galleries, it is dominated by an impressive central façade, surmounted by allegorical statues. A monumental composition (280 black and white columns of unequal height) by D. Buren fills the central space. Overlooking the garden is a double colonnade, the Orléans Gallery, built at the time of the Restoration (1814-1830) and formerly covered by an iron and glass roof. The Valois side gallery is known as the Prow Gallery because of its nautical decoration (Richelieu was minister for the navy). The sculptures in the fountains are by Pol Bury.

The garden. — It is overlooked by the elegant façades designed by the architect Louis. There are shops in the arcade specialising in the unique, the luxurious: decoration, medals, porcelain, stamp and antique shops.

On the grass by the palace, on a pedestal behind a statue, stands a toy cannon, known as the Palais-Royal cannon. From 1786 until 1914 it used to go off at midday provided the sun, when reflected through a magnifying glass, was hot enough to ignite the charge.

Leave the Palais Royal by the peristyle of the Beaujolais arcade.

From Palais-Royal to the Bibliothèque Nationale

On your way look through the grille at no **8**, Rue des Petits-Champs, to admire the courtyard and sombre brick and stone façade of the Tubeuf mansion built by Le Muet in 1633. Opposite stands Colbert's mansion (1665) now an annexe of the National Library. At street level the charming 19C **Colbert Arcade** illustrates by means of window displays the various activities of the National Library.

From Rue Vivienne turn into Rue Colbert which was spanned at the far end by the Hôtel de Nevers, a former literary salon. **Louvois Square** on the left, is adorned with a fountain by Visconti (1884). The Opera moved to the site of the former Hôtel de Louvois in 1793 and remained on this site until 1820 when the duc de Berry was assassinated by a certain Louvel after a performance. The theatre was destroyed and the company moved to Rue Le Peletier, before moving again in 1875 to the Garnier opera house, where the Emperor's Pavilion was equipped with a direct access for carriages.

★BIBLIOTHÈQUE NATIONALE □□ — fold 31: G 13

In the Middle Ages the kings of France collected manuscripts; Charles V mustered nearly 1 000 volumes in the Louvre Library *(p 30)*; Charles VIII and Louis XII had libraries at Blois; François I at Fontainebleau. A copyright act in 1537 ensured that a copy of every book printed enters the royal, now national, library — today extended to records and photographs.

In the 17C the Tubeuf Mansion was enlarged by Mansart and on coming into Mazarin's possession housed his 500 pictures and personal art objects. By 1666 the Royal Library numbered 200 000 volumes and Colbert decided to move it to his own mansion in the rue Vivienne; fifty-four years later, it was moved again when it was added to the original Mazarin collection. The Nevers and Chivry mansions were taken over in the 19C.

The Library today. — The Bibliothèque Nationale is divided into departments covering 16 500m²-177 600sq ft with several annexes elsewhere in Paris. It includes among others, the following departments:

Printed Books: About 12 million volumes dating from the 15C and including two Gutenburg bibles, first editions of Villon, Rabelais, Pascal... The central storeroom comprises 11 levels and 240km-149 miles of shelving. The reading room designed by Labrouste is a masterpiece of architecture (19C).

Manuscripts: papyri, Dead Sea scrolls, illuminated manuscripts including Charlemagne's Gospel, Charles the Bald's Bible and St Louis' Psalter; parchments, letters, MSS of Hugo, Proust, Pasteur and Marie Curie...

Engravings and Photographs: This is the richest collection in the world: 12 million engravings, 2 million photographs.

Maps and Plans: 13 — 20C.

Medals and Antiques: Coins, medals, cameos, bronzes and objets d'art. This department is also responsible for research into the treasure troves discovered in France.

Music and Record Library: Records, tapes and talking machines.

Tour. — The east side of the main courtyard is by the 18C architect, Robert de Cotte. The reading room (1868) — *members only* — can be seen through a window. At the end of the hall on the right is the Mansart Gallery *(free access during exhibitions)* and opposite, the State Room with the original plaster bust of Voltaire by Houdon (the marble original is at the Comédie-Française).

The great staircase leads to the **Medals and Antiques Museum★** (on the mezzanine): the art objects from royal and confiscated collections on display include ivory chess pieces, Dagobert's legendary throne and coins. *Open 1 to 5pm; 12noon to 6pm Sundays and holidays; closed 1 May; 20F; ☎ 47 03 83 34.*
On the floor above is the magnificent **Mazarin Gallery★** by Mansart *(access during temporary exhibitions).*

From the Bibliothèque Nationale to St-Roch Church

On leaving the library, walk left down Rue de Richelieu to Rue Molière.

Molière Fountain. — The 19C fountain by Visconti with statues by Pradier stands not far from what is now no **40** Rue de Richelieu, the site of Molière's house. It was there that he was taken when he collapsed on stage at the first Palais-Royal Theatre, on 17 February 1673. He was 51.
Make for Rue des Petits-Champs by way of Rues Thérèse and Ste-Anne — no 47 is the house Lulli had built in 1671, borrowing 11 000 *livres* from Molière to do so. Musical motifs can be seen upon the façade overlooking Rue Ste-Anne.
The Rue des Moulins gets its name from the windmills which stood upon a hillock built of public waste like the neighbouring Butte St-Roch. The mound was razed in 1668, but one of the mills, the Radet, was saved and transported to Montmartre *(p 90).*
The brief Rue Méhul leads to the old Ventadour Theatre where Victor Hugo's melodrama, *Ruy Blas*, was first played in 1838. It is now an annexe of the Bank of France.
Walk to Rue Monsigny and Rue St-Augustin on the left. Facing the **Gaillon fountain** (Fontaine Gaillon) erected in 1707 on the square of the same name (remodelled by Visconti in 1827), is the Restaurant Drouant, known in the world of letters as the place from which the names of the Goncourt prizewinners are announced annually in autumn.

On reaching Avenue de l'Opéra turn left.

★★**Avenue de l'Opéra.** — This luxurious thoroughfare was begun simultaneously at either end by Haussmann in 1854 and completed in 1878. The most serious obstacle in the road's path was the Butte St-Roch, which covered the area between what are now Rue Thérèse and Rue des Pyramides and rose to sufficient height for Joan of Arc to position her large supporting cannon upon it when her troops were preparing to attack the St Honoré Gate *(p 140).* The mound had been partly levelled off in 1615 but remained a poor area until the end of the 17C when the slums were demolished and the vast heaps of rubble were utilised to build up the lowlying areas around the Champ-de-Mars.
The Avenue de l'Opéra, just over a hundred years old, has become one of Paris' prestige streets where big business and commerce reign. For the tourist the avenue is the place for making purchases: perfume, scarves, gifts and *articles de Paris* (fancy goods). It is also a business district with many large banks, estate agents and international bookshops *(see Useful Addresses p 13).* More obviously the avenue and the streets off it have become the stronghold of the advertising and travel industries with the Havas Travel Agency at no **26**, and foreign tourist agencies and air and shipping lines occupying offices all around. No **27** is the National Centre for the Visual Arts with an entrance in *trompe-l'œil.*

Turn right into Rue des Pyramides and, after crossing Rue d'Argenteuil where Corneille died in 1684, continue to the square, **Place des Pyramides**, at the end of which there stands an equestrian statue of Joan of Arc by the 19C sculptor, Frémiet.

★**Rue de Rivoli.** — The Rue de Rivoli, between the Place des Pyramides and Rue de Castiglione on the right, crosses the site of the former Tuileries **Riding School**. In 1789 the school was hastily converted into a meeting place for the Constituent Assembly. Sessions were subsequently held there by the Legislative Assembly and the Convention, until on 21 September 1792, the day following the French victory over the Prussians at Valmy (commemorative tablet on a pillar in the Tuileries railings opposite no **230**), it became the setting for the proclamation of the Republic and the trial of Louis XVI (1792).
It was Napoleon who, in 1811, had this part of the avenue constructed, although it was not to be completed until nearly the middle of the century. The houses facing the Tuileries are of uniform design above arcades lined with both luxury and souvenir shops.
In 1944 Rue de Rivoli was the scene of a momentous decision in the capital's own history when the German General von Choltitz, Commandant of Paris, who had his headquarters at the Meurice Hotel at no 228, refused to obey Hitler's orders to blow up the capital's bridges and principal buildings when the tanks of General Leclerc's division and the Resistance were known to be approaching. He surrendered on 25 August and Paris was liberated intact.
Turn right up Rue de Castiglione, known formerly as the Passage des Feuillants after the Benedictine monastery which it skirted, and right again, into Rue St-Honoré. The crossroads of Rue de Castiglione and Rue St-Honoré affords a view of the Place and Colonne Vendôme *(p 84).*

Rue St-Honoré at the time of the Revolution. — The **Feuillants Monastery,** which had grounds extending to the Tuileries riding school, augmented its income by building an apartment house which can still be seen between nos **229** and **235** in the Rue St-Honoré. It was here that the short-lived Feuillants Club of moderates who, in line with La Fayette, Bailly, Sieyès and Talleyrand, disassociated themselves from the extremist Jacobin group, met in 1791.

No **211** is the former Noailles Mansion where General La Fayette married one of the daughters of the house in 1774. It is now the St James and Albany Hotel. On the left there used to be a **Jacobin Monastery** (a Dominican order of St James). In 1789 a club installed itself in the monastery and took its name, becoming famous during the Revolution under the leadership of Robespierre.

The Rue du Marché St-Honoré now cuts across the site of the monastery church and a market dating back to 1810 occupies the ground on which the monastery once stood.

St-Roch Church, on the left, was the site on 13 Vendémiaire — 5 October 1795 — of bloody fighting. A column of royalists leading an attack on the Convention, then in the Tuileries, aimed to march through the Rue St-Roch. Bonaparte, who was in charge of the defence, however, mowed down with gun fire the men massed on the church steps and perched on its façade. The bullet holes can still be seen.

Some idea of the scale of Baron Haussmann's earth-moving undertakings can be gained from the fact that to enter the church nowadays you have to walk up thirteen steps, whereas before the construction of the Opera Avenue, you had to go down seven.

★CHURCH OF ST ROCH ▣▣ — fold 31: G 13

The foundation stone of the church dedicated to the early 14C saint who tended those suffering from the plague in Italy, was laid by Louis XIV in 1653. The Moulins hillock site compelled the architect, Le Mercier, to reorientate the church so that it faces south to north.

Funds soon ran out but work was able to continue after a lottery had been organized in 1705. Instead of completing the nave, a series of chapels one behind the other were constructed beyond the apse, lengthening the church from the planned 80 to 125m-262 to 410ft (5m-16ft shorter than Notre-Dame) and obliterating all unity of design. In consequence, in line behind the altar are a Lady Chapel by Jules Hardouin-Mansart, with a tall richly decorated dome, a Communion Chapel with a flat dome and finally a Calvary Chapel *(closed for restoration)* rebuilt in the 19C.

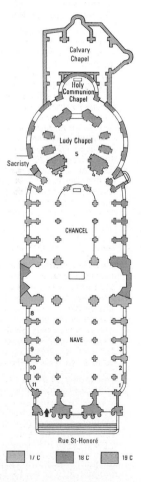

In 1719 a gift of 100 000 *livres* from John Law *(p 146)*, recently converted to Catholicism, enabled the nave to be completed. Robert de Cotte designed the façade in the Jesuit style in 1736. Among those buried in St-Roch in the Lady Chapel and side chapels are the playwright Corneille, the garden designer Le Nôtre, the Abbot de l'Épée *(p 202)*, the philosophers Diderot and d'Holbach and Mme Geoffrin, hostess of a famous 18C *salon*. The 17C mariner, Duguay-Trouin, has been transferred to Saint-Malo.

Works of Art:

1) Tomb of Henri of Lorraine, Count d'Harcourt by Renard (17C) and bust of the 17C Marshal de Créqui by Coysevox (17C).

2) Funeral monument of the astronomer, Maupertuis by d'Huez and statue of Cardinal Dubois by Guillaume Coustou.

3) Tomb of Duke Charles de Créqui.

4) Godefroy de Bouillon Victorious by Claude Vignon (17C). Funerary plaque to Duguay-Trouin.

5) The Triumph of the Virgin, painting by J. B. Pierre on the dome *(illumination: apply to the sacristan)*. The **Nativity**★ at the altar by the Anguier brothers, was brought from the Val-de-Grâce.

6) Resurrection of the Son of the Widow of Naïm by Le Sueur (17C).

7) Le Nôtre bust by Coysevox and funerary inscription.

8) Monument to the Abbot de l'Épée (19C).

9) Bust of the painter Mignard and statue of his daughter by Lemoyne (18C)

10) Baptism of Christ by Lemoyne. Medallion by Falconet.

11) Baptismal Chapel: frescoes by Chassériau (19C).

Continue left down Rue St-Honoré to Rue de l'Échelle, so called after the ladder or flight of steps leading to a scaffold which stood on the site during the Ancien Régime. The ecclesiastical courts then sent polygamists, perjurers and blasphemers to the steps where they were exposed in shame before the public.

On the right is the Marsan Pavilion, which, with the Flore Pavilion (reconstructed), are all that remain of the Tuileries Palace built by Philibert Delorme and Jean Bullant in the 16C for Catherine de' Medici and burnt down in 1871 *(p 32)*.

Costume and Fashion Museum (Musée des Arts de la Mode). — *Pavillon de Marsan, 109 Rue de Rivoli. Open 12.30 to 6pm; closed Tuesdays and certain holidays; variable admission fee.* ☎ *42 60 32 14.*
The collections comprising 12 500 dresses and over 100 000 textile samples dating from 18C to the present day, are exhibited in rotation on five floors.

★★MUSEUM OF DECORATIVE ARTS (MUSÉE DES ARTS DÉCORATIFS)
▦▦ — fold 31: H 13

107 Rue de Rivoli. Open 12.30 to 6pm; 11am to 6pm Sundays; closed Mondays, Tuesdays and certain holidays; 23F. ☎ *42 60 32 14.*
The temporary exhibitions organized by the museum are often extremely interesting (opening times as above; variable admission fee).
Art courses (drawing, modelling, metal engraving) are offered. *Information can be obtained at the Secrétariat des Ateliers:* ☎ *42 61 29 38.*
The numerous exhibits provide a vivid panorama of the evolution in form and taste in sculpture, painting, furniture, tapestry, banqueting settings and all forms of decoration in France.
First floor: 1950 to the present, including a reconstruction of Jeanne Lanvin's flat; Dubuffet Bequest including paintings, drawings and sculpture by the artist.
Second floor: objects from the Middle Ages to the Renaissance.
Third and fourth floors: reign of Louis XIV to the Second Empire — room settings with furniture and paintings.
Fifth floor: specialist departments (wallpaper, drawings...) and reference departments: fashion, textiles, glass, toys, crafts...

On leaving the museum, you pass on the right the latest Louvre façade (remodelled during the Third Republic). The statues are of the generals of the First Empire.

Turn left into Rue de Rohan, which leads to Place André-Malraux. The street runs over the original site of the Quinze-Vingts Hospital for the blind which in the reign of Louis XVI was transferred by Cardinal de Rohan, the institution's administrator, to barracks in Rue de Charenton where it remains to this day *(p 243)*.

★PLACE ANDRÉ-MALRAUX ▦▦ — fold 31: H 13

From this altogether Parisian crossroads — formerly known as the place du Théâtre-Français — created in the time of Napoleon III and decorated with attractive modern fountains there is a splendid view up the Avenue de l'Opéra.

Comédie-Française. — In 1680 Louis XIV combined the former Molière company with that at the Hôtel de Bourgogne *(p 145)* and granted it the sole right of performance in the capital. The new company took the name Comédie-Française. The company, however, found itself the butt of hostility simultaneously from the Sorbonne and the orthodox and was compelled to move home frequently — from the Guénégaud *(p 174)* to the Rue de l'Ancienne-Comédie *(p 174)*, the Palais des Tuileries *(p 31)* and the Odéon *(p 194)*.
At the Revolution a dispute broke out in the company between players who supported the Republicans and those favouring the Royalists. In 1792 the former, led by Talma, took over this theatre.
Napoleon showed a great interest in the Comédie-Française, in Talma — and also in the leading lady, Mlle Mars. In 1812 he presented the company with a foundation making it an association of currently acting and apprentice players and players on pension. Today the theatre is still under a director nominated by the state.
On 21 February 1830 the company, playing *Hernani*, was involved in the famous battle — a battle of taste — which marked Victor Hugo's triumphal *début* as a playwright.
The repertoire of the Comédie-Française has, by tradition, been classical, with set rules in style of acting and in interpretation — Molière, Corneille, Racine, Marivaux, Musset, Beaumarchais. Recently, however, works by foreign and 20C French authors have been admitted — Pirandello, Claudel, Giraudoux, Anouilh...
In the foyer are Houdon's famous bust of **Voltaire**★★ *(p 137)* and the chair in which Molière was sitting when taken fatally ill on stage *(p 137)*.
At no **161** Rue St-Honoré was the Café de la Régence founded in 1681 in the Place du Palais-Royal and forced to move in 1854 when the square was enlarged.

Memories of Joan of Arc. — Joan came to the gate in the Charles V perimeter wall which stood where no **163** Rue St-Honoré is now, when leading her attack on the capital in 1429. She had already freed Orléans *(see Michelin Green Guide Châteaux of the Loire)* and accompanied the King to Rheims for his coronation, but her task, as she saw it, was far from complete. Paris was still in the hands of the English under the Regent Bedford who wished not only to retain the city but to make it safe enough to bring over the young Henry VI and crown him in Notre-Dame, King of England and France.
The girl soldier paused to pray at the small St-Denis-de-la-Chapelle (the church, now remodelled, is at no 16, Rue de la Chapelle, 18e), before undertaking her attack on the gate fort defended by a moat. Realising this would have to be filled in, she moved to measure the water's depth with her lance when she was wounded in the thigh by an arrow. She was given first aid in what is now no **4** in the square while her men beat a hasty retreat. Henry VI was crowned in Notre-Dame (1431).
Although this is the only episode linking Joan of Arc with the capital there are, in addition to the medallion by Réal del Sarte on the Café de la Régence façade, four statues of her in the city — in the Place des Pyramides *(p 138)*, 16 Rue de la Chapelle, Place St-Augustin *(p 254)* and at 41 Boulevard St-Marcel.

The Halles-Beaubourg

Michelin plan **11** - folds 31 and 32: H 14, H 15

Distance 4.5km-3 miles – Time: 1 day
Start from Châtelet-les-Halles métro station
or R.E.R. station

After the demolition of the central market
a leisure and commercial centre has
been created. Also with the building
of the Pompidou Centre and the renovation
of the decrepit Beaubourg plateau, the character
of this old quarter has radically changed.

LES HALLES 🔲🔲 — fold 31: H 14

The Old Halles. — Paris' central market was on the Ile de la Cité; the second on the Place de Grève now the Place de l'Hôtel de Ville; the third settled on the present site around 1110. In 1183 under Philippe Auguste it was extended, permanent structures being erected and a surrounding wall built. The king levied sale and sales taxes.

Twice a week the city merchants and craftsmen were required to close their shops and conduct their business in the market where each street specialised in a trade.

By the 16C with a population of 300 000 in the capital the food market assumed a paramount importance, eventually replacing all other types of trade in the market. On the orders of Napoleon, the wine and leather markets were transferred to the Left Bank. Until the Revolution, close to the nearby St-Eustache crossroads was the market **pillory** where dishonest traders, thieves and prostitutes were publicly exposed.

By the 19C the great market was in urgent need of reconstruction. As Rambuteau and Haussmann thrust wide avenues through the quarter (Rues de Rivoli, du Pont-Neuf, du Louvre, des Halles, Étienne-Marcel), a stone pavilion was built by the architect **Baltard** commissioned by Louis Philippe, and being unsuitable, razed. He then designed plans of a hall of iron girders and skylight roofs, reminiscent of the Gare de l'Est, which were accepted by Napoleon III.

Ten halls in all were constructed between 1854 and 1866 and the buildings became the model for covered markets throughout France and abroad. Two further halls were opened in 1936. The animated market scene and the rich variety of colour and smell are vividly described by the writer Emile Zola as "the stomach of Paris" in his novel *Savage Paris (Le Ventre de Paris)*. The old tradition still exists of eating onion soup, snails and pig's trotters at 5am in simple but excellent restaurants with colourful names (Le Chien qui fume, le Pied de Cochon).

As the old buildings became inadequate, the market moved to Rungis (1969). One of the original halls has been reerected at Nogent-sur-Marne.

Forum des Halles. — An underground pedestrian concourse, lined with shops and with direct access to the metro stations, extends over 7 hectares — more than 17 acres to the east of the Commercial Exchange. At garden level, on the north and east sides, palm-shaped metal structures house public amenities (Pavillon des Arts, Maison de la Poésie...). There is a good view over the whole area from the upper terrace by the fountain.

Forum des Halles

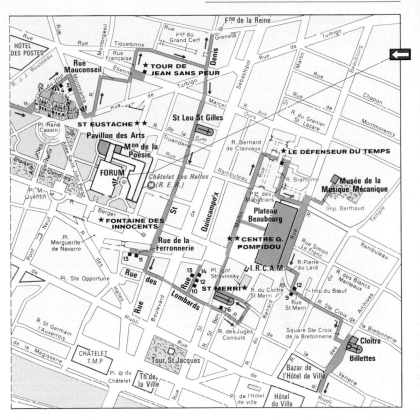

To the west, a garden (5 hectares-12 acres) includes pergolas along Rue Berger, children's play areas, a tree lined mall linking the semi-circular area by St-Eustache's, where stands a massive 70 ton stone head by H. de Miller, to the Fountain of the Innocents. The glazed galleries overlook the Place des Verrières; in the centre rises a pink marble sculpture by the Argentine Julio Silva, of **Pyegmalion**: next to a unicorn, the Buddha-like figure of the Dream-Keeper presenting her twin lunar and solar faces watches over the young girl asleep created by Pygmalion. The latter is depicted stilled for eternity in his fruitless quest while his desire is exemplified by a pig-headed man devouring the snake of temptation.

On level -4, on the Porte Lescot side, the theme of a **bronze low-relief** by Trémois representing a golden wall with amazing reliefs, is light travelling through the ages. On level -3 by Rue de l'Arc-en-Ciel, imaginary porticoes opening on to infinity painted by Attila, form a rainbow-coloured dome. **Moretti's fresco** (same level, by Rue des Piliers) in vivid colours evokes the evolution of man from prehistoric times (bronze human mask from Tautavel) to the age of writing including giant portraits of Victor Hugo and Louis Armstrong. On levels -2 and -1 Cueco's mosaic columns and Rieti's ceramics are decorated with wild and tame animals.

★**Grévin Museum's Forum Annexe.** — *Level -1. Open 10.30am to 6.45pm weekdays, 1 to 7pm Sundays and holidays; audioguides: 40 min; 38F, children 6-14: 26F; ☎ 40 26 28 50.*

The display, in this annexe of the waxworks museum on Boulevard Montmartre, portrays the Paris of the Belle Époque (1885-1900) by means of twenty-two scenes with animation and sound effects on the highlights of the capital: the opening of the Eiffel Tower, Montmartre cabarets, etc.

Holography Museum. — *Level -1 Porte Lescot. Open 10am to 7pm (1 to 7pm Sundays and holidays); 28F; ☎ 40 39 96 83.*

Holography is a process which uses coherent light or laser beams to create three-dimensional images known as holograms. It was invented in 1947 by Dennis Gabor and it experienced a rapid expansion with the invention of the laser beam. Among the many interesting exhibits are a series of disconcertingly lifelike portraits.

From level -3 go through the Place Carrée to gain access to the gallery leading to facilities open to the public in the fields of art (auditorium, video library, photographic studio), and sports (swimming-pool, gymnasium, billiard room). There is also a tropical glasshouse lit by four glass pyramids.

Cousteau Oceanic Centre. — *Open Tuesdays and Thursdays 10am to 5.30pm (last admission 4pm), Wednesdays, Fridays, weekends and holidays 10am to 7pm (last admission 5.30pm); closed Mondays except holiday Mondays; 75F, children 11 and under 50F; ☎ 40 26 13 78.*

The visit includes a dive to the ocean deep, a study of the anatomy of a 25m-82ft long whale, exhibitions on water as gas, ice and liquid and on Cousteau himself and his various oceanic explorations, discoveries and inventions.

Leave by the Porte du Louvre and cross to Rue Sauval, formerly Rue des Étuves (public baths had become places of ill repute by the end of the Middle Ages and were closed down under Louis XIII). From the entrance there is fine view of the Exchange and of St-Eustache's.

Rue St-Honoré. — This street, as of the 12C, was one of the quarter's major thoroughfares. The site of no 96 on the corner is where the poet and comedy writer Regnard was born in 1655 and where some historians allege Molière was born in 1662. Wagner lived there in 1839.

Further along, on the left, is an edifice built by Soufflot (1755). The sculptor Boizot reproduced a nymph by Jean Goujon on the façade and erected by the side of the building on the Rue de l'Arbre-Sec, a fountain adorned with a bronze mascaron surmounted by a marble plaque bearing France's coat of arms. This monument replaced the Croix-du-Trahoir fountain (**Fontaine de la Croix-du-Trahoir**), erected by François I but in no way resembles it. The original stood in the middle of the road, raised on a flight of steps on which vegetables were spread for sale. To one side stood the gallows from which the street on the left took its name of the Arbre Sec or withered tree. It is said also that in 613 at these crossroads, on the orders of her enemy, Frédégonde, the old Queen Brunehaut of Austrasia was tied by her hair to a wild horse's tail and broken. More than a thousand years later, on 26 August 1648, the arrest of the parliamentarian, Broussel, by Anne of Austria's forces in the same spot began a street row which, by the following morning, had developed into civil conflict: the Fronde had begun.

Oratory Church (Oratoire). — This was the site of Gabrielle d'Estrées' house in the 16C. In 1616 the Carmelite Oratorian Congregation, later to rival the Jesuits, had a church built by Le Mercier (1621-1630) which became the royal chapel in the reigns of Louis XIII, Louis XIV and Louis XV. Preachers such as Bossuet, Malebranche, Bourdaloue and Massillon attracted the royal family and court. The funerals of Louis XIII and his Queen, Anne of Austria, were held in the church. The Oratorians were suppressed at the Revolution; the chapel became an arms depot and in 1811, a Protestant church. The façade is 18C.

From the arches of the Rue de Rivoli there is a view of the church's east end which is well preserved, and of the statue of Admiral de Coligny placed there last century. He was assassinated on the night of the St Bartholomew's massacre (24 August 1572).

Take Rue Jean-Jacques Rousseau on the right where the philosopher lived at the end of his life (no 52). On the left is the former red light street, Rue du Pélican, and beyond the **Vero-Dodat arcade** (Galerie Vero-Dodat), created in 1822 by two pork butchers who installed gas lighting along it and let the shops for fabulous rents.

Commercial Exchange (Bourse du Commerce). — This circular building is hemmed in to the west by a semicircle of tall porticoed mansions and to the east by gardens and the Forum. It stands on a site where for the past 800 years French history has been made. Blanche de Castille, mother of St Louis, died in the first building (Hôtel de Nesle) in 1252 on a bed of straw as a sign of humility. It then became the Hôtel de Bohème, then Hôtel d'Orléans, Louis XII lost the mansion at cribbage to his chamberlain who converted it into a convent for repentant sinners. These were dislodged in 1572 when Catherine de' Medici left the Tuileries (p 30) and had a mansion, the Hôtel de la Reine, constructed by Delorme and Bullant. The building subsequently became the Hôtel de Soissons where in 1663 was born Prince Eugene of Savoy who served the Austrian empire and fought the infidels. Under the Regency it was turned into a gambling hall, then razed in 1748. A wheat market built in Louis XVI's reign was replaced in 1889 by the present rotunda.

Abutting on the market side wall to the south of the building, is a fluted column, 30m-98ft high, the only remaining feature of the mansion built by Bullant, which is thought to be the astrologer Ruggieri's observatory.

Inside, the vast circular hall lit by a glass dome is reserved for accredited commodity brokers. *Open 9am to 6pm; closed Saturdays, Sundays and holidays; proof of identity required.*

★★**ST-EUSTACHE CHURCH** ▯▯ — fold 31: H 14

St-Eustache, Gothic in plan and outline, Renaissance in decoration, is one of Paris' most beautiful churches. It has a long tradition of organ and choral music. Last century it was the setting for first performances of works by both Berlioz and Liszt.

Construction. — In 1214 a chapel, dedicated to St Agnes was built on this spot. A few years later, the chapel was rededicated to St Eustache, a Roman general converted, like St Hubert, by the vision of a cross between a stag's antlers. But the Halles parish, which had become the biggest in Paris, dreamed of a church worthy of its new status. Grandiose plans were made with Notre-Dame as the model. The foundation stone was laid in 1532. Construction was slow, however, in spite of liberal gifts and the church was only consecrated a century later, in 1637. The original plan had been adhered to, although the west front had never been completed, when in 1754 it was decided to replace this Renaissance front by a classical one with columns.

During the Revolution the church was renamed the Temple of Agriculture; in 1844 it was badly damaged by fire and subsequently reconstructed by Baltard.

St-Eustache, so close to the Louvre and the Palais-Royal, at the centre of everything going on in the capital and also the parish church of the Halles corporations, became a focal point of public ceremony — the baptisms of Armand du Plessis, the future Richelieu, of Jean-Baptiste Poquelin (Molière), the future Marquise de Pompadour, Louis XIV's first communion, the funerals of La Fontaine, Molière and the Revolutionary orator, Mirabeau.

The church was at one time paved with tombstones including those of Louis XIV's statesman, Colbert, Admiral de Tourville who beat the Anglo-Dutch fleets off Beachy Head in 1690 and was defeated, in turn, off La Hogue in 1692, and the composer Rameau.

Interior. — St-Eustache measures 100m long, 44m wide and 34m high-328 × 144 × 112ft. The church's majesty and rich decoration are striking.

The plan is that of Notre-Dame with nave and chancel encircled by double aisles and flat transepts. The vaulting above the nave, transept and chancel is Flamboyant, adorned with numerous ribs and richly carved hanging keystones.

The elevation, however, is entirely different to the cathedral's. The aisles, devoid of galleries, rise very high, the arches being so tall that between them and the clerestory windows there is only space for a small Renaissance style gallery.

The stained glass windows in the chancel are after cartoons by Philippe de Champaigne (1631). St Eustace appears at the centre, surrounded by the Fathers of the Church and the Apostles. The chapels are decorated with frescoes.

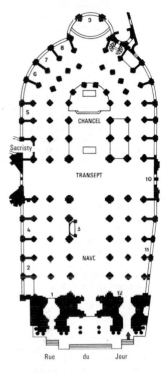

1) On the door tympanum: the *Martyrdom of St Eustace* by Simon Vouot (17C).

2) *Adoration of the Magi,* a copy of a painting by Rubens.

3) Churchwarden's pew presented by the Regent, Philippe of Orleans in 1720.

4) Colourful naive sculpture by R. Mason commemorating the fruit and vegetable market's move out of Paris on 28 February 1969.

5) *Tobias and the Angel,* by Santi di Tito (16C).

6) *The Ecstasy of Mary Magdalene,* painting by Manetti (17C).

7) *The Pilgrims at Emmaüs,* an early Rubens.

8) Colbert's tomb designed by Le Brun, Coysevox carved the statues of the minister and of Abundance; Tuby that of Fidelity (left).

9) Statue of the Virgin by Pigalle. Chapel frescoes by Thomas Couture (19C).

10) 16C statue of St John the Evangelist.

11) Bust of the composer Jean-Philippe Rameau who died in 1764.

12) Epitaph to 17C Lieutenant-General Chevert.

Exterior. — Take the narrow Rue du Jour. Opposite no **4** there is a good view★ of the buttresses and upper part of the church. No **4**, once the Paris seat of Royaumont Abbey, passed to Montmorency-Bouteville, who was executed in 1628 by Richelieu for contravening his edicts on duelling *(p 95)*; it then became the property of his son, Marshal of Luxembourg.

From no **3**, Rue Montmartre a blind alley ends at the beautiful north transept door.

★**Transept façade.** — This fine Renaissance composition is flanked by twin staircase turrets ending in pinnacles. Beneath the gable point is a stag's head with a Cross between the antlers recalling St Eustace's conversion. The statues on the door shafts are modern. The pilasters, niches, mouldings, grotesques and roses are delicately fashioned.

Chevet. — From the corner where the Rues Montorgueil and Montmartre meet there is a view of the church chevet and the final circular Lady Chapel. The bell tower's spire rising above the transept crossing was truncated in the 19C to house a signalling station.

Rue Mauconseil. — In 1548 a theatre was built on land belonging to the Hôtel de Bourgogne to the left of the street. The company had no women players until 1634 and all female roles were played by masked men. Racine first presented *Mithridate* and *Iphigénie* in this theatre. In 1680 the company, by royal command, merged with that of the Rue Mazarine *(p 174)*.

The Italians took over the theatre. Among the comedians was a clown, Scaramouche, who could still knock off his partner's hat with a high kick at the age of 83. The company was disbanded in 1697 after an attack on Mme de Maintenon. The last troupe to play the theatre before it disappeared was the Comic Opera (1716-1782).

★**John the Fearless' Tower (Tour de Jean-sans-Peur).** — Follow Rue Française (named after François I) on the left. At no **20** in Rue Étienne-Marcel, in a schoolyard, is a square machicolated tower *(not open)* built by John the Fearless for his own protection in 1408 following the assassination, on his orders, of the Duke of Orléans. The tower formed part of the **Hôtel de Bourgogne**, the former Artois mansion abutting on the Philippe Auguste perimeter wall.

Continue along Rue Française, then take Rue Tiquetonne (old houses with fine restored façades) on the right to Rue St-Denis.

Rue St-Denis. — The street, opened in the 7C, soon became the busiest and most prosperous in Paris. Kings rode along it when making solemn entries to the capital and visiting Notre-Dame; royal funerals followed it on their way to St-Denis Abbey. The new king was greeted with triumphal arches, porticoes and even fountains — the last much preferred as they played free wine or milk! One, much restored, remains from the time of Louis XI, the Queen's Fountain at no 142 (corner of rue Greneta).

At no 145, the Grand-Cerf Passageway was built in 1825 on the site of the inn of the same name, a staging point until the Revolution.

Church of St-Leu-St-Gilles. — *Open from 1.30pm.* Two 6C saints, Lupus (Leu in French), Bishop of Sens, and the Provençal hermit, Giles, are patrons of this church, built in 1320 and remodelled several times. A new east end and the north tower belfry were constructed in 1858 when the Sébastopol Boulevard was laid.

Inside the nave's Gothic bays contrast with the taller classical chancel. The keystones are interesting, also a 16C marble group by Jean Bullant of St Anne and the Virgin, 15C alabaster low reliefs, fragments of an altarpiece from the former Innocents' Cemetery *(at the sacristy entrance)* and a Christ Entombed *(in the crypt)*.

Walk left down Rue St-Denis, past Rue de la Grande-Truanderie — Vagabonds' Row, contemporary with the medieval Court of Miracles *(p 155)*, which gave sanctuary to miscreants up to the 17C.

★**Fountain of the Innocents (Fontaine des Innocents).** — The 19C square stands on the site of the Cemetery and Church of the Holy Innocents which dated back to the 12C.

The cemetery with its communal graves was encircled by a charnel house about which horrific tales were told of events during the siege of Paris in 1590 by Henri of Navarre; at other times, however, in spite of a famous illustration of the Dance of Death, the area was a popular place for a stroll. In 1786 the cemetery became a market after some two million skeletons had been transferred to a quarry, renamed the Catacombs *(p 240)*.

A Renaissance masterpiece, this fountain by Pierre Lescot, carved by Jean Goujon, stood in 1550, at the corner of Rue St-Denis. Backed against a wall, it had only three sides; when removed to its present site in the 18C, a fourth side was added; a new base was substituted in 1865 — the original low reliefs are in the Louvre.

Rue de la Ferronnerie. — It was while riding in this street in his carriage that Henri IV was assassinated on 14 May 1610 in front of no **11** (a marble slab marks the site). The sign at no **13** was a crowned heart pierced by an arrow — the witnesses to the murder felt this to be an omen. His assailant, Ravaillac, was later quartered on the Place de Grève.

Rue des Lombards. — Its name is a reminder of the medieval Lombard moneylenders. The right hand corner has remained empty since 1569 after a house on the site owned by two Huguenot merchants had been razed by decree.

Rue Quincampoix. — This street was the scene of the Scots financier, **John Law's** "South Sea Bubble". Law founded a bank there in 1719. Soon speculation began to be rife: the houses all around, the street itself were crowded with those making fortunes overnight — a hunchback was said to have gained 150 000 *livres* for the use of his back as a desk. The frenzy lasted until 1720 when the bank crashed and the speculators fled. Law's house was razed when Rue Rambuteau was built.

There are several old houses at nos **10, 12, 13, 14** with unusual paved courtyards, mascarons, intricate wrought iron balconies and nailed or craved doors.

Continue to Rue St-Martin, one of the oldest streets in Paris, now tree-lined, which affords a fine view.

From St Merry to the Georges Pompidou Centre

The St Merry presbytery *(76 Rue de la Verrerie)* with its fine 18C porch gives access to the church *(open daily 9am to 7pm)*.

★**St Merry Church (Église St-Merri).** — St Merry or Medericus who died on this spot in the 7C used to be invoked for the release of captives. The building although begun in 1520 and completed in 1612, is curiously, in the 15C Flamboyant Gothic style. It was formerly the rich parish church of the Lombard moneylenders (who gave their name to the nearby street — see above).

Outside, the west face stands directly on the narrow Rue St-Martin, and small houses and shops crowd the south wall and chancel.

The Flamboyant interior was remodelled under Louis XV by the architect Boffrand and the Slodtz brothers. There remain, nevertheless, good 16C stained-glass windows, in the first three bays of the chancel and transept, and fine ribbed vaulting at the transept crossing.

In addition to the majestic 17C organ loft — the organ *(concerts: Saturdays 9pm and Sundays 4pm except in August)* itself was at one time played by Camille Saint-Saëns — and the beautiful woodwork by the Slodtz brothers in the pulpit, sacristy and the glory at the back of the choir, the church has interesting pictures.

One bell dating from 1331, probably the oldest in Paris, remains from the medieval chapel which stood on the site of the present church.

Leave St Merry's to the left by Rue de la Verrerie; go round the church by way of Rue des Juges-Consuls (officers created by Charles IX to settle differences between merchants). At the corner of Rue du Cloître-St-Merri stands an 18C house.

In the square, the **Stravinsky fountain** with black and coloured mobile sculptures by Tinguely and Niki de Saint-Phalle respectively illustrating the works of the great composer (the Rites of Spring, Firebird...) is of interest.

The St Merry Quarter. — The quarter round the church has always been crowded with craftsmen, in the Middle Ages there were linen drapers, rivalling those of Flanders, haberdashers and hairdressers — Paris' taste and fashions had begun their influence throughout Europe.

At every political insurrection the barricades went up. In June 1832, a young boy and an old man, flourishing a tricolour, were killed near the Rue du Cloître-St-Merri — an event on which Victor Hugo based his description of the death of Gavroche in his novel *Les Misérables*. Today the quarter is adjusting to its new role as the cultural centre of contemporary art.

★★GEORGES POMPIDOU CENTRE ▥ — fold 32: H 15

Open 12noon to 10pm (10am to 10pm Saturdays and Sundays). Closed Tuesdays and 1 May. 24F National Museum of Modern Art only; 35F for special exhibitions in the Grande Galerie; 55F for a pass valid all day. ☎ 42 77 12 33.

Beaubourg is the name of an old village that was included within the Philippe Auguste perimeter wall at the end of the 12C. Situated in the heart of a very old quarter; cleaned up in 1936 of its decaying houses; included in 1968 in the redevelopment plan for the site of the former Halles market *(p 142)*, the plateau was to have been the site of a public library. However, in 1969, on the initiative of Georges Pompidou (1911-1974), the then President of France, a vast programme, which would change the whole aspect of the quarter, was envisioned — it was decided to create a multi-purpose cultural centre.

Pompidou Centre

Architecture. — The architects Richard Rogers, (British) and Renzo Piano (Italian) have achieved a building (1972-1977) totally futuristic in conception.

A gigantic parallelepiped unfolds its steel frame, glass walls and bright colours 166m long, 60m wide and 42m high (545 × 197 × 138ft). Devoid of any decoration, it stands a pile of steelwork, a surrealistic sculpture confronting its onlooker. The façade is a tangle of pipes and tubes latticed along its glass skin, giving an effect of a solid yet pliant superstructure. On the façade the caterpillar-like clear tube envelops the escalators.

The skeletal construction of the centre sheathed with tubes and funnels recalls a ship or factory — the past conception of a traditional museum is rejected in its entirety.

The elimination of all possible clutter brought on by the utilities — stairs, lifts, escalators, corridors, ventilation shafts, water and gas conduits — liberates 7 500m²-80 722 square feet of free space on each floor for research, animation and information.

A slightly inclined Piazza in front of the centre — the museum's outside reception area — is the playground of artists revealing their talents: whether it be the troubadour, fire-eater, poet, mime or juggler. On the right the Children's Workshop can be seen through the window.

On the ground floor, a large open area, the Forum, made up of several levels, contains temporary exhibits, a poster shop and book store. A large hexagonal portrait of *Georges Pompidou* by Vasarély and a yellow and white composition by Soto are noteworthy.

Activities. — The Centre seeks to demonstrate that there is a close correlation between art and daily activities. For both the specialists — artists, researchers — and the general public, this multi-purpose cultural centre offers an astonishing variety of activities and modern communication techniques encouraging curiosity and participation.

The Centre includes the following:

The **Public Information Library** (BPI) — entrance on 2nd floor — offers to the public a wide variety of French and foreign books, slides, films, periodicals, reference catalogue...

The **Industrial Design Centre** (CCI) on the ground floor and mezzanine, demonstrates the relationship between individuals and spaces, objects and signs through: architecture, urbanism, industrial design and visual communication.

The **National Museum of Modern Art** (MNAM) — entrance on the third floor — presents collections of paintings, sculptures and drawings from 1905 to the present time. Special exhibitions are held on the fifth floor (Grande Galerie).

The **Institute for Acoustic and Musical Research** (IRCAM) *(located underground, between the Centre and St-Merry Church)* bring together musicians, composers and scientists for the purpose of sound experimentation.

The Salle Garance on the ground floor holds three films shows daily as part of special programmes. ☎ *42 78 37 29*. There are also facilities for special shows, discussion groups and meetings and a bookshop.

★★★NATIONAL MUSEUM OF MODERN ART

The museum has gathered under one roof an exceptional quality and variety of painting and sculpture, tracing the evolution of international art beginning with Fauvism and Cubism and continuing through the entire contemporary art scene. The majority of the works were formerly in the Museum of Modern Art in the Tokyo Palace *(p 210)* complemented more recently by acquisitions and gifts.

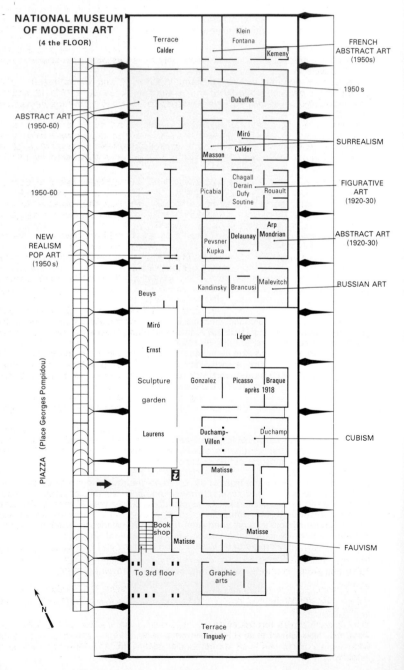

Ground floor. — *Access from the Piazza; open mornings by appointment only: extn. 4227.*
The reconstructed studio reveals where Constantin Brancusi (1876-1957), the pioneer of modern abstract sculpture, created.

4th Floor. — From 1905 to 1965. Sculptures are displayed throughout the galleries with the larger works on the **open-air terraces**: these include *Le Capricorne* by Ernst, *Une machine* by Tinguely, a Calder stabile as well as works by Miro and Laurens. To follow the chronological sequence of the movements turn right on entering, then take the galleries in an anti-clockwise direction.

To the right on entering are Matisse's *Nus de Dos*, four bronze reliefs showing a marked evolution in style between the earliest from 1909 and the latest dated 1930. The Graphic Art Room opposite has changing displays of photographs, collages and charcoal drawings.

Early 20C to post-First World War: Fauvism and Cubism. **Fauvism** (1903-10), a reactionary art movement, is characterised by a simplification of forms and strong colours. Colour and its decorative effects were used as the ultimate tool as illustrated by works such as *Rue de Marly-le-Roi* by Vlaminck, *Affiches à Trouville* by Dufy and *Les Deux Péniches* by Derain. Matisse, the leader of the movement, is represented by *The Violinist at the Window, The Roumanian Tunic, Arlequin* and his distinctive gouache cut-outs, "drawing with scissors" as the artist himself described it.

What the Fauves did for colour the **Cubists** did for form when they translated their pictorial vision by more or less geometrical forms to depict the volume or make-up of objects. The founders (1907) of the movement were Braque and Picasso, although for both of them Fauvism was only to represent a brief phase in their artistic development.

Other Cubists were the sculptor Duchamp-Villon (*Le Grand cheval majeur,* 1914), Juan Gris (*Le petit Déjeuner,* 1915) and Fernand Léger (*La Noce,* 1911-12, and the vast canvas typical of this monumental style, *Composition avec deux perroquets,* 1935-39).

The **Dada** movement came to fruition in Zurich during the First World War, in rebellion against what they saw as a civilisation intent on its own destruction; they rejected all ordinary values to create a deliberately anti-art movement (Arp). As early as 1913 Marcel Duchamp was creating his 'ready-mades' or works of art with everyday objects.

Artistic trends from post-First World War to the 1960s: Abstract Expressionism, Surrealism, New Figurative Art of the Fifties and Sixties, New Realism and Pop Art.

After the Second World War **abstraction** in one form or another became the most characteristic feature of art styles. Abstract artists generally abandoned figurative elements to concentrate on line and colour.

The movement was pioneered in 1910 by Kandinsky with his *Improvisations,* where the power of colour was given free reign, and evolved with Kupa's use of colour to suggest dynamic movement (*Autour d'un point* - 1911-30) and Mondrian's minimal geometry of horizontal and vertical lines (*Composition II,* 1937 and *New York City II,* 1942). Klee's poetic compositions remain in touch with reality while Brancusi's abstraction produced simple and highly polished sculptures *(Seal) (see the ground floor for his studio).*

Robert (*Manege de Cochons,* 1922) and Sonia Delaunay's (*Le Bal Bulier,* 1913) fascination with colour and movement, marks the intermediate stage between the geometric Cubist style and colour experimentation. Pevsner's spiral sculptures illustrate Constructivism.

From 1910 to 1930 Montparnasse was the centre of the **Paris School** formed by foreign artists to express intensity of feeling: Soutine developed a tormented expressionist style, Chagall portrayed a world of fantasy (*Autour d'Elle,*1945) and Modigliani evolved his decorative arabesques.

Rouault with his strongly religious works remained apart from the main artistic trends of the time and in contrast to his contemporaries developed a strangely sombre style.

The Dada creative techniques strongly influenced **Surrealism**, which viewed painting as a means of expressing the riches of the subconscious mind. The detailed and sometimes spontaneous works of Dali *(The ghostly cow),* Magritte, Míro (*La Sieste,* 1925) and Masson all depict the irrational and the incongruous.

In the 1950s Abstract art appealed to many French and foreign artists: some emphasised line (Hartung); others divided surfaces into large blocks of colour (Poliakoff, De Stael) or added a three-dimensional element: papier mâché on wood (*Messe de Terre,* 1959-60, by Dubuffet), interlocking sculptures (Kemeny). The COBRA movement (1948-51) advocated spontaneous expression through the use of bold colours and energetic brush strokes or footwork (*Planete nature,* 1960, by Kazuo Shiraga).

Pop' Art flourished in the United States with Rauschenberg's combine paintings (installation *Oracle,* 1962-65), Oldenburg's "sculpture objects" (*Ghost Drum Set,* 1972) and Andy Warhol's images from advertising (*10 Lizes,* 1963).

3rd Floor. — Contemporary art from 1965 to the present. This section is liable to regular rearrangement and is the place to see the works of contemporary and new generation artists.

New Realism, which expresses the prosperous urban society of the 1960s, introduced materials from everyday life which are piled up (*Home Sweet Home, Chopin's Waterloo,* 1961, by Arman), compressed (*Ricard* 1962, by César), or wrapped (Christo).

Conceptual art (1967 onwards) covers the often large-scale transitory installations such as Dubuffet's *Jardin d'hiver*, 1968-70 (take off your shoes); Joseph Beuys' *Plight*, 1985, using felt; Tetsumi Kudo's *Grafted Garden*, 1970-71; and Dorothea Tanning's *Chambre 202, Hotel du Pavot*, 1970. Jean Tinguely's *L'Enfer, un Petit Début*, 1984, is an entertaining installation of machinery in motion.

After visiting the museum, go up to the fifth floor.

From the top of the escalators a beautiful **view** of the rooftops of Paris can be seen — from right to left: hill of Montmartre and the Sacré-Cœur, St Eustache, the Eiffel Tower, Maine-Montparnasse Tower, St Merri and Notre-Dame.

THE HORLOGE QUARTER

To the north of the Georges Pompidou Centre, between Rue Beaubourg and Rue St-Martin, lies this recently renovated pedestrian quarter (colourful shops).

★**The Clock.** — *Rue Bernard-de-Clairvaux.* This unusual brass and steel clock is by Jacques Monestier. The electronically operated clock has a lifesize Jack known as the Defender of Time (Le Défenseur du Temps). With his double-edged sword and shield he gives battle on the hour with one of the three animals, symbolising the elements: a dragon (earth), a bird (air) and a crab (water). At noon, 6 and 10pm all three attack together.

At the corner of Rues Brantôme and Rambuteau stands Zadkine's Prometheus *(see museum p 259)* represented stealing fire from heaven.

Opposite Passage des Ménétriers and at the far end of Impasse Berthaud is another museum.

Musical Instruments Museum. — *Guided tours weekends and holidays from 2 to 7pm; 25F, children 15F; time: 1 1/4 hours; ☎ 42 71 99 54.*
The collection includes over 100 mechanical reproducers of music (late 19C-early 20C) all in good playing order.

From the Georges Pompidou Centre to the Hôtel de Ville

To the right, Rue Beaubourg runs along the façade of the Centre, which holds all the conduits used for the functioning of the building. Colours designate these functions: white conduits: ventilation system; blue conduits: air conditioning system; green conduits: fire prevention system; yellow conduits: electrical system; red conduits: transportation system.

Turn left into the narrow Pierre au Lard Alley. On the corner of Rue St-Merri there are two fine 17C houses (nos **12** and **9**), and a little along on the left is the sordid Cul-de-Sac du Bœuf, one of the oldest blind alleys in Paris. Rue St-Merri continues as Rue Ste-Croix-de-la-Bretonnerie. Take the road to the right called Square Ste-Croix-de-la-Bretonnerie, which opens into Rue des Archives, opposite the Billettes Church.

The Billettes Church (Église des Billettes). — *Open Sundays 10am to 12noon.* It is here, according to legend, that the miracle of the "boiled God" occurred in 1290: a usurer, Jonathan, cut a host and threw the pieces into a cooking pot; the water turned to blood and ran into the street attracting attention to the moneylender who was burned alive. In the 14C a monastery was erected on the site by the Brothers of Charity known as the Billettes on account of the heraldic billet on their habits. They were succeeded by Carmelites who in 1756 built the present sanctuary which became a Lutheran church in 1812.

The Billettes Cloister (Cloître des Billettes). — *1st door to the left after the Church.* The only remaining medieval cloister in Paris gives onto a small courtyard. Note the simplicity of its architectural elements: the ribbed vaulting of the galleries and corner bays rests on pendentives abutting the pillars.

14

★★

The
Grands Boulevards
and the
Sentier Quarter

Michelin plan **11** - folds 19, 20 and 31:
from F 13 to F 15 – from G 13 to G 17

*The following two walks will allow the tourist
to see the varying aspects of this quarter,
one of the liveliest in Paris. Well known
buildings, long tree lined vistas, a tide of
pedestrians moving earnestly on business or
idling slowly, wide café terraces with tables
overflowing onto the pavement, theatres, cinemas,
thousands of shops, in short the Boulevards –
their prestige as high, their fame as great as ever.*

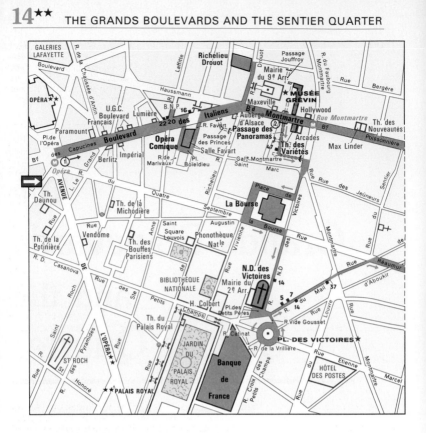

① **THE GRANDS BOULEVARDS** ▢▢ — folds 19 and 20: F 13 to G 17

Distance: 3km-2 miles — Time: 1 1/2 hours (not including the visit to the Grévin Museum). Start from the Opera métro station.

The ramparts transformed. — By 1660 Louis XIV had established himself firmly on the throne and the fortified perimeter walls around Paris had become obsolete and fallen into disrepair. The part of the Charles V wall between the Bastille and the St-Denis Gate, and the ramparts erected under Charles IX and Louis XIII *(p 20)*, were therefore knocked down, the moats filled in and a raised terrace thoroughfare constructed in their place. This fareway, sufficiently wide to allow four carriages to ride abreast, was bordered by side roads, lined by a double avenue of trees. Triumphal arches replaced the fortified gates.

The project, when it was finally completed in 1705, was known as the Boulevard. As it cut through open countryside it did not draw the crowds and was not safe after dark.

The place to take the air. — In about 1750 the Boulevard became fashionable: seated in the shade on straw-bottomed chairs Parisians watched horse carriages and riders pass by.

Gradually the west end became the area where the nobility and the rich built their private mansions; the east end, the Boulevard du Temple, almost a fairground, with crowds drawn to the theatres and dance halls, circuses, waxworks, puppets, dancers, acrobats, mechanical figures, cafés, restaurants, booths and barrows. For a hundred years the crowd rejoiced; by 1830 the local theatres had played violent melodrama for so long that the area was nicknamed the Criminal Boulevard.

Boulevard des Italiens, opened under the Directory, acquired an elegance which spread to Boulevard Montmartre and persisted until the middle of the 19C.

The roads were first paved in 1778 and about the same time street lights, burning animal fat, appeared and were declared altogether blinding; gas lamps were installed in the Passage des Panoramas *(p 154)* in 1817, and on the Boulevard in 1826. The first bus appeared on 30 January 1828 when it travelled from the Madeleine to the Bastille. Footpaths were surfaced.

Madeleine-Bastille Omnibus

The modern boulevard. — The creation by Haussmann of the Opera and Republic Squares and the wide highways leading to them, began the transformation which still goes on as crowds replace the fashionable; lights become more glaring; advertising irons out distinctive features; famous cafés disappear or are turned into anonymous brasseries and cinemas; the elegant carriages have given way to roaring traffic — and the only constant is the Parisian himself.

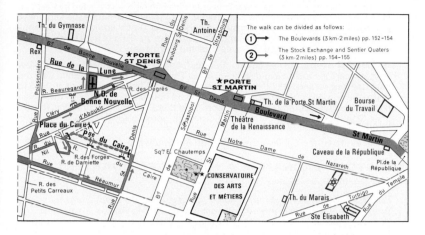

From the Opera to Richelieu-Drouot

Walk from the Opera Square *(p 82)* along the east end of Boulevard des Capucines *(p 82)* to Boulevard des Italiens.

The old Boulevard des Italiens. — The street's history is linked with fads and fashions. *Muscadins* and *Merveilleuses* haunted it at the time of the Directory; *Gandins* during the Restoration, were succeeded by Dandies who also followed English fashion and, in 1835, were the first to smoke in public. Waxed moustaches, imperials and crinolines appeared during the Second Empire when café society flourished.

The boulevard today. The uninspired Palais Berlitz, at the corner of the Rue Louis-le-Grand, has replaced the Pavillon de Hanovre, the favourite ice-cream restaurant of the *Merveilleuses*; no **22** is where the Café Tortoni stood; no **20**, the famous **Maison Dorée** restaurant (built 1839-1841) was once the meeting place for fashionable Paris; elegantly decorated façades line the boulevard and Rue Lafitte (view of the Sacré-Cœur); no **16** is where the Café Riche received its patrons from 1791 until early this century.

The Opéra-Comique. — The present building stands on the site of the theatre constructed by the Duke of Choiseul in 1782 in his own grounds for the Comic Opera company *(p 145)*, commonly called "the Italians". The boulevard took its name from the company.
The company gradually changed its repertoire from French to Italian light opera and ultimately, with Offenbach and Johann Strauss, included operettas.

Richelieu-Drouot Crossroads. — The Auberge d'Alsace, stands on the site of what was known, in the 17C, as the "modest and secluded" house of the poet, Regnard. Opposite, in 1796, was the famous Café Frascati which closed down when gambling was banned by Louis-Philippe.
To the left of the road junction at no 9 Rue Drouot is the new building, **Richelieu Drouot,** *(☎ 48 00 20 20; open daily 11am to 6pm; closed Sundays, holidays and in August)* of the Paris art auctioneer company. Reopened on 13 May 1980 the 16 auction rooms, with daily auctions at 2pm, provide a lively and interesting spectacle. Rue Drouot is also the haunt of stamp-collectors.

From Richelieu-Drouot to the Place de la République

Boulevard Montmartre. — On the right at no 11 is the Passage des Panoramas *(p 154)*. At no 7 stands the **Théâtre des Variétés** built in 1807, the home of light comedy and operetta presenting the wit and gaiety of Meilhac and Halévy, Offenbach, Flers and Caillavet, Tristan Bernard and Sacha Guitry.

★**Grévin Museum** (Musée Grévin). — *10 Boulevard Montmartre (see also p 143). Open 1pm (10am during holidays and school holidays) to 7pm (last admission 6pm); 46F; children 32F. ☎ 47 70 85 05.*
Grévin, a caricaturist, founded the museum in 1882. (The first waxworks were introduced to Paris in the 18C). In addition to likenesses of celebrities from the world of art, politics, sports, it contains historical scenes, distorting mirrors, conjuring sessions — amusement for one and all.

Continue along Boulevards Poissonnière and Bonne-Nouvelle. **Rue de la Lune,** to the right, forms a sharp angle with Rue de Cléry, typical of old Paris.
Further on, these boulevards become St-Denis and St-Martin Boulevards, each marked at its start by a monumental gate.

★**Porte St-Denis.** — The gate — 24m-75ft high — was erected by the city in 1672 in celebration of Louis XIV's victories on the Rhine — 40 strongholds captured in less than two months. On either side are carvings of the pyramids superimposed with trophies and on the boulevard side, allegorical figures representing Holland *(left)* and the Rhine *(right)*; above the arch can be seen the crossing of the Rhine; and on the faubourg side, the Fall of Maëstricht.

★**Porte St-Martin.** — The gate which is only 17m-56ft high was erected by the dean of the merchants' guild and the aldermen in 1674 to commemorate the capture of Besançon and defeat of the German, Spanish and Dutch armies. The carvings illustrate not only the taking of Besançon but also the breaking of the Triple Alliance, the capture of Limburg and the defeat of the Germans.

Boulevard St-Martin. — Built in an undulating area, the boulevard runs below the pavement in order to avoid steep inclines. Two adjoining theatres stand near the gate: the Renaissance (1872) and the Porte St-Martin. The latter was built in 1781 to house the company from the Palais-Royal opera house which had been destroyed by fire. The first masked Opera balls were held there. It became a dramatic theatre after 1814. Burned down during the Commune uprising *(p 106)*, it was rebuilt in 1873.

Continue down the Boulevard to Place de la République *(p 257)*.

② STOCK EXCHANGE AND SENTIER QUARTERS
🗺 — folds 19, 31, 32 and 20: F 14, G 14, G 15

Distance: 3km-2miles — Time: 2 hours (not including the Stock Exchange). Start from the Rue Montmartre métro station. Try to do this visit on a weekday.

No 11 Boulevard Montmartre is the **Passage des Panoramas** which was opened in 1799. The name comes from the two vast panoramas of capital cities and historic scenes painted and displayed in rotundas by the American, Henry Fulton, who also invented submarines and perfected steam ships. No **47** an engraver's shop, has kept its old aspect.

Turn right into Rue N.-D. des Victoires to reach Place de la Bourse.

Stock Exchange (Palais de la Bourse). — The building and the square stand on the site of a Dominican convent which was secularized in 1795 and became the seat of the royalist faction responsible for the insurrection of 13 Vendémiaire — 5 October 1795 — *(p 139)*.

Paris' first exchange was John Law's bank *(p 146)*. As a result of his bankruptcy, the public learned so much about shares and holdings that a public exchange was founded (1724). It was situated in the Mazarin Mansion *(p 137)*, then in the church of Notre-Dame des Victoires and in the Palais-Royal. The present building was begun by Brongniart in 1808, completed in 1826 and enlarged in 1902 and 1907. There is much activity in the square and in front of the building between 12.30 and 2.30pm on weekdays.

Inside the public may visit a gallery *(guided tours every 30 min from 11am to 1pm, except Saturdays, Sundays and holidays; 1 July to 15 September, two tours daily at 12noon and 12.30pm; time: 1 1/2 hour; 10F; for further information ☎ 42 33 99 83)*. From another gallery one can see the actual exchange.

Continue along Rue Notre-Dame-des-Victoires (note the 18C mansion at no **14**) to Place des Petits-Pères, which has been built on the site of the Monastery of the Barefoot Augustinians.

Basilica of Notre-Dame-des-Victoires. — The basilica (built 1629-1740) served as the monastery chapel and later, was occupied by the Exchange from 1795-1809. Inside are 17C panelling in the chancel, seven paintings by Van Loo (*Louis XIII dedicating the church to the Virgin,* scenes from the *Life of St Augustine*), a fine 18C organ loft and a monument to the 17C composer, Lulli *(2nd chapel on the left)*. The church is famous for its annual pilgrimage to the Virgin which goes back to 1836; some 35 000 ex-votos cover the walls.

From the church, walk along the short Rue Vide-Gousset (Pickpocket Street) to Place des Victoires.

★ **PLACE DES VICTOIRES** 🗺 — fold 31: G 14

In 1685 Marshal de la Feuillade, to curry favour with Louis XIV, commissioned a statue of the king from the sculptor, Desjardins. The statue, unveiled in 1686, showed the king, crowned with the laurels of victory, standing on a pedestal adorned with six low reliefs and four captives representing the vanquished Spain, Holland, Prussia and Austria. Mansart designed the façades overlooking the square where the statue was erected.

The statue was melted down in 1792; a new figure by Desaix replaced it in 1806 only to be melted down in turn in 1815 (and reappear as Henri IV on the Pont Neuf!). The present equestrian statue of the Sun King was sculpted by Bosio in 1822.

The side of the square with even numbers is the least damaged and gives some idea of the intended 17C elegance although its harmony was impaired by the construction of Rue Etienne Marcel in 1883.

One of the façades of the **Bank of France** can be seen on looking along Rue Catinat, from the entrance of Rue d'Aboukir. The Bank on Rue de la Vrillière was founded at the instigation of Napoleon in January 1800. First housed at no **4** Rue d'Aboukir, it moved in 1812, to the mansion *(not open)* built in 1635 by François Mansart and remodelled by Robert de Cotte. The present building dates mostly from the 19C.

From Place des Victoires to Boulevard Bonne-Nouvelle

Walk out of Place des Victoires along Rue Vide-Gousset and turn into Rue du Mail. At nos **5** and **7** (both 17C) belonging to Louis XIV's minister, Colbert, are, on the upper capitals, a faun's mask and cornucopias and interlaced snakes (the snake — *coluber* in Latin — Colbert's emblem), respectively. At no **14**, an 18C hôtel, lived Madame Récamier.

The Sentier. — The Sentier quarter begins on the other side of Rue Montmartre. It is the centre of the wholesale trade for materials, trimmings, hosiery and ready-made clothes.

After Rue de Cléry, turn right into Rue Réaumur, continue to Rue St-Denis, where you turn left to reach the Passage du Caire.

Caire Passage and Square. — Napoleon's victorious campaign in Egypt in 1798 aroused great enthusiasm in Paris — architecture and fashion were greatly influenced and streets and squares in this area (formerly convent grounds) were given names in memory of his successes.
Walk under the covered arcades of the strange Passage du Caire to the square (the heart of the old Court of Miracles) where the outlet is overlooked by a house with a façade decorated with Egyptian motifs.

The Court of Miracles. — A Court of Miracles was a place where, in the Middle Ages, miscreants lived out of the reach of the authorities. Blind alleys and passage-ways, easily defended, opened off the muddy courtyard and the police did not often venture inside the area. It was the refuge of well organised bands of rogues led by their own elected king.
During daylight, the lame, the blind and the maimed went out to beg in town; at night they returned, shed their wooden legs and other props and indulged in the orgies described vividly by Victor Hugo in the *Hunchback of Notre-Dame*. It was this nightly miraculous cure from infirmity that gave the court its name.
Turn left onto Rue des Forges which runs into Rue de Damiette and Rue du Nil. The crowded Rue des Petits-Carreaux leads to Rue de Cléry.

Mount Orgueil. — The Rue de Cléry is the old counterscarp of the Charles V perimeter wall; turn left into Rue des Degrés which now crosses the houses by means of steps which once crossed the ramparts. The whole quarter stands on Mount Orgueil, a natural mound used as a redoubt and which, in the 16C, afforded a good viewpoint over the capital — hence the name of the street, Beauregard, which you follow to Notre-Dame de Bonne-Nouvelle.

Notre-Dame-de-Bonne-Nouvelle. — *Closed 1pm to 3.30pm.* The classical belfry is all that remains of the church restored by Anne of Austria — the remainder of the building dates from 1823-1829. Inside numerous paintings decorate the walls. Note the one by Mignard above the door in the south aisle of Anne of Austria and Henrietta-Maria, wife of Charles I of England, at the end of the north aisle showing Henrietta of England and her three children before St Francis of Sales, an Annunciation by Lanfranco *(centre of the chancel, light-switch on the right)*, and a painting by Philippe de Champaigne *(to the right)*. In the Lady Chapel there is a fine 18C Virgin and Child attributed to Pigalle.
A small museum contains works of art: 17C alabaster statue of St Jerome; two Descents from the Cross, an 18C silk vestment.

By taking Rue de la Lune *(p 153)* on the right one arrives at Boulevard Bonne-Nouvelle.

Place des Victoires

15

★★

La Villette

Michelin plan **11** - folds 10 and 11: B 20, B 21, C 20, C 21

*Métro station: Porte de la Villette
(north – City of Science and Industry)
and Porte de Pantin (south – Great Hall)*

*La Villette cattle market and slaughter houses
formerly occupied the area between the Porte de
la Villette and the Porte de Pantin bordered
by the St-Denis Canal and traversed by the
L'Ourcq Canal which was dug in 1812 to feed all
the Paris fountains. In winter it was turned
into a skating-rink.
On its banks were stored coal transported in
winter from the coalmines of northern France and
goods from the French colonies.*

During the Second Empire the slaughter houses and the cattle market with its three halls (including the Great Hall) were built and were soon in full operation; these buildings were to remain in use for over a hundred years. In 1969 work started on a vast auction hall to replace the old buildings but under increasing pressure from the refrigeration industry the work stopped and in 1974 operations were moved to the new Rungis market.

An urban complex has been created on the 55 hectare-136 acre site: the City of Science and Industry, the Géode, the Great Hall, the Paris-Villette theatre (former exchange), the Zenith, the Music City, and the park.

Public housing, restaurants, baths and a hotel complete the project.

★★★THE CITY OF SCIENCE AND INDUSTRY
(CITÉ DES SCIENCES ET DE L'INDUSTRIE)

Open daily 10am to 6pm; closed Mondays; ☎ 40 05 70 00; groups ☎ 40 05 70 70; Minitel: 36 15 VILLETTE. Inventorium: 15F; City day-pass: 35F; Planetarium (supplement to City day-pass): 15F; hire of infra-red hedset: 15F; yearly season ticket: 200F.

All floors are accessible to wheelchairs.

A reception team fluent in 18 languages (including sign language) and a videoguide are available to visitors at the four reception counters.

Explora: for an in-depth tour of the exhibition, allow one day for each of the four sectors.

The City of Science and Industry was inaugurated in 1986. The architect Adrian Fainsilber converted the shell of the former auction hall to house the project devised by Maurice Lévy. Fainsilber was awarded the Prize for Architecture in 1987.

The building. — This massive structure made of granite, steel and glass rises on a 4 hectare-10 acre site. The building, framed by massive pillars marking four large bays and crowned by blue girders, is reflected in the surrounding water-filled moat. The south façade, which is mirrored in the Géode's globe, is enhanced by three square bio-climatic glasshouses (32m-105ft across) with panes of clear tempered glass suspended one above the other on high-technology runners. Hydraulic glass lifts with a telescopic jack move up and down among the plants.

Inside the 100m-328ft long hall escalators — with the mechanism encased in glass — lead up to the Explora exhibition. At a height of 40m-131ft two rotating domes — 17m-55ft in diameter — track the course of the sun and computer-controlled mirrors reflect sunlight throughout the building.

Many contemporary art works inspired from the world of science come into their own in this museum devoted to science and industry: *Souvenirs* by J. Monory around the Planetarium or *Inventing the Earth* by Jeffrey Shaw where visitors look through a periscope to view a series of images recorded on videodisc.

TOUR

The City of Science and Industry invites visitors to participate in the great scientific, technological and industrial adventure of modern times. The scientific and industrial displays have been devised for amusement, information and learning purposes. As the City of Science and Industry is a progressive undertaking with new displays and activities presented at intervals, return visits are recommended to keep up with new developments.

The planetarium. — *Level 2.* Scientific and imaginative presentation of the solar system combining true pictures, an astronomical simulator and a triphonic system. The shows include "Children of the Sun" and "The adventures of Starball".

Children's activities. — Introduction to science and technology for children 3 to 12 years old and multi-media library *(mediathèque) (basement 1)*.

"The adventures of Starball". — *Level 2.* Show for 5 to 10 year olds at the planetarium.

Inventorium. — *Level 0.* Two large areas reserved for children aged 3 to 6 years and 6 to 12 years. Workshops and special equipment help to gain an understanding of the world.

Mediathèque. — *Basement 1.* This multi-media library contains a large collection of books, magazines, videodiscs and educational software. It is open to all but there is a specialist section for professional visitors; it offers a wide range of services from assistance to readers to access to external data banks. Card holders can make an electronic reservation for documents available on loan from outside terminals.

Other facilities. — The science newsroom *(level 0)* presents an interactive introduction to economic and scientific activity.

The Louis Lumière cinema *(level 0)* which aims to make science accessible to a wide public is counterbalanced by a research centre in the history of science and technology (from 1789 to the present day) and an international conference centre *(basement 1)* open to research scientists and industrialists from all over the world.

Temporary exhibitions on current topics are changed every 3 to 5 months.

If you are only staying a few days in Paris, the map on p 6 shows you how to see the capital's unique sights in four days.

The Géode

★★★The Géode (La Géode)

Opposite the south façade of the City of Science and Industry.
Film shows every hour from 10am to 9pm; closed Mondays; 45F; reduced
admission (excluding weekends and holidays): 35F. ☎ 40 05 80 00 or for groups
only: ☎ 40 05 06 07; Minitel 36 15 VILLETTE, code GEODE. Tickets for sale on the
premises or through Minitel.
The shining steel globe, 36m-118ft in diameter, designed by Adrien Fainsilber,
which is mirrored in a sheet of water, is a brilliant feat of engineering both in terms
of structure and equipment.

Boldness and perfection. — The 6 000 tons of seating in the auditorium are
supported by a single pillar and a fine web structure while the globe built
independently by Chamayou combines a complex structure and sophisticated
technology.
The geodesic mesh frame, assembled to a degree of precision of less than 1/10mm
is sheathed in steel. The perfect globe is composed of 6 433 stainless steel triangles
and expansion is absorbed by the fastenings.

The auditorium. — The hall which has an inclination of 30°, is equipped with 357
reclining seats from which can be seen a hemispherical 1 000m² screen in perforat-
ed aluminium for sound reproduction. The equipment comprises a multi-media
system, an Omnimax projector (70mm film running horizontally to project a picture
nine times bigger than the 35mm film) and a sound capacity of 16 800w reproduced
by 12 quadrophonic amplifiers and 6 low frequency modules.
The distortion occurring from the curved screen, 26m-85ft across is unusual but the
panoramic views are very realistic. The wide-angle lens and the 180° projection field
which is higher than the human field of vision (140°), create a bird's-eye view.

Programme. — About 50 films on science are shown at the Geode.

★★★Explora

The permanent exhibition on three upper levels of the City of Science and Industry
presents scientific knowledge in an enjoyable and attractive fashion which encour-
ages experimentation as this is not a traditional museum. The exhibition is
organised in four sectors introducing concrete data, scientific principle and technology: From the Earth to the Universe, The Adventure of Life, Matter and the Work
of Man, and Language and Communication.
Each sector covers a number of themes in a vertical progression on three levels.
Visitors may be inclined to wander freely rather than follow the strict order of
presentation and it is advisable to hire an infra-red headset which picks up the
appropriate commentary for each display *(available in 4 languages — hire on levels*
0 and 1).
Explora is aimed at all types of visitors through three different approaches: firstly an
easy, direct contact with the exhibits, secondly an interactive stage with active
involvement through the use of touch screens and simulators, and finally a
conceptual approach based on information panels and computerized data.

A quick tour. — Visitors who are pressed for time should see the sector "The
Adventure of Life" (meteorological station, aquaculture, greenhouse bridge), the
sector "From the Earth to the Universe" (*Nautilus* submarine, Ariane rocket and
orbital space station) and the sector "Language and Communication" (tracking of
eye movement, odorama) and finally the science newsroom. If there is time take in a
show at the Planetarium or the Géode.

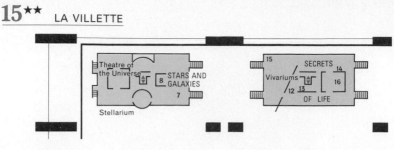

LEVEL 2a

Theatre of the Universe
8 STARS AND GALAXIES
7
Stellarium

15 SECRETS 14
Vivariums 16
12 13
OF LIFE

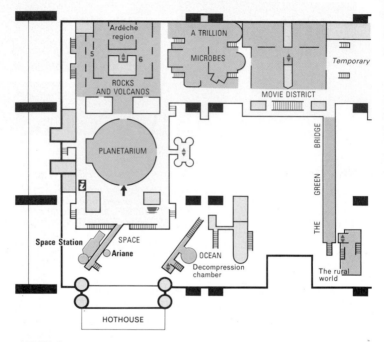

LEVEL 2

Ardèche region
5 6
ROCKS AND VOLCANOS

A TRILLION MICROBES

Temporary

MOVIE DISTRICT

PLANETARIUM

THE GREEN BRIDGE

Space Station
SPACE
Ariane

OCEAN
Decompression chamber

The rural world

HOTHOUSE

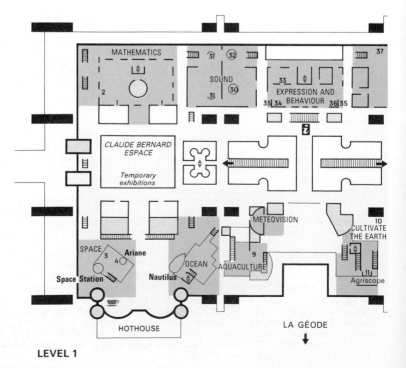

LEVEL 1

MATHEMATICS
2
1 1

31 32
SOUND
30
31

37

33
EXPRESSION AND BEHAVIOUR
35 34
36 35

CLAUDE BERNARD ESPACE

Temporary exhibitions

METEOVISION

10
CULTIVATE THE EARTH

SPACE
3 Ariane
4
Space Station

OCEAN
Nautilus
AQUACULTURE
9

11
Agriscope

HOTHOUSE

LA GÉODE
↓

CITY OF SCIENCE AND INDUSTRY «EXPLORA»

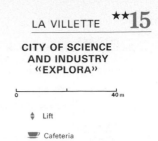

0 ————————— 40 m

⇕ Lift

☕ Cafeteria

Some sections of Explora may be temporarily closed for rearrangement or for large-scale reorganization. Therefore the location of certain exhibits may change and the following descriptions are accordingly subject to change.

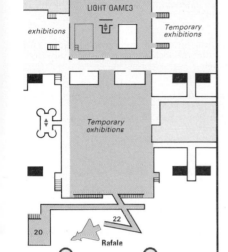

COMMUNICATIONS ORIENTATION TABLE

LIGHT GAMES

exhibitions

Temporary exhibitions

Temporary exhibitions

20

22

Rafale

HOTHOUSE

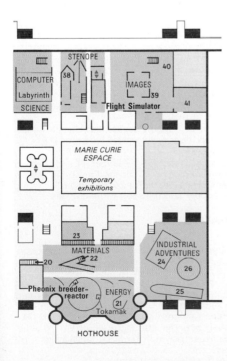

STENOPE

COMPUTER 38

Labyrinth

SCIENCE

IMAGES 39

40

Flight Simulator

41

MARIE CURIE ESPACE

Temporary exhibitions

23

MATERIALS

22

20

INDUSTRIAL ADVENTURES

24

26

25

Pheonix breeder-reactor

ENERGY 21

Tokamak

HOTHOUSE

Ariane rocket

General presentation of the exhibition. — The following table lists the highlights to enable the visitor to plan a tour to suit his own tastes and time available. In each sector there is a qualified attendant.

Sectors of EXPLORA	Selected exhibitions

FROM THE EARTH TO THE UNIVERSE

level 1

The Ocean — The Nautilus: full-scale model of the latest French submarine which can reach a depth of 6 000m-19 700ft.

Mathematics — Fresco of the history of mathematics (1), the shortest distance (2).

levels 1 and 2

Space — Third stage of Ariane rocket, orbital space station *(10 min)*. Games: the MMU space (3), living in space (4).

level 2

Rocks and Volcanos — Geological history of the Ardeche region *(1/4 hour)*. Mineral clock (5). Movements of the continents (6).

level 2a

Stars and Galaxies — Theatre of the Galaxies *(1/2 hour)*, the Big Bang theory (7), stellarium *(10 min)*. Theatre of the Sun (8) *(1/4 hour)*.

THE ADVENTURE OF LIFE

level 1

Meteovision — Weather forecasting centre *(1/4 hour)*.

Aquaculture — Fish hatchery (9).

Cultivate the Earth — Wheat futures (10), Agriscope (history and modernization of agriculture - *40 min*), forest display (11) *(11 min)*.

The Green Bridge — Hi-tech glasshouse: crops grown in media other than soil and in-vitro. Biotechnology techniques.

level 2

A Trillion Microbes — A trillion living species: enemies as agents of illness and allies in disease control (penicillin and vaccination), creation of new micro-organisms.

level 2a

The Secrets of Life — Bio-Meter (12), Evolottery (14) (evolution of human population), stress (13), genes (15), cine-bio (16) *(20 min)*.

MATTER AND THE WORK OF MAN

level 1

Energy: management of resources — A dispatching centre (20): hydraulic and nuclear power plants *(10 min)*. The Shadocks (21): energy and Entropy, perpetual motion. Particle accelerator: nuclear reaction (Tokamak). Debate on the nature of matter *(3/4 hour)*.

Materials: old and new — Section of Renault Espace (22), Rafale fighter plane. A modern automated workshop (23) *(1 1/2 hours)*.

Industrial Adventures — Industrial case studies: Dumper (24) and Michelin tyre technology, TGV or the French high-speed train (25) and Gaz de France (26) exhibit illustrating the supply and transport of natural gas.

LANGUAGES AND COMMUNICATION

level 1

Sound — Sound bubble (30), sound refraction and propagation. Parabolic sound dishes (31). Sound in space, loss of hearing, speed of sound (32).

Expression and Behaviour — The Eye Tracker (33), *(1/4 hour)*, Odorama (34) (sound images with smells released in the room *10 min*). Hall of Greetings (35) (how people of different cultures greet each other), rituals (36).

Computer Science — Colour a graph (37), flight simulator *(10 min)*. Daedelus: labyrinth (artificial intelligence - *1/4 hour*). Expert systems, programming.

| Images | Photography, cinematography, videoscopy. Reality on screen **(41)** *(14 min)*, film projections **(39)** *(1/4 hour)*, film clip **(40)** *(5 min)*. Electronic microscopy, X-rays, scanner. |
| Stenope | Pinholes to demonstrate the representation of space: double perspective room **(38)** *(20 min)*, optical illusions and perspective. |

level 2

| Movie District | Science in our civilization: historical mural illustrating the inventions and discoveries of man. The image of man *(20 min)*. |
| Light Games | Propagation of light, the origins of colours, 3-D vision, optical illusions. |

level 2a

| Communications Orientation Table | Evolution of communications: Morse telegraph to a video-phone prototype. Applications in different domains: geopolitics, economics and society. |

★★LA VILLETTE PARK *time: 2 hours*

La Villette park, the largest park within the city walls, is more than just an open space. It is a new dynamic quarter combining science and technology, art and gardens and it is the setting for all sorts of events and activities.

Galleries and follies. — The park designed by B. Tschumi comprises a geometric structure, the La Villette and L'Ourcq galleries intersecting at right angles, and a promenade meandering through green spaces, gardens and recreation areas.

Follies. — There are 9 red-roofed pavilions, built of enamelled iron over a concrete frame, laid out 120m-394ft apart in a grid pattern throughout the park. The word "folly", used to denote 18C pavilions, is here given a scientific dimension harmonising with the nearby City of Science and Industry to describe varied cubical structures with a cross-section of 10.80m-36ft. Each has a distinctive feature: a slide, weather vane or belvedere... Some, like the children's pavilion, are reproductions of structures designed by Le Corbusier in the 1930s.

Galleries. — La Villette gallery is a direct link between the Porte de la Villette and the Porte de Pantin. The undulating canopy is suspended from a beam which also supports the deck of the bridge spanning the Ourcq, along the latter stands the gallery de l'Ourcq. The galleries which bound two sides of the triangular meadow are lined with 52 fifty-year-old plane trees which have been transplanted from the Lion Fountain Square.

The great hall. — The hall (Grande Halle) built by J. de Merindol (1867) is a modern construction combining cast-iron columns, an iron frame and lead roof. Cattle auctions were held there for over a hundred years, from 1867 to 1974. Then it was the setting for various events and rock concerts until 1983 when it was converted by the architects B. Reichen and P. Robert into a multi-purpose venue with moveable partitions and a capacity of over 15 000.
Overlooking the Lion Fountain Square (Place de la Fontaine aux Lions), the main glass façade opens into a vast hall complemented by three 200m²-2 152sq ft platforms on wheels and the North Hall which can be completely partitioned off. The Boris Vian Gallery in the basement is reached from the middle of the hall.

Activities. — A full programme of artistic and popular events includes the following which are held on a regular basis: Housing *(mid-April)*, Sound and Image Technology Show (SATIS) *(late April)* and the Music Show *(mid-September)*.

La Villette Centre (Veterinarians' Rotunda). — Housed in the central part of the Maison de la Villette, a local history exhibition presents documentary information on the slaughter houses and adjoining areas. The latest techniques are used to feature oral history and the testimony of local people through a resource centre, workshops and meetings.

Le Zenith. — This hall which can accommodate 6 000 spectators is used mainly for variety and rock concerts. Its light structure covered with a canopy is also suitable for business meetings and conferences.

Tour of the Garden. — A promenade is laid out through the grounds which are planted with 18 000 young trees, mainly willows (15 500), hornbeams, some white willows as well as golden and Pennsylvania ash.

Energy garden (Jardin de l'Energie). — This garden by A. Chemetoff, laid out in a 6m-19ft pit to create a micro-climate and encourage the growth of bamboo, is enhanced by a composition by D. Buren who is also responsible for the black and white columns at the Palais Royal *(p 137)*. Alternate bands of black and white pebbles, black and green bamboo extend to the energy wall which dispenses heat and humidity through a system of superimposed gargoyles. At the far end of the garden, B. Leitner's sound cylinder is an experiment relating to the perception of sound in space.

Garden (Jardin de la Treille). — This conventional garden is by A. Vexlard.

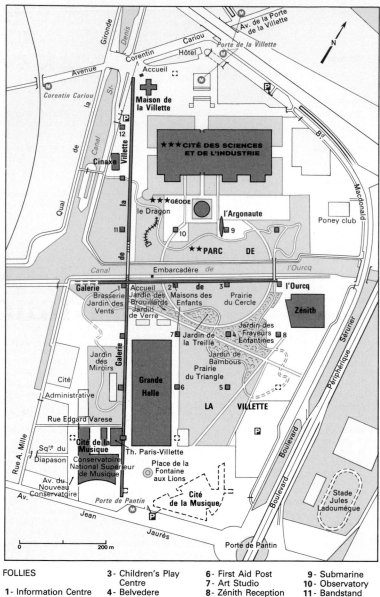

FOLLIES

1- Information Centre
2- Video Studio
3- Children's Play Centre
4- Belvedere
5- Café
6- First Aid Post
7- Art Studio
8- Zénith Reception and Ticket Office
9- Submarine
10- Observatory
11- Bandstand
12- Fast Food

The sections under construction or at planning stage are indicated by a broken line.

Meadows (Prairies). — The triangular meadow along the Great Hall and the half-moon meadow between the hall and the Géode have been created using the techniques developed for sports grounds: drains, slits, sand and clay mix for drainage, retractable automatic sprinklers which dispense 5mm of water daily.

Music City (Cité de la Musique). — South of the park, on either side of the Lion Fountain, this complex by C. de Portzamparc will include the Higher National Music Conservatory. The west side will be devoted to a music school while the east wing will house a concert hall, an instruments gallery displaying the collections of the museum of musical instruments and a school of music.

Activities

For children. — A pony-club and two pavilions have been planned for children.

Children's centre (Maison des Enfants). — *Open Wednesdays and during school holidays.* There are two workshops in two separate buildings; introduction to video and plastic arts with qualified staff.

The Dragon. — This gigantic coloured slide by François Ghys towers above the intersection of the two canals.

For all. — A gallery of video art is located in one of the pavilions. Cinemas, baths, restaurants and a neighbourhood centre are also planned.

At the Great Hall. — Concerts, plays, salons and exhibitions.

At the Paris-La Villette Theatre. — Performances by a theatre company.

16
★★

The Faubourg St-Germain

Michelin plan **11** - folds 29 and 30: from H 10 to J 12

Distance: 4km-2 1/2 miles — Time: 3 1/2 hours
Start from the Assemblée Nationale métro station

The « noble faubourg » which lies off the far bank of the Seine from the Tuileries and east of the Invalides, includes many fine old 18C town houses and monuments. The stately private residences have been converted to government offices and embassies and it remains as difficult as ever to see the houses behind the monumental gateways.

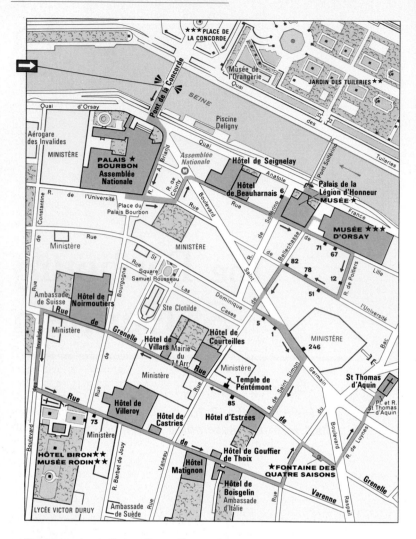

Only through a half-open door will you glimpse the beautiful façades erected by Delisle-Mansart, Boffrand or other 18C architects. The faubourg St-Germain was originally, as its name implies, the suburb *(faubourg)* of the town which developed round the Abbey of St-Germain-des-Prés *(p 176)*. Until the end of the 16C the surrounding countryside was used for farming and hunting, except for a strip of meadow at the river's edge finally won from the abbey by the University and named the Clerks' Meadow.

In the 17C Marguerite of Valois, first wife of Henri IV, took the east end of the meadow from the University as part of the grounds in which to build a vast mansion with a garden running down to the Seine. The acquisition was made so casually that the embankment came to be called the Malacquis (distorted to Malaquais) or Misappropriated Quay. On the death of Queen Marguerite in 1615 the University tried to reclaim the land but, after twenty years of legal proceedings, succeeded only in having the main street of the new quarter named the Rue de l'Université.

The district was at its most fashionable in the 18C. Noble lords and rich financiers built houses which gave the streets an individual character: one monumental entrance followed another, each opening on a courtyard closed at the far end by the façade of an elegant mansion behind which lay a large garden.

The Revolution closed these sumptuous town houses and although they reopened their doors at the Restoration, the quarter never fully regained its status, as the fashionable, at the time of Louis-Philippe and Napoleon III, migrated to the Champs-Élysées. Several mansions were pulled down when Boulevard St-Germain and Boulevard Raspail were opened. The finest houses remaining now belong to the state or serve as ambassadorial residences. Something of the quarter's great days can, however, still be recalled in the Rues de Lille, Grenelle and Varenne.

Join us in our neverending task of keeping up to date.
Send us your comments and suggestions, please.

Michelin Tyre Public Limited Company
Tourism Department
Lyon Road — HARROW — Middlesex HA1 2DQ.

From Concorde Bridge
to the Palace of the Legion of Honour

Pont de la Concorde. — The bridge was designed by the civil engineer, Perronet, in 1787 when he was 79. It was completed by 1791, the stones from the Bastille having been used in its construction so that, it was said, "the people could forever trample the ruins of the old fortress". During Louis-Philippe's reign the bridge was decorated with 12 colossal statues of famous men but the ornament was not liked and the figures were dispatched first to Versailles and subsequently dispersed to provincial towns!

Walk to the centre of the bridge, which was doubled in width in 1932, for remarkable **views**★★ along the Seine and across Place de la Concorde to the Madeleine.

★PALAIS BOURBON 🔟 — fold 30: H 11

In 1722 the Duchess of Bourbon, daughter of Louis XIV and Mme de Montespan, acquired land on which to build a house fronting on the Rue de l'Université. By 1728 the palace and terraced gardens running down to the Seine were complete.

Twenty-eight years later Louis XV bought the property so that it could be altered to form part of the general scheme of the Concorde Square; in 1764, however, Louis XVI sold it to the Prince of Condé who enlarged and embellished it. Finally, the adjoining **Hôtel de Lassay** was added and renamed the Petit or Little Bourbon.

Work was almost finished when the Revolution broke out. The palace was confiscated to serve as a chamber for the Council of the Five Hundred. Next it was used to house archives and Lassay House and its outbuildings as accommodation for the École Polytechnique. In 1807 Napoleon commissioned Poyet to design the present façade overlooking the Place de la Concorde in harmony with the Greek plan of the Madeleine. At the Restoration the palace was returned to the Condés only to be bought back in 1827 and converted for use by the Legislative Assembly.

Exterior. — The antique style façade with a portico is decorated with an allegorical pediment by Cortot (1842), statues (copies), on high, of Minerva by Houdon and Themis by Roland, and below, among other figures, those of Henri IV and Louis XIV's ministers, Sully and Colbert. The allegorical low reliefs on the wings are by Rude *(right)* and Pradier *(left)*.

Take Rue Aristide-Briand, on the left, to Place du Palais-Bourbon from which you will get a good view of the 18C palace.

Interior. — *Guided tours Saturdays 10am, 2pm and 3pm; entrance: 33 Quai d'Orsay; some form of identification is required;* ☎ *40 63 63 08..*

Among the most impressive of the many rooms decorated with paintings and sculpture, are the lobby, with its ceiling by Horace Vernet, the Council Chamber and the **Library**★★. This is a fine room in itself and, in addition, magnificently decorated with a History of Civilisation, painted by Delacroix between 1838 and 1845. Houdon's portrait busts of Voltaire and Diderot are also in the library.

Council Chamber. — *Apply to 33, Quai d'Orsay when the Assembly is in session, to attend a debate in the National Assembly.* Proceedings are conducted by the President of the **National Assembly** from the bureau formerly used for the Council of the Five Hundred *(see above)*. He faces the deputies — 577 when all are present — seated on benches arranged in a semicircle. Government members occupy the front bench below the speaker's stand (N. B. the political right and left are as viewed by the president and therefore the reverse as seen from the gallery).

Walk out of Place du Palais-Bourbon, along Rue de l'Université, down Rue de Courty across Boulevard St-Germain to Rue de Lille and turn right.

This street, named after the town of Lille, is typical of the old "noble faubourg". Nos 80 and 78 were designed by the architect, Boffrand in 1714. The first, the **Hôtel de Seignelay**, occupied by the Ministry of Commerce and Tourism, was owned originally by Colbert's grandson, then by the Duke of Charost, tutor to the young Louis XV and aristocrat philanthropist who was saved from the guillotine by his own peasants. By 1839 it had passed to Marshal Lauriston, a descendant of John Law, the Scots financier *(p 146)*.

The **Hôtel de Beauharnais**, next door, received its name when Napoleon's son-in-law bought it in 1803 and redecorated it sumptuously for his own and his sister, Queen Hortense's, use. Since 1818 the house has been the seat of first the Prussian, and later, the German diplomatic missions to France. Now restored, it is the residence of the German ambassador.

The writer Jules Romain lived at no **6** Rue Solférino from 1947 to his death (1972).

PALACE OF THE LEGION OF HONOUR 🔟 — fold 30: H 11

The **Hôtel de Salm** was built in 1786 for the German Prince of Salm who, finding himself in straitened circumstances organised a lottery with the property as prize to settle his debts but the lottery was cancelled. The prince lost his life during the Revolution. The mansion was occupied by various tenants until it was acquired by Napoleon, who made the mansion the Palace of the Legion of Honour in 1804. It was burnt during the Commune of 1871 and rebuilt, in 1878, by the members of the Legion to the original plans. The only parts remaining of the early building are the low reliefs on the outside walls.

Turn left down to Quai Anatole-France to look at the back of the palace where there is a delightful semicircular pavilion in complete contrast to the severe lines elsewhere.

★**The Legion of Honour Museum.** — *2 Rue de Bellechasse. Open 2 to 5pm; closed Mondays, 1 January, Easter and Whit Tuesdays, 1 May, 14 July, 15 August, 1 November, 25 December; 10F. ☎ 45 55 95 16.*

The museum presents original documents, decorations, pictures, uniforms and arms illustrating the orders of chivalry and nobility of Pre-Revolutionary France (the Star, St Michael, the Holy Spirit, St Louis), and the creation of the Legion of Honour by Napoleon on 19 May 1802, its rapid expansion during the Empire (personal decorations of Bonaparte and his brothers), educational establishments and its subsequent history.

Further galleries show other French civil and military decorations: academic awards, the Military Medal, Military Cross, the Cross of the Liberation, Order of Merit, Order of Malta and foreign orders.

From the Legion of Honour Palace to the Hôtel Biron

Across Rue de Bellechasse, the former Orsay Station (Gare Paris Quai d'Orsay) is now a museum *(p 125)*.

Continue down Rue de Lille where no **71, Hôtel de Mouchy** dates from 1775 and no **67, President Duret's house,** from 1706. Turn right down Rue de Poitiers where at no **12** the **Hôtel de Poulpry** (1700), the monarchist group known as the Poitiers Street Committee used to meet in 1850.

Turn right in Rue de l'Université, at one time the quarter's main street and still lined with interesting houses: no **51**, the **Hôtel de Soyécourt** was built in 1707; no **78** in 1687; no **82** is where the poet Lamartine lived from 1837 to 1853 (inscription).

Turn left in Rue de Bellechasse.

As you emerge on Boulevard St-Germain, look right to see the more modern — 1877 — part of the Ministry of Defence. The old part overlooking Rue St-Dominique includes the **Hôtel de Brienne** which consists of two houses and a former monastery. Cross the boulevard and continue down Rue de Bellechasse before turning left in Rue St-Dominique.

This street, which got its name from a former monastery for Dominican novices, was amongst the quarter's most interesting before a large part of it was swept away to make way for the Boulevard St-Germain. No **5**, the **Hôtel de Tavannes**, has a fine round arched doorway surmounted by a scallop and crowned by a triangular pediment. It housed a literary salon in the early 19C. The artist, Gustave Doré, died in the house in 1883. Inside *(open 20 August to 30 September, 10am to 12noon and 3 to 6pm)* there is a fine stairwell with a wrought iron balustrade, no **1**, the **Hôtel de Gournay**, was erected in 1695.

The Rue St-Dominique ends on Boulevard St-Germain on which you turn right. No **246**, now with no 244 the offices of the Secretary of State for Transport, was formerly the **Hôtel de Roquelaure** (fine courtyard), the residence of the statesman Cambacérès (1753-1824) and later the seat of the Council of State.

Take Rue St-Simon opposite then turn right into Rue de Grenelle.

Rue de Grenelle. — At no 79 stands the great **Hôtel d'Estrées** (1713); no **85** is the **Hôtel d'Avaray** (1728), the Royal Netherlands Embassy. **Pentémont Temple** with its Ionic cupola of 1750 was at one time a convent chapel; then the nuns were replaced by the Imperial Guard and these, by the civil servants of the Ministry of War Veterans. No 110, the **Hôtel de Courteilles** (1778), dominating the street with its massive façade, is now the Ministry of Education; no 116 was built in 1709 for Marshal de Villars and considerably remodelled. No 118, is the much smaller, **Hôtel de Villars**, built in 1712 and extremely elegant with twin garlanded, oval windows. Continue to no 136, the **Hôtel de Noirmoutiers** (1722), at one time the army staff headquarters and the house in which Marshal Foch died on 20 March 1929. The mansion now serves as the official residence of the *Préfet* of the Ile-de-France Region.

Turn left into Boulevard des Invalides and walk to the Hôtel Biron on the corner of Rue de Varenne.

★★HÔTEL BIRON ⬛⬛ — fold 29: J 11

The house and garden enable one to see Rodin's sculptures in a perfect residential setting.

In 1728, one Abraham Peyrenc, a wigmaker who had accrued a fortune and aggrandised his name to Peyrenc de Moras, commissioned Gabriel the Elder to build him a house in the Rue de Varenne. In time the beautiful building came into the hands of the Duchess of Maine, grand-daughter of the great Condé and wife of the son of Louis XIV and Madame de Montespan, and then of Marshal Biron, a general in the Revolutionary government who died, decapitated, in 1793.

In 1797 the house was turned into a dance hall. Under the Empire it reverted to its role of residence, first of the papal legate then of the ambassador of the Tsar. In 1820 it was taken over by the Convent of the Sacred Heart as an educational establishment. Madame Sophie Barat, the mother superior (canonised: 1925), had the neo-Gothic chapel constructed (1871) and the greater part of the residence's panelling ripped out, seeing in the wood carving a symbol of the vanities of the age — a few ornamented rooms, nevertheless, do still remain.

After the Congregation Law of 1904, under which many convents were dispersed, the educational part of the building and the gardens were converted into the Lycée Victor-Duruy and the house was made available to artists. Thus Auguste Rodin came to live in and enjoy the house until his death in 1917, presenting his work by way of rent. The house has since been converted into a museum and the gardens restored.

★★Rodin Museum (Musée Rodin).

— Open 10am to 6pm (last admission 5pm); 1 October to 31 March 10am to 5pm (last admission 4.30pm); closed Mondays and certain holidays; 20F, Sundays 10F; gardens only 2F; ☎ 47 05 01 34.

Rodin's sculpture, primarily in bronze and white marble, is immensely striking, vital, life-like. Creation in the guise of figures emerging from the living rock was a favourite theme **(The Hand of God)** although he excelled in studies of the nude **(St John the Baptist).**

On the ground floor are some of the most expressive works: **The Cathedral, The Kiss, The Walking Man** and **The Man with a Broken Nose.** At either end of the gallery, in corresponding rotundas which have kept their fine panelling, are **Eve** and the **Age of Bronze.** One room is devoted to drawings by the artist which are exhibited in rotation.

The Cathedral by A. Rodin

At the top of the beautiful 13C staircase, on the first floor, are the smaller works, the plasters for the large groups and for the statues of **Balzac** *(p 207)* and **Victor Hugo** *(p 249).*

Finally, in the garden, can be seen the sculptures which made Rodin's reputation during his lifetime. **The Thinker** (right), **The Burghers of Calais** and **The Gates of Hell** (left) and the **Ugolin group** (in the centre of the pool).

The personal collections of the artist (furniture, pictures, antique) are displayed in the house and in the former chapel *(temporary exhibitions).*

From the Hôtel Biron to St Thomas Aquinas Church

Rue de Varenne. — The street was laid along a rabbit warren — *garenne* which evolved, in time, to Varenne — belonging to the Abbey of St-Germain-des-Prés. There are attractive old houses in this street also: no **73** the great **Hôtel de Broglie** (1735); nos 80-78, the **Hôtel de Villeroy** (1724), now the Ministry of Agriculture; no 72, the large **Hôtel de Castries** (1700).

The most famous, of course, is the **Hôtel Matignon** at no 57. The house was built by Courtonne in 1721 and has since been considerably remodelled. Talleyrand, diplomat and statesman to successive regimes, owned it from 1808 to 1811, then Madame Adelaïde, sister to Louis-Philippe. Between 1884 and 1914 it housed the Austro-Hungarian Embassy and in 1935 it became the office of the President of the Council of State and in 1958 the Paris residence of the prime minister.

No 56, the **Hôtel de Gouffier de Thoix,** has a magnificent doorway ornamented with a shell carving. No 47, the **Hôtel de Boisgelin** is now the Italian Embassy.

Turn left into Rue du Bac, then right into Rue de Grenelle.

★**Fountain of the Four Seasons (Fontaine des Quatre-Saisons).** — The beautiful Four Seasons' Fountains, carved by Bouchardon between 1739 and 1745, was commissioned by Turgot, the dean of the local merchants' guild and father of Louis XVI's minister. The commission was undertaken in answer to complaints that the stately quarter was almost totally without water!

A seated figure of Paris looking down on reclining personifications of the Seine and the Marne adorns the ornate Ionic pillared fountain front. The sides are decorated with figures of the Seasons and delightful low reliefs showing cherubs performing the seasons' labours.

The Romantic poet, Alfred de Musset, lived at no 59 from 1824 to 1839, when he wrote most of his plays and dramatic poetry. The Hôtel Bouchardon will house an art foundation.

Cross Boulevard Raspail and take Rue de Luynes before crossing Boulevard St-Germain to Place St-Thomas d'Aquin.

St Thomas Aquinas Church (Église St-Thomas d'Aquin). — The church, formerly the chapel of the Dominican novitiate monastery, was begun in 1682 in the Jesuit style to plans by Pierre Bullet. The façade was only completed in 1769. Inside are 17 and 18C paintings and a ceiling (apsidal chapel) painted by Lemoyne in 1723 of the Transfiguration. The sacristy has Louis XV panelling.

17
★★

The
Institut de France
and
Beaux-Arts Quarter

Michelin plan **11** - fold 31: J 13, J 14 – K 13, K 14

Distance: 3km-2 miles – Time: 2 1/2 hours
Start from the Odéon métro station

On this walk the Institute of France, with its famous dome, the School of Fine Arts and the Mint are the principal monuments. The quays (Quai de Conti, Quai des Grands Augustins) are lined with bookstalls and provide the best vantage points.

From the Carrefour de l'Odéon to the École des Beaux-Arts

Cross Boulevard St-Germain and opposite Danton's statue, by no **130**, cut into the Commerce-St-André Court, opened in 1776 on the site of a real tennis court.
It was in this passage that a Dr. Guillotin perfected, on some sheep in 1790, his "philanthropic decapitating machine" and at a small printers, no **8**, that Marat produced his paper, *The People's Friend*. Take the first alleyway (grilles) to the right: one of the towers of the Philippe Auguste wall can be seen on the corner.

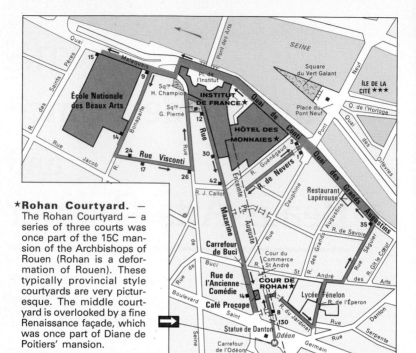

★Rohan Courtyard. — The Rohan Courtyard — a series of three courts was once part of the 15C mansion of the Archbishops of Rouen (Rohan is a deformation of Rouen). These typically provincial style courtyards are very picturesque. The middle courtyard is overlooked by a fine Renaissance façade, which was once part of Diane de Poitiers' mansion.

Continue along the peaceful Rue du Jardinet, built on the site of former gardens, into Rue de l'Éperon where the Lycée Fénelon stands, the first girls' school to be opened in Paris (1893).
Bear right *(Rue St-André-des-Arts)* then left into Rue Séguier, dating back to 1179 and lined still by old houses.

Quai des Grands Augustins. — Built in 1313, it is the oldest in Paris. It got its name from the Great Augustine Monastery established by St Louis in the 13C on the site which extended along the waterfront and between Rue des Grands-Augustins and Rue Dauphine. Note, as you pass, two 17C mansions no **35**, and no 51 now the famous Lapérouse Restaurant.

Quai de Conti. — It begins at the Rue Dauphine. Between nos **1** and **3**, is the curious **Rue de Nevers**, a blind alleyway hollowed out in the 13C and remaining medieval in character which ends abruptly at the Philippe Auguste wall.

★THE MINT (HÔTEL DES MONNAIES) ▯▯ — fold 31: J 13

A succession of buildings have stood between the Rue Dauphine and the Philippe Auguste wall since the Nesle Mansion was first erected on the site in the 13C. The house was rebuilt by Luigi di Gonzaga, Prince of Nevers, in 1572, remodelled in 1641 and renamed by the Princess de Conti when she came to live there in 1670.
In the 18C Louis XV transferred the Mint to the mansion, selecting the architect, **Antoine**, to design the workshops built between 1768 and 1775. The simplicity of line, sober bossage and decoration pleased the public after the surfeit of classical orders and colonnades. The architect lived in the building until he died in 1801.

Tour. — *Open 1 to 6pm (9pm Wednesdays); closed Mondays and holidays, excluding 8 May, 1 and 11 November; 15F; audio-visual presentation;* ☎ 40 46 55 35. A staircase rising from the beautiful coffered entrance hall, circles twice before reaching the suite of panelled rooms, overlooking the Seine, which are used for temporary exhibitions.
The **Coin Museum** occupies the refurbished minting and milling halls on the far side of the main courtyard. The exhibits retrace the history of French coin-making and mints from 300BC as well as the art of medal-making which developed in the 16C under Italian influence. A fine collection of coins, medals, banks, paintings, engravings and drawings illustrate various political, social and financial events.
In the rolling workshop note several coining presses and the 1807 Uhlhorn press which was steam-driven.
Medals and coins are on sale at no 2 Rue Guénégaud *(Mondays to Fridays 9am to 5.45pm, Saturdays 10am to 1pm and 2 to 5.30pm; closed Sundays and holidays).*

The pressing of blanks into French and other coins has been transferred to Pessac in the Gironde. However, collectors' pieces, dies for the Assay and Weights and Measures offices, medals and decorations are still produced here *(guided tours of the medal and decoration workshops Tuesdays and Fridays, 2pm and 2.15pm except 1 January, 1 May, 25 December and in August)*.

A pyramid in the second court on the left is a former meridian bearing *(see map p 198)*.

★THE INSTITUTE OF FRANCE (INSTITUT DE FRANCE) ▢▢ — fold 31: J 13

The Academy dome marks the building from afar. Long before the present building, the site formed part of the Philippe Auguste perimeter wall which at its end on the Seine was defended by the **Nesle Tower**, standing where the left wing of the institute has since been erected (the Mint side). The tower's history became widely known when Alexandre Dumas dramatized it in a play.

In 1661, three days before he died, Cardinal Mazarin, when making final bequests from his immense wealth, left 2 million *livres* for the foundation of a college of sixty scholars from the provinces acquired by France under his ministry. The College of Four Nations — Piedmont, Alsace, Artois and Roussillon — was opened in 1688 and closed in 1790 when the building was successively used for various ends.

The building next became the home of the Institute, a body founded by the Convention and transferred from the Louvre by Napoleon in 1805. It incorporates the French Academy, founded by Richelieu in 1635 and the Academies of Inscriptions and Belles Lettres (1663), Science (1666), Fine Arts (1803) and Moral and Political Sciences (1832).

The French Academy (l'Académie Française). — Membership of the French Academy is limited to forty and since 1980 is no longer exclusively masculine. The admission ceremony, following election and approval by the head of state, the Academy's patron, is made a great Paris occasion.

Members are commonly known as "immortals" although the wearing of a green robe at solemn meetings and collaboration in the production of the Dictionary of the French Language have not saved the majority from total obscurity — whereas those refused admission include: Descartes, Pascal, Molière, La Rochefoucauld, Rousseau, Vauvenargues, Diderot, Beaumarchais, Balzac, Maupassant, Proust, Zola...

The majority of present academicians are writers — Julien Green, Ionesco and Marguerite Yourcenar the first woman to be admitted — but also represented are the Church, the army, diplomacy, medicine and technology.

Exterior. — The rounded wings ending in square pavilions and framing the Jesuit style chapel at the centre, were designed by Le Vau to harmonize with the Louvre, of which he was also an architect, on the far bank of the Seine. The cupola drum is adorned with Mazarin's coat of arms.

The courtyard through the gate to the left of the cupola, is lined on either side by twin porticoes which precede respectively, left, the Mazarin Library, originally the cardinal's own collection and, right, the ceremonial hall.

A second courtyard, is surrounded by the buildings where the scholars used to live. The third smaller courtyard was the old kitchen yard. The well is still visible. At the far end is the Bureau des Longitudes which houses: laboratories and offices for a group of research workers specialising in astronomy.

Interior. — A tour of the interior *(apply in advance; 10F; ☎ 43 29 55 10)* includes the academy council chambers and the former Mazarin Chapel beneath the dome which, since 1806, has been the ceremonial hall. Outstanding among the statuary, pictures and tapestries is Mazarin's tomb by Coysevox.

Beyond the Place de l'Institut, at the corner of Rue Bonaparte and Quai Malaquais stands a 17C stone and brick house (no **9**). Further along is the École Nationale des Beaux-Arts. The writer Anatole France was born at no **19** (plaque on no **15**).

Take Rue Bonaparte which follows the course of the canal which fed water from the Seine to the moat surrounding St-Germain-des-Prés Abbey *(p 176)*.

ÉCOLE NATIONALE DES BEAUX-ARTS ▢▢ — fold 31: J 13

A monastery dedicated to the Patriarch Jacob was founded in 1608 by Marguerite of Valois, Henri IV's first wife, when she regained her freedom, and was occupied by the Augustine order.

The monastery was closed down in 1791 and the building was used to store works of art from other monuments which had been destroyed or were no longer in use. The archaeologist **Lenoir** founded the Museum of the French Monuments where 1 200 small busts, statues etc. were displayed. Some of the treasures from St-Denis, the Louvre, Versailles and from many churches were thus saved.

The museum was closed in 1816 and replaced by the School of Fine Arts. The church and cloister are all that remain of the monastery. In 1860, the school annexed the **Hôtel de Conti** (11 Quai Malaquais) and in 1885, the Hôtel de Chimay (nos 15 and 17).

Tour. — The courtyard and some monuments are open at no **14**, Rue Bonaparte. These include the doorway from the Château d'Anet, the retreat of Diane de Poitiers, fragments from the Hôtel Legendre, demolished in 1841 and low reliefs from the Louvre's south wing. There are casts and copies in the courtyards and galleries.

From the École des Beaux-Arts to Carrefour de l'Odéon

Turn left into the narrow alleyway, **Rue Visconti**, which was known in the 16C as « Little Geneva » since many Protestants including the artist Bernard Palissy, lived in this area. The playwright Racine died at no **24** in 1699. Balzac founded a printing-house at no **17** in 1826 but it did not enjoy much success. Delacroix had a studio there from 1836 to 1844.

Before you turn left into Rue de Seine which is lined with art galleries, look on the right at the sign of a famous 17C nightclub, Le Petit Maure, at no **26**.

Rue Mazarine. — Molière's first appearance as an actor was made in 1643 at the theatre which stood at no **12**. He had joined the company which lodged next door, at no **10**, and included the Béjart family of two brothers and two sisters, on inheriting some money from his mother. He was 21, had always been stagestruck and gladly abandoned the legal career chosen for him by his father. Symbolically he changed his name from Poquelin to Molière.

The company leased the real tennis court at no 12 and built a theatre inside it which Molière and his companions, with youthful audacity, named the Illustrious Theatre. But the venture failed and a year later, the company moved to Quai des Célestins. The first Paris **fire station** home of the capital's first fire brigade which was created in 1722, was at no **30**. It was mustered by François Dumouriez du Perrier, onetime valet to Molière, and later member of the Comédie-Française.

No **42**, again an indoor real tennis court converted into the **Guénégaud Theatre**, was where in 1671, opera was presented for the first time in France. The work, *Pomone* by Perrin and Cambert, played for eight months before the rival composer, Lulli, jealous of its success, had the theatre closed. After Molière's death in 1673, his company, evicted from the Palais-Royal by Lulli again, made the theatre their home until 1689 *(see below)*.

Carrefour de Buci. — By the 18C the Buci crossroads had become the focal point of the Left Bank with bustling pedestrians, wheeled traffic and a sedan chair rank, a guard post, a gibbet and a pillar to which miscreants were attached by an iron collar. There were several **real tennis courts** in the area, including three in the Rue de Buci. It was a very popular game. Until the 15C the ball was thrown by hand, then a glove was used and finally the racket was introduced. In 1687, the best players received a fee for appearing in public.

Rue de l'Ancienne-Comédie. — The street got its present name in 1770, the date the Comédie-Française left.

When the Four Nations College opened in 1688, the austere Sorbonne teachers at its head disapproved of the proximity of the Comédie-Française and forced the company to leave the Rue Mazarine *(see above)*. The players amongst whom was Molière's widow, Armande Béjart sought another real tennis court and finally found one at no **14** — the façade between the 2nd and 3rd floors in adorned with a reclining figure of *Minerva* by Le Hongre. The painters David, Gros and Horace Vernet had studios overlooking the court. The theatre opened in 1689 with *Phèdre* by Racine and Molière's *Le Médecin Malgré lui*. Eighty-one years later, in 1770, the company, by this time once more in low financial waters, left for the Tuileries Palace Theatre before finally moving to the Odéon.

The old **Café Procope**, at no **13** goes back to 1686 when it was founded by a Sicilian of that name. The establishment's popularity knew no bounds: throughout the centuries, it has been a meeting-place for writers, poets, revolutionaries, philosophers etc.

★★

St-Germain-des-Prés

Michelin plan **11** - folds 30, 31: J 12, J 13 – K 13

Distance: 2km-1 mile – Time: 1 1/2 hours
Start from St-Germain-des-Prés métro station

This old quarter on the Left Bank is known for its beautiful church as well as for its narrow streets, antique shops, restaurants, cafés and cellars. The church, the oldest in Paris, and the abbatial palace are all that remain of the famous Benedictine abbey.

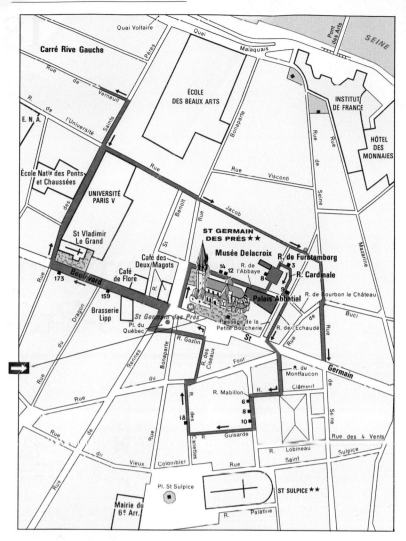

★★ST-GERMAIN-DES-PRÉS CHURCH ▯▯ — fold 31: J 13

In 542 King Childebert, son of Clovis, on his return from Spain with a piece of the True Cross and St Vincent's tunic, had a monastery built in the open field *(prés)* to shelter the relics. He was buried in the church as were subsequent members of his line until King Dagobert (639) who is buried in St-Denis Cathedral. Also interred here in 576 is St Germanus, Bishop of Paris, after whom the church had taken its name of St-Germain-des-Prés or St Germanus in the Fields.

A powerful abbey. — St-Germain-des-Prés was from the 8C, a link in the prodigious chain across Europe of 17 000 Benedictine abbeys and priories and in its own right, sovereign ruler of a domain of some 17 000ha-42 000 acres. Spiritually it acknowledged only the pope.

The monastery was sacked four times in forty years by the Normans and the present church is, therefore, a rebuilding dating in its earliest parts from 990 to 1021. There followed enlargement of the chancel in 1163 — an addition consecrated in person by Pope Alexander III at a service from which the bishop of Paris was excluded — as a mark of the order's independence — the building of Gothic cloisters and refectory, and a Lady Chapel in the 13C by Pierre of Montreuil, making the monastery a most beautiful medieval group.

In the 14C while Paris was being given its third defence perimeter by Charles V *(p 20)*, the abbey surrounded itself with a crenellated wall intersected by towers and preceded by a moat connected with the Seine. These fortifications remained until the end of the 17C when they were replaced by houses, so creating the district of St-Germain *(p 166)* which extends to the west.

A centre of learning. — The Cluniac rule was followed in the abbey from the 11 to the 16C when it became debased under the rule of commendatory abbots, often lay persons appointed by the King; it was reformed in 1515 and in 1631 and then attached itself to the austere Congregation of St Maur which earned the community a reputation for holiness and learning until 1789. The monks devoted themselves to the study of inscriptions (epigraphy), ancient writing (paleography), the Church Fathers, archaeology, archives and medieval documents.

Decadence. — The abbey was suppressed at the Revolution: the rich library was confiscated, the church, from which the royal tombs disappeared, turned into a saltpetre work and the greater number of its buildings sold, knocked down or burnt. In spite of everything, however, the nave was saved although the twin transept towers disappeared. The vessel received a decoration of somewhat stiff frescoes between 1841 and 1863 by the painter, Flandrin.

Exterior. — With all that has happened to it, inevitably the 11C Romanesque church has altered considerably in appearance. Of the three original towers there remains only the massive one above the façade, one of the oldest in France. The top arcaded storey, rebuilt in the 12C was restored by the architect Baltard in the 19C and, in the same century, crowned with the present steeple. The original porch is hidden by an outer door added in 1607; the presbytery is an 18C addition.

The twin square towers at the end of the chancel were truncated in 1822. The chancel itself, rebuilt in the middle of the 12C when its buttresses were strengthened by flying buttresses, is contemporary with Notre-Dame.

The small square to the south is on the site of the monks' cemetery and in September 1792 was the setting for the massacre of the 318 priests and monks who had been locked up in the adjoining abbey prison.

The glazed limestone portico placed against the far wall was executed by the Sèvres factory for its pavilion at the 1900 Universal Exhibition.

Interior. — St-Germain, built as a monastery chapel, is not large — it measures 65 × 21 × 19m - 213 × 69 × 62ft high. Proportions and carving are diminished by the unfortunate 19C multicolour restoration.

To the right of the cradle vaulted porch is the St Symphorian Chapel *(not open)* where St Germanus was buried in Merovingian times. Excavations in the chapel have uncovered several decorated stone and plaster sarcophagi and also a fragment thought to be part of the 11C church or the Merovigian edifice.

The Gothic vaulting above the nave and transept, similar to that in the chancel, replaced an earlier wooden roof in 1646; the capitals are copies of the 11C originals now in the Cluny Museum *(p 183).*

The frescoes above the arches are by Flandrin, a student of Ingres, and depict scenes from the life of Christ together with the parallel episodes from the Old Testament, e.g. The Resurrection and Jonah and the whale.

The chancel and ambulatory remain 12C. Originally the arches, some of which are still semi-circular, supported galleries but in 1646 these were converted into a purely ornamental triforium; the 6C marble shafts in the slender columns are from the original Childebert church and along with the remains found in St Symphorian Chapel and Notre-Dame are the only traces of Merovingian buildings in Paris. The capitals in the chancel are Romanesque and depict traditional themes: foliage, birds, monsters.

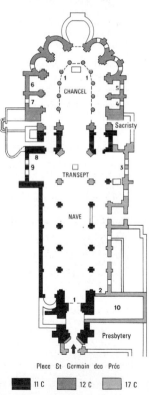

Place St Germain des Prés

■ 11 C ■ 12 C □ 17 C

1) Modern wrought iron grille by Raymond Subes.
2) Our Lady of Consolation (1340).
3) Tomb by Girardon (17C).
4) Mausoleum of James Douglas, a 17C Scottish nobleman attached to the court of Louis XIII.
5) Descartes' and the learned Benedictines, Mabillon and Montfaucon's tombstones.
6) Boileau, the poet and critic's tombstone.
7) Tomb of William Douglas, a Scottish nobleman attached to the court of Henri IV.
8) Statue of St Francis Xavier by N. Coustou.
9) Tomb of John Casimir, King of Poland, who died in 1672, Abbot of St-Germain-des-Prés.
10) St Symphorian Chapel *(closed).*

A Picasso sculpture, *Homage to Apollinaire,* has been placed in a small square on the corner of Place St-Germain-des-Prés and Rue de l'Abbaye amidst fragments of the Lady Chapel built by Pierre of Montreuil and removed from the church in 1802 (the portal is in the Cluny Museum, *p 183).*

Walk along the quiet Rue de l'Abbaye. The refectory designed in 1239 by Pierre of Montreuil and burnt down in 1794 stood at nos **14-12** and the chapter-house at no 11.

Abbatial Palace. — The abbatial palace (nos 5 to 1) is an impressive brick and stone edifice, constructed in 1586 by the Cardinal-Abbot Charles of Bourbon, proclaimed King of France in 1589 during the League. His reign, as Charles X, however, was shortlived since he died the following year, a prisoner of his nephew Henri IV. The palace was remodelled in 1699 by the Cardinal de Fürstemberg and sold in 1797. The angle pavilion and the Renaissance façade have been restored to their original aspect. The severity of the façade is tempered by the twin-casement windows and, above, the alternate round and triangular pediments.

THE ST-GERMAIN QUARTER

★The Old Streets. — Turn left into **Rue de Fürstemberg**, an old fashioned street with a charming square shaded by paulownia and white-globed lamp-posts. The street was built in 1699 by the cardinal of the same name, through the acquisition of the monastery stableyard. The nos **6** and **8** are the remains of the outbuildings.

Delacroix, leader of the Romantic painters set up his studio in no **6** which is now the **Eugène Delacroix Museum** *(open 9.45am to 12.30pm and 2pm to 5.15pm; closed Tuesdays and certain holidays; 11F, 6F on Sundays;* ☎ *43 54 04 87).* He died there in 1863.

Bear right into the curious winding **Rue Cardinale**, again opened (1700) by Fürstemberg, this time overlooking the monastery tennis court and still partially lined by old houses (nos **3** to **9**). From Rue Cardinale you can enjoy an overall view of the Abbatial Palace and of the picturesque crossroads of Rue de l'Échaudé (1388) and Rue Bourbon-le-Château. Continue past the Petite Boucherie passage to Rue de l'Abbaye on the left and subsequently turn right into Rue de l'Échaudé (1388).

The construction of the Boulevard St-Germain brought about the disappearance, in about 1870, of the meeting point of several small roads which had served as the abbey's place of public chastisement. Justice was meted out on thieves, counterfeiters, pimps, who were punished by gibbet and pillory — a penalty suppressed by Louis XII in 1636.

The old St-Germain Fair. — Cross the boulevard into Rue de Montfaucon which at one time led to the St-Germain fairground. Then take Rue Clément to the right. Gangways leading up to the road from nos **6, 8** and **10** in Rue Mabillon show that the ground level has been raised.

The fair, founded in 1482 by Louis XI for the benefit of the abbey, lasted until the Revolution (1790), its annual celebration an important event in the Paris economy. In 1818 the site was made over to the local market. A part was taken in 1900 to built university examination halls (Hôtel des Examens) with premises for the market's stall holders on the ground floor. A sports centre is housed in the basement of the remaining section.

Take Rue Guisarde on the right. Built in the 17C, it derives its name from the secret meetings of the League formed by the Duke of Guise's supporters.

Return in the direction of St-Germain-des-Prés by way of Rue des Canettes, so named after the low-relief depicting ducklings at no **18**, and Rue des Ciseaux where there are still some old houses.

Turn left into Rue Gozlin, cross Place du Québec with its fountain and then left again along Boulevard St-Germain.

Boulevard St-Germain. — Near the Place St-Germain-des-Prés you will see on the right the famous Café des Deux-Magots and the Café de Flore where intellectuals and artists meet. Opposite is no 151, the Brasserie Lipp, a popular venue with politicians, writers and celebrities. Further on some 18C mansions remain standing (nos **159** and **173**).

The antiquarian quarter. — The numerous art galleries and antique shops in the streets (Rue des Saints-Pères, Jacob, Bonaparte, de Seine) between the boulevard and the river will delight art lovers and collectors. The area known as the **Carré Rive Gauche** organises a five day antiques fair in May to present a selection of objects outstanding for their rarity, craftsmanship or beauty.

Turn right into Rue des Saints-Pères.

On the right stands the former St-Pierre Chapel (17C) which was part of the Charity Hospital; its name was distorted to Saints-Pères. It is now the Ukrainian church of St Vladimir the Great. The Engineering School is housed in the 18C mansions at no 28. Opposite, the great buildings erected on the site of the Charity hospital are the premises of the Paris V University. The fine bronze doorway is by Paul Landowski. Beyond at no 13 is the National Administration School (E.N.A.).

Continue along the pretty Rue de Verneuil with its old houses and 18C mansions. Return to Rue Jacob and walk along the left hand side of the road (publishing houses, antiquarian shops). Then turn right into the old Rue de Seine, built in the 13C, which leads back to Boulevard St-Germain.

19
★★

The St-Séverin
and
Maubert Quarters

Michelin plan **11** - folds 31 and 32: K 14, K 15

Distance: 2 1/2km-1 1/2 mile – Time: 2 1/2 hours.
Start from the St-Michel métro station

This is one of Paris' medieval quarters with narrow, winding streets, old and modern schools, university buildings, churches and the treasure filled Hôtel de Cluny.
Start from Place St-Michel and take Rues de la Huchette, de la Harpe (an old Roman way) and St-Séverin to reach the Church of St-Séverin. The area is a pedestrian precinct.

★★CHURCH OF ST-SÉVERIN

⬛⬛ — fold 31: K 14

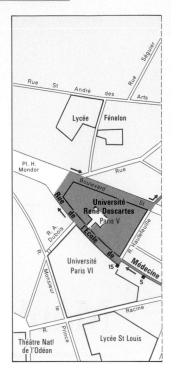

In the 6C there lived in this area, which was then open country, a hermit by the name of Séverin who persuaded Clodoald, grandson of King Clovis and future saint (St Cloud in France), to take holy orders. An oratory, in due course, was raised to his memory but was burned down by the Normans. It was replaced first by a chapel and later by a church dedicated not to the original Séverin but to a Swiss namesake, St Severinus.

By the end of the 11C, St-Séverin was serving as the parish church for the Left Bank; in the 12C, Foulques, a parish priest of Neuilly-sur-Marne, preached from his pulpit the Fourth Crusade, which was to found the Latin Empire of Constantinople (1204).

Building of the present church began in the first half of the 13C when a master builder, maintaining the Romanesque façade, began to reconstruct the first three bays of the nave in the Gothic style. This substitution of Romanesque by Flamboyant Gothic continued until 1530. In 1681 the capricious Grande Mademoiselle, cousin to Louis XIV, who had broken with her own parish church of St-Sulpice, adopted St-Séverin and, pouring moneys from her vast fortune, had the chancel modernized by the architect, Le Brun. Under his supervision pillars were faced with marble and wood; pointed Gothic arches were transformed into rounded arcades.

Exterior. — Chapel and aisle bays are covered by ridge roofs, each gable being ornamented with mouldings and monster gargoyles.

The west door, which is 13C, comes from the Church of St-Pierre-aux-Bœufs which stood on the Ile de la Cité and was demolished in 1839. Above, windows, balustrades, the rose window, are all 15C Flamboyant Gothic.

The original porch can be seen on the north side of the tower (the tympanum has been recarved). Still on the north side, in the corner formed by the chapels, is a niche containing a statue of St Severinus. The tower superstructure and spire are both 15C.

Ground plan. — *Open Mondays to Saturdays 11am to 7.45pm (excluding Thursday afternoons), Sundays 9am-8pm.* The width of the building compared to its length, strikes one immediately on entry. This extra breadth occured in the 14 and 15C when the church's enlargement was being mooted but land was only available on either side. The original building with single side aisles was, therefore, flanked by outer aisles and a series of chapels. There is no transept. The Communion chapel, on the southeast side, is a 17C addition.

The actual dimensions are: length 50m, width 34m and height 17m-164 × 112 × 56ft (*cf. the proportions of Notre-Dame, p 111*).

Nave. — The first three bays of the nave are far superior to the rest. Their short columns are ornamented with capitals while above the broken arch arcades rises the triforium, a narrow gallery replacing an earlier wide tribune similar to those of Notre-Dame. The bays of the triforium are filled, like those of the windows above, with a regular tracery of trefoils and roses.

In the following Flamboyant style bays, the columns lack capitals; the tracery in the arcades is angular and complicated.

The capitals along the aisles are carved on the nave side with the figures of angels, prophets and urchins.

The organ is as outstanding as the Louis XV organ loft. The two apostle paintings in the north aisle are 17C.

Chancel. — The chancel's five apsidal arches stand higher than those lining the chancel; the Flamboyant vaulting follows a single, much compartmented, design.

The church's wonder is the Flamboyant double **ambulatory**★★, circling the chancel. As you walk, the fall of the rib tracery onto the column stems recalls strolling through a grove of palm trees. On the central pillar the ribs continue in further ornament as spirals down the shaft.

In the chapel adjoining the sacristy is a late 15C mural, the Last Judgment.

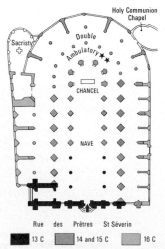

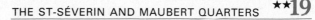

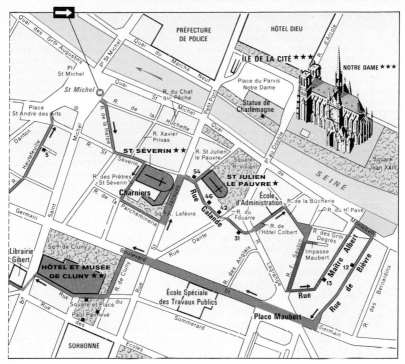

★**Windows**. — The beautiful stained glass in the upper windows is late 15C; the bay in the west end illustrating a Tree of Jesse behind the organ is 16C; the modern glass in the east end chapels is by Bazaine.

Charnel House. — *Not open to the public.* A small garden exists, where there was formerly a burial ground surrounded by a charnel house *(charniers).* Part of the galleries although restored, look much as they did in medieval times. They are the only ones still extant in Paris today. (The practice was to remove the bones of the dead from their graves and put them in cavities in the charnel house walls as the burial ground became overcrowded).

It was in this burial ground that in 1474 the first operation for gall stones was performed. An archer, who had been condemned to death, was a sufferer and was offered his freedom by Louis XI should he survive an experimental operation that a surgeon of the time wished to try out. The operation was successful; the archer was cured and freed.

Walk left round the church by way of Rue des Prêtres-St-Séverin and Rue de la Parcheminerie or Parchment Street, so called after public letter writers and copyists who lived there. Once past the east end of the church in Rue St-Jacques, bear right into Rue Galande leading to St-Julien-le-Pauvre and René-Viviani Square *(p 104)*

★ST-JULIEN-LE-PAUVRE CHURCH ⬜⬜ — fold 31: K 14

This corner of Paris has an appeal all its own with its small local church in a picturesque setting and an unforgettable view of Notre-Dame.
Several of the chapels which have stood successively on this site since the 6C have been named St Julian — after the 3C Martyr, Bishop of Brioude; after the Confessor, the medieval Bishop of Le Mans, who was also known as the Poor because he gave so much away that his purse was always empty; and finally after the ferryman and Hospitaller. In the end it was the name of the medieval bishop which prevailed: St Julian the Poor.
The present building was constructed by the monks of Longpont, a monastery a few miles outside Paris, between 1165 and 1220 (when Notre-Dame was being built). From the 13 to the 16C the University held its assemblies, including the election of chancellor, in the church, but in 1524 the students made such a rumpus and damaged the interior so gravely that university proceedings were barred henceforth. In 1655 the priory was suppressed and the church attached as a chapel to the Hôtel-Dieu Hospital. Since 1889 it has been a Melchite Chapel.

The square. — The square, on the site of a couple of the church's bays, is more a close than a square. It is bordered to its right by a night-club in the cellars of an old house. The **view★★** across the opening of Rue Galande to St-Séverin is one of the best known of old Paris and is still being faithfully reproduced by painters. An iron wellhead, originally over a well inside the church, now stands against the doorway near two paving stones from the Old Orleans-Lutetia Roman road (Lutetia was the Roman name for Paris).
No 14 in Rue St-Julien-le-Pauvre dates form the 17C and was at one time the house of the governor of the Petit Châtelet or lesser Barbican.

The Church. — The portal onto the square was constructed only in 1651 when two bays of the nave and the south aisle were removed. The north face and chancel, flanked by twin apsidal chapels, overlook the Square René-Viviani.

Inside, although the nave, which lacks a transept, was recovered with cradle vaulting in 1651, the Gothic vaulting over the aisles was left. The chancel, the most beautiful part of the building, is closed by a wooden iconostasis on which hang icons or holy pictures. The two chancel pillars have **capitals★** remarkably carved with acanthus leaves and harpies. There is also an unusual 15C tombstone in the south aisle.

From the church, take Rue Galande on the left.

Maubert Quarter. — This old quarter with its small winding streets, the haunt of students, has been restored. The **Rue Galande** where cellars and pointed medieval arches have been unearthed at nos **46** and **54** and a carved stone above the door of no **42** shows St Julian the Hospitaller in his boat, was the Lyons-Paris Roman road. The Rue du Fouarre on the left was one the places where university lectures were given in the open air in the Middle Ages when students sat on bundles of straw *(fouarre)*; hence the street's name. Dante is said to have attended lectures in this street in 1304.

Follow Rue Galande (15C gable at no **31**) to Rue Lagrange. Cross Rue Lagrange and take Rue de l'Hôtel-Colbert.

At the corner of Rue de la Bûcherie is situated the Paris Administration School on the premises of the first Medical School founded in the 15C. The rotunda dates from the 17C.

Turn right into Rue de la Bûcherie.

By the corner of Rue Frédéric-Sauton, take a few steps to the right into Impasse Maubert where the first Greek College was founded in 1206, and also the laboratory where the infamous Marquise de Brinvilliers concocted her poisons *(p 233)* was situated in the 17C.

On the right is the small **Rue Maître-Albert** named after the Dominican Albert the Great who taught in the square in the 13C (Maubert is probably a contraction of his name). Its old houses rise above an underground network which led to the banks of the Seine and to the adjoining alleyways where rogues and conspirators found shelter. Mme du Barry's negro attendant, Zamor, who denounced her and caused her to be sent to the guillotine, died in 1820 at no **13**. Continue along Quai de Montebello, an embankment which protected the low lying areas from high tides; lovely views of Notre-Dame to the left. Turn right into **Rue de Bièvre** named after a tributary of the Seine. This quarter was frequented by boatmen and tawers. The entrance of the former St-Michel College at no **12** is surmounted by a statue of St Michael slaying the dragon.

Since the early Middle Ages, the **Place Maubert** has been a traditional meeting-place where barricades have gone up in times of popular uprising.

Rue des Anglais, off Boulevard St-Germain, was named after the English students who lived there in the Middle Ages.

Rue de Cluny leads to Place Paul-Painlevé and the Hôtel de Cluny.

★★HÔTEL DE CLUNY AND ITS MUSEUM ▯▯ — fold 31: K 14

The old residence of the Abbots of Cluny, the ruins of the Roman baths and the wonderful museum, make a supremely interesting group.

The Roman baths. — The present ruins cover about one third of the site which must have been occupied at the beginning of the 3C by a vast Gallo-Roman public bath house, constructed by the powerful guild of Paris boatmen. By the end of the 3C it had been sacked and burnt to the ground by the Barbarians.

Residence of the Abbots of Cluny. — About 1330, Pierre of Châlus, Abbot of Cluny-en-Bourgogne bought the ruins and the surrounding land on behalf of the influential Burgundian Abbey to build a residence for abbots visiting the college founded by the abbey near the Sorbonne. Jacques of Amboise, Bishop of Clermont and Abbot of Jumièges in Normandy, rebuilt the residence to its present design between 1485 and 1500.

The house received many guests including in 1515 Mary Tudor, eldest daughter of Henry VII who at 16 had been married to Louis XII of France, a man in his fifties who only survived three months. The queen passed her period of mourning in the residence strictly watched by Louis' cousin and successor, François I, lest she should bear a child which might cost him his throne. In fact when Mary was discovered one night in the company of the young Duke of Suffolk the king compelled her to marry the Englishman there and then in the chapel and then despatched her straightaway to England.

In the 17C the house served as residence for the papal nuncios, the most illustrious being Mazarin.

Abandonment. — At the Revolution the residence was sold for the benefit of the state. It had a variety of owners — a surgeon who used the chapel as a dissecting room, a cooper, a printer. The navy installed an observatory in the tower and discovered 21 planets. The baths were covered with six feet of soil and vegetables and an orchard planted.

Founding of the museum. — In 1833 a collector by the name of Alexandre Du Sommerard came to live in the house. On his death in 1842 the mansion and its contents were purchased by the state and opened as a museum in 1844; the gardens opened in 1971.

★★ HOUSE

The Hôtel de Cluny with that of Sens and Jacques Cœur's house, is one of the three large private houses dating back to the 15C to remain in Paris. The medieval tradition can be seen in several features such as the crenelations and turrets although these have only a decorative function. Comfort and delicate ornament are important elements in the mansion's design.

Enter the main courtyard where there is a beautiful 15C well curb. The left wing is decorated with arches; the central building has mullioned windows while above, a frieze and Flamboyant balustrade, from which gargoyles spurt, line the base of the roof which in its turn is ornamented with picturesque dormer windows swagged with coats of arms. A pentagonal tower juts out from the central building to contain a wide spiral staircase. There are other staircases in the corner turrets.

★★ MUSEUM

Open 9.30am to 5.15pm; closed Tuesdays ; 16F (8F on Sundays). ☎ 43 25 62 00. Guided tour of baths on Wednesdays at 3pm; 22F.

The museum's twenty-four galleries are entirely devoted to the Middle Ages; the collection as a whole, gives an outstanding picture of the period.

★**Baths (Thermes).** — Excavations have determined the plan of these public baths dating from 200 AD. The best preserved area, the frigidarium (room XII) which measures 21 × 11m-69 × 36ft, was 14.5m-47 1/2ft high and had walls 2m-6 1/2 thick, was built of small quarry stones divided by red brick courses. The ribbed vaulting rests on consoles carved as ships' prows — an unusual motif which has inspired the idea that the building was constructed by the Paris boatmen. This same guild, in the reign of Tiberius, (14-37 AD), dedicated a pillar to Jupiter which was discovered beneath the chancel of Notre-Dame *(map p 186)* and is now on view in the court; known as the **Boatmen's Pillar (1)** it is Paris's oldest sculpture.

The tapestries. — Several rich series of tapestries, woven in the south of the Netherlands in the 15 and early 16C, are of the « thousand flower » type, which is typified by harmony and freshness of colour, love of nature, and the grace of the people and animals portrayed by the artist. In Room IV the series "Aristocratic Life" depicts the life of a noble couple *c* 1500.

The most perfect example is **The Lady and the Unicorn**★★★ series (room XIII rotunda, 1st floor). In the six hangings the lion (chivalric nobility) and the unicorn (bourgeois nobility), standing on either side of a richly clad lady, probably symbolize the armorial bearings of different members of the Le Viste family from Lyons. Five of the hangings are believed to depict allegories of the senses but the sixth remains unexplained. Note the blue-green grass and uniform red backgrounds, the lack of decoration, the richness of the animal and plant life. Fine tapestries from Auxerre Cathedral illustrating the life of St Stephen hang in the chapel and adjoining rooms (XX, XIX, XVIII).

The decorative arts of the Middle Ages. — In addition to the tools and utensils of everyday life, the museum displays great art treasures: illuminated manuscripts, furniture, arms and armour, ironwork, stained glass (medallions from the Sainte-Chapelle — Room VI), ce-

The Lady and the Unicorn — detail

ramics, liturgical vestments and furnishings (lectern — Room XXIII), ivories (casket — Room XIX), sculpture (capitals from St-Germain-des-Prés and Ste-Geneviève, statues from the Sainte-Chapelle — Rooms IX and X, stalls from Beauvais — Room XVIII).

Room VIII contains fragments of sculpture from Notre-Dame including 21 heads from the King's Gallery. Discovered during the restoration of a mansion in the 9th arrondissement, these works date from the mid-12C to the mid-13C and in spite of their condition, the heads evoke an unexpected freshness and a surprising intensity. The doorway belonged to the Lady Chapel of St-Germain-des-Prés Church.

Some of the finest masterpieces of the late Middle Ages are grouped in Room XIV: paintings of the Life of the Virgin (England) and the Tarascon Pietà; a tapestry depicting the story of the Prodigal Son; sculptures in stone, marble and wood including two Flemish altarpieces: the Passion and the Averbode retables, a statue of Mary Magdalene thought to be a portrait of Mary of Burgundy.

A splendid gold altar frontal from Basle Cathedral is presented in Room XIX; in addition gold ware is displayed in Room XVI: rare votive crowns of the Visigoths, gold rose from Basle, reliquaries in *champlevé* enamel from Limousin.

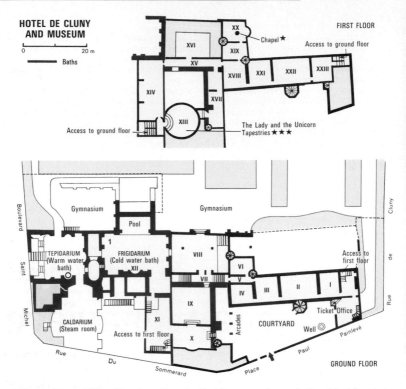

HOTEL DE CLUNY AND MUSEUM

Baths

★ **Chapel (room XX)**. — The chapel, on the first floor, was formerly the abbots' oratory. It has elegant Flamboyant vaulting which falls upon a central pillar and twelve niches, each with its console and carved canopy and formerly containing the statue of a member of the Amboise family. A stone staircase with an open well leads down to the garden.

On leaving the Hôtel de Cluny, continue along Rue Du Sommerard and across Boulevard St-Michel to Rue de l'École-de-Médecine, another old Gallo-Roman road.

Rue de l'École-de-Médecine. — At no 5 the long-gowned Brotherhood of Surgeons, founded by St Louis in the 13C, performed anatomical operations of every kind until the 17C. Barbers or short-gowned surgeons were only allowed to undertake bleeding and confinements. The 1695 lecture theatre has been incorporated in the Paris III University.

At no **15** stood a Franciscan monastery of high repute in the Middle Ages for its teaching. In Louis XVI's reign, the geometrician **Verniquet** worked there on the first trigonometrical plan of Paris. Shortly afterwards, in 1791, the revolutionary group formed by Danton, Marat, Camille Desmoulins and Hébert took over both the monastery and its name, the Cordeliers. Marat lived opposite and it was there that he was stabbed in his bath by Charlotte Corday on 13 July 1793.

The present buildings, now a university centre (Paris VI), were built between 1877 and 1900 to house the School of Practical Medicine. Of the vast conventual buildings, only the monks' Flamboyant Gothic refectory-dormitory remains in the courtyard.

The central part of the former Medical School (no 12), now known as the **René Descartes University** (Paris V), dates back to 1775. An Ionic colonnade precedes a large courtyard at the centre of which stands a statue of the 18C French anatomist, Bichat, by David d'Angers. In pre-revolutionary times students of medicine and surgery were taught separately; they were united in 1808. All students now complete their practical studies in the eleven university medical centres of the Paris region.

Continue round the school and along Boulevard St-Germain to Rue Hautefeuille, on the left. The old street, in which no **5**, with an attractive 16C turret, was once a residence of the abbots of Fécamp, ends in Place St-André-des-Arts, a square with picturesque houses on the site of a church of the same name.

Montagne Ste-Geneviève

Michelin plan **11** - folds 43 and 44: K 14, K 15: L 14, L 15

Distance: 3 1/2km 2 miles — Time: 2 1/2 hours
(tour of the Police Museum not included)
Start from the Maubert-Mutualité métro station

This is an unusual walk among university faculty buildings and famous schools with the Sorbonne, the Pantheon and St-Étienne du-Mont Church as the principal landmarks.

Gallo-Roman Lutetia. — *In the 3C Lutetia was a small town of some six thousand inhabitants: Gauls occupied the Ile de la Cité, Romans the summit and some slopes of what was later known as Mount St-Geneviève.*

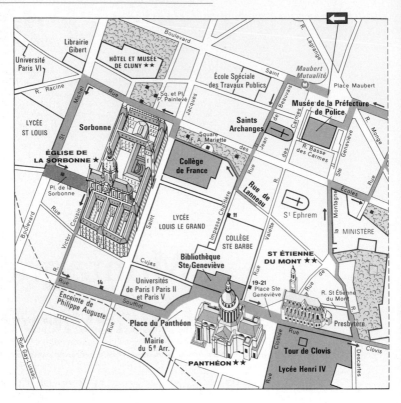

All the usual public monuments associated with any city colonized by the Romans are to be found: an aqueduct, in this case 15km-9 miles long from the Rungis plain, to bring water to the public baths, a network of paved roads to serve the first Latin quarter, a temple to Mercury crowning Montmartre Hill, an important crossroads. Lutetia itself was crossed by the great Soissons-Orleans road, so heavily congested with traffic that it was made one way.

The preaching of St Denis on the Ile de la Cité would lead one to presuppose the existence of a Christian church of some kind from the year 250 AD, although no trace of such a building has been discovered. Shortly afterwards the Barbarian invasions ravaged the entire Left Bank with fire (276-280).

The medieval Alma Mater.

— In the 12C teachers, clerks and students threw off the tutelage of the bishops of the Ile de la Cité *(p 117)* and moved to the area around the St-Genevieve and St-Victor Monasteries on the Left Bank.

In 1215 Pope Innocent III authorised the group's incorporation and this led to the founding of the University of Paris, the first in France.

Students came from provincial France and abroad, registering under disciplines — theology, medicine, the liberal arts, canon law — or by "nationality", in the colleges founded upon the hill: Sorbon College, 1253; Harcourt College, 1280 on the ruins of the Lutetia Theatre and now St Louis Lycée; Coqueret College *(p 187)*; Scottish College *(p 191)*; Clermont College, founded by the Jesuits in 1550 and now Louis-le-Grand Lycée; St Barbara's, Navarre and many others.

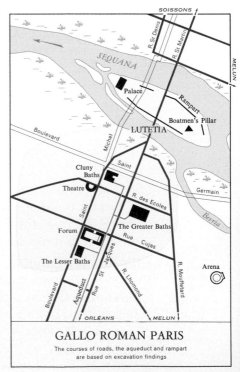

GALLO ROMAN PARIS
The courses of roads, the aqueduct and rampart are based on excavation findings

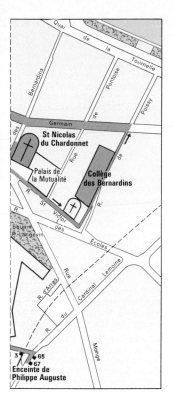

The youthful student crowd, turbulent and a terror to the local populace, did not even hold the king in respect. The University had its own jurisdiction of which it was extremely jealous, in 1407 even compelling the royal marshal, who had hanged several students, to come personally and cut down the corpses from the gibbet before seeking the Sorbonne's pardon. The Franciscans (St Bonaventura), Dominicans (St Albert the Great, St Thomas Aquinas) and later the Oratorians (Malebranche, Massillon) and the Jesuits also drew thousands of students and although the University tried, on several occasions, to prevent their following courses, it failed.

From tutelage to autonomy. — In 1793, the Convention disbanded all universities; Latin ceased to be the official language of scholarship.

In 1806 Napoleon founded the Imperial University of France, with a series of academies as the actual bodies of instruction. But university tradition and the enormous influx of students made the system unwelcome and finally unworkable...

New buildings were erected in Rue des Saints-Pères, Halle aux Vins, Censier and elsewhere and lately in the suburbs: Orsay, Nanterre, Châtenay-Malabry... but still did not prevent the student uprising of May 1968.

October 1970 saw the disappearance of the University of Paris as such and the creation, in its place, for a present student population of about 295 000, of thirteen autonomous universities in the Paris region, each with a full range of disciplines, its own curricula and examinations.

The Latin Quarter. — It is so named because teaching was officially carried out in Latin as well as exchanges between masters and students until the Revolution. The quarter remains the home of students and younger people of all nationalities, of Bohemianism and fantasy. The Boulevard St Michel, or Boul'Mich, as it is known, is the heart of the area with its café terraces, publishing houses and bookshops, particularly around the Librairie Gibert, selling new and secondhand books, textbooks, French and foreign language editions, luxury volumes and paperbacks.

In the surrounding streets "cellars", night-clubs, exotic restaurants, experimental cinemas provide night long entertainment.

From Place Maubert to Place de la Sorbonne

Leave Place Maubert *(p 182)* by Rue Jean-de-Beauvais where, in the 14C, the **Beauvais College Chapel** was erected. Since 1882 the much restored chapel has been the seat of the Romanian Orthodox Church in Paris *(no 9 bis; to visit phone in advance; ☎ 43 54 07 47)*.

The street crosses Rue des Écoles which, when it was laid in 1651, caused the 150-year-old print shop of the erudite publishing house of Estienne to be pulled down.

Coqueret College, where in the 16C under the Hellenist master, Dorat, the students included the poets Ronsard, Antoine de Baïf and, later, Rémy Belleau, Jodelle, Pontus de Tyard and du Bellay, who together formed the Pléiade literary group, stood at no **11** in Impasse Chartière. It has been incorporated in St Barbara's.

The **Rue de Lanneau,** by the entrance to the Chartière blind alley, is picturesque with 16C houses. Turn left for the Collège de France.

COLLÈGE DE FRANCE □□ — fold 43: K 14

The Collège de France has a great past and an equal reputation in present times. The building stands on the site of large Gallo-Roman baths discovered in 1846 *(map opposite)* of which nothing remains.

Three Language College. — The medieval university spoke only Low Latin; the Classical authors were proscribed; Virgil was unknown. In 1530, at the suggestion of the great humanist, Guillaume Budé, François I created a new centre of learning with twelve "king's readers" freed from the constraints of Sorbonne intolerance, scholasticism and disdain of pagan literature. The teachers received payment from the king and so could give instruction free.

In the "three language college" students learned to read the greatest Latin, Greek and Hebrew authors. Henri II installed the staff and students in two colleges, Cambrai and Tréguier which were replaced on the same site in the 17C by Louis XIII, with the Royal College of France. New subjects of study were added: mathematics, medicine, surgery, philosophy, Arabic, Syriac, botany, astronomy, canon law and, in the reign of Louis XV, French literature.

The college today. — In 1778 the building was reconstructed by Chalgrin and, at the Revolution, took its modern name of Collège de France. 19C reconstructions have been replaced in the 20C by vast additions. The ill-equipped labs, at the corner of Rue des Écoles and Rue St-Jacques in which Claude Bernard worked on the function of the pancreas from 1847 to 1878 have disappeared in favour of new halls and laboratories and equipment such as the cyclotron on which Frédéric Joliot-Curie produced fission in a uranium particle. Other outstanding members of the College have been Cuvier (zoologist), Ampère (physicist), Michelet (historian), Champollion (Egyptologist), Renan and Bergson (philosophers), Marcelin Berthelot (chemist), Paul Valéry (poet) and more recently François Jacob (physician). The college retains total scholastic independence although dependent financially, since 1852, on the state.

THE SORBONNE Ⅲ — fold 43: K 14

Foundation. — In 1253 a college for sixteen poor students who wished to study theology was founded by a Paris canon, Robert of Sorbon — named, in accordance with medieval custom, after his native village of Sorbon in the Ardennes — and the King, Saint Louis, to whom the priest was confessor. From such a simple beginning was to develop the Sorbonne, the centre of theological study in pre-Revolutionary France and the seat of the University of Paris.
It was in the same buildings that three printers summoned from Mainz by Louis XI established the first printing house in France in 1469.

Political and religious struggles. — The theological faculty at Philip the Fair's request condemned the Templars which resulted in their dissolution; in the Hundred Years War, the Sorbonne sided with the Burgundians and the English, recognising Henry V of England as King of France and seconding one of their greatest advocates, Bishop Pierre Cauchon as prosecutor in the trial of Joan of Arc. The Sorbonne steadfastly opposed all Protestants and, in the 18C, the philosophers.

From Richelieu to the present day. — Richelieu, on his election as Chancellor of the Sorbonne, put in hand reconstruction of the buildings and church (1624-1642). In 1792 the Sorbonne and University were suppressed; in 1806 they were re-established by Napoleon. Between 1885 and 1901 the Sorbonne underwent great change due to a large-scale rebuilding and expansion programme.

THE PRESENT BUILDING *Entrance: 47 Rue des Écoles*

The building is a remarkable feat of design: it includes twenty-two lecture halls, two museums, sixteen examination halls, twenty-two lecture rooms, thirty-seven rooms for the teaching staff, two hundred and forty laboratories, a library, a physics tower, an astronomy tower, offices, the chancellor's lodge, etc.
The most interesting areas are the entrance hall, the main staircase and great lecture theatre *(to visit apply in writing to Service des Visites de la Sorbonne, 47 Rue des Écoles, 75005 Paris; ☎ 40 46 20 15)* with Puvis de Chavannes' famous painting, the **Sacred Wood★**. The lecture rooms, galleries and halls are decorated with historical and allegorical paintings.
The main courtyard, lined on the left by the library wing, is dominated by the chapel's classical pediment and cupola. Decorative panels by Weerts beneath the arches illustrate the traditional Lendit Fair held at St-Denis and formerly a great university occasion (11 June).

★**The Sorbonne Church (Église de la Sorbonne).** — *Open only when there are temporary exhibitions or cultural events.*
The church was erected by Le Mercier between 1635 and 1642 in the Jesuit style. The façade, unlike St-Paul-St-Louis *(p 94)*, is not so proportioned as to overwhelm the rest of the building and its design of two (instead of three) superimposed orders became the style model.
The **face★** overlooking the main courtyard of the Sorbonne is completely different: above the ten Corinthian columns marking the doorway, rise, first the transept, then the cupola. The effect is outstanding and worth walking into the courtyard to see.
Inside, in the chancel is the **tomb★** of Cardinal Richelieu, the white marble magnificently carved by Girardon in 1694 to drawings by Le Brun. The tomb was violated in 1794 when the church became the Temple of Reason.
The cupola pendentives were painted with Richelieu's coat of arms, angels and Church Fathers by Philippe de Champaigne.
The Duke of Richelieu, minister to Louis XVIII, is also buried in the church. In the crypt are the tombs of faculty members who died for their country.

From Place de la Sorbonne to Place du Panthéon

On leaving the church take Rue Victor-Cousin on the left and then Rue Soufflot. The **Jacobin Monastery** Church, founded by the first brothers of the Dominican order, who arrived in Paris in 1217, on the site of a former Chapel to St James, stood at no **14**. Jacques Clément who assassinated Henri III in 1589 was a brother in the monastery, also Humbert II, last of the line of Dauphiné princes who, by taking holy orders, brought his province under the French crown.
The Rue Soufflot and the semicircular square are lined by the symmetrical building of the former Law Faculty (by Soufflot, 1772) now the offices of Paris I, Paris II and Paris V Universities, and buildings by Hittorff, 1844.
On the left is the **St Genevieve Library** (Bibliothèque Ste-Geneviève) which replaced the Montaigu College in the 19C. The college was known for its teaching, its austere discipline and its squalor — its scholars were said to sleep on the ground amidst

lice, fleas and bugs. Manuscripts, incunabula and 16-18C works from St-Genevieve Abbey were transferred to the new building designed by Labrouste, a master of steel architecture, in 1850 to form the nucleus of the new library (some 2 700 000 volumes). *Reader's ticket holders and students only.* Behind the library is St Barbara's College, founded in 1460 and the last of the Latin Quarter Colleges to survive.

A hexagonal tower (1560), known as Calvin's Tower, stands in the courtyard at nos **19-21** Rue Valette. It is all that remains of Fortet College where, in 1585, the Duke of Guise founded the Catholic League which was to expel Henri III from Paris.

★★ THE PANTHEON ▢▢ — fold 43: L 14

The Pantheon's renown makes it one of the capital's most popular sights.

A royal vow. — Louis XV, when he fell ill at Metz in 1744, vowed that if he recovered he would replace St-Genevieve Abbey's half ruined church by a magnificent edifice. He entrusted the fulfilment of his vow to the Marquis of Marigny, brother to the Marquise de Pompadour.

Soufflot, Marigny's *protégé*, was charged with the plans. In his effort to combine the nobility and purity of Antiquity and the sweeping lines of the Middle Ages, he designed a vast church 110m long by 84m wide by 83m high-361 × 276 × 272ft — in the form of a Greek cross with a vast crypt. At the centre of the chancel he placed a huge dome beneath which would lie the saint's shrine. The foundations were laid in 1758 but financial difficulties intervened and it was only completed after Soufflot's death (1780) by his pupil, Rondelet, in 1789.

The Pantheon

The Temple of Fame. — In 1791 the Constituent Assembly decided that the now closed church should henceforth "receive the bodies of great men who died in the period of French liberty" — the church thus became the national Pantheon. Voltaire and Rousseau were buried there, and for a short time, Mirabeau and Marat also. Successively the Pantheon has been a church under the Empire, a necropolis in the reign of Louis-Philippe, a church again under Napoleon III, headquarters of the Commune and finally a lay temple (Victor Hugo was buried within it in 1885).

Exterior. — The Assembly ordered the blocking of Soufflot's forty-two windows which has deadened the design in spite of the frieze and garland which encircle the building. Two storeys were also removed from the towers flanking the apse.
The **dome**★★ with its iron framework, can only be appreciated from a distance. The peristyle is composed of fluted columns supporting a triangular pediment, the first of its kind in Paris. In 1831 David d'Angers carved a representation upon it of the Nation distributing palms presented by Liberty to great men: civilians on the left, the military led by Napoleon on the right. The central doorway is framed by marble groups depicting Clovis' Baptism, St Genevieve and Attila.

Interior. — *Restoration work in progress — only the crypt and upper areas are open to the public.* Flattened domes and, to divide the nave from the aisles, a line of columns supporting a frieze, cornice and balustrade, were used by Soufflot instead of more orthodox elements. The great central dome was also intended to be supported on columns but Rondelet substituted heavy masonry, so spoiling the effect; it weighs about 10 000 tons. The upper cupola has a fresco commissioned by Napoleon in 1811 from the artist, Gros, of *St Genevieve's Apotheosis.*
In 1849 Foucault took advantage of the dome's height to conduct an experiment proving the rotation of the earth *(see Conservatoire des Arts et Métiers, p 237).* The walls are decorated with **paintings**★ dating from 1877 onward: *Scenes from St Genevieve's Life* (right wall), the *Saint watching over Paris and Bringing Food to the City* — left wall beyond the dome *(p 108)* are by Puvis de Chavannes.

Crypt. — *Open 10am to 6pm in summer, 10am to 12noon and 2 to 5pm 1 October to 31 March; closed 1 January, 1 May, 1 and 11 November, 25 December; 25F;* ☎ *43 54 34 51.* The crypt extends under the whole building and contains the tombs of great men in all walks of life throughout France's history: La Tour d'Auvergne, Voltaire, Rousseau, Victor Hugo, Émile Zola, Marcelin Berthelot, Louis Braille (inventor of a system of writing for the blind), Jean Jaurès, the explorer Bougainville. Steps lead up to the dome: fine view over Paris.

★★ST-ÉTIENNE-DU-MONT CHURCH ▯▯ — fold 44: L 15

Closed on Mondays in July and August.

It is in this church that St Geneviève is venerated particularly. Both outside and inside, the church building is unique.

Until 1220 the servants of the Abbey of St Geneviève attended services in the church crypt then, their number becoming too great, a parish church, dedicated to St Stephen, was built adjoining the abbey church. By the end of the 15C St-Stephen's had become too small. Rebuilding began in 1492 with the belfry tower and apse; in 1610 the foundation stone for the new façade was laid by Queen Margot, first wife of Henri IV, and in 1626 the new church was consecrated.

The **façade**★★ is highly original. Three superimposed pediments stand at the centre, their lines emphasized by the upward sweep of the belfry. The south aisle rises to a considerable height above the chapels. The chancel, the first part to be built, has Flamboyant style broken arch bays, the nave, the later, rounded windows of the Renaissance.

The interior of the church is Gothic although it is 16C. The height of the arches over the nave and chancel, however, prevented the usual triforium being constructed and instead there is a line of windows. The walls along the aisles are also tall enabling wide, luminous bays to be hollowed out. An elegant balustrade course cuts the height of the tall pillars.

The Flamboyant vaulting above the transept catches the eye with its multiple ribbing and 5.50m-18ft intricately carved hanging keystone.

The 17C organ loft is highly ornate. Recitals are given regularly on the organ (90 stops).

The stained glass, which for the most part dates from the 16 and 17C is worth looking at in detail, particularly in the ambulatory and chancel.

The **roodscreen**★★ is the only one in existence in Paris. In the 15 and 16C all the major churches possessed roodscreens from which the Epistles, the Gospels and sermons were delivered. The screens' disadvantage, however, was that they hid all liturgical ceremony performed in the chancel from the faithful in the nave and in Paris they were, therefore, all removed apart from this one in which the wide arch gave a clear view.

The centre is decorated in the Renaissance style; the twin side doors are classical. Two lovely open spiral staircases lead to the rood loft and the course along the chancel pillars. Delightful feminine figures adorn the arch at either end.

Place Ste Geneviève

1) Marble slab marking the spot where an archbishop of Paris was stabbed to death by an unfrocked priest (3 January 1857).

2) 1650 **pulpit**★ supported by a figure of Samson.

3) **Stained glass window**★ of 1586 illustrating the parable of those invited to the feast.

4) 16C Entombment.

5) Over the arch, two ex-votos offered by the City of Paris: on the right, the City giving thanks to St Geneviève, painted by de Troy in 1726; on the left, an earlier painting by Largillière (1696).

6) The epitaphs of Racine (by Boileau) and Pascal.

7) **St Geneviève's shrine.** — St Geneviève's relics, originally buried in the crypt of the neighbouring abbey *(p 191)*, were exhumed and burnt upon the Place de Grève in 1793. When the abbey church was pulled down in 1802, the saint's sarcophagus stone was found and is now encased by the modern gilded copper shrine containing a few small relics.

8) Pascal (1623-1662) and Racine (1639-1699) lie buried near the pillars to the Lady Chapel. Racine was originally interred at Port-Royal-des-Champs and translated in 1711.

Cloister. — It is sometimes called the Charnel House Cloister. At one time the church was bordered to the north and east by two small burial grounds in which lay the remains, notably, of Mirabeau and Marat after they had been removed from the Pantheon.

The right side of the ambulatory opens onto the cloister which surrounded the burial ground at the church's east end and which, it is thought, may at one time have been used as a charnel house. At the beginning of the 17C, the cloister's main gallery at the end and on the left was glazed with **stained glass**★ beautiful in vitality and colour.

The small Cathechism Chapel was added by Baltard in 1859.

From Place du Panthéon to St-Nicolas-du-Chardonnet

Take Rue Clovis.

Henri-IV Lycée (Lycée Henri-IV). — It was on this site that Clovis, following his victory over the Visigoths at Vouillé near Poitiers, had a rich basilica erected in 510 in which he and his wife Clotilda were both buried and also St Geneviève. The widespread devotion to the saint soon called for the foundation of an abbey which came under the rule of Augustine canons and rivalled the Abbey of St-Germain-des-Prés in spiritual, juridical and territorial power. Medieval piety was expressed on all occasions by fasting and vast processions walking behind the saint's shrine through the decorated streets of Paris to the sound of ringing church bells.

The Revolution suppressed such festivities and even the abbey so that there remain only the refectory (along Rue Clotilde), Gothic cellars and the church belfry, known as **Clovis' Tower** (Tour de Clovis). Since 1796 the buildings have been occupied by the Henri-IV Lycée.

On the corner of Rue Descartes is St-Etienne's presbytery erected by the Duke of Orleans when he retired to the St-Geneviève Abbey where he died in 1752.

Further along, a large section of the **Philippe Auguste perimeter wall** (Enceinte Philippe-Auguste — *p 20*) can be seen at no **3** Rue Clovis. It originally stood 10m-33ft high and here lacks only its crenelations. Opposite, at no **65**, Rue du Cardinal-Lemoine is the **Scottish College**, a building with a noble façade which has belonged to the Roman Catholic Church of Scotland since the 14C. Inside, a magnificent staircase leads to the classical style chapel where a royal relic was deposited in 1701 on James II's death in exile *(p 201)*. The building is now a girls' hostel, the Foyer Ste-Geneviève. *Apply at the porter's lodge a few days in advance (☎ 43 54 11 41) to visit the chapel; closed 1 July to 9 September.* The philosopher Pascal died in 1662 at no **67**.

Return to Rue Descartes and turn right to skirt the former Ecole Polytechnique (moved to the outskirts of Paris in 1977) which replaced the earlier Navarre College, founded in 1304 by Jeanne of Navarre, wife of Philip the Fair, and is now the Ministry for Research and Technology. The institution, originally intended for seventy poor scholars, later numbered among its students Henri III, Henri IV, Richelieu and Bossuet. The École Polytechnique, founded by the Convention in 1794, moved to this site in 1805. Two years of military discipline and scholarship "for country, science and glory" ensure a high standard of technical knowledge among the few selected. The "X", as they are known, have included such diverse personages as Foch, the positivist philosopher Auguste Comte, Borotra, André Citroën and the French Presidents, Albert Lebrun and Valéry Giscard d'Estaing. Women were admitted for the first time in 1972.

Return to Rue de la Montagne Ste-Geneviève, then take Rue des Ecoles on the right and Rue des Bernardins on the left to the Church of St-Nicolas-du-Chardonnet.

St-Nicolas-du-Chardonnet Church. — A chapel was constructed on this site in a field planted with thistles *(chardons)* in the 13C. In 1656 it was replaced by the present north to south oriented building; the façade was completed only in 1934. It is dedicated to St Nicholas, the patron saint of boatmen.

The **side door★** (Rue des Bernardins), with remarkable wood carving after designs by Le Brun, a parishioner, is the best exterior feature.

The Jesuit style interior is liberally decorated with paintings including works by Restout, Coypel, Claude, Corot and Le Brun (his funeral monument, by Coysevox, stands in an ambulatory chapel on the left near Le Brun's own monument to his mother). There is an interesting monument by Girardon to the right of the chancel. The 18C organ loft is from the former Church of the Innocents *(p 146)*.

From St-Nicolas-du-Chardonnet Church
to Place Maubert

On leaving the church, walk left along Rue St-Victor. In the Middle Ages, **St-Victor Abbey** with its monastery buildings, gardens and church where Bishop Maurice of Sully was buried, extended from this area as far as the Seine. Walk past the Palais de la Mutualité.

Turn left into Rue de Poissy constructed in 1772 on the site of the **Bernardins College** gardens. Founded in 1246 it was a school for monks and was taken over by the Cistercians in the 14C. After it was closed down at the Revolution, the building was used as a staging-point for prisoners condemned to the galleys. Since 1845 it has been a fire-station (18-24 Rue de Poissy). From the road, one can catch a glimpse of the upper part of the refectory with its three ogive-vaulted aisles divided into seventeen bays. It is one of the finest Gothic halls in Paris. *Not open to the public.*

Continue to Boulevard St-Germain and walk left to Place Maubert. Then take Rue des Carmes to visit the Police Museum.

POLICE MUSEUM (MUSÉE DE LA PRÉFECTURE DE POLICE) ☐☐ — fold 44: K 15

1 bis Rue des Carmes; 2nd floor. Open Mondays to Fridays 9am to 5pm, Saturdays 10am to 5pm. ☎ 43 29 21 57. extn 336.

The **Historical Collections of the Police Museum** display the evolution of the Paris police from the watch in the early Middle Ages to the creation of the police force in 1870. There are also interesting legal documents such as *lettres de cachet* or royal warrants, decrees, prison registers as well as weapons and souvenirs of famous criminals and conspirators.

The **Luxembourg Quarter**

Michelin plan **11** - folds 31, 43: K 13, L 13

*Distance: 3km-2 miles – Time: 2 hours
(tour of the Luxembourg Palace not included)
Start from the Odeon métro station*

*This pleasant walk takes in one of the city's finest
gardens and the most extensive green
open space with harmonious lines and vistas
on the Left Bank. On summer afternoons
the trees provide welcome shade for children
and adults alike.*

From Carrefour de l'Odéon to the Luxembourg

Take Rue de Condé. It was in this street, lined with old houses, that Beaumarchais wrote the *Barber of Seville* in 1773 (no **26**). Continue along Rue Crébillon to the Place de l'Odéon.

Place de l'Odéon. — This semicircular square was created in 1779 in the former Condé house grounds and has remained unchanged. The houses surrounding it have plain façades; the roads leading to it were named after famous writers: Corneille, Racine, Voltaire (now renamed Casimir-Delavigne), Molière (Rotrou), Crébillon, Regnard. No **1**, the Café Voltaire, was frequented by the Encyclopaedists and, at the turn of the 20C, by famous writers and poets: Barrès, Bourget, Mallarmé and Verlaine.

Théâtre National de l'Odéon. — In 1782 a theatre was built in the gardens of the former Condé mansion to accommodate the French Comedians who for the past twelve years had been installed in the Tuileries Palace Theatre. The new theatre, built in the antique style of the day, was given the name Théâtre Français.

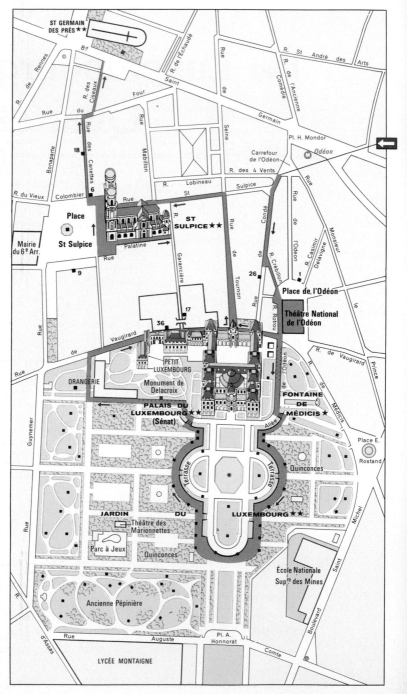

Luxembourg Palace and Gardens

Came the Revolution; the company divided and in 1792 those for the Republic left under Talma for the theatre in Rue Richelieu, the present Comédie-Française *(p 140)*. The Royalists who remained were soon removed to prison.

In 1797 a new company took over the theatre, renamed it the Odeon and failed. In 1807 the building was burned down but was reconstructed and the company started up again. In spite of the success of the play by Alphonse Daudet, the *Arlésienne* (1872) to music by Bizet, the theatre never became popular until 1946 when it began to specialize in 20C plays. It changed its name to Theâtre de France and for several years, with a company headed until 1968 by Jean-Louis Barrault and Madeleine Renaud, became the best filled theatre in Paris. Inside is a modern ceiling designed in 1963 by André Masson.

Walk down Rue Rotrou and turn right for the Luxembourg Palace.

★★LUXEMBOURG PALACE AND GARDENS
▣▣ — fold 43: K 13, L 13

The site, after the abandonment of the encampment and villas of Gallo-Roman times, became a desert and later the haunt of a ghostly highwayman named Vauvert, after his lair in an old ruin. Terror spread until in 1257 the Carthusians, installed by St Louis at Gentilly, suggested to the king that they rid the neighbourhood of the outlaw. They succeeded and built a vast monastery in the area.

Marie de' Medici's Palace. — After the death of Henri IV, his Queen, Marie de' Medici decided to build a palace which would recall the house of her youth in Tuscany. In 1612 she bought the mansion of Duke François of Luxembourg and a considerable adjoining area; in 1615 her architect, Salomon de Brosse, began to construct a palace inspired by the Pitti Palace of Florence. The building was much admired and in 1621 Rubens was commissioned to paint a series of 24 large pictures retracing allegorically the queen's life — the pictures now hang in the Medici Gallery in the Louvre *(p 48)*.

The day of deceit. — In 1625 the queen installed herself in the palace but her joy was short-lived for she had entered into opposition with Richelieu. She extracted a promise from her son, Louis XIII, on 10 November 1630 to dismiss the Cardinal but it was revoked twenty-four hours later and she was banished to Cologne where she died penniless in 1642. The palace reverted to its original Luxembourg title and, although abandoned, remained crown property until the Revolution.

The palace as parliament. — In 1790 when the monastery was suppressed, the gardens were enlarged and the palace vista extended the full length of the Avenue de l'Observatoire. Under the Terror the palace became a prison. The building next became a parliamentary assembly for the Directory, the Consulate, the Senate and its successor the Peers' Chamber. Chalgrin, architect of the Arc de Triomphe and the Odéon, completely transformed the interior, while from 1836 to 1841 Alphonse de Gisors enlarged it on the garden side by the addition of a new front to the main building and two projecting wing pavilions. At various dates Marshal Ney, the conspirator Louis-Napoleon Bonaparte (the future Napoleon III) and members of the Commune who turned against it, were all tried in the palace. In the Second World War the building was occupied by the Germans. On 25 August 1944 it was freed by Leclerc's Division and the French Resistance. Over the years much of the grounds has been taken over for the building of new roads.

The palace is now the seat of the **Senate** (Sénat), the French Upper House. The Senate is composed of 319 members chosen by an electoral college consisting of deputies, departmental and municipal councillors. Should the Presidency of the Republic fall vacant, the Senate President will exercise the functions of Head of State in the interim.

PALACE

Open first Sunday of every month at 10.30am; apply to the Caisse Nationale des Monuments Historiques, 62 Rue St-Antoine, 75004 Paris; ☎ 42 74 44 50.

To give a Florentine air to his design for the palace, Salomon de Brosse employed bosses, ringed columns and Tuscan capitals but he kept the French style ground plan of a courtyard surrounded by a central building, two wings at right angles and closed by twin arcaded galleries meeting in a central gateway surmounted by a cupola. The fine balustraded terrace has been recently reconstructed according to Brosse's original plan.

The Petit Luxembourg, now the residence of the president of the Senate, comprises the original Hôtel de Luxembourg presented to Richelieu by Marie de' Medici and also the cloister and chapel of a convent founded by the queen.

The former Luxembourg museum houses temporary exhibitions.

Interior. — The library is decorated with **paintings**★ by Delacroix *(Dante and Virgil walking in Limbo, Alexander placing Homer's poems in Darius' gold casket)*. The ceiling of the library annexe is decorated with a painting of the *Signs of the Zodiac* by Jordaens. In the Golden Book Room are the 17C panelling and paintings which once adorned Marie de' Medici's apartments. The Senate council chamber, the state gallery and most of the salons were furnished during the reign of Louis-Philippe. The main staircase by Chalgrin leads to the gallery in which the Rubens paintings were hung at one time.

Exterior. — Two inner courts, below the level of the Allée de l'Odéon, are decorated in the French garden style.

The Senate has extended its premises to a series of buildings across Rue de Vaugirard. In the ground floor galleries can be seen exhibitions of Coins and Medals and Sèvres Porcelain. Incorporated in the new building are no **36**, the doorway of a mansion built by Boffrand for the Palatine princess Anne of Bavaria in 1716 and round the corner at no **17** Rue Garancière, the façade of another mansion adorned with mascaroons representing the Seasons.

GARDENS

Basically the design is formal, the only free, more English style garden being along Rue Guynemer and Rue Auguste-Comte.

The **Medici Fountain**★ (Fontaine de Médicis) (1624) which stands in a green setting at the very end of a long pool shaded by plane trees, shows obvious Italian influence in its embossed decoration and overall design. In a niche the jealous cyclops, Polyphemus, waits to crush Acis and Galatea (by Ottin, 1863) while on the Rue de Médicis side is a low relief of Leda and the Swan (1807).

Statues began to invade the lawns under Louis-Philippe and today have reached such numbers that they seem to confront one at every step. The best, among this not artistically impressive crowd of figures, is the Delacroix group by Dalou. Queens and illustrious women of France line the terrace.

From the Luxembourg Palace to St-Germain-des-Prés

Walk to Place St-Sulpice by way of Rue de Vaugirard and Rue de Tournon and, on the left, Rue St-Sulpice.

Place St-Sulpice. — Started in 1754, it was originally intended that the square should be semi-circular with uniform façades modelled on that at no **6** (at the corner of Rue des Canettes), designed by Servandoni, the 18C Italian architect and painter who worked principally in France *(see below)*. The project for the uniform square fell through.

At the centre of the square stands a fountain erected by Visconti in 1844. It is so fashioned that it includes at the cardinal points of the compass, the portrait busts of four great men of the church: Bossuet, Fénelon, Massillon and Fléchier. None were ever made cardinals and in a play upon words — *point* in French means: both point and never — the fountain is known as Fontaine des Quatre Points Cardinaux — the Fountain of the Cardinal Points or the Four Cardinals who never were.

No **9** was the site of a former seminary.

★★CHURCH OF ST-SULPICE ▢▢ — fold 31: K 13

The church, dedicated to the 6C Archbishop of Bourges, St Sulpicius, was founded by the Abbey of St-Germain-des-Prés as a parish church for the peasants living in its domain. It has been rebuilt several times and was enlarged in the 16 and 17C, reconstruction beginning in 1646 with the chancel. Six architects were in charge successively over a period of one hundred and thirty-four years.

By 1732 work was due to begin on the façade but it was felt that a different style was required from the Graeco-Roman which had been adopted up till then. A competition was organized which was won by the Florentine, Servandoni, who proposed a fine antique style façade in contrast to the rest of the edifice. Servandoni's project was adopted but modified first by Maclaurin and then by Chalgrin. Delacroix' genius dominated the twenty artists who worked on the interior mural decorations.

Exterior. — The final façade differs considerably from Servandoni's original concept. The colossal pediment has been abandoned; the belfries are crowned not by Renaissance pinnacles but by balustrades; the towers are dissimilar, the one on the left being taller and more ornate than the one on the right which was never completed.

Walk back along the south side of the church, down Rue Palatine. The transept façade is in the Jesuit style with two superimposed orders and heavy ornaments. Seen from the corner of Rue Palatine and Rue Garancière, St-Sulpice is a building of some size, shouldered by massive buttresses designed as inverted consoles and ending in the dome and corbelled apse of the Lady Chapel.

Interior. — The interior, which measures 113m long by 58m wide by 34m high-371 × 190 × 112ft — is extremely impressive.

In the transept, a copper band oriented from north to south and inlaid in the pavement, crosses from a plaque in the south arm to an obelisk in the north arm. During the winter solstice a ray of sunshine, passing through a small hole in the upper window in the south transept, strikes marked points on the obelisk in the far transept at midday exactly. At the spring and autumn equinox the ray falls on the copper plaque. This 1744 meridian *(p 202)* also serves daily as a midday timepiece. The Christ against the Pillar, the Mater Dolorosa and the Apostles beside the chancel columns are by Bouchardon.

The decoration of the **Lady Chapel**★ at the centre of the east end of the church, was supervised personally by Servandoni. In the altar niche is a Virgin and Child by Pigalle; on the walls hang paintings by Van Loo and on the dome is a fresco by Lemoyne.

The **organ loft**★ was designed by Chalgrin in 1776. The organ itself was rebuilt in 1862 and is considered one of the finest in France. The church has a long and august musical tradition.

Mural paintings★ full of Romantic ardour were carried out by Delacroix between 1849 and 1861 on the walls of the first chapel on the right. On the vaulting is St Michael killing the demon; on the right wall Heliodorus is being driven from the Temple (the story is that Heliodorus, a minister of the King of Syria, coveted the treasures of the Temple and was struck down by three avenging angels, one of whom is riding a horse); on the left wall Jacob struggles with the Angel.

Two stoups against the second pillars of the nave have been made from giant shells given to François I by the Venetian Republic and then Louis XV to St-Sulpice Church in 1745. Their rock supports were carved by Pigalle.

Return to St-Germain-des-Prés by Rue des Canettes, Duckling Street, which takes its name from the low relief at no **18** — and Rue des Ciseaux with its many old houses.

The **Val-de-Grâce Quarter**

Michelin plan **11** - fold 43: L 13, L 14 – M 13, M 14

*Distance: 3.5km-2 miles – Time: 2 1/2 hours
Start from Port-Royal métro station*

*This former « Valley of Grace » is now devoted
to medical care and higher education. The first
half of the 17C saw the establishment of
religious communities: in 1605, the **Carmelites**
(no 284 Rue St-Jacques) — Louise de
la Vallière retreated to the convent when no
longer favoured by Louis XIV; in 1612, the
Ursulines; in 1622, the **Feuillantines** founded by
Anne of Austria; in 1626, the **Visitandines.**
The same year, Mother Angélique Arnauld
ordered the construction of **Port-Royal,** the
dependency of the Jansenist Port-Royal-des-
Champs. Her tomb lies in the chancel of the
church at no 123 Boulevard de Port-Royal.*

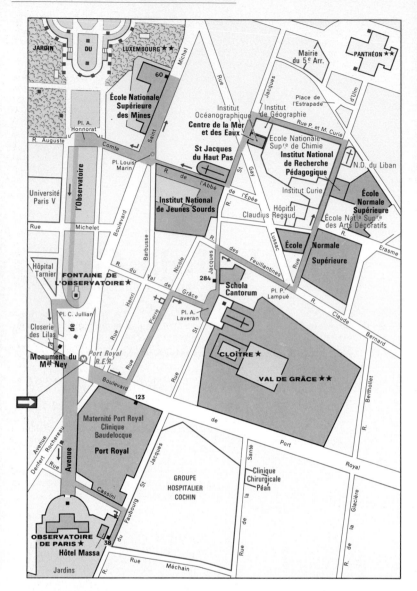

★★VAL DE GRÂCE ⬜⬜ — fold 43: M 14

All the 17C buildings of the former abbey remain. A few years after the foundation of the new Oratory congregation *(p 144)* in Rue St-Jacques in 1611, Anne of Austria bought the mansion to establish in it a Benedictine community which took the same name as its provincial convent, Val-de-Grâce. Anne visited the community frequently to pray and discreetly to intrigue against Richelieu. At 37, Anne, who had been married twenty-three years, was still without a child. She promised the gift of a magnificent church if her prayers were answered and kept her vow on the birth of Louis XIV in 1638. The plans for the Val-de-Grâce Church were drawn by François Mansart.

The foundation stone was laid by the young king himself in 1645. Anne of Austria, finding Mansart too slow, replaced him by Le Mercier, who, until his death, executed his predecessor's plans. The building was at last completed in 1667 and consecrated in 1710 (Louis XIV was 72). Val-de-Grâce became a military hospital in 1795 and a medical school in 1850. The new buildings house a military hospital once again.

★★**Church.** — The church, probably the most Roman in appearance in France, was erected in the Jesuit style after the Sorbonne *(p 188)* and before the Invalides *(p 73)*. Above the two tier façade with a double triangular pediment is a dome, which is less tall but more ornate than its Paris rivals and obviously inspired by St Peter's basilica in Rome.

Inside, the Baroque influence appears in the sculptured vaulting over the nave, the monumental baldachin with six twisted columns framing the altar and the magnificent **cupola**★★ decorated with a fresco by Mignard in which there are 200 figures each three times lifesize. The outstanding carvings are by Michel Anguier and Philippe Buyster.

The St-Louis Chapel (*right*) was originally the Benedictine chancel. From 1662 the hearts of members of the royal and Orleans families were deposited in the St-Anne Chapel, on the left. When the caskets were desecrated at the Revolution there were 45, including those of Queen Marie-Thérèse, "Monsieur" (Philippe, Duke of Orleans), the Regent, Philippe of Orleans and Marie Leczinska. Most have disappeared.

Former Convent. — *Restoration work in progress.* Go through the porch to the right of the church. The **cloister★**, which opens off the end of the court, is classical in style with two superimposed galleries and a mansard roof. The gardens, through the court's second arch, give a good view of the convent's majestic rear façade, the pavilion in which Anne of Austria stayed, distinguished by a porch with ringed columns, and the rear of the church dome.

Museum. — *Closed for restoration.* Displays include documents and mementoes of the great military physicians (Parmentier, premier pharmacist during the Empire; Villemin, Roussin, Broussais, Vincent, Laveran, Nobel prizewinner, 1907) and the French Health Service. Models and equipment indicate treatment meted out to the wounded during the Empire and the First World War.

From the Val-de-Grâce to the Observatory

Schola Cantorum. — *269 Rue St-Jacques.* The conservatory was founded privately in 1896 by Ch. Bordes, Guilmant and the composer Vincent d'Indy, to restore church music. The buildings formerly belonged to a community of English Benedictines who sought refuge in Paris after the Anglican Schism of 1531; the body of James II, who died in exile at St-Germain-en-Laye in 1701, rested in the chapel (now secularised) until the Revolution when the building was desecrated. It is now a music, dance and drama school.

Bear right in Rue des Feuillantines then left into Rue d'Ulm.

École Normale Supérieure. — *45 Rue d'Ulm.* The school of higher studies for those entering the teaching profession was created by the Convention in 1794. It transferred to these buildings in 1847. For many university and other learned men and politicians, the "Normale" has proved to be the springboard to a brilliant career. The **French Office for Modern Methods of Teaching** (Institut National de Recherche pédagogique) is at no 29 Rue d'Ulm. It houses temporary exhibitions on education (*open 8.45am to 6pm; closed weekends and holidays; ☎ 46 34 90 02*).

Turn left into Rue Pierre-et-Marie-Curie and left again into Rue St-Jacques.

Marine and Freshwater Centre (Centre de la Mer et des Eaux). — *195, Rue St-Jacques. Open 10am to 12.30pm and 1.15 to 5.30pm; 10am to 5.30pm Sundays and holidays; closed Mondays, 1 January, 1 May, 14 July, 15 August and 25 December; 18F. Film shows on Wednesdays, Saturdays and Sundays, 3 and 4pm. ☎ 46 33 08 61.*

The centre which is part of the Oceanographic Institute founded at the beginning of the 20C by Albert I of Monaco, is devoted to the study of the ocean, its role and resources, and holds exhibitions and audio-visual presentations. Aquariums.

The Observatory Fountain

Church of St James of the High Pass (St-Jacques-du-Haut-Pas). — *Closed 12.30 to 4pm and Monday mornings; in July and August closed 12.30 to 5pm and all day Monday.* The church, built in the classical style between 1630 and 1685, became a Jansenist centre. The astronomer, Cassini *(see below)*, is buried inside.

National Institute for the Deaf (Jeunes Sourds). — A hospital to succour pilgrims on their way to Compostela in Spain was established on this site in the 14C by monks from Altopascio (High Pass) near Lucca in Italy. In 1790, one year after the death of the Abbot de l'Épée *(p 139)* who had worked on the education of deaf mutes, the hospital took up his work.

Rue de l'Abbé-de-l'Épée leads to Boulevard St-Michel.

School of Advanced Mining Engineering (École Supérieure des Mines). — *Enter through no 60.* The school was founded in 1783 and moved to the present buildings, the former Hôtel de Vendôme, in 1815.
The **mineralogical collection★★** is among the world's richest. *Open Wednesdays to Fridays 2 to 5pm; Tuesdays and Saturdays 10am to 12.30pm and 2 to 5pm; closed Sundays, Mondays and holidays; 10F; ☎ 40 51 91 39.*

Avenue de l'Observatoire. — The wide avenue with its central flower borders is lined by the buildings of Paris V University. The **Observatory Fountain★** (1873) by Davioud is known for its decoration of the four quarters of the globe by Carpeaux (Oceania was omitted for reasons of symmetry!). The view towards Montmartre is attractive.
Before the Closerie des Lilas café, so famous in the 1920's, stands the vigorous François Rude's **statue of Marshal Ney** (1853) — executed nearby in 1815 for his support of Napoleon — greatly admired by Rodin.

★THE OBSERVATORY
⬚⬚ — fold 43: N 13

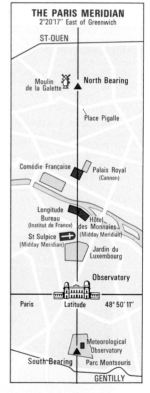

THE PARIS MERIDIAN
2°20'17" East of Greenwich

ST-OUEN

Moulin de la Galette

North Bearing

Place Pigalle

Comédie Française

Palais Royal (Cannon)

Longitude Bureau (Institut de France)

Hôtel des Monnaies (Midday Meridian)

St Sulpice (Midday Meridian)

Jardin du Luxembourg

Observatory

Paris   Latitude   48° 50' 11"

Meteorological Observatory

South Bearing   Parc Montsouris

GENTILLY

The Observatory's construction, on orders from Colbert and to plans by Claude Perrault, was begun on 21 June 1667, the summer solstice, and was completed in 1672. The Cassinis, a family of four astronomers of Italian origin, continued in succession as directors until the Revolution. The dome and wings were added under Louis-Philippe.
The research conducted at the Observatory has included the calculation of the true dimensions of the solar system (1672), of the meridians of longitude, until then more than a little exaggerated — Louis XIV commented that the Academician's calculations had considerably reduced the extent of his kingdom! — the speed of light, the production of a large map of the moon (1679), the discovery by mathematical deduction of the planet Neptune by Le Verrier in 1846, the invention of new instruments...

The building. — The building's four walls are oriented to the cardinal points of the compass, the south face also determining the capital's latitude. The meridian of longitude, calculated in 1667, which passes through the building was known as the Paris Meridian, until 1884 when the Greenwich mean was adopted generally with the exception of France and Ireland, which only followed suit in 1911. Midday bearings are to be found elsewhere in Paris besides on the actual meridian *(see diagram)*.
The Observatory has been the seat of the International Time Bureau which since its inauguration (1919) sets Coordinated Universal Time (UTC) and is itself based on International Atomic (IAT). The speaking clock (☎ 36.99) gives Coordinated Universal Time accurate to one millionth of a second.
Guided tours: first Saturday in the month at 2.30pm on written application to the Service des visites, 61 Avenue de l'Observatoire 75014 Paris, enclosing S.A.E.; ☎ 40 51 21 74: small museum of old instruments, modern equipment in the park and dome of the upper terrace.
From the Observatory, walk up Rue du Faubourg St-Jacques to no **38**, the **Hôtel Massa** (*p 56* — the Men of Letters Society).

Montparnasse

Michelin plan **11** - folds 41 and 42: L 11, L 12 – M 11, M 12

Distance: 4km-2 1/2 miles – Time: 4 hours
Start from the Montparnasse-Bienvenüe métro station

This crowded quarter, which traditionally belonged to artists and the working class, is today the scene of one of the major urban renewal projects to be undertaken within the heart of Paris.

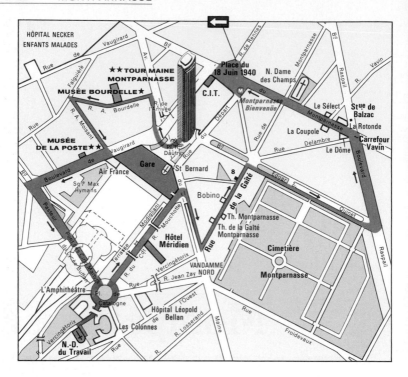

Mount Parnassus. — The debris from age-old quarries formed a heathlike grass covered mound. For students, chased away from the Pré-aux-Clercs by Queen Margot *(p 166)*, it became a favourite haunt to declaim poems away from the confines of the city — they nicknamed it Mount Parnassus after the mountain of Apollo and the muses.

In the 18C the mound was razed but the boulevard laid across its site, a fragment of the Farmers General perimeter wall, complete with toll-booths, kept the name alive.

A pleasure ground. — The Revolution saw the springing up of cafés and cabarets on the city outskirts and revellers enjoying the Montagnes-Suisses and Élysée-Montparnasse gardens and the dancing at the Arc-en-Ciel and Grande Chaumière. The polka and the can-can were first seen here before they became the rage of Paris. At the Observatory crossroads, where Marshal Ney was executed *(p 202)* were, first, the Bullier Hall, then, a few years later, the Closerie des Lilas café. Crowds gathered at the Constant Dance Hall and in the inns of the village of Plaisance to dance the mazurka between sips of tart Suresnes wine.

As the quarter began to spread out, Haussmann intervened, he planned to create an entirely built-up area which included the old villages of Plaisance, Vaugirard and Montrouge. He then proceeded to divide it up with the Rue de Rennes, the Boulevard Arago and the Boulevard d'Enfer (now Boulevard Raspail).

Bohemian Montparnasse. — At the turn of the century avant-garde artists, poets and writers, moved to the Left Bank of the Seine, particularly Montparnasse. The atmosphere had already been described by Henri Murger many years earlier in his *Scenes of Bohemian Life* on which Puccini had based his opera *La Bohème*. The 1900 Exhibition Wine Pavilion was reconstructed at no 52 Rue de Dantzig, renamed the **Ruche** or Beehive, and replaced the Bateau-Lavoir of Montmartre *(p 87)*, providing lodging and studios for Modigliani, Soutine, Chagall, Zadkine and Léger. Talk went on for hours in the café-restaurants (le Dôme, la Rotonde, le Sélect and La Coupole) among the Russian political exiles — Lenin, Trotsky — musicians — Stravinsky, Satie and "the Six" — poets — Cocteau — and foreigners — Hemingway, Foujita, Picasso, Eisenstein, Blasco Ibanez... It was the golden age of the **Paris School** and it lasted into the mid-thirties, ending only with the outbreak of war in Spain and Western Europe.

Montparnasse today. — This former international Bohemian quarter is entirely Parisian. Anonymous crowds of revellers and artists attracted by the cafés, cinemas and night-clubs rub shoulders with the local population of workers, shopkeepers and artisans.

Since redevelopment the Maine-Montparnasse complex has become the nucleus of a business area while the Vandamme-Nord section has a mixture of offices, housing, sporting facilities and hotel accommodation. Beyond the old village of Plaisance, part of Paris for less than a century, is transformed by the presence of modern high-rise blocks.

To choose a hotel or restaurant, use the small, **MICHELIN Red Guide:**
PARIS, Hotels and Restaurants,
an extract from the current **MICHELIN Red Guide FRANCE.**

★THE MAINE-MONTPARNASSE COMPLEX
⊞ — fold 42: L 11 — M 11

Dating from 1934 the original plan for this area was revised in 1958 when it became a major urban renewal project with the aim of creating a high density business area on the Left Bank. Work began in 1961 and the tower was completed in 1973.

Place du 18-Juin-1940. — Until 1967 this site, lined by cafés, was occupied by the old 19C station, the Gare Montparnasse which will be remembered as the headquarters of General Leclerc at the time of the liberation of Paris and the place where, on 25 August 1944, the German military governor signed his garrison's surrender. A mural plaque at the entrance to the commercial centre *(left side)* commemorates this event.

At the corner of Boulevard du Montparnasse and Rue de l'Arrivée, stands the cube shaped building of the **International Textile Centre** (CIT), which houses over 200 firms.

The Commercial Centre. — The podium extending from the Place du 18-Juin-1940 to the foot of the tower consists of 8 levels, 6 of which are underground. On the upper three floors are department stores, 60 or so luxury shops presenting the latest fashions, cafés and restaurants. The remaining floors are occupied by parking space, the technical installations and a sports centre *(entrance Rue du Départ)* with swimming pool.

★★**Montparnasse Tower (Tour Montparnasse).** — This 209m-688ft high tower, dominating the whole quarter — adds a new landmark to the Paris skyline and is the most spectacular and controversial feature of the project. The strictly geometrical lines of the façades are softened by the harmonious curved form. This tower, the tallest office building of the complex is the design of a group of French architects. The building with 52 floors given over to office space has a working population of 5 000. The technical installations — heating, lighting, etc. — and security systems are controlled by a computer. The foundations go down 70m-230ft to support the 120 000 tons of masonry and shafts. The weight load of the building is distributed between two different structures: a central reinforced concrete core, of the same shape as the building, and the outer "walls" of closely spaced vertical columns. These are linked by horizontal beams. The curtain walls are covered with bronze tinted glass.

The building is separated from the new railway station, by a parvis paved with pink Sardinian granite under which passes the Avenue du Maine.

Ascent. — *Open 1 April to 30 September 9.30am to 11.30pm; 1 October to 31 March 10am to 10pm; (11pm Fridays and Saturdays); last admission 1/2 hour before closing time; 35F, children, 21F;* ☎ 45 38 52 56. The 56th floor observatory affords a magnificent **panorama★★★** of Paris and its suburbs. Viewing tables help you to pick out the main landmarks: the Eiffel Tower with the skyscrapers of the new Défense quarter in the distance, the Louvre, the Sacré-Cœur, Notre-Dame, the Bois de Vincennes, Orly Airport and the Bois de Boulogne. By night Paris becomes a fairytale wonderland. There is also a bar and panoramic restaurant at this level. From the 59th floor the view can extend as far as 49km-30 miles.

Montparnasse Tower

The Station (Gare). — Trains from southern and western France now run into a U-shaped terminus surrounded on three sides by immense 18 storey glass, steel and concrete blocks. The station proper, on five levels, occupies the central area — a vast concourse connects with the métro and supplies every amenity, even a small chapel to St Bernard *(entrance at no 34)* — the lectern was carved from a railway sleeper. The longer sides of the U, extending nearly 250m-275 yds back along the track, are occupied by 1 000 flats and a major postal sorting office on the left and, on the right, the Air France and other offices, overlooking the Square Max-Hymans and Boulevard de Vaugirard.

The station has been redeveloped to cater for the French high-speed train on the southwest line (TGV Atlantique) and also to absorb some of the traffic from Austerlitz Station. Porte Océane, the main entrance, is a vast glass-clad arch linking the city to the station. Hanging gardens and tennis courts have been laid out on the concrete podium spanning the tracks.

From Maine-Montparnasse to the Montparnasse Cemetery

Walk left along Avenue du Maine, then turn left into Rue Antoine-Bourdelle.

★**Bourdelle Museum (Musée Bourdelle).** — *No 16. Open 10am to 5.40pm; closed Mondays and holidays; 12F. Temporary exhibitions: 20F. ☎ 45 48 67 27.*
Bourdelle's (1861-1929) house, garden and studio have been converted to display the artist's sculptures, paintings and drawings. In the great hall are the original plaster casts of his great sculptures — many of which may also be seen at the Champs-Élysées Theatre and in the Alma Quarter. The most outstanding items among his immense output are the huge bronzes, now in the garden, his portrait busts of his contemporaries, including his master, Rodin, the writer Anatole France and the **portraits of Beethoven**★ of whom he made 21 different studies.

Continue along Rue Antoine-Bourdelle and turn left into Rue Armand-Moisant which leads back to Boulevard de Vaugirard.

At no 34 Boulevard de Vaugirard stands the **National Postal and Philatelic Centre.** The unusual façade has five decorative panels of light reflecting prisms to break the monotony of the windowless walls of the five exhibition floors.

★★**Postal Museum (Musée de la Poste).** — *Open 10am to 5pm; closed Sundays and holidays; 18F. Library, photographic library, lecture theatres, temporary exhibition galleries and a stamp counter. ☎ 42 79 24 24.*
The museum presents an attractive account of the postal services through the ages. Start on the 5th floor. In Gallery 2 note the parchment scroll, used by religious orders in the Middle Ages as a means of communication between abbeys and the balloon used during the 1870-71 siege of Paris. Gallery 3 shows the development of the postal network in France, from the early relay posts for mounted carriers to the 18 000 post offices of today. The next two galleries display models of different means of postal transport.
Galleries 10-12 are of special interest. Note the model of a present day stamp printing machine. Next comes a complete collection of French stamps since the first issue in 1849 and finally other national collections, displayed in rotation. The final two galleries show the present sorting and franking methods and machines.
The Cinq-Martyrs-du-Lycée-Buffon Bridge, overlooked by two modern buildings, links the redeveloped Montparnasse quarter with the Plaisance quarter. In the mid-19C Plaisance was one of the villages surrounding Paris. Note on the right the two strikingly modern buildings in stone and glass respectively, by Ricardo Bofill, linked by a neo-classical semicircular façade and a vast disc-shaped fountain in the centre of the square.
Continue to **Notre-Dame-du-Travail Church** (1900) unusually built in the metallic architectural style with the iron girders visible on the façades in an attempt to bring together the notions of work and worship.
After the bridge turn left into Rue du Commandant-René-Mouchotte, which passes one of the main postal sorting offices and on the right the elegant white building of the Méridien-Montparnasse Hotel, which contrasts with the surrounding buildings. The architect Pierre Dufau was also responsible for two of the towers at La Défense (the Septentrion and Assur towers). The hotel with its 1 000 rooms and conference hall is part of a larger complex comprising office and housing space, a commercial centre and a bowling alley. Two overhead passageways link the Vandamme-Nord centre to the Modigliani Terrace.

Turn right into Avenue du Maine then left into Rue de la Gaîté.

Rue de la Gaîté. — This old country road has, since the 18C, been lined throughout by cabarets, dance halls, restaurants and other pleasure spots — hence its name. The street's tradition which began with the Mère Cadet, the Veau qui Tète and the Gigoteurs Dance Hall, is maintained today by the Gaîté-Montparnasse (no 26), the Grand Edgar Theatre (no **8**) the Montparnasse Theatre (no 31). The theatre's reputation for popular drama was revived in the 1930's.

Turn right into Boulevard Edgar-Quinet for the cemetery's main entrance.

Montparnasse Cemetery (Cimetière Montparnasse):

1) J.-P. Sartre, philosopher, and Simone de Beauvoir, writer.
2) Soutine *(p 204)*, painter.
3) Baudelaire, poet.
4) Laurens, sculptor.
5) Bourdelle (no inscription), sculptor.
6) Dumont d'Urville, admiral.
7) Tristan Tzara, Romanian Dadaist poet.

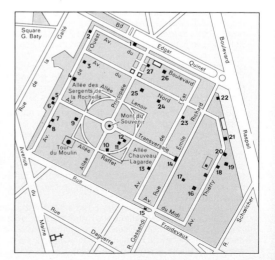

8) Zadkine, sculptor.

9) Mounet-Sully, actor.

10) Houdon, sculptor.

11) Jussieu *(p 237)*, botanist.

12) Rude *(p 59)*, sculptor.

13) Le Verrier *(p 202)*, astronomer.

14) Baudelaire's Cenotaph.

15) Henri Poincaré, mathematician.

16) Cesar Franck, composer.

17) Guy de Maupassant, writer.

18) Bartholdi, sculptor.

19) Kessel, writer.

20) André Citroën, engineer and industrialist.

21) Pigeon, sculptor.

22) The Kiss by Brancusi, Romanian sculptor.

23) Sainte-Beuve, writer-critic.

24) Saint-Saëns, composer.

25) Vincent d'Indy, composer.

26) Leon-Paul Fargue, poet.

27) Boucicaut, businessman.

From the Montparnasse Cemetery to Place du 18-Juin-1940

Make for Boulevard Raspail built in 1760 and extended a hundred years later beyond Boulevard Montparnasse towards Boulevard St-Germain. Turn left towards **Vavin Crossroads** (Place Pablo Picasso). This crossroads, originally the summit of the Parnassus Mound, bustles with life and is now the heart of the old quarter. In 1939 the famous statue of **Balzac** by Rodin was placed on an island site in the Boulevard Raspail. Walk up Boulevard Montparnasse which is lined with big café-restaurants and cinemas. Pass the Church of Notre-Dame-des-Champs (Our Lady of the Fields) whose name recalls a much older country church before reaching Place du 18-Juin-1940.

The
Chaillot Quarter
and
Avenue Montaigne

Michelin plan **11** - folds 16, 17, 28 and 29: G 8, G 9

Distance: 3km-2 miles – Time: 4 hours
Start from the Alma-Marceau métro station

This walk travels through one of the most luxurious quarters of Paris where the wealthy residential section mingles with the elegance of the couturiers and perfumers.

The Alma Square and Bridge. – *The square and bridge created in the time of Napoleon III, are named after the first Franco-British victory in the Crimean War (1854).*

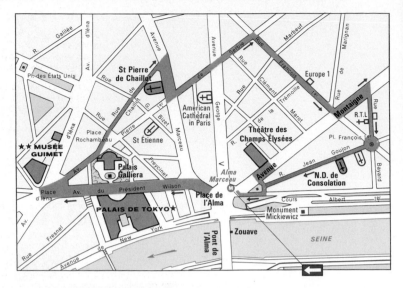

The original bridge, slowly undermined by the Seine, was replaced in 1972 by an asymmetrical steel structure with a 110m-361ft span.

Only the **Zouave** (upstream by the single pile) remains of the four Second Empire soldier statues which decorated the old bridge; he serves as a high water marker and is very popular with Parisians — once in January 1910, the water came up to his chin.

★ PALAIS DE TOKYO ⊡⊡ — fold 28: G 8 — H 8

The Palais was built for the 1937 World Exhibition, replacing the Savonnerie Carpet Workshop *(p 245)*. The two wings linked by a portico, look down over a series of terraces, which are adorned by low reliefs and statues by Bourdelle *(p 206)*, including his **France★** *(in the centre)*.

The **west wing** houses a European Foundation (FEMIS) which offers courses in film making and audio-visual techniques. There are temporary exhibitions devoted to the cinema and photography.

Museum of Modern Art of the City of Paris (Musée d'Art Moderne de la Ville de **Paris**). — *Enter on Alma side. Open 10am to 5.30pm (8.30pm on Wednesdays); closed Mondays and 1 January, 1 May and 25 December; 15F; temporary exhibitions: 20F* ☎ *47 23 61 27. Library.*

The collection illustrates the main trends in 20C art. Fauvism which is characterized by flat bright colours is represented by Matisse and Derain. Picasso and Braque, the leading exponents of Cubism, experimented with geometrical lines and volumes and influenced Delaunay, Léger, Gromaire and Ozenfant. Rouault, Utrillo and Suzanne Valadon developed their own individual style. The Paris school was created by foreign artists who came to live in Paris at the turn of the century: Modigliani, Soutine, Foujita, Chagall. The main movements evolved after the First World War: abstract art, surrealism, figurative art, new realism.

Abstract art dismissed figurative elements in favour of the interplay of line and colour (Fautrier, Helion, Arp, Magnelli, Domela) while surrealism introduced a dreamlike dimension to the real world. One gallery is devoted to Brauner's preliminary sketches and to his unusual *"conglomeros"*. Most modern artists are advocates of abstraction. One room displays furniture and objets d'art of the period between 1920 and 1937.

Dufy's *The Good Fairy Electricity*, the biggest picture in the world comprising 250 panels (600m-6 095sq ft), represents the scientists and thinkers, who mastered this form of energy. Other large-scale canvases are *La Danse* by Matisse and decorations by Delaunay.

The museum displays works illustrating the trends and techniques of contemporary art. The experimental centre (A.R.C.) presents innovations in the fields of plastic art, music and poetry.

★★ GUIMET MUSEUM (MUSÉE GUIMET) ⊡⊡ — fold 28: G 7

Open 9.45am to 5.15pm. Closed Tuesdays and holidays; 16F (8F Sundays). ☎ *47 23 61 65.*

The museum, founded by Émile Guimet, a 19C collector from Lyons contains Oriental works of art.

The ground floor is reserved for Far Eastern art: Khmer art (Cambodia), is well represented by intricately carved temple pediments and a series of **heads of Buddha** in the typical pose with eyes half-closed and a meditative smile. The seated Shiva with ten arms is an example of central Vietnamese art.

The Lamaist section includes a remarkable collection of Tibetan and Nepalese banners *(thanka)* as well as ceremonial objects and gilded bronzes; of the latter the most noteworthy is the graceful **dancing Dakini**.

The first floor shows the evolution of Indian art from the 3C BC to the 19C. There are the carved low reliefs from Northern India and the Hindu sculpture and bronzes originating from the southeast. Outstanding among the sculpture is the beautiful **Cosmic Dance by Shiva**. The art of both Pakistan (represented here by the famous Bodhisattva from Shabaz-Garhi) and Afghanistan (the Begrâm treasure: sculptured ivories of Indian origin and Hellenistic plasters) are of special interest.

The Chinese collection includes ceremonial bronze objects, jade and laquer ware, Buddhist sculpture and funerary statuettes.

On the second floor are the exceptional displays of **Chinese ceramics** from the Calmann and Grandidier collections (18C *"famille rose"* set) and the series of Buddhist banners (8C-11C) which was discovered in a cave of Dunhuang. The jewels from Korea include a funerary crown.

From Japan can be seen dance masks *(gigaku)* and the "Portuguese Screen" (16C) depicting the arrival in Japanese waters of a Portuguese ship.

Buddhist Pantheon. — *19 Avenue d'Iéna*. This annexe now recreates Emile Guimet's original conception of a Buddhist pantheon of Japan. The works date in the main from the 17C and 18C and were collected in 1876 by Guimet during a five-month visit to Japan. The main displays on the first floor represent the first two of six categories of "venerated beings" according to their progress along the path to the deathless state of Enlightenment: the Buddhas (the Enlightened One) and the bodhisattvas (Buddhas to be), or helpers along the way. In the reliquary, Mandala of the Lotus Sutra (12), two Buddhas flank the tablet of hommage of the sutra (sacred text) and are accompanied by other attendants. Amida, the Buddha of the Western Pure Land is portrayed in a typical seated position on a lotus pedestal (18) and in the Amida Triad (21) flanked by the bodhisattvas Kannon and Seishi descending on clouds to welcome the deceased into paradise or the "Pure Land". The rare 13C bronze statue alongside is of the bodhisattva Seishi (24). In the next room Kannon, the popular bodhisattva of compassion and mercy, is shown in a variety of forms. The other exhibits on this floor illustrate the influence that Chinese Buddhism had on its Japanese counterpart.

The downstairs gallery with the remaining four categories of divinities is dominated by the striking mandala with its twenty-three statues, a replica of the early 9C masterpiece of Buddhist art the Mandala Tôji in Kyoto. Conceived as an aid to meditation this grouping of Buddhist deities shows Buddha encircled by five secondary bodhisattvas, the guardian kings of the cardinal points, the warlike kings of wisdom and other attendants.

From Place d'Iéna to Place de l'Alma

On leaving the Guimet Museum, on Place d'Iéna, note the concrete Economic and Social Council Building (Palais du Conseil Économique et Social) designed by Auguste Perret (1937).

In this residential quarter of private mansions *(hôtels)* and luxurious apartment houses live many foreigners.

Palais Galliera. — *10 Avenue Pierre-Ier-de-Serbie*. The Duchess of Galliera, wife of the Italian financier and philanthropist, had this building built (1878-1888) in the Italian Renaissance style. The mansion houses a Costume Museum.

Costume Museum. — *Open 10am to 5.40pm; closed Mondays, holidays and between exhibitions; for further information ☎ 47 20 85 23; 28F.* Revolving exhibitions (twice yearly) present men, women and children's fashion and dress from 1735 to the present. This vast collection comprises almost 12 000 complete outfits and an additional 60 000 articles.

Follow — on the left — Rue de Chaillot, the main street of the old village of Chaillot.

Church of St Peter of Chaillot. — The church was rebuilt in the neo-Romanesque style in 1937. Overlooking its façade, on which the life of St Peter has been carved by Bouchard *(p 240)*, is a 65m high-213ft — belfry.

Take Avenue Pierre-Ier-de-Serbie leading to a bustling quarter dotted with banks, art galleries, luxury boutiques, couturiers and perfumers. After crossing Avenue Georges-V turn right into Rue François Ier (further left the Europe No 1 broadcasting station) to reach the elegant **Avenue Montaigne**. Until 1870 crowds flocked to the Mabille dance hall in this former gallant Widows' Alley. Nowadays it is lined with great buildings and famous couturier shops.

At no 22, Rue Bayard is the Radio-Télé-Luxembourg station. Note the façade of the building which was decorated by Vasarely.

Church of Notre-Dame de Consolation. — *23 Rue Jean-Goujon*. A fire at a charity bazaar in 1897 killed 117 people on the site on which this memorial chapel, designed by Guilbert, was erected (1901).

The decoration is neo-Baroque: note the handsome marble columns at the entrance to the side chapels and supporting the entablatures. Niches contain urns and cenotaphs. It is the Italian church in Paris.

The statue in the Cours Albert Ier is of the Polish poet and patriot, Mickiewicz (1798-1855) by Bourdelle *(p 206)*.

Champs-Élysées Theatre. — *13 Avenue Montaigne*. The theatre, the work of the Perret brothers was in 1912 one of the first large reinforced concrete buildings to be erected in Paris. The high reliefs on the façade are by Bourdelle; the decoration on the ceiling is by Maurice Denis. At times, Diaghilev and his Russian ballet company, the Marquis de Cuevas and his dancers, and the actor Louis Jouvet all starred at the theatre. After renovation it is one of the finest theatres in Paris.

The Bois de Boulogne

Michelin plan **11**: detailed map

*This vast park of 846 ha-2 100 acres
is cut by wide shaded roads (speed limit),
rides and cycle tracks (bicycles for hire
opposite the Jardin d'Acclimatation's main entrance
at the Carrefour des Sablons and near the
Royal Pavilion at the Carrefour du Bout-des-Lacs,
daily 15 April to 15 October, Wednesdays,
Saturdays and Sundays, the rest of the year).*

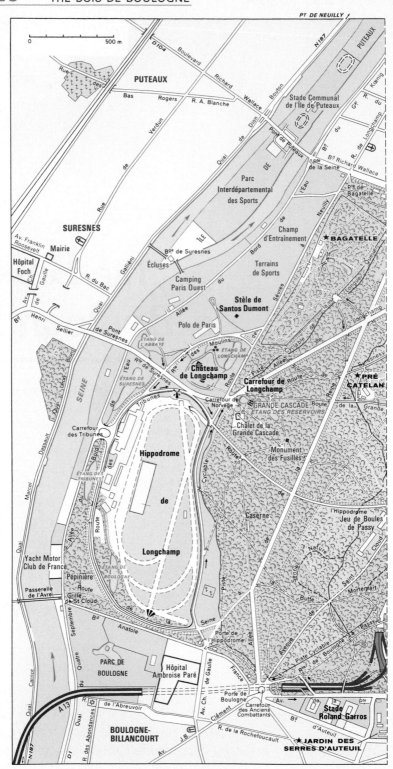

Many roads are now reserved for pedestrians; boating is allowed on the Lower Lake. There are lakes, waterfalls, gardens, lawns and woodland, two racecourses, cafés and restaurants for the enjoyment of the public. Race meetings at Longchamp and Auteuil attract large numbers of racegoers and roads tend to be busy. The best time for a pleasant stroll is on weekdays, in the morning. There are two waymarked paths: the round tour (red and yellow) and the short one (yellow and blue).

A royal forest. — In Merovingian times the forest was hunted for bear, deer, wolves and wild boar; in 1308 local woodmen went in pilgrimage to Our Lady of Boulogne and, on their return, built a church with funds provided by Philip the Fair, which they called Our Lady of Boulogne the Lesser.

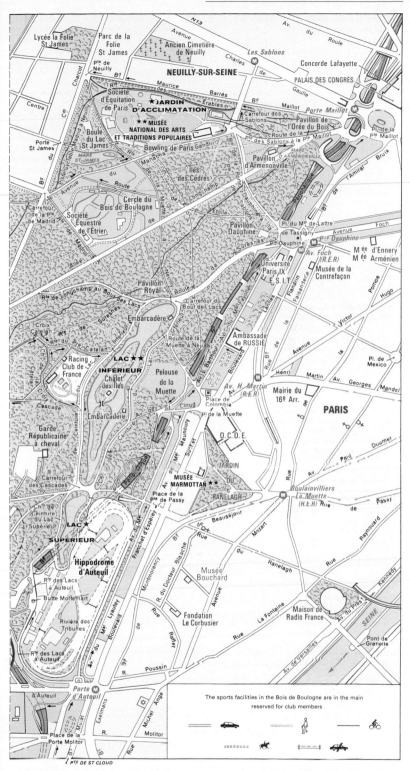

As the forest had become a refuge for bandits, in 1556 Henri II enclosed it with a wall pierced by eight gates; the most important are the Porte Maillot and Porte de la Muette.

In the 17C Colbert converted it into a Royal Hunt with straight rides marked at their meeting points by crosses, as at the Croix Catelan. Louis XIV opened the wood to the public but it was not until the Regency that it became highly fashionable and great houses were built: Neuilly, La Muette, Bagatelle, St-James' Folly and Ranelagh.

Decline. — During the Revolution the forest became the refuge of the pursued, the destitute and poachers. In 1815, the English and Russian armies bivouacked in the forest and because of the resulting devastation, new plantings were carried out.

The wood today. — When Napoleon III gave the forest to the capital in 1852, Haussmann demolished the surrounding wall, landscaped the area after Hyde Park creating winding paths, ornamental lakes and ponds, and built the Longchamp racecourse, restaurants, kiosks and pavilions. 1854 saw the opening of the Avenue de l'Impératrice (now the Avenue Foch); the wood became the fashionable place to take the air. The Auteuil racecourse, famous for its jumps, was built after 1870. The construction of the ring road round Paris and of the Parc des Princes stadium, and other planning decisions have caused some disruption but the wood is once again the capital's main recreation area.

The **Parc des Princes** sports stadium, dating from 1972, is the scene of many of the capital's important sporting events (rugby and football cup finals). The **Sports Museum** *(24, rue du Commandant Guilhand, third floor; open 9.30am to 12.30pm and 2 to 5pm; closed Wednesdays, Saturdays and holidays; 20F; ☎ 40 45 99 12)* illustrates the historical development of several sports with tableaux, posters, works of art and memorabilia of famous champions (Suzanne Lenglen, Charpentier...). Pride of place goes to the tennis-playing Four Musketeers (Henri Cochet, Jean Borota, René Lacoste and Jacques Brugnon), who in the days of long trousers and wooden rackets, collected the Davis Cup six years running (1927 to 1932). The cycling section is particularly interesting with a detailed description of technical developments in the domain of the bicycle.

TOUR

Métro station: Les Sablons. A miniature train links the park entrance and Porte Maillot on Wednesdays, Saturdays, Sundays and holidays (daily during school holidays) from 1.30pm to 6pm; 8F.

★**Children's Amusement Park (Jardin d'Acclimatation).** — *Entrance: Carrefour des Sablons. Open 10am to 6pm; 8F. Special attractions on Wednesdays, Saturdays, Sundays and school holidays from 1.30pm. ☎ 40 67 90 82.*
This park, primarily arranged as a children's amusement park (the enchanted river and miniature railway), includes a small zoo with a pets corner, a typical Norman farm and an aviary. The **Musée en Herbe** *(open 10am-2pm Saturdays except during Parisian school holiday periods - to 6pm; closed morning of 1 January and 25 December; 13 F; ☎ 40 67 97 66)* is an art museum cum workshop designed for youngsters.

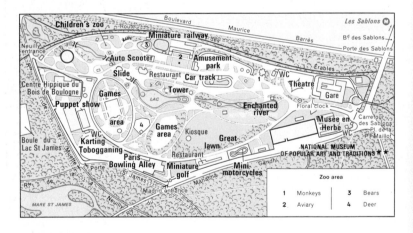

★★**National Museum of Popular Arts and Traditions** (Musée National des Arts et Traditions Populaires). — *Description p 253.*

★★**Lower Lake (Lac Inférieur).** — This lake is very popular on Sundays. It has a landing stage for the motor boat to the islands *(café-restaurant)* and boats for hire *(42F an hour)*.

★**Upper Lake (Lac Supérieur).** — A pleasant recreation area.

Auteuil Racecourse (Hippodrome d'Auteuil). — *Métro station: Porte d'Auteuil.* The racecourse is famous for its jumps including a 8m-28ft water jump. The main events are listed in the Calendar of Events *(p 15)*.

Garden (Jardin des Serres d'Auteuil). — *Métro station: Porte d'Auteuil. 3 Avenue de la Porte d'Auteuil. Open 10am to 6pm (5pm 1 October to 31 March); certain glass houses close at 4pm; 3F; ☎ 40 71 75 22.*
The formal garden which still retains its 19C charm is surrounded by hothouses growing azaleas, palm trees and ornamental plants for public buildings and official occasions. The central building contains a palm house and a tropical house with banana trees, papyrus plants and giant strelitzias. The other buildings house rare species (orchids, begonias...) The azalea and crysanthemums displays draw large crowds.

Beyond the garden is the **Roland-Garros stadium** where the French Open Tennis Championships are held every year *(late May-early June)*.

Tour of Longchamp. — A picturesque although man-made waterfall (Grande Cascade) graces the crossroads (**Carrefour de Longchamp**). Beyond the pond is a monument to 35 young people who lost their lives in 1944.

Longchamp Chateau was given to Haussmann by Napoleon III and now houses the International Children's Organisation.

An abbey, Our Lady of Humility, was founded in 1255 by St Isabel, sister to St Louis, on a site between Longchamp Pool and the Carrefour des Tribunes. This in time became known as Longchamp. By the 18C, austerity had disappeared from the nunnery. Services at the end of Holy Week were crowded by the fashionable Longchamp procession took place regularly until the last days of the Second Empire — even though the abbey had been suppressed in 1789.

The buildings were razed in 1795. The **mill** at the far end of the racecourse has been rebuilt. A tower, one of the few remains of the abbey, can be seen from Rue des Moulins. Near the Paris Polo Club, a stele marks one of the early aviation records established by the Brazilian flier Santos-Dumont on 12 November 1906.

Longchamp racecourse (**hippodrome**), opened by Napoleon III in 1857, is the setting for famous racing events *(p 15)*. The Route des Tribunes skirts the course. A panoramic restaurant *(open on race days only)* offers a good view of the course.

★**Bagatelle.** — *Bus: No 43 (stop: Place de Bagatelle). Route de Sèvres-à-Neuilly. Open 16 May to 31 July, 8.30am to 8pm; 1 to 15 May and August 8.30am to 7.30pm; September 8.30am to 7pm; the rest of the year closes at dusk; 6F, 3F November to end of February;* ☎ *40 /1 75 22.*

The first house to be built on the site was in 1720; it fell into ruin and in 1775 the Count of Artois, the future Charles X, bought it, betting his sister-in-law, Marie-Antoinette, and winning, that he would have a house designed and built within three months, complete with its landscaped garden.

It was owned by Napoleon after the Revolution and at the Restoration returned to the Duke of Berry. By the 19C it had come to be owned by the Hertfords of whom the third and fourth marquesses and the latter's son, Sir Richard Wallace, formed a large collection of 17 and 18C French paintings, furniture and art objects. The City of Paris bought the house from the family in 1905. The art collection had already been transferred to London where, since 1897, it has been on view as the Wallace Collection, Hertford House.

Bagatelle is well known for its beautiful garden, particularly its walled iris garden *(May)*, roses *(June to October)* and water lilies *(August)*. Exhibitions of paintings and sculpture are held *(May to October)* in the Trianon and Orangery.

★**Pré Catelan.** — This attractive well-kept park is named after a court minstrel from Provence murdered there in the reign of Philip IV. It includes a luxurious café-restaurant, lawns and shaded areas and a copper beech nearly two hundred years old with the most widespread branches in Paris.

A **Shakespeare garden** *(guided tour 3 to 3.30pm and 4.30 to 5pm; no tours on certain summer weekends when there are theatre performances; 3F)* is planted with flowers, herbs and trees mentioned in his plays. There is also an open air theatre.

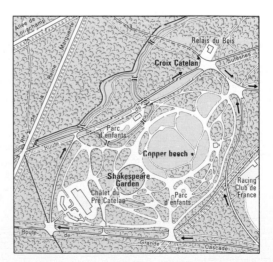

26

★★

Vincennes

Michelin plan **11**: detailed map,
and plan **23** - Banlieue de Paris Sud-Est

*Vincennes – a fortress, the focal point of
many events in French history, picturesque
lake-scattered wood, the largest zoo in France,
a delightful floral garden – takes a day to
discover and enjoy fully, whether by car or
on foot.*

219

Vincennes Château

★★THE CHÂTEAU plan 23: B8, B9
Métro station: Château de Vincennes or RER Vincennes

This "medieval Versailles" has two distinct aspects within its walls where a tall forbidding keep stands close to a majestic group of 17C buildings.

The manorhouse. — In the 11C the crown acquired Vincennes Forest from St Maur Abbey; in the 12C Philippe Auguste built a manorhouse within its confines to which St Louis added a Holy Chapel. This king also forbade anyone to hunt the animals of the forest while, seated at the foot of an oak, he received his subjects without let or hindrance of ushers.

The castle. — The castle was constructed by the Valois: Philippe VI, John the Good and finally Charles V who completed it in 1369. Charles further invited the members of his court to build themselves houses within the walls to create a royal city, but it was not until the reign of Louis XIV that the nobility sought to live in the king's shadow.

The classical château. — Mazarin, appointed governor of Vincennes in 1652, had symmetrical royal pavilions designed by Le Vau and built to frame the main courtyard which faced south overlooking the forest. In 1660, one year after the pavilions' completion, the young Louis XIV spent his honeymoon in the King's Pavilion but subsequently preferred other royal domains.

The prison. — From the beginning of the 16C to 1784, the keep, no longer in favour as a royal residence, was used as a state prison. Supporters of the League, of Jansenism, of the Fronde, libertines, lords and philosophers were held; the disgrace of detention in Vincennes was far less than at the Bastille and, among the many held, the famous included the Great Condé, the Prince de Conti, Cardinal de Retz, Fouquet (guarded by d'Artagnan), the Duke of Lauzun *(p 123)*, Diderot, Mirabeau...

The porcelain factory. — In 1738, quite by chance, the château became a porcelain factory when two craftsmen, dismissed from Chantilly, sought refuge at Vincennes and began to practise their skill.
A company was formed which produced painted objects in soft paste, including sprigged flowers in natural colours. Porcelain bouquets and even "gardens" became highly fashionable before the factory was transferred to Sèvres in 1756. *(See Michelin Green Guide Ile-de-France.)*

The arsenal. — Under Napoleon the château was converted into a formidable arsenal. The towers were lopped to the height of the perimeter wall and mounted with cannon, the rampart crenelations removed, and the keep once more converted to a prison.

Daumesnil's Refusals. — In 1814 when the Allies called for the surrender of Vincennes, the governor, General Daumesnil, known as Peg Leg since the loss of his leg at the Battle of Wagram, retorted "I'll surrender Vincennes when you give me back my leg".
At the end of the Hundred Days, the castle was again invested and there came a second refusal to surrender. Five months later, however, the doors were opened to Louis XVIII.
1830 found Daumesnil still governor and insurgents attempting to attack Charles X's ministers detained in the keep. The governor refused them entry, announcing that before giving in he would blow himself and the castle sky high.

The military establishment. — Under Louis-Philippe, Vincennes was incorporated in the Paris defence system; a fort was built beside it, outer openings were blocked up, the ramparts reinforced with massive casemates and the complex virtually interred by glacis.

On 24 August 1944 the Germans, before their departure from the castle, shot 26 resistance fighters, exploded three mines, breaching the ramparts in two places and damaging the King's Pavilion, and set fire to the Queen's Pavilion.

Restoration. — The restoration of Vincennes was begun by Napoleon III who commanded Viollet-le-Duc to begin the work which lasted a century, and is now completed.

The main courtyard looks again much as it did in the 17C since the moat round the keep has been redug, the 19C casemates removed and the pavilions restored. The château, in fact, is being revealed, once more, as one of the great historic royal houses of France.

TOUR OF THE EXTERIOR *(plan below)*

We suggest you begin by walking right round the outside of the château, following the embankment round the moat.

★★**The Keep** (**Donjon** — exterior). — This magnificent construction epitomizes the greatness of 14C military architecture. The 52m tall-170ft — tower, quartered by turrets, with a spur to the north for outbuildings, attiring room and a small oratory, was encircled by a sentry path protected by now vanished battlements and machicolations.

The keep proper was surrounded by a fortified wall and a separate moat. The base of the wall was protected against sappers by massive stonework, corner turrets and a covered watch path, complete with battlements, machicolations and gun embrasures.

The Tour du Bois and the Colonne du Duc d'Enghien. — The arcades of the classical Vincennes portico overlooking the forest and closing the perimeter wall on the south side, come into view as you arrive on the Château Esplanade. The Bois Tower at the centre was reduced by Le Vau in the 17C when he transformed the gate into a state entrance (it appears as a triumphal arch from inside).

From the bridge over the moat can be seen, at the foot of the Tour de la Reine (Queen's

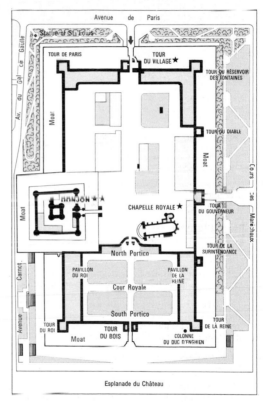

Tower) on the right, the column marking the spot where the **Duke of Enghien**, Prince of Condé, accused of plotting against Napoleon, was executed by firing squad on 20 March 1804. (His body was exhumed on the orders of Louis XVIII and reinterred in the Royal Chapel).

The Cours des Maréchaux. — Continue along the perimeter wall; the avenue was built in 1931 on the site of various outbuildings. It was in the penultimate of the five truncated towers of the east wall, the Devil's Tower (Tour du Diable), that the porcelain factory was established.

TOUR OF THE CHÂTEAU

Guided tours of the keep and chapel 10am to 6pm; closed on certain holidays; Time: 3/4 hour; 24F. ☎ 43 28 15 48.

★**Tour du Village.** — This massive tower 42m high-138ft — the only one beside the keep not to have been lopped in the 19C, served as the governor's residence in the Middle Ages. It was a good place from which to survey the entrance and conduct the defence of the fortress. Although the statues which graced the exterior have disappeared, some defensive features are still visible: slits for the drawbridge

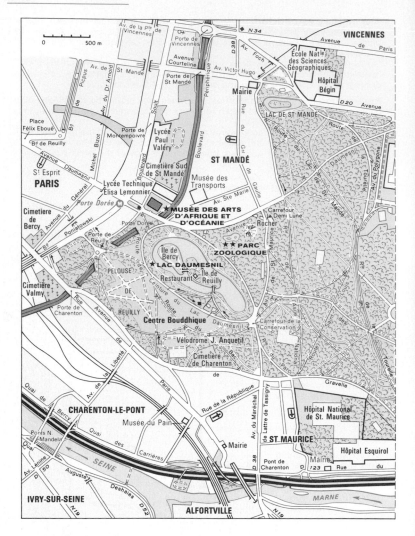

chains, groove of the portcullis, loopholes. Within the wall, on the left, is a military **museum** *(guided tour Wednesdays 10am to 12noon and 2 to 6pm — 5pm in winter and first and third Saturdays of the month 2 to 6pm — 5pm in winter: closed holidays excluding 11 November;* ☎ *49 57 32 00)*: documents, paintings and mementoes.

To the left of the paved alleyway is the site of St Louis' manorhouse (tablet on small building which has 17C foundations).

★**Chapelle Royale.** — The Royal Chapel, modelled on the Sainte-Chapelle *(p 119)* and begun by Charles V in the 14C in place of the one built by St Louis, was only completed in the 16C in the reign of Henri II. The building, apart from the windows and some decoration, is pure Gothic; the façade with its beautiful stone rose windows is Flamboyant. The interior consists of a single elegant aisle with highly decorative consoles and a frieze running beneath the windows which, in the chancel, are filled with unusually coloured mid-16C **stained glass**★ featuring Scenes from the Apocalypse. The Duke of Enghien's tomb is in the north chapel.

★★**The Keep (Donjon).** — The fortified wall, after the removal of the additional works, is protected by a barbican which guarded the drawbridge. The keep is in the centre of a courtyard. There is a small **museum** *(audio-visual presentation)* retracing its history. Each of the keep's floors, except for the topmost one, is the same with a main chamber with vaulting resting on a central pillar and four small dependent rooms in the turrets serving as waiting room, oratory, attiring room and treasury. These were later converted into prison cells (graffiti on the walls).

First floor. — A gangway provided direct access from the barbican to the first floor which was originally a royal reception room hung with tapestries to brighten the stone walls. Charles V received the Holy Roman Emperor here with great ceremony. Fouquet was imprisoned in this room while Mirabeau was held prisoner for three years in one of the towers where he wrote a scathing condemnation of royal warrants. Another prisoner in Napoleon's reign painted his cell walls.

Second floor. — A wide spiral staircase leads to what was once the royal bed-chamber. Henry V of England, Charles VI's son-in-law, died of dysentry in this room in 1422 and in 1574, Charles IX also died here at the age of twenty-four.

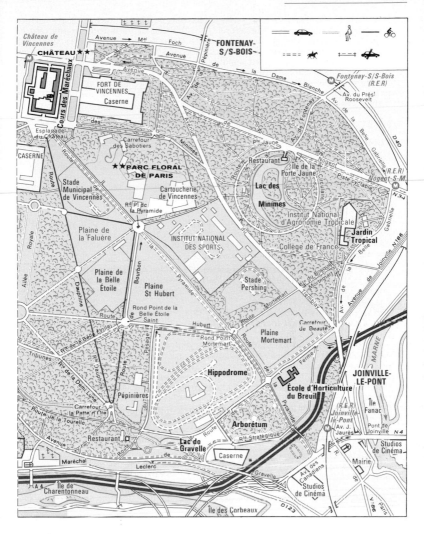

Ground floor. — This was the kitchen. In the great south hall there is a well 17m-56ft deep and a gate which was that of the Temple Tower brought here after the demolition of the prison in which Louis XVI and his family were held *(p 259)*.

★**Classical Vincennes.** — The main courtyard (Cour Royale) is once more closed to the north by a portico, as Le Vau intended, and is framed by the two royal pavilions. Anne of Austria and Louis XIV's brother lived in the **Queen's Pavilion** (Pavillon de la Reine). The governor, Daumesnil, died there in 1832; and the last royal occupant was the Duke of Montpensier, Louis Philippe's youngest son. Mazarin died in the **King's Pavilion** (Pavillon du Roi) in 1661 while awaiting the completion of his apartment in the Queen's Pavilion. On the ground floor there is a **museum** displaying 8 500 army insignia from 1920 to the present day *(open Wednesdays 2 to 5pm; ☎ 49 57 32 85)*.

At the far end of the court, the triumphal arch built onto the Tour du Bois by Le Vau and the colonnades on either side have restored this part of the château to its former glory.

★★THE BOIS 🔟 detailed map

The Bois de Vincennes with its natural attractions, its famous zoo and beautiful flower garden, is a popular recreation area. In addition to facilities for sport there are two waymarked paths: red for the complete tour and yellow and blue for the shorter one.

The Royal Forest. — Philippe Auguste enclosed the wood as a royal hunt with a wall 12km-7 miles long and stocked it with game. Charles V built the small Beauté Château within it on a low hill overlooking the Marne.

In the 17C it became a fashionable place to take the air. Strollers gained access to the wood through six gates pierced in the wall. The Pyramid monument commemorates the new plantations which were carried out in Louis XV's reign.

The military firing range which opened in 1798 was the first of a series of enclaves to be created in the forest, a practice which is still current to this day for military and sporting purposes.

The Bois in Modern Times. — Napoleon III ceded Vincennes in 1860 — except the château and military installations — to the City of Paris to be made into an English style park. Haussmann created the Gravelle Lake which was filled with water diverted from the Marne and in turn it fed the lakes and rivers flowing through the woods. The National Sports Institute dominated by a modern covered stadium offers training facilities for athletics and swimming.

The hundred-year old **Throne** (or Gingerbread) **Fair** is held each spring *(Palm Sunday to end of May)* on the Reuilly Lawn near Lake Daumesnil. This colourful event is the capital's main fair attraction *(p 250)*.

WEST SIDE

★★**Zoological Garden.** — *Métro station: Porte Dorée. Entrance: Avenue Daumesnil. Open 1 April to 19 November 9am to 6pm (6.30pm on Sundays and holidays); the rest of the year 9am to 5.30pm (5pm 19 November to 20 January); 35F;* ☎ *43 43 84 95.*

550 mammals and 700 birds of some 200 different species live in natural surroundings close to their familiar habitat. At the centre is an artificial rock 72m-236ft high inhabited by wild mountain sheep.

★**Lake Daumesnil.** — *Métro station: Porte Dorée.* A great many people flock to the lake shore and its two islands *(bridge across — café on Reuilly Island). For hire: bicycles 15 April to 15 October daily, the rest of the year Wednesdays, weekends and holidays, 26F per hour; boats 40 to 46F.*

★**African and Oceanian Art Museum (Musée des Arts africains et océaniens).** — *Métro station: Porte Dorée. 293 avenue Daumesnil. Open Mondays and Wednesdays to Fridays 10am to 12noon and 1.30 to 5.30pm, weekends 12.30 to 6pm; closed Tuesdays; 24F;* ☎ *43 43 14 54.*

The façade of the building, erected for a Colonial Exhibition in 1931, is decorated with a great sculptured frieze illustrating the contributions made by the overseas territories to France.

The ground floor and the right side of the main hall are devoted to Oceanian art: large collection of painted bark (Australia), masks (New Guinea), strange funerary figures and root sculptures. On the left side of the hall are exhibited examples of African art; its themes are life and death: masks, wood and copper figures (Gabon). On the first floor are dance masks, ceremonial masks (Mali, Ivory Coast), gold pendant masks (Ivory Coast, Ghana), and magical statues (Congo).

On the second floor, the North African countries are represented by fine **jewellery**★, ceramics, embroidery from Fez, Algerian headdress, Tunisian pottery, furniture (carved or inlaid with mother of pearl and ivory), and large wool carpets.

In the basement there are a tropical **aquarium**★ and two terrariums.

Buddhist Centre (Centre bouddhique). — *Guided tours during Buddhist festivals;* ☎ *43 41 54 48.*

South of Lake Daumesnil is the Buddhist Temple of Paris housed in one of the 1931 Colonial Exhibition buildings. The new roof with 180 000 tiles carved out of a chestnut tree with an axe is noteworthy. Inside is a monumental statue of Buddha (9m-30ft) in gold leaf.

EAST SIDE

★★**Paris Floral Garden (Parc Floral de Paris).** — *Métro station: Château de Vincennes. Route de la Pyramide. Open 9.30am to 6pm (8pm 1 April to 30 September; 5pm 1 November to 28 February). 5F, 10F at weekends and holidays from 1 May to 30 September;* ☎ *43 43 92 95.*

The garden which extends over 30ha-75 acres includes hundreds of species. The Valley of Flowers is delightful all year round. The Pavilions dotted in a setting of pine trees and round the lake and the Hall de la Pinède house exhibitions and shows

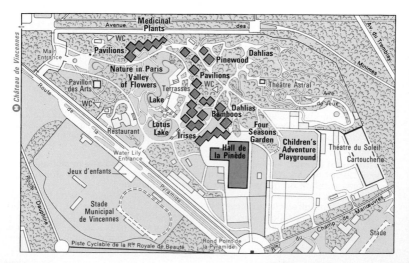

(photographs, dance, posters and horticulture). Alleys lined with modern sculpture lead to the children's adventure playground. The Dahlia garden from Sceaux, south of Paris, has been recreated near the Pyramid *(in flower September-October)*. The water garden with its water-lilies and lotus is at its best from July to September. There are also a Four Seasons Garden, and gardens growing medicinal plants *(best seen from May to October)*, irises *(May)* and bamboo. Flower shows are held throughout the year: Orchids *(early March)*, tulips *(from April)* and rhododendrons and azalea *(from May)*.

Minimes Lake. — *Station: Fontenay-sous-Bois (R.E.R.)*. The lake, named after a monastery on the same site which formed an enclave in the royal forest, includes three islands, of which one, the Porte Jaune, is accessible across a bridge *(café-restaurant, boats for hire 40F per hour)*.

Tropical Garden (Jardin tropical). — *Station: Nogent-sur-Marne (R.E.R.)*. The garden, in which stand the Institute of Tropical Agronomic Research and the Tropical Forestry Centre *(no 45 bis, Avenue de la Belle-Gabrielle)*, has a Chinese gate by the main entrance . On the far side of the garden, a Temple to the Memory of the Indochinese killed in the 1914-1918 War was destroyed by fire in 1984. The nearby alley is inspired by the famous avenue at Angkor Watt.

Breuil School of Horticulture (École de Breuil). — *Station: Joinville-le-Pont (R.E.R.)*. Horticulture and landscape design. Beautiful gardens. The arboretum *(entrance: Route de la Pyramide; open March to October 10am to 6pm; April and September 10am to 7pm; November to February 10am to 5pm; 5F on weekends and holidays, free weekdays; ☎ 43 28 28 94)* extends over 12ha-30 acres and includes 2 000 trees of 80 different species.

Hippodrome. — *Station: Joinville-le-Pont (R.E.R.)*. The main racing events are listed in the Calendar of Events *(p 15)*. Evening race meetings are also held.
On the other side of Route de la Ferme is **Gravelle Lake** dotted with waterlilies.

27

★★

La Défense

Michelin plan **11**: detailed map

*Distance: 3.5km-2 miles from Porte Maillot.
Central Parking area: access road Défense 4
from the ring road
Access also by the R.E.R. or bus No. 73*

*The quarter gets its name from a monument
commemorating the defence of Paris
of 1871. The bronze statue by Barrias has
been returned to its original site beside the
Agam pool.*

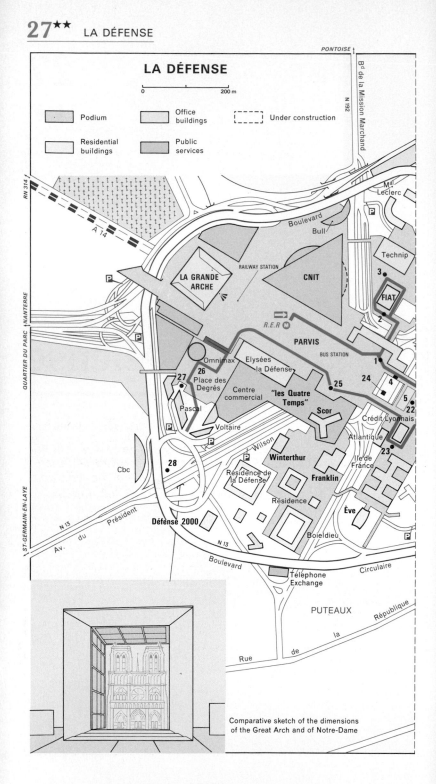

LA DÉFENSE

0 — 200 m

- Podium
- Residential buildings
- Office buildings
- Public services
- Under construction

Comparative sketch of the dimensions of the Great Arch and of Notre-Dame

The urbanisation of the area west of Paris and the creation of a new business and residential centre are the most ambitious town planning projects ever undertaken in the Paris region. The coordinating body EPAD (Établissement Public pour l'Aménagement de la Défense) set up in 1958, is responsible for the management of the project which covers an area of 800ha-1976 acres divided into two zones.

The business sector. — This zone of 130ha-321 acres comprising parts of the **Puteaux** and **Courbevoie** districts and the continuation of the Champs-Élysées-Pont de Neuilly axis, has as its centrepiece, a vast concrete **podium** rising in steps from the Seine and forming a central mall with patios and squares on different levels.

A complex network of communications exists underneath the podium: local access and link roads, national roads, a ring road, the R.E.R. express metro, suburban line and bus stations, parking areas, basement floors of the towers, air ducts, stairs and lifts, and galleries (15km-9 miles) used for cables and pipes.

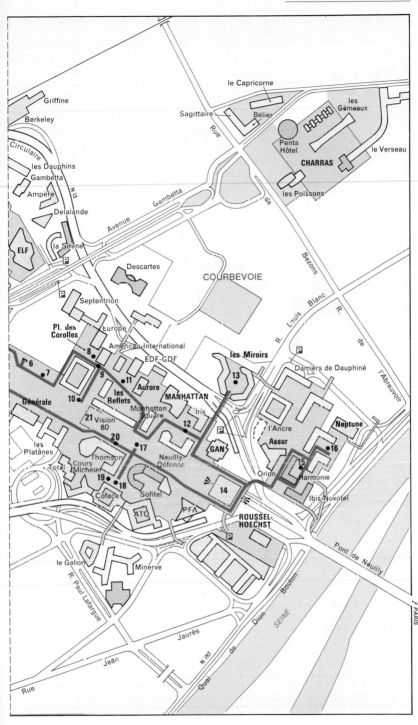

Experts from all corners of the world come to visit this development which represents a new building concept.

The skyline all around the podium is broken by towers, with the tallest rising 45 storeys high. Since 1964 when the Esso building first opened, 47 towers have been completed and provide office space for over 400 companies, including some of France's most important ones. The towers are equipped with air conditioning, automated mail sorting, close circuit television and open plan offices. In 1988 over 70 000 people worked at La Défense.

Most of the smaller tower blocks are residential. The exceptions are: Eve, Défense 2000 and Gambetta.

At the foot of the business and residential towers are the commercial, leisure and sports complexes. The shopping centre covering 120 000m² is the largest in Europe.

The park area. — The 90ha-222 acre area further to the west in the Nanterre plain includes offices, housing, sports facilities and a park.
The Hauts-de-Seine **Police Headquarters** (Préfecture) and the **School of Architecture** were both completed in 1972.
At the heart of this new urban development is a 24ha-59 acre **park** which includes a botanical garden which is overlooked by office buildings, flats, a theatre with a capacity of 900 and the Opera Ballet School. Some of the towers have unusual curved walls pierced by odd-shaped windows set in an irregular pattern.

TOUR

The new business district of La Défense, with its assortment of tower blocks, has acquired a outstanding architectural work of fittingly monumental proportions to embellish the western end of the historic axis running from the Louvre. Although this overtly contemporary monument dominates the podium, the visitor's eye is often attracted by the striking form or movement of one of the many works of art commissioned by the official authority EPAD. Many of today's better known artists and sculptors (Miró, Moretti, Calder, César...) are represented in this open-air-gallery.

Parvis. — From the podium there is a fine **vista**★ down the opening between the towers in the direction of the Étoile.

The Great Arch. — *Open July and August Mondays to Thursdays 9am to 7pm; Fridays, Saturdays and holidays 9am to 9pm, Sundays 10am to 7pm; the rest of the year Mondays to Fridays 9am to 5pm, Saturdays, Sundays and holidays 10am to 7pm; 30F; ☎ 43 28 28 94.*
At the western end of the podium towers the great arch known as the Tête Défense designed by the Danish architect Otto von Spreckelsen. This gigantic open cube (106m-348ft wide) with its prestressed concrete frame faced in glass and white Carrara marble rises sheer without expansion joints. For technical reasons it is slightly out of alignment in relation to the La Défense-Louvre axis; the 300 000 tonne weight is carried on 12 piles sunk in the below-ground area which is criss-crossed by communications systems. The cathedral of Notre-Dame with its spire could fit into the space between the walls of the arch. Scenic lifts will whisk visitors to the roof to enjoy a unique view of the Paris area from the terrace.
The south vertical wall of the arch houses government offices and the north wall major French and international companies. The three-storey thick roof is occupied by the International Foundation for Human Rights.
From the terrace there is a view of the historic axis right down to the Louvre as well as of the capital and its suburbs. Also at this level is a suite of galleries for temporary exhibitions, arranged around several patios. The marble and granite mosaic paving of the patios represents a chart of the heavens.
The theme of the internal decoration of the side walls of the arch by Jean Dewasne is languages and communication to recall the now abandoned project for an International Communications Centre.
To the right of the Arch is a metal sculpture by the Japanese artist Aiko Miyawaki. She has linked the twenty-five metal columns with a spidery web of curving wires.
The **Point Info-Défense** *(open daily 10am to 7pm; ☎ 47 74 84 24)*, in front of the CNIT, provides tourist and cultural information as well as giving details concerning the companies located at the Défense.

Palais de la Défense (CNIT). — The Centre for Industry and Technology, the earliest (1958) and one of the most famous edifices of the complex, is remarkable for its dimensions and the boldness of its architecture. Its concrete vaulting in the form of an inverted shell has only three points of support, each poised on the apex of a triangle.
The building which originally served as a venue for major trade exhibitions, is now a business centre (offices, auditoriums, conference rooms, hotel, exhibition centre for new technology).
Further on, to the left, the Place de la Defense is dominated by Calder's last work, a red stabile **(1)** 15m-49ft high. Go through an opening on the left to the Fiat Tower.

Fiat Tower. — Designed by a team of French and American architects, this is the tallest building, along with the Elf Tower, with its 45 storeys rising 178m-584ft above the podium. Its massive but harmonious lines are particularly attractive at night with its polished granite and black tinted façade looking like a giant chess-board. Contrary to the other towers built with curtain walls, the Fiat tower has load-bearing walls. Another unusual feature is the widening of the windows near the top to avoid a tapering effect.
From inside there is direct access to the public transport system.

At the foot of the tower, The Great Toscano **(2)** a bronze bust by the Polish artist Mitoraj, evokes some antique giant. Pass round the tower to the left to see a sculpture **(3)** in polyester resin by Delfino inspired from the world of science-fiction.

Elf Tower. — Similar in height to its neighbour the Fiat Tower, the impressive Elf building is by a team of French and Canadian architects. The three glass curtained towers of varying height are a blue colour which changes with the light.

Return to the esplanade.

The Art Gallery 4 **(4)** *(open daily except Tuesdays 12noon to 7pm)* presents works from countries all over the world.
In the centre of the esplanade, the monumental **fountain by Agam (5)** plays with music and illuminations *(Friday evening at 8.30pm, Saturdays at 3 and 8pm and Sundays at 3pm)*.

Opposite the Esso building, the underground Gallery (6) holds art exhibitions. Pass in front of the "Midday-Midnight" Pond (7) where the artist Clarus has decorated a ventilation shaft to represent the trajectory of the sun and moon in a trompe-l'œil rock setting.

Bear left on the esplanade and pass round a small building to reach the **Place des Corolles** named after a sculpture, Corolla (8), adorning the copper fountain by Louis Leygue. A ceramic fresco, The Cloud Sculptor (9), by Attila ornamenting a low wall adds its dreamlike quality and vivid colours to the concrete environment.

The **Reflets** terrace is adorned with a sculpture by Philolaos, The Mechanical Bird (10), depicted with its great steel wings tucked in.

Beyond the Vision 80 tower, built on stilts, is the **Place des Reflets** overlooked by the shimmering **Aurore** Tower, the rose-coloured Manhattan Tower and the green GAN Tower. Note the work by Derbré entitled The Earth (11).

Manhattan Tower. — This is one of the most original structures of the whole complex in terms of shape, colour and materials used. The building attracts the eye with its undulating design, its smooth glazed façade harmonising with the colour of the sky, and its pure, elegant lines. The S-shaped plan comprises two adjoining structures with the concrete pillars of the framework placed away from the façade to avoid any projections which would break the harmony. Each storey is made up of 4 000 transparent, reflecting glass panes.

In Place de l'Iris the slender silhouette of the Moonwalker (12) balanced on a sphere poised on the ridge of a cubic volume, is by H de Miller.

GAN Tower. — This green tower in the form of a Greek cross, houses a group of insurance companies. This metallic structure with a reinforced concrete core has 42 storeys soaring 166m-545ft above the podium. Black aluminium rails make a delicate pattern on the glazed façade.

The Iris passageway above the ring road leads to the **les Miroirs** building by H. La Fonta: the fountain (13) in the courtyard is enhanced by four cylindrical volumes decorated with mosaics. From the patio area there is a view of the Poissons Tower in the distance; its giant clock-barometer gives a weather reading for the Paris region (blue — variable, green — fine, red — rainy) and a flashing light marks the hours.

On the way note the unusual Assur Tower (UAP), shaped like a three-pronged star, designed by Pierre Dufau and further on residential buildings in a chequer-board layout.

East of the esplanade the Takis pond (14) comprises a mirror of water with 49 multi-coloured lights set at the top of flexible metal rods at different heights. Wonderful views of the arch and of Paris.

On Square Vivaldi the Conversation Fountain (15) by Busato represents two bronze figures in animated conversation.

In the Place Napoleon I at the foot of the Neptune Tower, a cross-shaped monument (16) commemorates the return of the Emperor's remains from St Helena. The imperial eagle came from the railings of the Tuileries.

Return to the Takis pond.

Roussel-Hoechst Tower. — This attractive blue-green, steel and glass tower was the first to be built (1967) at La Défense.

The triangular PFA Tower has sharp-angled curtain walls. The bronze low relief Ophelia (17) is by the Catalan sculptor Apel les Fenosa.

Go around the Sofitel Hotel on your left. From the terrace overlooking the square, Cours Michelet you can see Venet's 14m-46ft high painted steel sculpture (18) and further on to the right Jakober's assemblage of welded iron ressemble an American footballer's protective mask (19).

Further on stands a large frog-shaped fountain (20). Thirty-five flower-stands (21) decorated with faces and clasped hands mark the boundary of the small square situated below the esplanade. The decorative aluminium façade and vivid colours of the Générale Tower contrast with surrounding buildings.

By the Agam fountain, a stairway (signpost) leads down to a gallery where is displayed Moretti's monster (22), a sculpture featuring different textures and symbolizing the artist's wide-ranging experiments *(open 11am to 4pm except Sundays, Mondays, holidays and during the caretaker's holidays; ☎ 47 76 18 84.)*

A white marble sculpture "Lady Moon" (23) by Julio Silva can be seen between the Atlantique and Crédit Lyonnais Towers; further to the right rise the pyramid-like Defense 2000 and the white elliptical outline of the Eve Tower south of the Villon quarter.

The Scor Tower in the form of a tripod partly hides the fortress-like Winthertur and Franklin Towers (the latter comprises two abutting structures) with dark glazed façades in a severe architectural style.

Barrias' bronze group entitled "La Défense" (24); once again stands on its original site at the foot of the monumental Agam fountain, facing westwards from where no invader has ever come.

The Quatre Temps shopping centre comprises department stores, over 250 shops, restaurants and cinemas on two levels. The building above, Élysées-La Défense, has an interior garden.

In front of the centre is a brightly coloured monumental sculpture (25) of two figures by Miró. On the Place des Degrès, the sculptor Kowalski has created a mineral landscape (26): parts of pyramids, wave of granite...

A bronze "Icarus" (27) by César stands at the foot of the elegant IBM building. A short distance away, "Slat" (28) a sculpture by R. Serra consisting of five sheets of steel weighing 100 tons and 11m-36ft high, has been installed at a crossroads.

Additional Walks and Sights

Buttes-Chaumont Park

THE ARSENAL

Michelin plan **11** - folds 33 and 45: K 17

Métro Station: Sully Morland — Entrance: 1 Rue de Sully.

From 1352 the site was occupied by a Benedictine community, the Celestines. Proximity to the royal residences such as the Hôtels St-Paul *(p 94)* and des Tournelles *(p 95)* brought considerable patronage. The monastic church accumulated great riches, in particular works of art and royal tombs which are now in the Louvre, St-Denis or at Versailles.

In 1512, despite strong opposition from the Celestines, the city requisitioned the riverside stretch of land for the purpose of manufacturing cannon. Henri II purloined the workshops and founded a royal arsenal. Gunpowder was one of the products and the famous explosion of 1563 was heard as far afield as Melun to the south. Philibert Delorme rebuilt the arsenal and it was here that Sully, Grand Master of Artillery, established his residence. Under Louis XIII the manufacture of cannon was discontinued and the production of gunpowder was transferred to the Salpêtrière.

Fouquet's Trial. — In 1631 Richelieu established the Arsenal as a court for special hearings. It was the scene of the three-year trial for embezzlement of Fouquet, Louis XIV's finance minister. Colbert energetically packed the magistrate's court, but the verdict was only banishment (1664). Displeased Louis XIV changed the sentence to life imprisonment and banished the chief magistrate to his estate.

The Poisoners' Court. — Following the affair of the notorious poisoner, the Marquise de Brinvilliers *(p 100)*, who dispatched her father and two brothers, the art of poisoning became extremely popular in the capital. A certain La Voisin masterminded the dealings in the lethal potions commonly known as "inheritance powder". In the face of a growing scandal the Arsenal court became the Poisoners' court in 1680. On being questioned La Voisin implicated many princesses, duchesses... Her fate was quickly sealed by her being burned at the stake.

The Library. — *It is possible to visit the library by joining a guided tour; time: 1 1/2 hours; apply in advance by phoning ☎ 42 77 44 21; closed Sundays, holidays and 1 to 15 September; 12F.*

The library, created in 1757, was established as a public one in what remained of the Arsenal building in 1797. In the 19C it became the early meeting-place of the Romantics: Lamartine, Hugo, Vigny, Musset, Dumas... Around 1900, it housed a literary circle. The library possesses more than a million and a half volumes, 15 000 MSS, 120 000 prints and a large collection on the history of the theatre, which belongs to the National Library. The building also includes rooms and an oratory with fine 17C paintings and ceilings as well as 18C salons. On the doors of the 18C music room are drawings of Bouchardon's low reliefs decorating the sides of the Four Seasons Fountain in Rue de Grenelle *(p 169)*.

Along Boulevard Morland one should note the cannon and mortar of the roof-top balustrade, recalling the early role of the building.

The statue of the 19C poet, Arthur Rimbaud, in the square is by Ipousteguy.

The barracks, **Caserne des Célestins,** (1892) stand on the site of the convent gardens. On the right is a late 19C iron and glass building, the **Pavillon de l'Arsenal** *(21 Boulevard Morland; open Tuesdays to Saturdays 10.30am to 6.30pm and Sundays 11am to 7pm; closed 1 May; ☎ 42 76 33 97).* This exhibition centre presents architecture and urbanism in the capital from the earliest city walls to the grand projects of today (Bercy, La Défense and La Villette) which have propulsed Paris to the forefront of modern architecture. A model of the city locates the various parks and open spaces, new development areas and public services.

AUTEUIL

Michelin plan **11** - folds 26, 27, 38 and 39: K 4, K 5 - L 4

Distance: 4km-2 1/2 miles — Time: 1 1/2 hours (excluding Radio-France House). Buses nos 70, 72 and 52.

During the Second Empire Auteuil became part of the city of Paris but it was only at the turn of the century that the last vineyards disappeared. Many of the houses of this desirable residential area have retained good-sized gardens.

On the midstream island, below the Pont de Grenelle, is a smaller version of Bartholdi's **Statue of Liberty**, which stands at the entrance to New York harbour. It was donated by the American colony in Paris in 1885 and placed on this spot four years later at the time of the 1889 Universal Exhibition.

The towers on the far bank of the Seine are part of the Front de Seine *(p 244)*.

★**Radio-France House.** — *Guided tours of museum, 10.30 and 11.30am and 2.30, 3.30 and 4.30pm daily except Sundays and holidays. Time: about 1 hour; 10F; ☎ 42 30 21 80.*

One concentric building 500m-547yds in circumference and a tower 68m-223ft tall, covering in all 2ha-5 acres, go to make up Radio-France House. It was designed and erected by Henry Bernard in 1963 and until 1975 housed the Paris offices of the French Broadcasting Service. It is here in the 60 studios and the main auditorium (studio 104) that the programmes of French radio stations are produced.

A museum traces the evolution of communication and the development of transmitters and receivers from the 1793 Chappe telegraph and crystal sets to the latest transistors. The research carried out by scientists such as Maxwell, Hertz, Branly, Popov, Marconi and Lee de Forest (inventor of the three-electrode tube) into wave propagation brought about the invention of the wireless. There are also some experimental television sets and the reconstruction of a studio.

On leaving the Radio-France House take Rue de Boulainvilliers.

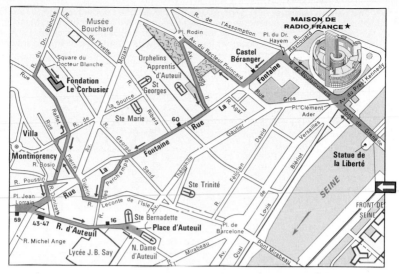

Rue La Fontaine. — The street takes its name from the spring which supplied the village of Auteuil. Here, as in Rue Agar, there are several buildings by Hector Guimard, the famous *art nouveau* architect *(p 23)*. His best-known block of flats, **Castel Béranger,** is at no 14.

Take Avenue du Recteur-Poincaré to reach the calm of Place Rodin, the setting for *The Age of Bronze (p 169)*. Return by Avenue Léopold-II. The building at the junction with Rue La Fontaine is an orphanage (Orphelins Apprentis d'Auteuil).

Turn right. No **60** another work by Guimard was built in 1911.

Having passed Rue George-Sand, turn left into Rue des Perchamps. Before taking Rue Leconte-de-Lisle to the right, glance at the elegant rear façade of what was once one of Auteuil's finest mansions, the Hôtel de Puscher.

Take Rue Pierre-Guérin. Beyond Rue de la Source, this dead end street retains the aspect of a village lane.

Via Rue Raffet make for Rue du Dr.-Blanche.

Le Corbusier Foundation. — *8-10 Square du Dr.-Blanche. Open 10am to 12.30pm and 1.30 to 6pm (5pm on Fridays); closed weekends, all public holidays, in August and between 25 December and 1 January; 5F. ☎ 42 88 41 53.*

Two buildings, namely Villas La Roche and Jeanneret, dating from 1923, serve as a documentation centre for the work of the famous architect, Le Corbusier (1887-1965). Villa La Roche houses a permanent exhibition, a library and photographic collection.

Retrace your steps. To the right is the exclusive **Villa Montmorency** which was laid out on the site of the park of the former Hôtel de Montmorency. One notable owner was the Comtesse de Boufflers, mistress of the Prince de Conti and fervent admirer of Rousseau.

Rue Donizetti leads to Place Jean-Lorrain. The modern building at no **59** Rue d'Auteuil marks the site of a literary salon of a certain Madame Helvetius, who was better known as "Notre-Dame d'Auteuil". The salon was frequented by philosophers and writers in the period from 1762 to 1800.

Rue d'Auteuil. — Follow the narrow Rue d'Auteuil with its many shops.

At nos **43-47** is an 18C mansion.

At no 11 bis a 17C château is now occupied by a school.

Admire at no **16** the main front of the Hôtel de Puscher.

Place d'Auteuil. — The church of Notre-Dame (1880) is a Romano-Byzantine pastiche.

The obelisk opposite the Ste-Bernadette Chapel is the last remaining tomb from the onetime cemetery. The monument commemorates the chancellor Aguesseau and his wife (1753).

PLACE DE LA BASTILLE

Michelin plan **10** - fold 33: J 17 - K 17 — *Métro Station: Bastille*

The vast crossroads, scene of the historic events of 1789, is dominated by the July Column.

Construction of the Bastille. — The first stone of the Bastille, which was intended to provide Charles V, who lived at the Hôtel St-Paul *(p 94)*, with a fortified residence, was laid in 1370 and the last in 1382. All men caught loitering were press-ganged. Its history is far from heroic: besieged seven times in periods of civil strife, it surrendered six times. An interesting episode occurred in 1652 when the Grande Mademoiselle Louis XIV's cousin, opened the St-Antoine gate to the Fronde and fought the royal army.

The prison regime. — Prisoners were usually detained under the notorious *lettre de cachet* or royal warrant, and included the enigmatic Man in the Iron Mask and Voltaire. In 1784 *lettres de cachet* were abolished: the Bastille was cleared and its demolition planned. The governor had only 32 Swiss guards and 82 invalid soldiers left under his command.

The Taking of the Bastille. — In July 1789 trouble broke: the popular minister, Necker, was dismissed by the king; the Exchange closed and the militant crowd marched first on the Invalides to capture arms *(p 70)*, then on the Arsenal and the Bastille. By late afternoon the Bastille had been seized and the prisoners — only seven in number — symbolically freed.

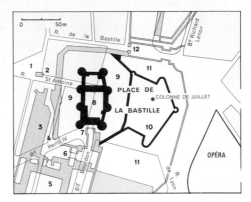

Site of the Bastille in the 18th century

1 Former Place de la Bastille	7 Main drawbridge
2 Guardroom	8 Great Courtyard
3 Barracks	9 Bastille defence ditches
4 Outer Courtyard	10 Bastion
5 Arsenal	11 Paris perimeter ditches
6 First drawbridge	12 St-Antoine Gate

Demolition. — The fortress was immediately demolished, 83 of its stones being carved into replicas and sent as dire reminders of the evil of despotism to the provinces. The following year there was dancing on the site.

The Square Today. — Paving stones mark out the ground plan of the Bastille on the square which was modified in appearance by the opening of the Rue de Lyon in 1847, the Boulevard Henri-IV in 1866 and the building of the station in 1859. The latter was converted into an exhibition hall in 1970, then demolished in 1984. The site was then earmarked for another of the grand urban projects which have brought Paris to the forefront of contemporary architecture *(see below)*. Even today the square has remained a symbolic rallying point for demonstrations, marches and public celebrations (the election in 1981 of the Socialist President François Mitterrand).

Opéra de la Bastille. — On the site now rises a massive but harmonious building in terms of form, proportions and materials, designed by the Uruguay-born Canadian, Carlos Ott. The curvilinear, utilitarian design accommodates a 2 700 seat auditorium with several revolving stages for quick scene changes, workshops and rehearsal rooms. The opera had its gala opening on Bastille Day 1989 to commemorate the Bicentenary of the French Revolution. The first production was Berlioz' massive work *Les Troyens* with Myung-Whun Chung as the music director.

The **July Column** (Colonne de Juillet), a bronze column 52m-171ft high, crowned by the figure of Liberty (built between 1831 and 1840), stands in memory of Parisians killed in July 1830 and 1848. They were buried underneath the column and their names carved on the shaft.

★**St Martin's Canal.** — This canal dating from the Restoration flows under the Place de la République to reappear at the Arsenal basin *(p 255)*.

BERCY QUARTER

Michelin plan **⊞** - fold 46: M 19, N 19 and N 20 — *Métro station: Bercy*

Under a development plan for a 50ha-123 acre site to the east of Paris, the Bercy quarter is changing rapidly with the building of new offices for the Ministry of Finance, residential accommodation and the creation of a 13ha-32 acre riverside park between the sports complex and the wine warehouses *(also scheduled for refurbishment)* to the east. The Bercy office complex — one of the largest of its kind — houses the Ministry of Finance, transferred from the Rivoli wing of the Louvre. In contrast to other riverside office blocks this futuristic ensemble thrusts away from its foothold in the Seine, over the embankment expressway, to spread out over the former industrial site.

Palais Omnisports de Paris-Bercy. — On the eastern side of the capital, this new sports complex was built to stage international indoor sporting events. From the outside the appearance is somewhat surprising with grass-covered walls sloping away at 45 degrees. The glass roof is sheathed with a network of girders. The project was the result of collaboration between the architects Andrault, Parat and Guvan.

Sport takes first place with facilities catering to 22 different activities, but the centre's versatility is such that it can stage a variety of entertainments from opera, theatre and ballet to rock concerts. In addition to the adaptable main arena there are two multi-purpose halls and two warming-up or rehearsal halls.

In the square to the east an unusual fountain with a deep gully, the "Canyon Eaustrate" by Gérard Singer recalls the landscape of the North-American continent.

★★ THE BOTANICAL GARDENS QUARTER

Michelin plan **11** - folds 44 and 45: K 16 - L 15, L 16, L 17

Métro Station: Gare d'Austerlitz

This area bordered by the Latin Quarter, the Gare d'Austerlitz and the banks of the Seine offers varied sights: a Gallo-Roman arena, the Botanical Gardens, and the Arab mosque and cultural institute.

★★BOTANICAL GARDENS (JARDIN DES PLANTES)

Michelin plan **11** - fold 44: L 16

In 1626 Hérouard and Guy de la Brosse, physicians to Louis XIII, obtained permission, firstly, to establish in the St-Victor suburb, the Royal Medicinal Herb Garden which had previously been on the Ile de la Cité *(p 122)* and subsequently, to found a school of botany, natural history and pharmacy. In 1640 the garden was opened to the public.

After Fagon, Louis XIV's first physician, the botanist Tournefort, and the three Jussieu brothers journeyed widely to enrich the Paris collection.

It was during the curatorship of Buffon from 1739-1788, assisted by Daubenton and Antoine-Laurent de Jussieu, nephew of the earlier brothers, that the gardens were at their greatest. Buffon's 36 volume *Natural History* was equalled by his expansion of the gardens to the banks of the Seine, planting of lime trees along the avenues, creation of the maze, amphitheatre and museum galleries... so great indeed, was his prestige that a statue was erected to him in his lifetime.

The National Natural History Institute. — At the Revolution the gardens' name was changed to that of Natural History Institute and a menagerie was created by transporting the animals from private zoos and circuses. This enabled Parisians to see for the first time such wild animals as elephants (brought from Holland in 1795), bears (all the animals which have occupied the pit have been called after the first one which was known as Martin), giraffes (1827) etc. In 1870, however, when Paris came under siege, the citizens' hunger exceeded their curiosity and most of the animals were slaughtered for food. With Geoffroy-Saint-Hilaire, Lamarck, Lacépède, Cuvier, Becquerel and many other great names, the institute won international recognition in the 19C which it maintains today through its teaching and research.

Tour. — In the 17C a tall mound built up from public waste was converted by Buffon into a **maze**. At the summit is a small kiosk overlooking the rest of the gardens and the mosque. A column nearby marks the grave of Daubenton, naturalist and Buffon's collaborator.

The famous cedar of Lebanon is one of two planted by Bernard de Jussieu in 1734 on the hillside facing the Seine. They were brought back, so the story goes, by the scientist from England — he was said to have kept the plants in his hat. In fact, he was given two plants in a pot by Kew Gardens and the pot fell and broke near the gardens in Paris; he carried the plants in his hat only for a short distance.

The Ginkgo Biloba and the iron tree from Persia are also of interest.

1) Sea-lions	5) Waterfowl	9) Reptiles
2) Ibex	6) Bear pit	10) Birds of prey
3) Deer	7) Lamas	11) Ginkgo
4) Bison	8) Foxes, Jackals	12) Iron-bark tree

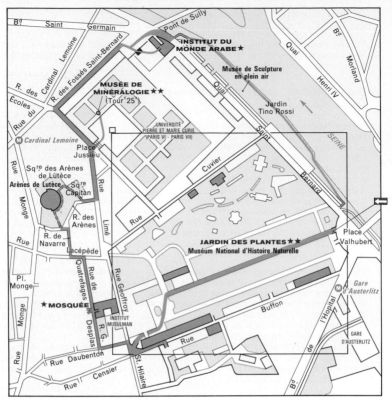

The oldest tree in Paris, a Robinia or false acacia planted here in 1635, can be seen near the Allée des Becquerel. Opposite the Winter Garden, the Australian House contains Mediterranean and Australian species.

Winter Garden (Jardin d'Hiver). — *Open 1 to 5pm; closed Tuesdays and holidays; 12F.* ☎ *40 79 30 00.*
This garden contains a large collection of tropical plants. Further on, the Mexican Garden is planted with succulents: cacti, euphorbia.

Alpine Garden (Jardin Alpin). — *Open 1 April to 30 September 8am to 11am and 1.30pm to 5pm; closed weekends and holidays;* ☎ *40 79 30 00.*
It includes plants from mountain regions: Corsica, Morocco (south face), the Alps and the Himalayas (north face). There is also a pistachio tree (*c*1700) and a tall deciduous conifer (metasequoia).

Menagerie, vivarium, reptiles. — *Open 1 April to 30 September 9am to 6pm; 1 October to 5 November and 5 February to 30 March 9am to 5.30pm; 6 November to 4 February 9am to 5pm; 25F;* ☎ *40 79 37 94.*
Big reptiles, birds and wild beasts are shown in an old-fashioned setting in which they nevertheless appear contented and their presence adds interest to the garden.

Botanical School (École de Botanique). — *Open 8 to 11am and 1.30 to 5pm; closed weekends and holidays.* ☎ *40 79 30 00.*
The garden contains more than 10 000 classified plants including plants grown for food and medicinal purposes. Rising above everything is the Corsican Pine grown from seeds brought from the isle by Turgot in 1774.

★**Mineralogical Gallery.** — *Open 10am to 5pm (11am to 6pm on weekends from 1 April and 30 September); closed Tuesdays and holidays; 25F including the Palaeobotanical Gallery;* ☎ *40 79 30 00.*
Minerals, meteorites and precious stones.
In the entrance hall of the Mineralogical Gallery can be seen a cross-section of the trunk of an American sequoia tree more than 2 000 years old. It is inlaid with tablets describing events contemporary to its growth.

Palaeobotanical Gallery. — *Same admission times and charges above.*
Evolutionary trends of flora and specimens of fossil plants.

Entomological Gallery. — *Open 2 to 5pm; closed Tuesdays and weekday holidays; 12F.* ☎ *40 79 30 00.*
Selection of insects from all over the world.

Paleontological Gallery. — *Open 10am to 5pm; closed Tuesdays and holidays, 18F.* ☎ *40 79 30 00.*
The gallery of comparative anatomy comprises 36 000 specimens.
Fossils are displayed on the first and second floors with large prehistoric animals and casts of extinct species in the centre.

Take Rue Daubenton and Rue George-Desplas to the Paris Muslim Institute (Institut Musulman de Paris) and its facilities: cafe, restaurant, market and baths.

THE MOSQUE Michelin plan ⅡⅡ - fold 44: L 16 - M 16

Entrance: Place du Puits-de-l'Ermite. Guided tours (3/4 hour) 9am to 12noon and 2 to 6pm; closed Fridays and Moslem holidays; 15F; ☎ 45 35 97 33.

The white buildings overlooked by a minaret, making one feel far from home, were erected between 1922 and 1926.

Three holy men supervise the enclave: the *muphti*, lawyer, administrator and judge; the *iman* who looks after the mosque; and the *muezzin* or cantor who calls the faithful to prayer twice a day from high up in the minaret.

Native craftsmen from the Mohammedan countries have contributed to the decoration of the halls and courts with Persian carpets, copper from North Africa, cedarwood from Lebanon, a dais from Egypt, etc. A Hispano-Moorish style courtyard has a garden at its centre — a symbol of the Muslim Paradise. At the heart of the religious buildings is a patio, inspired by that of the Alhambra in Granada. The prayer chamber is outstanding for its decoration and magnificent carpets.

From the Mosque to the Mineralogical Museum

On leaving the Mosque take Rue de Quatrefages on the right, turn left into Rue de Lacépède (18C mansion at no 7) then right into Rue de Navarre where one finds the entrance to the square surrounding the arena.

Lutetia Arena (Arènes de Lutèce). — The exact date of the Gallo-Roman arena remains unknown. This is one of two Parisian monuments from this period, the other being the Cluny public bath house. The arena, destroyed in 280 by the Barbarians, lay buried for fifteen hundred years before being rediscovered by accident when the Rue Monge was laid in 1869. Only since the beginning of this century has the site been methodically excavated and restored.

The arena was constructed for circus and theatrical presentations; although many of its stone tiers have now vanished, the stage and wings remain.

Standing against a wall in Square Capitan are the engraved stones which indicated the seats of notables of the period.

Leave the arena by Square Capitan with its formal garden and fountain, take Rue des Arènes and turn left into Rue Linné to Place Jussieu which is lined by the modern façades of the Pierre and Marie Curie University (Paris VI and VII) buildings built on the site of the former wine market.

★★**Mineralogical Museum (Musée de Minéralogie).** — *Tower 25, ground floor, take the lift. Open Wednesdays and Saturdays 2 to 6pm; closed during university vacations; 10F; ☎ 44 27 52 88.*

The museum presents in a most attractive fashion its collections of minerals. Here in dazzling array are cut and uncut gemstones and rock crystal.

Take Rue des Fossés-St-Bernard to the Institute of the Arab World on the corner of Quai St Bernard.

★ **INSTITUTE OF THE ARAB WORLD (INSTITUT DU MONDE ARABE)**
Michelin plan ⅡⅡ - fold 44: K 16

Open 1 to 8pm except Mondays and Moslem holidays; 25F; annual pass 100F; ☎ 40 51 38 38.

The aim of the Institute set up by France and twenty Arab countries is to promote Arab culture, cultural exchanges and cooperation. The two ranges of the glass and aluminium building are separated by a very narrow inner courtyard decked in translucent marble.

The curved upper north face of the building bears a photographic print of the Ile St-Louis buildings opposite, while on the straight south face 240 geometric panels open and shut to let in the right amount of light in the manner of Arab blinds. Behind the glass on the west side a cylindrical white marble Book Tower evokes the Samarra mosque minaret.

The Institute includes a museum, a library, a reference department and an audiovisual studio.

Museum. — *7th floor.* On display are works of art from countries ranging from Spain to India to illustrate Arab history from the 9C to the 19C: cut and glazed glass, metallic glaze ceramics, chased bronze, wood and ivory sculpture, geometric or floral carpets. The architecture of palaces and mosques and scientific achievements in the fields of medicine, astronomy and mathematics are also featured. There is a fine collection of astrolabes which are greatly valued by Arab astronomers. On the lower level an exhibition of contemporary art from the 1950s comprises paintings, sculpture, graphic arts, photographs...

Cross Rue St-Bernard to the riverside, Square Tino Rossi, the setting for an open-air **sculpture museum**: *Chronos 10* by Schoffer, *Bell II* by Kiyomizu, *Development of Form* by Zadkine.

If you are interested in contemporary architecture then visit one or two of the capital's Grand Projects:

The Great Arch in La Défense business district
The Pyramid at the Louvre
The Opera House at the Bastille.

BOUCHARD STUDIO AND MUSEUM

Michelin plan **11** - fold 26: J 4 — *Métro Station: Jasmin*

25 Rue de l'Yvette. Open Wednesdays and Saturdays 2 to 7pm; closed last fortnight of every quarter; 20F. ☎ *46 47 63 46.*

The work by the sculptor, Henri Bouchard (1875-1960) varies from medals and statuettes to imposing memorials. Stone and bronze were his favourite materials. The studio display includes the plaster cast of *Apollo (p 63)*, the monumental bronze in front of Chaillot Palace, and the materials used in the creation of low reliefs, in particular those of the Church of St-Pierre de Chaillot *(p 211)*.

★ BUTTES-CHAUMONT PARK

Michelin plan **11** - fold 22: D 19, D 20 - E 19, E 20
Métro Station: Buttes Chaumont

Until 1864-1867 when Napoleon III and Haussmann converted the area into a park, Paris' first open space to the north, Chaumont, the bare or bald *(chauve)* mound, was a sinister area of quarries and rubbish dumps.
Haussmann took full advantage of the differences in ground level and of the quarries to dig a lake, fed by St-Martin's Canal, in which he massed part-natural, part-artificial rocks 50m-150ft high. Two bridges lead to the island which he crowned with a temple commanding an extensive view of Montmartre and St-Denis.

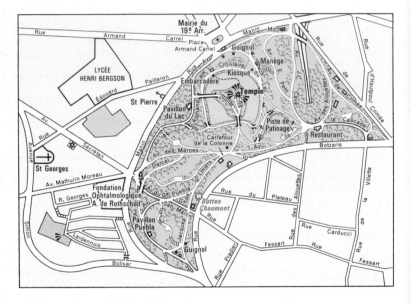

At the corner of Rue Manin and Avenue Mathurin-Moreau stands the A.-de-Rothschild Ophtalmic Foundation, home of the French eye bank.
Steps lead up to the streets overlooking the hospital and affording an attractive view of Montmartre.

★ THE CATACOMBS

Michelin plan **11** - fold 42: N 12 — *Métro Station: Denfert-Rochereau*

In the middle of **Place Denfert-Rochereau** is a small bronze version of Bartholdi's *Lion* in commemoration of Colonel Denfert-Rochereau's successful defence of Belfort in 1870-71. The two elegantly-proportioned buildings adorned by sculpted friezes are examples of Ledoux' city gates and toll-houses *(p 20)*, which punctuated "the wall walling in Paris".

Tour. — *Entrance: 1 Place Denfert-Rochereau. Open Tuesdays to Fridays, 2 to 4pm; Saturdays and Sundays, 9 to 11am and 2 to 4pm; closed Mondays and holidays; time: 1 hour; 15F.* ☎ *43 22 47 63; numerous stairs; take a torch.*
In 1785 it was decided to take the disused parts of the quarries formed by excavation since Gallo-Roman times at the bases of the three "mountains" — Montparnasse, Montrouge and Montsouris — and turn them into ossuaries. Several million skeletons from the Innocents and other cemeteries were thereupon transported to Montrouge where the bones were stacked against the walls, the skulls and crossed tibias forming a macabre decoration.
On the liberation of Paris in August 1944 it was found that the Resistance Movement had established its headquarters within the catacombs.

*Use **Michelin Maps** with your **Michelin Guide**.*

CERNUSCHI MUSEUM

Michelin plan **11** - fold 17: E 10
Métro Station: Monceau or Villiers

7 Avenue Vélasquez. Open 10am to 5.40pm; closed Mondays and holidays; 12F. ☎ *45 63 50 75.*

The banker Henri Cernuschi donated to the City of Paris, on his death in 1896, his house and extensive collection of Oriental art.
The museum is devoted to ancient Chinese art and includes Neolithic terracottas, archaic bronzes and jade, ceramics, funerary statuettes and ink drawings. A 5C stone Bodhisattva and an 8C Tang painting on silk, *Horses and their Grooms,* are outstanding.
On the first floor temporary exhibitions alternate with showings of traditional Chinese painting.

Horseman, Han dynasty

★★ CONSERVATOIRE NATIONAL DES ARTS ET MÉTIERS

Michelin plan **11** - fold 32: G 15, G 16
Métro Station: Réaumur-Sébastopol or Arts et Métiers

The Conservatory, an institution for technical instruction, a considerable industrial museum and a laboratory for industrial experiment, has incorporated in its present buildings the old church and refectory of the St Martin in the Fields priory which once stood on the site.
This Benedictine priory had developed around the original chapel built in the 4C, dedicated to St Martin, the Bishop of Tours. In 1273 the precincts were enclosed by a fortified wall, parts of which can still be seen by continuing around to Rue du Vertbois (watch tower). The Conservatory, created by the Convention in 1794, was installed five years later in the priory.

★★**Refectory.** — *Open Mondays to Fridays 1 to 8pm, Saturdays 9am to 7pm; closed Sundays, holidays and in August.* Enter the courtyard where on the right is the former monks' refectory by Pierre of Montreuil (13C), now the library. The interior is true Gothic with pure lines, perfect proportions and seven slender columns down the centre. On the right is a door with delightful carvings.

★★NATIONAL TECHNICAL MUSEUM
(MUSÉE NATIONAL DES TECHNIQUES)

292 Rue St-Martin. Open 10am to 5.30pm; closed Mondays and holidays; 20F, 10F on Sundays; ☎ *40 27 23 31.* The museum illustrates technical progress in industry and science and displays large-scale machines and models.

Ground Floor: 10. — the former **Church of St Martin in the Fields**★ (St-Martin-des-Champs — *exterior: p 258*) where, below the early 12C vaulting in the ambulatory showing clearly the transition from Romanesque to Gothic are exhibits on locomotion — cycles, cars, aircraft, etc. Foucault's pendulum, which demonstrated the rotation of the earth (19C), is suspended from the roof;

9, 8 and 5. — railways from the 19C: steam, electric and diesel; model trains;

4. — agricultural machinery;

2. — at the foot of the staircase is the Echo Room with apparatus and mementoes of the 18C chemist, Lavoisier;

21. — weights and measures: 1551 measure, 15C standard;

20. — mathematics, astronomy, geodesy: examples of Pascal's arithmetic machine, early instruments (astrolabes, globes, sun dials, pendulums, chronometers...);

19 to 15. — horology: fine collection with a particularly good 18C section;

13. — automata: Marie-Antoinette's clockwork dulcimer-playing puppet of 1784;

11 to 12. — *Temporary exhibition area;*

Return to Gallery 2. The double flight staircase is by the 18C architect of the Mint, Jacques Antoine.

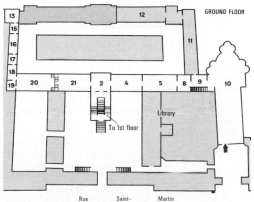

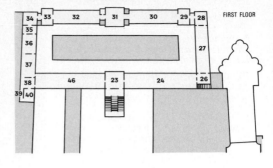

FIRST FLOOR

First Floor: 23. — in the stateroom at the top of the stairs: models based on the Encyclopaedia (late 18C) mostly of craft workshops;

24. — energy: mills, model of the Marly machine (1678-1655), turbines, boilers;

26 and 27. — physics and electricity: early scientific instruments, calorimeter;

28. — glass from the greatest European glassworks: pieces by Gallé in central display case;

29. — Laboratories of the physicists Charles and Nollet;

30. — acoustics and optics: microscopes, spectacles;

31. — music: experimental and early instruments;

32. — mechanics: machine tools, gears;

33 to 37. — radio, television, electronic acoustics: telecommunications systems for transmitting signals, images, sound, including the techniques of today's radar, laser and satellite; the transmitting station from the Eiffel Tower; Edison's phonograph; sound recording (records, tapes, film soundtracks);

38 and 39. — photography, cinema, cameras of Niepce, Daguerre and Edison; the magic lantern used by the Lumière brothers in 1895 *(p 82);*

46. — graphic arts (printing, duplicators, typing machines), telecommunications (Chappe telegraph, Morse telegraph) and technology of everyday life (heating, elevation, lighting, domestic equipment).

EXPIATORY CHAPEL (CHAPELLE EXPIATOIRE)

Michelin plan **11** - fold 18: F 11 — *Métro Station: St-Augustin*

Square Louis XVI (entrance: 29 rue Pasquier)
Open 10am to 12.30pm and 1.30 to 4.45pm (3.45pm from 1 October to 31 March); closed 1 January, 1 May, 11 November and 25 December; 20F. ☎ *42 65 35 80.*

A small cemetery, opened in 1722, was used as burial ground first for the Swiss Guards killed at the Tuileries on the 10 August 1792 *(p 31)* and then for the victims of the guillotine which stood in the Place de la Concorde *(p 55)*. These last numbered 1 343 and included Louis XVI and Marie-Antoinette. Immediately on his return to Paris, Louis XVIII had the remains of his brother and sister-in-law disinterred and transported to the royal necropolis at St-Denis (21 January 1815). Between 1816 and 1821 the chapel was erected according to Fontaine's plans.
The cloister occupies the site of the old burial ground. Charlotte Corday, who stabbed Marat in his bath to avenge the Girondins, and Philippe-Égalité are buried on either side of the steps leading to the chapel in which two marble groups show Louis XVI and an angel (by Bosio) and Marie-Antoinette supported by Religion symbolised by a figure with the features of Madame Elisabeth, the king's sister (by Cortot). The crypt altar marks the place where Louis XVI's and Marie-Antoinette's bodies were found.

THE FAUBOURG ST-ANTOINE

Michelin plan **11** - folds 33, 34 and 46: K 18, K 19

Distance: 3km-2 miles — Time: 1 3/4 hours — Start from the Bastille métro station.

The old streets of the Faubourg St-Antoine have been the centre of the cabinet-making industry for centuries.

HISTORICAL NOTES

The community grew up round the fortified Royal Abbey of St Anthony, founded in 1198.

Privileges. — Louis XI added to the abbey's privileges by giving it power to dispense justice locally and allowing the craftsmen in the vicinity to work outside the established powerful and highly restrictive guilds. The cabinet-makers of St-Antoine thus became free to design furniture and, from the 17C, copied or adapted pieces from the royal workshops and began to employ mahogany, ebony, bronze and produce marquetry.

Industrial progress. — By the time of the Revolution, workshops had developed in size, in the case of Réveillon, populariser of painted wallpapers, to 400 employees. The sheer numbers were a cause for social unrest and in April of 1789 the factory, at **31** Rue de Montreuil, was the scene of rioting and Réveillon was obliged to flee. In October 1783 **Pilâtre de Rozier** *(p 249)* made the first aerial ascent from Réveillon's factory yard in a balloon of paper made on the spot, inflated with hot air and secured by a cable.

The Revolution abolished the guilds, thereby reducing the local craftsmen's advantage which suffered further with 19C mechanisation. Small workshops, nevertheless, abounded. With the abolition of the national workshops in June 1848 the faubourg was the setting for the erection of numerous barricades.

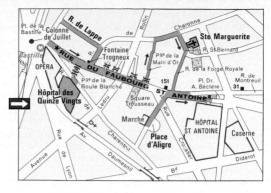

TOUR

★Rue du Faubourg St-Antoine.

— The street is lined with furniture shops and honeycombed with courts and passages, often with picturesque names (Le Bel Air, l'Étoile d'Or, les Trois-Frères, l'Ours, la Bonne-Graine...), where timber is matured and carpenters and cabinet makers can be seen at work.

The Passage de la Boule Blanche at no 50 opens onto the entrance (no 28) of the **Quinze Vingts Hospital** in Rue de Charenton. St Louis founded the hospital for 300 (15 × 20) blind persons and located it in the vicinity of the Louvre (p 140). It was later transferred to these 18C buildings which were formerly barracks, erected by Robert de Cotte.

At the corner with Rue de Charonne is the Trogneux Fountain (1710). Continue up this side street until you reach the picturesque **Rue de Lappe** on the left, which was famous for its dance halls and Auvergne shops and which now boasts some art galleries.

Return to the main street; the Main-d'Or Passage at no 133, typical of the old quarter, comes out onto Rue de Charenton.

St Margaret's Church.

— Open 9am to 12noon and 5 to 7pm; avoid visiting during services.

Built in the 17C and enlarged in the 18C, the interior is disparate in style, the nave low and plain with basket handle arching, the chancel tall and light. The marble pietà (1705) behind the high altar is by Girardon; the false relief frescoes (1765) in the Souls in Purgatory Chapel, left of the chancel, are by Brunetti. The transept chapels contain 18C paintings which originally came from the Lazarus House (p 251).

The small cemetery is presumed to be the burial place of Louis XVII who is said to have died in the Temple in 1795 (p 259).

From St Margaret's to the St Anthony Hospital.

— Return to the main street by the Rue de la Forge Royale. Opposite no **151** a barricade was erected in protest against the dissolution of the Assembly and Napoleon III's coup d'état in December 1851. **Place d'Aligre** is the site of a daily market (mornings only).

At no 184 is the St Anthony Hospital on the site of the old abbey which gave the quarter its name.

Adjoining these 18C buildings is the modern building (1965), the work of the architect Wogenscky. Not open.

★ FLEA MARKET (MARCHÉ AUX PUCES)

Michelin plan **11** - fold 7: A 13, A 14 — Métro Station: Porte de Clignancourt
Open Saturdays, Sundays and Mondays.

In the 19C it was the site of the bastions marking the city limits (p 20). The market developed from the casual offering of their wares by hawkers to the curious at the end of the 19C, to an established trading centre in the 1920s. A lucky few picked up masterpieces from the then unknowing sellers; now more than 2 000 stalls attract a motley throng to pick over every imaginable type of object.

The stalls are grouped:

Vernaison: period furniture, ornaments.

Biron: antiques and valuables.

Cambo: furniture, paintings.

des Rosiers: furniture, ornaments, paintings.

Serpette: country furniture, antiques, ornaments.

Paul-Bert: secondhand goods, bronzes.

Jules-Vallès: country furniture, curios.

Malik: secondhand clothes, spectacles, records.

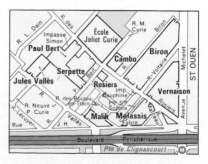

A variety of less permanent stalls is to be found in the neighbouring streets: Rue J.-H.-Fabre, Rue des Rosiers, Rue Voltaire, and Avenue Michelet.

★ AVENUE FOCH

Michelin, plan **11** - folds 15 and 16: F 5, F 6 and F 7

Métro Station: Charles-de-Gaulle-Étoile

Avenue Foch, radiating from the Étoile to the Place du Maréchal-de-Lattre-de-Tassigny, is one of Haussmann's most magnificent roadways. This 120m-393ft wide thoroughfare was laid out in 1854 as the Avenue de l'Impératrice and quickly became adopted by fashionable society as the way to the Bois de Boulogne. Today lawns and trees separate the avenue from the parallel side roads which are overlooked by elegant mansions. On the death of Marshal Foch in 1929 the avenue was renamed.

At no 59 Avenue Foch Adolphe d'Ennery's mansion now houses two museums.

Armenian Museum. — *Ground floor. Open Thursdays and Sundays 2 to 6pm; closed certain holidays and in August;* ☎ *45 56 15.88.*
The collection includes Amenian jewels, religious and folk art objects as well as modern paintings, sculpture and drawings.

Ennery Museum. — *First floor. Open Thursdays and Sundays 2 to 5pm; closed holidays and in August;* ☎ *45 53 57 96.*
The rich collection of the dramatist and librettist, Adolphe d'Ennery (1811-99), are displayed in their original Second Empire setting. Chinese and Japanese furniture, ceramics, bronzes, lacquerwork, jade and several hundred **netsuke**★ (small carved wood, ivory or bone belt ornaments) are displayed in showcases inlaid with mother-of-pearl.

Near the Manufacturer's Syndicate at 16 Rue de la Faisanderie is the small but interesting **Counterfeit Museum** (Musée de la Contrefaçon) *(open Mondays and Wednesdays 2 to 4.30pm; Fridays 9.30am to 12noon; closed Tuesdays, Thursdays, weekends and holidays;* ☎ *45 01 51 11).* The exhibits include commercial forgeries and non-copyright publicity material.

★ THE FRONT DE SEINE

Michelin plan **11** - folds 27 and 39: K 6 - L 5, L 6

Métro Station: Charles-Michels or Javel

The area bordered by Avenue Émile-Zola, Rue du Docteur Finlay and the embankment is another urban renewal project. This area has been the theatre for architectural innovation, and several generations of high-rise buildings have mushroomed in the twenty years between 1967 and 1986. The modern tower blocks demonstrate a variety of silhouettes and embellishments; high-rise flats are integrated with office towers, public buildings and a shopping centre, **Beaugrenelle**. A vast concrete podium, above the road network, ensures a traffic-free zone which is given over to spacious gardens and children's playgrounds.

GEORGES-BRASSENS PARK

Michelin plan **11** - folds 52: N 8 — *Métro Station: Convention*

At the foot of a wooded hill lies the largest park created in Paris this century on the site of the Vaugirard slaughter-houses of which some features remain: the horse market, two bronze bulls at the main entrance and the auction bell tower by the pond in the centre. There is also a belvedere, a beekeeping school, a garden with scented plants for the blind and a vineyard where the grape harvest is celebrated gaily at the beginning of October.

THE GOBELINS QUARTER

Michelin plan **11** - folds 44 and 56: N 15 - P 15

Distance: 2.5km-1 1/2 miles — Time: 2 hours — Start from the Place d'Italie métro station

This walk leads from the Place d'Italie via La Butte-aux-Cailles to the famous Gobelins' Tapestry Factory.

Place d'Italie. — The square marks the site of one of the toll-houses built by Ledoux and is today on the edge of an area of high-rise buildings. From the Avenue des Gobelins there is a good view of the Pantheon.
At the corner of Avenue d'Italie and Rue Bobillot stands the new film centre by the Japanese architect Kenzo Tange. This audio-visual centre will house France's largest cinema screen.
Take Boulevard Auguste-Blanqui and turn left into Rue du Moulin-des-Prés.

La Butte-aux-Cailles. — On 21 November 1783, having taken off from the vicinity of La Muette, the physicist **Pilâtre de Rozier** landed his hot air balloon on this mound, then occupied by several solitary windmills. This was the first free flight *(p 249).*
Today the district is one of surprising contrasts although the small houses and cobbled streets are slowly giving way to modern blocks of flats. A new quarter is growing out of the old village. In Place Paul-Verlaine turn right into Rue de la Butte-aux-Cailles. Rue des Cinq-Diamants has retained a certain old-world charm. The peaceful Passage Barrault and then the street of the same name lead to Boulevard Auguste-Blanqui.

From La Butte-aux-Cailles to the Gobelins' Tapestry Factory. — On the far side of the boulevard take Rue Corvisart, then cross the park, Square René-Le-Gall. The far end of the park is overlooked by Auguste Perret's 1935 building, the **National Furniture Storehouse** (Mobilier National).

The river **Bièvre** flows under Rue de Croulebarbe and Rue Berbier-du-Mets. Ice taken from the marshes was packed into wells and then covered with earth. This activity gave the district its name La Glacière (ice house). Up to the 17C this willow-bordered stream was of sparkling clear water but dyeing, tanning and bleaching soon turned it into a murky evil-smelling stream. In 1910 the stream was filled in.

A plaque on the wall of an old house opposite the Mobilier National recalls the famous 15C Gobelins dyeworks.

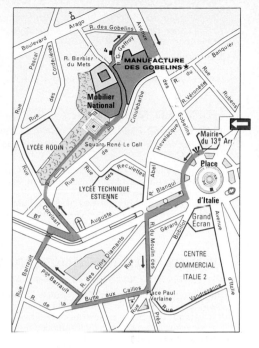

Take to the right the narrow but twisting Rue Gustave-Geffroy. At No 4 stands the old **Hôtel de la Reine-Blanche** which was no doubt named after Philippe VI's widow, Blanche d'Evreux. According to the chronicler Juvénal des Ursins, it was here in 1393 that Charles VI was almost burnt alive at one of the many festivities organised on his physicians' orders to attempt to cure his insanity. His hairy costume caught fire with near dire results! The house rebuilt in the 16C was taken over by the Gobelins in the 18C and today it is a dismal-looking industrial building.

★**Gobelins' Tapestry Factory (Manufacture des Gobelins).** — *42 Avenue des Gobelins.* In about 1440 the dyer, Jean Gobelin, who specialised in scarlet, set up a workshop beside the Bièvre which was to be used by his descendants until the reign of Henri IV in the early 17C when it was taken over by two Flemish craftsmen, summoned by the king. Colbert, charged by Louis XIV with the reorganisation of the tapestry and carpet weaving industry, grouped the Paris and Maincy shops around the Gobelins workshops thus creating, in 1662, the Royal Factory of Tapestry and Carpet Weavers to the Crown. At the group's head he placed the artist, Charles Le Brun. Five years later the group was joined by the Royal Cabinet-Makers. The greatest craftsmen, including also gold and silversmiths, were therefore working side by side and in an atmosphere propitious to the evolution of the Louis XIV style. In the last 300 years more than 5 000 tapestries have been woven at the Gobelins factory after cartoons by the greatest painters — Le Brun, Poussin, Mignard, Boucher, Lurçat, Picasso...

The **Savonnerie** (1604-1826) *(p 177)* and **Beauvais** (1664-1940) carpet and tapestry factories have, over the years, been incorporated to form the present single unit.

Tour. — *Guided tours of the workshops, Tuesdays, Wednesdays and Thursdays at 2 and 3pm; time 1 1/2 hours; 25F.* ☎ 48 87 24 14.

The factory, although in a modern building (1914), has retained 17C methods: warp threads are set by daylight, the colours being selected from the factory's range of 14 000 tones. Each weaver, working from mirrors, completes from 1 to 8m²-1 to 8 sq yds each year depending on the design. All production goes to the state.

The four great French Tapestry workshops

Aubusson: producing less fine hangings for the lesser 17 and 18C aristocracy and bourgeoisie; floral and plant, animal, Classical fable and, later, landscape designs. Chinoiseries and pastoral scenes (after Huet) were the most used motifs.

Beauvais: very finely woven in the 18C often with vividly dyed silks which, unfortunately, have faded. Motifs include grotesques, Fables after La Fontaine (by Oudry), Boucher's Italian Comedy, Loves of the Gods, Chinoiseries, and pastoral scenes (after Huet). 18C designs continued into 19C.

Felletin: coarser weave hangings with rustic motifs.

Gobelins: sumptuous quality hangings often with gold interwoven. Renowned for originality, series include The Life of the King, The Seasons and Elements, Royal Residences, Louis XV at the Chase. Motifs also after Oudry and Boucher (Loves of the Gods — p 50). Neilson, a Scot, became the most influential weaver in late 18C.

When sightseeing in the Paris region
then use the **Michelin Green Guide Ile-de-France.**

GRAND ORIENT LODGE MUSEUM

Michelin plan **11** - fold 19: F 14 — *Métro Station: Cadet*

16 Rue Cadet. Open 2 to 6pm; closed Sundays and holidays and first two weeks in September; ☎ *45 23 20 92 extn 303.*

The museum occupies a vast hall in the modern premises of the Grand-Orient-Lodge, an association of French provincial lodges. Documents, emblems and portraits retrace the history of this Grand Lodge and its freemason members.

HENNER MUSEUM

Michelin plan **11** - fold 17: D 9 — *Métro Station: Malesherbes*

43 Avenue de Villiers. Open 10am to 12noon and 2 to 5pm: closed Mondays; 13F. ☎ *47 63 42 73.*

Paintings, drawings and sketches by the Alsatian artist Jean-Jacques Henner (1829-1905) are the subject of this museum. An audio-visual display describes the artist's work and its evolution.

During a trip to Italy Henner was greatly influenced by the works of both Titian and Correggio and following this visit his landscapes were to include figures of nymphs and naiads. In his numerous portraits he employed vigorous brushwork.

CHURCH OF THE HOLY SPIRIT

Michelin plan **11** - fold 47: M 11 — *Métro Station: Daumesnil*

Off the usual tourist trails, this church is impressive for its sheer size. It was designed by Tournon and decorated by well-known artists of the inter-war period. It is a good example of concrete-built religious architecture of the 1930s although the basic forms are still greatly influenced by Gothic and Byzantine styles. In terms of form the Holy Spirit recalls the Church of St Sophia in Constantinople. Dark inside, the little light there is, is shed by a circlet of stained-glass windows by Barillet at the base of the dome and those of the low bays. In the apsidal chapel a vast fresco by Maurice Denis portrays the "work" of the Holy Spirit throughout the world. In the ambulatory the Way of the Cross by Georges Desvallières portrays a sober style with dull colours and tormented forms, developed by religious artists in reaction to the frivolous and carefree works of the Années Folles. At the far end of the north aisle a low relief by Roger de Villiers demonstrates the same restraint.

JEWISH ART MUSEUM

Michelin plan **11** - fold 7: C 14 — *Métro Station: Lamarck-Caulaincourt*

42 Rue des Saules. Open 3 to 6pm; closed Fridays and Saturdays, in August and on Jewish holidays; 15F. ☎ *42 57 84 15.*

On the third floor of the Montmartre Jewish Centre, this small museum contains in addition to devotional objects, works by Chagall and other contemporaries. Models of Polish and Lithuanian synagogues give some idea of the architectural styles current in the 17C and 18C in those countries.

★ MONCEAU PARK

Michelin plan **11** - fold 17: E 9, E 10 — *Métro Station: Monceau*

This elegant quarter includes one of Paris' rare green open spaces.
In 1778 the Duke of Orléans, the future Philippe-Egalité, commissioned the painter-writer Carmontelle to design a garden on the Monceau Plain, then rich in game.

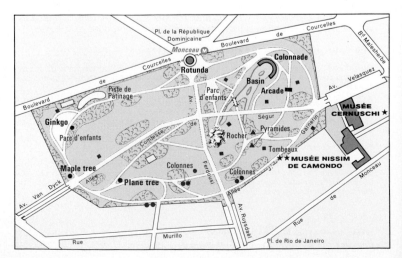

The artist produced a land of dreams, scattered with pavilions and landscaped after the fashion of the English and German gardens of the time. He constructed a pyramid and a pagoda, a Roman Temple, feudal ruins, Dutch windmills, a Swiss farm, naumachia and mounds, linked by a network of rising and falling paths. Some still remain.

At the Revolution, Monceau Park — in which Garnerin, the first parachutist, had landed on 22 October 1797 — passed to the lawyer and statesman Cambacérès. It returned briefly to the Orléans before, in 1852, the financier, Pereire, sold part of the park for the building of luxurious houses. In 1862, the engineer Alphand laid out a farther area after the style of an English park.

The rotunda at the entrance, known as the Chartres Pavilion, was originally a toll-house in the Farmers-General perimeter wall *(p 20)* and has fine wrought-iron gates. The many statues in the park take second place to the trees. The oval **naumachia basin** is modelled on the Roman pools constructed for the simulation of naval battles; the colonnade brought to adorn it was from the never-completed mausoleum of Henri II at St-Denis while the nearby Renaissance arcade stood before the Hôtel de Ville.

Nearby are the Cernuschi *(p 241)* and Nissim de Camondo *(p 250)* museums.

★ MONTSOURIS PARK and UNIVERSITY RESIDENTIAL CAMPUS

Michelin plan **⅒** - fold 55: R 13 - S 13, S 14

Métro Station: Porte d'Orléans or RER Station: Cité Universitaire

The Montsouris Park and the Paris University Residential Campus form a large green open space to the south of the city, which is highly appreciated by Parisians.

★**Montsouris Park.** — Haussmann began work on this nondescript area, which was undermined by quarries and capped by dozens of windmills in 1868. By 1878 he had turned it into a park: the 16ha-50 acres had been landscaped and paths constructed to climb the mounds and circle the cascades and large artificial lake (the engineer personally involved in the construction committed suicide, when the lake suddenly dried out on opening day).

The park is dominated by the **south bearing** of the old Paris meridian *(plan p 202)*. The municipal meteorological observatory is in a nearby building.

In the vicinity. — Several of the smaller streets, some still cobbled, retain a peaceful aspect of former times, notably Rue des Artistes and Rue St-Yves with Cité du Souvenir at no **11**.

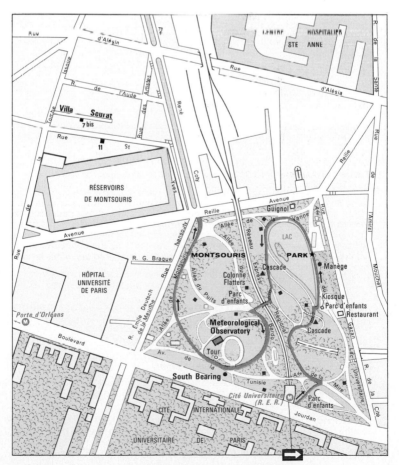

Painters, attracted by the park's peace and proximity to Montparnasse at the beginning of the century, left their mark on the area, as, for instance, the Douanier Rousseau and Georges Braque who had a studio (west of the park) in a street which now carries his name.

During the inter-war period some of the most famous residents of the **Villa Seurat** were the artist Gromaire, Lurçat, Orloff the sculptor, Henry Miller and Soutine. No **7 bis** is the work of Auguste Perret.

The grass-covered sides and rooftops of the Montsouris reservoirs overlook the Avenues Reille and René Coty. The waters of the Vanne, Loing and Lunain collect in these 100-year-old reservoirs.

★**Paris University Residential Campus** (Cité Internationale Universitaire de Paris).
— *Main entrance: 19-21 Boulevard Jourdan.*

The "city" on the edge of Monsouris Park spreads over an area of 40ha-100 acres, housing over 5 500 students from 120 different countries in its 37 halls of residence. Each hall forms an independent community, reflecting in its architecture an individual character, frequently inspired by the country which founded it.

The first hall, the **E.-and-L.-Deutsch-de-la-Meurthe Foundation** was opened in 1925. The **International Hall** (1936) with a swimming pool, theatre and vast rooms was presented by John D. Rockefeller Jr; the **Swiss Hall** and **Franco-Brazilian Foundation** were designed by Le Corbusier. The **Persian Foundation** (1968) is interesting.

The **Sacred Heart Church** (Sacré-Cœur — *open daily on request 9am to 11am and 3 to 5pm*) stands on the far side of the ring road and is reached by a footbridge. Built between 1931 and 1936 in neo-Romanesque style, it is plain with preponderantly blue stained-glass windows.

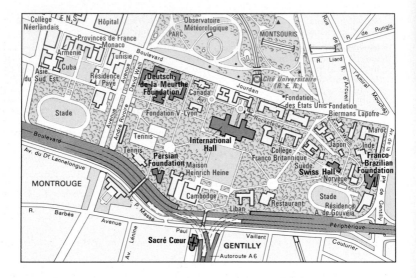

MOREAU MUSEUM

Michelin plan **11** - fold 19: E 13 — *Métro Station: Trinité*

14 Rue de La Rochefoucauld. Open 10am to 12.45pm and 2 to 5.15pm; closed Tuesdays, 1 January and 25 December; 16F; 8F Sundays; ☎ 48 74 38 50.

On his death the artist Gustave Moreau (1826-1898) left his house and collection of some 11 000 paintings, drawings and water colours and wax sculptures, to the nation. Moreau, influenced by Delacroix and his master Chassériau, delighted in lending a touch of fantasy to biblical and mythological subjects.

On the third floor note *The Triumph of Alexander the Great* (opposite the spiral staircase), dated 1890, where the countries traversed by the conqueror are over-painted in black; a moving *Orpheus by Eurydice's grave*; and one of his last works, *Jupiter and Sémélé* (1895).

THE MUETTE QUARTER
and RANELAGH GARDENS

Michelin plan **11** - folds 26 and 27: H 4, H 5 - J 4, J 5

Distance: 1.5km-1 mile — Time: approx. 45 min (excluding the Marmottan Museum) — Start from the Muette métro station.

The original Muette Estate was developed as an elegant quarter. Today it enjoys the green open space of the Ranelagh Gardens as well as the added attraction of the Marmottan Museum with its rich collections.

La Muette. — Take the Chaussée de la Muette. It was here that Charles IX had a hunting lodge where he kept his falcons when in moult (french *en mue*), hence the name Muette. This name was also used for the replacement château built by Philibert Delorme and set in a park extending to the Bois de Boulogne.

The château had many royal owners from Queen Margot, first wife of Henri of Navarre, Louis XIII to the Duchesse de Berry. It was here, knowing her days to be numbered, that she lived up to her motto "short and sweet" dying aged 24. Both Louis XV and the Marquise de Pompadour appreciated the château as a clandestine meeting place. The future Louis XVI and Marie-Antoinette spent the first years of their married life here.

At the Revolution the estate was subdivided and in 1820 the piano maker Sébastien Erard purchased the château and part of the park. A century later the property was sold off as building lots.

At no 2 Avenue Mozart is an unusual museum set up by a collector.

Museum of Spectacles (Musée des lunettes et des lorgnettes). — *Open 10am to 6pm; closed Sundays, holidays and in August;* ☎ 45 27 21 05.

The museum presents the history of spectacles, opera and field glasses, lorgnettes and other aids to sight from the 13C. There are many rare and precious specimens: gold lorgnettes and magnifying glass with automata, carved boxwood cases, etc.

Walk back and make for the Ranelagh Gardens. At the entrance is a statue of the 17C French poet La Fontaine with two of the famous animal characters from his Fables at his feet.

Ranelagh Gardens (Jardin du Ranelagh). — The gardens, on the far side of Avenue Raphaël, date from 1860 when they were laid out on the site of an earlier garden and café of high revelry. This had been established in 1774 and called in the spirit of Anglomania of the time, after the gay London pleasure gardens established by Lord Ranelagh.

★★**Marmottan Museum (Musée Marmottan).** — *2 Rue Louis Boilly. Open 10am to 5.30pm; closed Mondays, 1 May and 25 December; 25F;* ☎ 42 24 07 02.

In 1971 the Marmottan Museum was transformed, by an outstanding bequest by Michel Monet of 65 paintings by his father. The museum had developed from the bequest in 1932 by the art historian, Paul Marmottan, of his house and Renaissance (tapestries, sculpture), Consular and First Empire collections (portraits, medallions, paintings, furniture) to the Academy of Fine Arts. The Donop de Monchy legacy in 1950 added works by Claude Monet including the famous *Impression — Sunrise (stolen 1985)* which gave the Impressionist Movement its name. The majority of the Monet paintings, acquired in 1971 and for which a special underground gallery has been built, were painted at the artist's Normandy home at Giverny. They form a dazzling series of water lily, wisteria and garden scenes and with canvases by Renoir, Sisley, Pissarro, Boudin and Signac, make a perfect complement to the Orsay and Orangery Museums *(pp 54, 125)*.

A small gallery houses the 13-16C illuminated MSS of the Wildenstein Bequest. The Duhem Bequest of about 60 paintings, drawings and watercolours includes Gauguin's splendid *Bouquet of Flowers* painted in Tahiti and an interesting pastel by Renoir: *Seated Girl in a White Hat*.

From the Marmottan Museum to Square Lamartine. — Cross the Ranelagh Gardens and Avenue Prudhon to reach Allée Pilâtre-de-Rozier, named after the hot air balloonist *(pp 242, 244)* who made his first free flight from here on 21 November 1783. This alley skirts a park.

The Rue André-Pascal is named after the pen name of the banker cum author Baron Henri de Rothschild and builder of the adjacent sumptuous mansion. Since 1948 the mansion has been international territory as the seat of the Organisation for European Cooperation and Development (in French the O.C.D.E.); *not open to the public.*

The marble relief at the end of the alley by Victor Hugo is entitled *The Poet's Vision*. Cross Place de Colombie, overlooked by the statue of Peter I of Serbia and his son Alexander I of Yugoslavia, before turning right into Avenue Henri Martin, formerly Avenue de l'Empereur. Once over the Auteuil railway track Avenue Victor Hugo is on the left. The monumental statue is Rodin's *Victor Hugo and The Muses*.

The calm **Square Lamartine** is the site of the Passy artesian wells (600m-1970ft deep) dug in 1855. Residents came for a supply of sulphur-rich water at a temperature of 28°C (82°F).

★ PLACE DE LA NATION

Michelin plan **11** - fold 47: K 21 - L 21 — *Métro Station: Nation*

The square was originally named the Throne Square in honour of the state entry made by Louis XIV and his bride, the Infanta Maria-Theresa, on 26 August 1660, when a throne was erected at which the king received due homage. It was renamed, by the Convention in 1794, the Square of the Overturned Throne when they placed a guillotine upon it and it was renamed a third time, on 14 July 1880, during the first anniversary celebrations of the Revolution. The bronze group by Dalou illustrates the **Triumph of the Republic★** and was originally intended for the Place de la République *(p 257)*.

The columns on either side of Avenue du Trône, supporting statues of Philippe Auguste and St Louis, and the pair of toll booths were by Ledoux *(p 20)*.

The **Throne** or **Gingerbread Fair** was held on the nearby Cours de Vincennes for over 1 000 years. The fair recalls the concession obtained in 957 by the monks of St Anthony's Abbey to sell a rye, honey and aniseed bread in memory of their saint in Holy Week. The piglet-shaped breads were a reminder of St Anthony's faithful companion in the desert. The present-day funfair is held in the Bois de Vincennes *(p 224)*.

★★ NISSIM DE CAMONDO MUSEUM

Michelin plan **11** - fold 17: E 10 — *Métro Station: Monceau or Villiers*

63 Rue de Monceau. Open 10am to 12noon and 2 to 5pm. Closed Mondays, Tuesdays, 1 January, 25 December; 18F; ☎ 45 63 26 32.

In 1936 Count de Camondo presented his house and 18C art collection to the nation in memory of his son Nissim, who had died in the First World War. The house built in 1910 stands in grounds adjoining Monceau Park *(p 246)*.

The mansion presents an elegant Louis XVI interior with panelled salons, furniture made by the greatest cabinet-makers (Riesener and Weisweiler), Savonnerie carpets and Beauvais tapestries *(p 245)*, paintings by Guardi and Hubert Robert and gold and silver ornaments by the royal goldsmith, Roettiers. Among the outstanding pieces are tapestries of the *Fables* of La Fontaine after cartoons by Oudry, a roll-top desk by Oeben and a splendid Sèvres porcelain service, known as the Buffon service, in which every piece is decorated with the design of a different bird.

★ PALAIS DES CONGRÈS

Michelin plan **11** - fold 15: E 6 and plan p 141 — *Métro Station: Porte Maillot*

The Paris Conference Centre, situated near the Bois de Boulogne on the Champs-Élysées-Défense axis, provides a modern conference centre (Palais des Congrès) in addition to other business and recreational facilities and hotel accommodation. On several floors around the main conference hall there are exhibition halls *(1st floor)*, other smaller conference and meeting rooms, business suites and offices and around 80 shops lining the Rue Basse and the Rue Haute. In addition there are restaurants, cinemas, a discotheque, a bus station, parking space and on the seventh floor spacious kitchens, restaurants and function rooms.

The terraces on the 5th and 7th floors afford fine views of the Bois de Boulogne and La Défense.

The **Conference Hall★★** *(to see inside go to a performance)* within the centre is unique in Europe. This dual-purpose hall for conferences and entertainment has a convertible stage and a seating capacity of 3 700. The decorative forms of the walls, the specially designed seats, and the roof ensure acoustic uniformity.

Concorde-La Fayette Hotel. — Dominating the centre is the 33-storey hotel, Concorde-La Fayette. This 1 000 room hotel communicates directly with the conference centre. On the top floor there is a panoramic bar *(open 11am to 2am, access is reserved for customers only)* which affords an extensive **view★** of Paris, the Bois de Boulogne and at the far right La Défense.

Behind the Palais des Congrès, in Place du Général Koenig near the ring road, the **Notre-Dame-de-Compassion Chapel** has interesting stained glass by Ingres.

★ RUE DE PARADIS

Michelin plan **11** - fold 20: E 15 - F 15, F 16 — *Métro Station: Gare de l'Est*

The street is known today for its shops of beautiful tableware, the chief points of sale of the French glass, china and porcelain factories.

The group of buildings at nos 30-32, houses the International Tableware Centre (trade only) which regroups the best-known names in porcelain and glass-making.

At no 30 *bis* is **Baccarat**, the glassmakers who have supplied royal palaces and state residences throughout the world for the last 150 years.

★**Glass Museum (Musée du Cristal).** — *Exhibition and shop on the first floor. Open Mondays to Fridays 9am to 6pm, Saturdays 10am to 12noon and 2 to 5pm; closed Sundays and holidays; ☎ 47 70 64 30.*
Some of the workshops' finest pieces illustrating the development of style are on display (chandeliers, vases, perfume bottles).

THE QUARTER

Maison St-Lazare. — *107 Rue du Faubourg St-Denis.* In the Middle Ages this was the capital's leper house. St Vincent of Paul, the founder of the Priests of the Mission (known today as Lazarists), died here in 1660.

At the time of the Revolutionary troubles the building became a prison and the poet André Chénier, one of its most industrious inmates, was here prior to his execution. Changed to a women's prison, it once again became a hospital in 1935.

St-Laurent Church. — *68 Boulevard de Magenta. Closed weekends 2 to 4pm.* The belfry is all that remains of the 12C sanctuary. The nave was rebuilt in the 15C and the church altered in the 17C (chancel sculpture and woodwork). The west front and spire date from the Napoleon III period.

Tho **St-Laurent Fair** was held for over 600 years in the grounds of what is now the Gare de l'Est railway station. Over a hundred stalls and booths offered their goods duty free. It was on one of these make-shift stages that the first presentation of the new dramatic form, comic opera, took place around 1720.

St-Vincent-de-Paul Church. — *Place Franz-Liszt. Closed Sundays 12noon to 3.30pm.* The church is the work of the architect Hittorff (1824-1844) who was also responsible for the final decoration of Place de la Concorde. Basilical in form, the church has a columned portico and two tall towers. Inside, Flandrin's fresco runs around the nave, dividing the elevation in two. A bronze calvary by Rude stands on the high altar.

PASSY

Michelin plan **11** - fold 27: H 5, H 6 - J 5, J 6

Distance: 2km-1 1/4 miles — Time: approx. 1 1/2 hours (excluding the museums) — Start from the Trocadéro métro station.

In the 13C Passy was a woodcutters' hamlet; in the 18C it became known for its ferruginous waters and in 1859 it was incorporated into the city of Paris.

The "Fellows of Chaillot" or *bonshommes* was the familiar name by which the Minim Friars, whose monastery stood on the hill until the Revolution, were known, presumably because of the red wine produced by the community and still recalled in the names of the Rue Vineuse and Rue des Vignes.

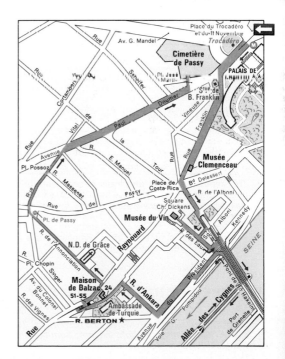

Today the houses in their own gardens that used to make up the peaceful residential quarter are being replaced by large blocks of flats.

Make your way from Place du Trocadéro et du 11-Novembre *(p 63)* along Rue Franklin.

Clemenceau Museum (Musée Clemenceau). — *8 Rue Franklin. Guided tours 2 to 5pm; closed Mondays, Wednesdays, Fridays, August and Christmas; time: 1 hour; 15F. ☎ 45 20 53 41.* The great man's apartment is as it was on the day of his death in 1929. Mementoes in a gallery on the first floor recall George Clemenceau's career as a journalist and statesman: the Montmartre mayoralty, the Treaty of Versailles and the premiership.

Continue down Rue de l'Alboni, to the right of the high-level métro station, and bearing right, turn into Rue des Eaux, at the end of which are a small street and square named after Charles Dickens.

No **5** Rue des Eaux marks the original entrance to the quarries. Under the Empire they were converted into France's first sugar beet refinery. The underground galleries now house a **wine museum** (musée du vin) *(open 2 to 6pm; closed Mondays, 1 January, and 25 December; 21F; tour and wine tasting: 26F; ☎ 45 25 63 26)* with waxwork figures and implements recalling the days of the wine-producing monks.

Allée des Cygnes. — Continue along Rue des Eaux and over Bir-Hakeim Bridge to the islet which divides the Seine at this point. The Allée des Cygnes, or Swans' Walk, which was built up on the riverbed at the time of the Restoration, makes a pleasant stroll with a good view of the Radio-France House *(p 233)* on the right and of the Front de Seine *(p 244)* on the left. The figure of *France Renaissante* at the upstream end of the island is by the Danish sculptor, Wederkinch (1930) and downstream is the Statue of Liberty *(p 233)*.

Rue d'Ankara. — The former château park of Marie-Antoinette's devoted friend, the Princess of Lamballe, at the end on the left, is now occupied by the Turkish Embassy and private houses. In the 19C it belonged to Doctor Blanche, a specialist in mental illnesses who converted it into a home for the insane.

★**Rue Berton.** — The Rue Berton, on the left, is one of the most unexpected in Paris — its ivy-covered walls and gas brackets giving it an old country town atmosphere. No **24** was the back entrance to Balzac's house *(see below)*.

Rue Raynouard. — This street is full of historical interest. Many famous people have lived in this street named after an obscure academician of the Restoration: Louis XIV's powerful financier, Samuel Bernard, the Duke of Lauzun, Jean-Jacques Rousseau, the song writer Béranger and Benjamin Franklin, when in France negotiating an alliance for the new republic of the United States with Louis XVI. It was at this time that he erected over his house, no 66, the first lightning conductor in France. The modern blocks of flats in reinforced concrete at nos **51** to **55** are by Auguste Perret who died here in 1954.

No **47**, half-hidden in its garden, was **Balzac's house** (Maison de Balzac) from 1840 to 1847 *(open daily 10am to 5.40pm; closed Mondays and holidays; 12F, free Sundays, except during exhibitions; ☎ 42 24 56 38)*. Manuscripts, caricatures and engravings in the house reflect the Human Comedy described in his novels which can be seen in an adjoining museum-library.

Turn left into Rue de l'Annonciation, the former name of the 17C chapel, much restored and now known as Our Lady of Grace. Cross the square and Rue de Passy, the old village main street, to go along Rue Vital and Avenue Paul-Doumer, on the right.

Passy Cemetery (Cimetière de Passy). — The cemetery above Trocadero square, contains, amid the greenery, the remains of many who have died since 1850 from the world of literature (Croisset, T. Bernard, Giraudoux), painting (Manet, Berthe Morisot), music (Debussy, Fauré), aviation (Henry Farman) and films (Fernandel).

If you plan to visit some of the sights in the outskirts of Paris
*then use the **Michelin Green Guide Ile-de-France.***

PASTEUR INSTITUTE

Michelin plan **⑪** - fold 41: M 10 — *Métro Station: Pasteur*

25 Rue du Docteur-Roux. Museum and crypt open Mondays to Fridays 2 to 5.30pm; closed weekends, holidays and in August; film and lecture on the Institute available on appointment, same hours, ☎ 45 68 82 82; 12F.

This internationally famous Institute has laboratories for pure and applied research, lecture theatres, a reference section, a vaccination centre, a hospital for the treatment of infectious diseases and a serum and vaccination production plant (at Louviers-Incarville).
The Institute and its Lille, Lyons and other auxiliary institutes abroad continue the work of Louis Pasteur (1822-1895), whose tomb is in the crypt and whose apartment has been converted into a museum.

★★ PÈRE-LACHAISE CEMETERY

Michelin plan **⑪** - folds 34, 35; H 20, H 21 — *Métro Station: Père Lachaise*

Open 7.30am to 6pm, 16 March to 8 November; 8am to 5.30pm, 9 November to 15 March: Saturdays open from 8.30am; Sundays and holidays 9am. Main entrance: Boulevard de Ménilmontant.

In 1626 the Jesuits bought in this country area, a site on which to build a house of retreat. This became a frequent visiting place of Louis XIV's confessor, Father La Chaise, who gave generously to the house's reconstruction in 1682. The Jesuits were expelled in 1763. Forty years later, the city acquired the property for conversion to a cemetery.
The cemetery was the scene of the Paris Commune's final and bloody stand on 28 May 1871. The last insurgents were cornered and attacked on the night of the 27th, fierce fighting taking place among the graves. At dawn the 147 survivors were stood against the wall in the southeast corner — the **Federalists' Wall** (Mur des Fédérés) — and shot. They were buried where they fell in a communal grave which remains a political pilgrimage for many.
Paris' largest cemetery, designed by Brongniart, is on rising and falling ground. Only some of the tombs of the famous are marked on the plan. A sculpture by Paul Landowski in the basement of the **Columbarium** is noteworthy.

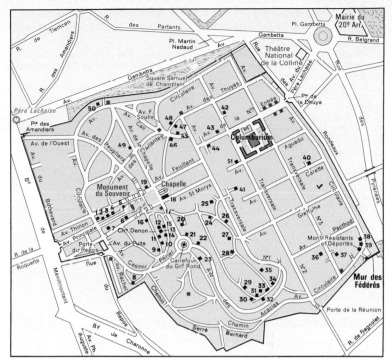

1 Colette
2 Rossini (cenotaph)
3 A. de Musset (in the shade of a willow, as he requested)
4 Baron Haussmann
5 Generals Lecomte and Thomas
6 Félix Faure
7 Arago
8 Abélard and Héloïse (p 112)
9 Gustave Charpentier
10 Chopin (p 84)
11 Cherubini
12 Boïeldieu (cenotaph)
13 Bernardin de St-Pierre
14 Grétry. — 15 Bellini
16 Branly
17 Géricault. — 18 Thiers

19 David. — 20 C. Bernard
21 Monge
22 Champollion
23 Auguste Comte
24 Gay-Lussac
25 Corot
26 Molière and La Fontaine
27 Alphonse Daudet
28 Hugo family (p 95)
29 Bibesco family (Anna de Noailles)
30 Marshal Ney (p 202)
31 Beaumarchais (p 100)
32 Larrey
33 Marshals Davout, Masséna, Lefebvre
34 Murat and Caroline Bonaparte
35 David d'Angers
36 Modigliani (p 204)

37 Édith Piaf
38 Henri Barbusse
39 Paul Éluard, Maurice Thorez
40 Oscar Wilde
41 Sarah Bernhardt
42 Marcel Proust
43 Guillaume Apollinaire
44 Allan Kardec (founder of spiritualist movement — the tomb is always a mass of flowers)
45 Delacroix (p 178)
46 Michelet
47 G. de Nerval
48 Balzac and the Countess Hanska
49 Georges Bizet
50 Georges Méliès
51 Simone Signoret, Yves Montand

PICPUS CEMETERY

Michelin plan **11** - fold 47: L 21, L 22 — *Métro Station: Nation or Picpus*

35 Rue de Picpus. Guided tours 2 to 6pm (4pm 15 October to 15 April); closed Mondays, holidays, 4 July and in August; guided tours at 2.30pm and 4pm apply in advance ☎ 45 48 81 63.

In 1794 the guillotine on the Place de la Nation fell on the heads of 1 306 people, including André Chénier and 16 Carmelite nuns, whose bodies were thrown into two communal graves. The ground, known as the Martyrs' Field, was later enclosed by a wall and an adjoining cemetery opened in which relatives of those guillotined on the square could be buried. At the far end of the cemetery the Martyrs' Field can be seen through a gate.

★★ NATIONAL MUSEUM OF POPULAR ARTS AND TRADITIONS

Michelin plan **11** fold 14: E 4 — *Métro Station: Les Sablons*

Open 9.45am to 5.15pm; closed Tuesdays, 1 January, 1 May and 25 December; 16F, 8F on Sundays; ☎ 40 67 90 00.

Two galleries give a glimpse of day-to-day life in pre-industrial France.
The **Cultural Gallery** *(ground floor)* evokes man's environment, the technical progress made by man to enable him to exploit the natural resources and the institutions he created for community living.
The **Study Gallery** *(basement)* has displays concerning agriculture, husbandry, domestic life, crafts, local beliefs and customs, games, music and local folklore. An audio-visual show and slides add interest to the visit.

ROMANTIC MOVEMENT MUSEUM

Michelin plan **10** - fold 19: E 13 — *Métro Station: Pigalle or St-Georges*

Maison Renan-Scheffer, 16 rue Chaptal. Open 10am to 5.40pm; closed Mondays and holidays; 12F. ☎ *48 74 95 38.*

This was the charming house where **Ary Scheffer** (1795-1858) lived and worked for nearly thirty years. This artist of Dutch origin was influenced by the Romantics and greatly admired by Louis-Philippe.
On Friday evenings his home was the meeting-place for a group of painter and literary friends (Delacroix, Ingres, Liszt, Chopin, George Sand and Ernest Renan who married Ary's niece).
Paintings, jewellery and drawings bring to life memories of George Sand, her family and friends. Canvases by Ary Scheffer and a selection of portraits depict the literary and artistic members of the 19C French Romantic movement.

ST ALEXANDER NEWSKY CATHEDRAL

Michelin plan **10** - folds 16 and 17: E 8, E 9
Métro Station: Courcelles or Ternes
12 Rue Daru. Guided tours on Tuesdays and Fridays between 3 and 5pm.

This, the Russian Orthodox Church of Paris, was erected in 1860 in the Russian neo-Byzantine style with a typical Greek cross plan. The main features of the exterior are gilded onion-shaped domes while the interior is decorated with frescoes, gilding and icons. The services are magnificently sung in the tradition of Holy Russia.

ST AUGUSTINE'S CHURCH

Michelin plan **10** - fold 18: E 11 — *Métro Station: St Augustin*
Closed weekends 12noon to 3.30pm and holidays.

Both the church and the imposing 1927 building of the Cercle Militaire border the Place St-Augustin with in the centre a replica of the statue of Joan of Arc by Paul Dubois. The original is in Rheims.
Baltard, the architect of the old covered market (the Halles), who designed this church in 1860, employed for the first time in such a building a metal girder construction which enabled him to dispense with the usual buttressing. The triangular shape of the site dictated the church's unusual form, widening out from the porch to the chancel crowned by a dome.

★ ST-GERMAIN-DE-CHARONNE CHURCH

Michelin plan **10** - fold 35: H 22
Métro Station: Gambetta or Porte de Bagnolet

At the heart of the old village of Charonne which was surrounded by vineyards in the past and where a meeting is said to have occurred between St Germanus of Auxerre and St Geneviève *(p 112)* in 429, are the church and St-Blaise square. Rue St-Blaise, the former high street with its small houses, is in sharp contrast to the high-rise buildings nearby.
The church and cemetery crown a hillock. The squat 13C tower supported by massive pillars has interesting capitals.

★ ST MARTIN'S CANAL

Michelin plan **10** - folds 21 and 33: E 17 to K 17 — *Métro Station: Jaurès*

The peaceful, old-fashioned reaches of the 4.5km-2 3/4 mile canal, dug at the time of the Restoration to link the Ourcq Canal with the Seine, are still navigated by numerous barges. The embankments where the water course is above the surrounding plain, the nine locks and bordering trees, make an unusual landscape.

From Place de Stalingrad to the marina

Following a programme of urban renewal the toll-house now stands on an esplanade bordered by two terraces which overlook the Villette Basin with its traffic of passing barges going to and from the St Martin's Canal.

Rotonde de la Villette. — *Place de Stalingrad*. The rotunda, another of Ledoux' toll-houses *(p 20)* serves as a storehouse for archaeological finds.

Follow Quai de Jemmapes between Place de Stalingrad and Square Frédéric-Lemaître.

Montfaucon Gallows. — The canal and the Rues Louis-Blanc, de la Grange-aux-Belles and des Écluses-St-Martin delimit an area that was the site of the gallows notorious for being able to hang sixty condemned at once. Various finance ministers died by it, notably Marigny, the builder, during the reign of Philip the Fair, Montaigu, the repairer, and the unlucky Semblançay who had nothing whatsoever

St Martin's Canal

to do with it. Following the assassination (1572) of Admiral Coligny his body was displayed here. Although already in disuse during the 17C it was 1760 before the gallows were dismantled.

By Rue de la Grange-aux-Belles two footbridges span the canal, forming a charming setting.

St-Louis Hospital. — *Entrance: Rue Bichat.* One of the oldest Parisian hospitals, St-Louis specialises in dermatology. The brick and stone buildings, reminiscent of the Places des Vosges and Dauphine with their steeply pitched roofs and dormer windows, are divided by flower-lined courts.

The canal disappears in Frédéric-Lemaître Square (beyond the Quai Valmy) to flow underground and reappear beyond the Place de la Bastille as the Arsenal Basin. The basin followed the line of the moat skirting Charles V's ramparts and has been developed as a pleasure boat harbour, the **Arsenal Marina** (Port de Plaisance de Paris-Arsenal), to accommodate over 200 boats. The quaysides have been landscaped as terraced gardens.

Boat trips. — *Half day excursions between La Villette and the Seine. For further information apply to Paris-Canal, 19-21 quai de la Loire, Paris 19th, ☎ 42 40 96 97 or to Canauxrama, 13 quai de la Loire, Paris 19th, ☎ 42 39 15 00.*
The boat passes through nine locks including four double locks. The finest is the Recollets; its name is derived from a Franciscan convent which stood nearby. Next comes an underground gallery 1 854m-6 082ft long, lit by air-vents, built by Baron Haussmann in 1860. Underneath the Bastille vault on either side of the July Column *(p 236)* plinth can be seen the railings of the crypt where the victims of the 1830 and 1848 revolutions were buried.

★ THE ST-MÉDARD QUARTER

Michelin plan 🔟🔟 - fold 44: L 15 - M 15
Distance: 2km-1 1/4 miles — Time: 1 hour. Start from Censier-Daubenton métro station.

The Church of St Medard marks the opening of the unique Rue Mouffetard.

St Medard's. — St Medard's was originally the parish church of a small market town on the River Bièvre. Its patron, Saint Medard, counsellor to the Merovingian kings of the 6C, was also the author of the delightful custom of giving a wreath of roses to maidens of virtuous conduct. The church, started in the mid-15C, was completed in 1655.

The « Convulsionnaires ». — In 1727 a Jansenist deacon with a saintly reputation died at the age of 36 of mortification of the flesh and was buried in the St Medard churchyard beneath an upraised black marble stone. Sick Jansenists came to pray before the tomb, to lie upon and underneath it giving rise to a belief in miraculous cures which led to massive scenes of collective hysteria.
In 1732, Louis XV decreed an end to the demonstrations: the cemetery was closed: an inscription nailed to the gate:
> By order of the King, let God
> No miracle perform in this place!

Tour. — *Closed Mondays.* The exterior is interesting. From the front with the great Flamboyant window overlooking the Rue Mouffetard, continue right, along the narrow and picturesque Rue Daubenton where at no **41** a gate and passage lead to a small side entrance to the church. The famous cemetery surrounded the apse.

Return to the façade by way of Rues de Candolle and Censier.

The Flamboyant Gothic nave has modern stained glass; the unusually wide chancel is Renaissance-influenced with unsymmetrical semicircular arches and rounded windows. In 1784 the pillars were transformed into fluted Doric columns. There are paintings of the French school, a remarkable 16C triptych *(behind the pulpit)* and, in the second chapel to the right of the chancel, a *Dead Christ* attributed to Philippe de Champaigne.

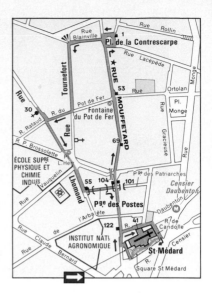

★**Rue Mouffetard.** — The Rue Mouffetard, downhill, winding, lined with old houses and crowded with life, is one of Paris' most original streets. The bustle is greatest in the morning particularly at the lower end where the street climbs between small domestic shops distinguished by painted signs which date from far back and are sometimes picturesque as "At the Clear Spring" at no **122** where a well has been carved on the façade, and no **69** where a tree in relief surmounted the now vanished sign of the Old Oak.

Nos **104** and **101**, on opposite sides of the street, mark the entrances to quiet passages — Passages des Postes and Patriarches.

The Iron Pot Fountain — Pot-de-Fer — at the corner, like others in the district, runs with surplus water from the Arcueil Aqueduct which Marie de' Medici had constructed to bring water to the Luxembourg Palace. Its Italian style bossages are reminiscent of the Medici Fountain *(p 196)*.

When no **53** was demolished in 1938, a cache was discovered in the ruins of 3 350 gold coins bearing the head of Louis XV, placed there by Louis Nivelle, the king's bearer and counsellor.

An inscription at no **1 Place de la Contrescarpe** recalls the Pinecone cabaret — Pomme-de-Pin — described by Rabelais.

Other streets in the vicinity. — During the Middle Ages the area abounded in student colleges. One of the rare examples is the **Scottish College** *(p 191)*.

Continue along Rue Blainville (glance to the right at the Pantheon dome) and left down the old and quiet **Rue Tournefort**. Turn right into Rue du Pot-de-Fer then left into **Rue Lhomond** which descends the Montagne Ste-Geneviève (the steps beside the road indicate the mound's original height). The richly decorated chapel at no **30** was built by Chalgrin in 1780. Turn up by no **55**, into the picturesque **Passage des Postes**, to return to Rue Mouffetard and St Medard's Church.

★ THE SALPÊTRIÈRE HOSPITAL

Michelin plan **11** - fold 45: M 17 — *Métro Station: St-Marcel*

Entrance: Square Marie-Curie.

The hospital has all the grandeur of the Grand Siècle. In the time of Louis XIII a small arsenal on the site manufactured gunpowder from saltpetre. In 1656 Louis XIV established a General Hospital for the Poor of Paris in the saltpetre works in the hope of clearing the capital's streets of beggars and the more vicious characters — fifty-five thousand beggars were known to exist in Paris at the time.

By 1662, 10 000 pensioners had been taken in, but following the cleaning up of the Courts of Miracles *(p 155)* in 1667, the buildings had to be enlarged — a project undertaken by Le Vau and Le Muet. In 1670, a chapel was added, designed by Libéral Bruant at the same time as he was building the Invalides *(p 69)*.

Gradually the hospital began to take in indiscriminately the mad, the infirm, the orphaned and prostitutes — the hospital, in fact, became a prison with all subject to the same harsh regime. At last, at the end of the 18C, one of the doctors, Philippe Pinel (1745-1826) began the work on a reformed treatment for the insane which was to win him and the hospital wide acclaim; a century later Professor Charcot, under whom Freud came to study, was to further the hospital's reputation with research and treatment in advanced neuro-psychiatry.

Tour. — A formal garden precedes the central wing of the immense, austere and majestic edifice which has a certain resemblance to the Invalides.

At the centre is the octagonal dome of the **St-Louis Chapel** surmounted by a lantern. The chapel ground plan is unusual with a rotunda encircled by four aisles forming a Greek cross and four chapels at the angles of the crossing. Eight areas were thus formed in which the inmates could be placed separately: women, girls, the infectious, etc.

The ensemble, with the exception of one of the chapels which is still used by the hospital, now serves as a cultural centre.

THE SEITA GALLERY MUSEUM

Michelin plan 🔟 - fold 29: H 9

Métro Station: Invalides - 12 Rue Sur-couf. Open 11am to 6pm; closed Sundays and holidays. ☎ 45 56 60 17.

The building at no 12 stands on the site of France's first cigarette factory (1845). The museum traces the history of tobacco from its original medicinal use as snuff, then through the various modes of being chewed, snuffed and smoked.

The tobacco trade flourished between the old and new continents and outward cargoes of this American plant were paid for by return loads of manufactured goods. The French Ambassador to Portugal, Jean Nicot introduced Marie de' Medici to snuff-taking. The various ways of enjoying tobacco are illustrated and accompanied by a variety of pipes, tobacco pouches and pots, snuff boxes, cigarette cases, holders, lighters, matches, cigar cutters...

French tobacco shop sign — late 19C

THE SEWERS (LES ÉGOUTS)

Michelin plan 🔟 - folds 28 and 29: H 8, H 9 — *Métro Station: Alma-Marceau*

The Paris sewer system was initially the giant undertaking of the engineer Belgrand at the time of Napoleon III. 2 100 km — 1 305 miles of underground tunnels, some passing under the Seine, channel sewage towards Achères, Europe's largest biological purification station or to the treatment plants (Achères, Pierrelaye and Triel) on the outskirts of Paris.

Tour. — *Entrance: corner of Quai d'Orsay and Pont de l'Alma. Open 11am to 5pm (6pm in summer) last admission 1 hour before closing time; closed Thursdays, Fridays and three weeks in January; 22F; ☎ 47 05 10 29; 20 min audio-visual presentation; no tour during storms, after a heavy rainfall or when the Seine is in flood.*

The tour of part of the sewer system includes an overflow outlet, sand filtering basins, a secondary conduit and holding and regulatory reservoirs. The larger mains also contain pipes for drinking and industrial water and telephone and telegraph cables. Explanatory panels in the Belgrand Gallery explain the historical development and workings of the Paris sewer system (water supply, purification and evacuation).

*To choose a hotel or restaurant, use the small, **MICHELIN Red Guide:***
PARIS, Hotels and Restaurants,
*an extract from the current **MICHELIN Guide FRANCE.***

★ THE TEMPLE QUARTER

Michelin plan 🔟 - folds 32 and 33: G 15 to G 17

Distance: 2km-1 1/4 miles — Time: 2 1/2 hours — Start from the République métro station.

This quarter was the domain of the Knights Templar and the Benedictines from St Martin's in the Fields.

PLACE DE LA RÉPUBLIQUE

Michelin plan 🔟 - fold 33: G 17

The original square was named Place du Château-d'Eau. On it stood the Théâtre Historique, built in 1847, by Alexandre Dumas as a setting for his historical dramas — it opened with his *Queen Margot* for which crowds queued for seats for two days and nights.

In 1854 Haussmann decided to replace the small square with the present vast expanse as part of his anti-revolutionary street planning scheme. The diorama built in 1822 by Daguerre, of daguerreotype fame, was knocked down in favour of barracks for 2 000 soldiers and wide avenues cut through turbulent areas — the Boulevard Magenta, Avenue de la République, Boulevard Voltaire and Rue de Turbigo. The Boulevard du Crime was razed.

The square was completed by 1862 and the **Statue to the Republic** by Morice erected in 1883. The best part is the base by Dalou *(p 250)* on which are bronze low reliefs of the great events in the history of the Republic from its inception to 1880 when the 14 July was celebrated as a national holiday for the first time in the Place de la Nation.

Place de la République to St Nicholas in the Fields

At 195 Rue du Temple stands **St Elizabeth's** *(closed Sunday afternoons)*, a 17C convent chapel now the Church of the Knights of St John of Malta and outstanding for the hundred 16C Flemish **low reliefs**★ of biblical scenes around the ambulatory. Turn left in Rue de Turbigo to approach the former **St-Martin-des-Champs**★ with its Romanesque east end (1130 — restored), fine capitals, belfry of the same period and Gothic nave.

Turn right into Rue St-Martin.

★★**Conservatoire National des Arts et Métiers.** — *Description p 241.*

★**St Nicholas in the Fields** (St-Nicolas-des-Champs). — *Closed Sunday afternoons.* The church, built in the 12C by the priory of St Martin in the Fields for the monastery servants and neighbouring peasants, was dedicated to one of the most popular medieval saints, Nicholas, 4C Bishop of Myra in Asia Minor and patron saint of children, sailors and travellers. It was rebuilt in the 15C and enlarged in the 16 and 17C. The Revolution rededicated it to Hymen and Fidelity.

The façade and belfry are Flamboyant Gothic, the south **door**★ Renaissance (1581).

Inside, the nave is divided into five by a double line of pillars; the first five bays are 15C; the vaulting in the aisles beyond the pulpit rises in height, semicircular arcs succeed pointed arches; the sides of the pillars towards the nave have been fluted. The chancel and chapels contain a considerable number of

Statue to the Republic

mostly French 17, 18 and 19C paintings; the twin sided high altar is adorned with a retable painted by Simon Vouet (16C) and four angels by the 17C sculptor, Sarrazin. The best point from which to see the forest of pillars and double ambulatory is the Lady Chapel (Adoration of the Shepherds by Coypel).

The typically Parisian organ is 18C; the organist was for a time Louis Braille *(p 189)*.

From St Nicholas to Place de la République

Continue left down Rue St-Martin and along to the Temple Square. On the way you pass no **51** Rue de Montmorency, the oldest house (1407) in Paris, once the **house of Nicolas Flamel**, legal draughtsman to the university and bookseller who made a fortune copying and selling manuscripts. He used the proceeds in good works, including setting up above his shop (now a restaurant) an "almshouse" in which the high rent charged for the lower floors allowed the upper rooms to be given rent free to the poor who were asked to say a prayer for their benefactor.

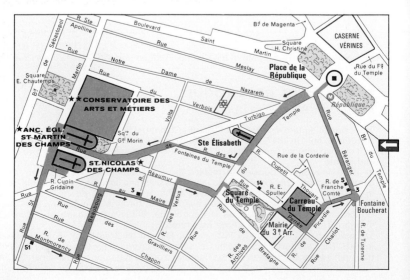

Turn left in Rue Beaubourg, scene of street fighting in 1834, and right into the old Rue au Maire. Off this, at no **3** Rue Volta, is a **house**, dating from the 17C, which reveals a timbered façade (gable now gone).

Continue along Rue au Maire before turning left into the narrow Rue des Vertus. This, in turn, leads to Rue Réaumur and Square du Temple.

The Former Templar Domain. — In 1140 the religious and military order, founded in 1118 in the Holy Land by nine knights to protect pilgrims and known as the Order of Knights Templar, established a house in Paris. By the 13C the order had achieved great power with 9 000 commanderies throughout Europe and an un-rivalled international banking system. In France the knights had become independent of the crown and had acquired possession of one quarter of the land area of Paris — including all the Marais quarter.

The Templars fortified their domain and its keep became a refuge for local peasants and those fleeing royal jurisdiction. Craftsmen also congregated, exempt from guild taxes, until there were 4 000 within the walls where even kings were known to seek shelter.

Philip the Fair decided to suppress this state within a state and one day in 1307 had all the Templars in France arrested (150 knights were imprisoned in Paris); the order dissolved; the leader and fifty-four followers *(p 122)* were burnt at the stake and the property divided between the crown and the Knights of St John of Jerusalem, later known as the Knights of Malta.

The Templar Prison. — The Knights of Malta were suppressed in their turn at the Revolution and the Temple Tower, as it is known, was used as a prison for Louis XVI, Marie-Antoinette, the king's sister Madame Elisabeth, the seven-year-old Dauphin and his sister, on their arrest on 13 August 1792 *(see Carnavalet Museum, p 95)*.

The king was held in the tower and it was from here, therefore, that he went to the guillotine on 20 January 1793 following his trial and conviction by the Convention. The following July the Dauphin was separated from his mother, who, in August, was transferred with her sister-in-law to the Conciergerie *(p 120)* which she was to leave only to go to the guillotine on 16 October. Two years later, on 8 June 1795, a young man in the Temple Tower died and the mystery arose which has never been solved, of whether he was Louis XVII, the son of Louis XVI or who he was. In 1808 the tower was razed to prevent Royalist pilgrimages and the domain converted into an open air secondhand clothes market known as the Carreau du Temple or Temple Stones. In 1857 Haussmann laid out the covered market, the town hall, on the other side of Rue Perrée, and the present square.

Square and Carreau du Temple. — Cross the square where, on the left at no **14**, is the Assay Office (Hôtel de la garantie) for precious metals. At the far end, left of the town hall, is the Carreau, still lined, like the surrounding Picardie, Corderie and Dupetit-Thouars streets, with clothes, costume and fancy clothes shops and stalls *(market except Mondays: 9am to 1pm)*

Continue along Rue de Franche-Comté and, leaving the 1699 Boucherat Fountain on the right at the end of the street, turn left up Rue Béranger. At nos **3** and **5** there is an 18C hôtel where in 1857 the poet and writer of popular songs, Béranger, died.

ZADKINE MUSEUM

Michelin plan **11** - fold 43: L 13 — *Métro Station: Vavin or Port Royal (R.E.R.)*
100 bis, Rue d'Assas. Open 10am to 5.40pm; closed Mondays and holidays; 12F (free on Sundays). ☎ 43 26 91 90.

Russian by birth and French by adoption, the sculptor Ossip Zadkine (1890-1967) came to Paris in 1909, after a stay in London. His works in wood and stone expressed his anguish and anxiety. This house, now presented as a museum, was his home from 1928 to his death.

Amongst the works on display note in particular the *Woman with a Fan,* from his Cubist period, the elm wood sculpture of *Prometheus* and the model of his memorial to the destruction of Rotterdam *(The Destroyed City)*. In the last room the exhibits include the artist's materials and easel along with several busts and portraits of Van Gogh as well as the plaster cast of Zadkine's statue of the great man, now in Auvers-sur-Oise.

A variety of sculpture stand in the garden.

Index

A

B

C